BARBARA BAYNTON

UQP AUSTRALIAN AUTHORS

General Editor: Laurie Hergenhan
Reader in Australian Literature
University of Queensland

Also in this series:

Marcus Clarke edited by Michael Wilding
Henry Lawson edited by Brian Kiernan
Five Plays for Stage, Radio and Television edited by Alrene Sykes
The 1890s: Stories, Verse and Essays edited by Leon Cantrell
Rolf Boldrewood edited by Alan Brissenden
The Jindyworobaks edited by Brian Elliott
Hal Porter edited by Mary Lord
Henry Kingsley edited by J.S.D. Mellick
Joseph Furphy edited by John Barnes
New Guinea Images in Australian Literature edited by Nigel Krauth
Australian Science Fiction edited by Van Ikin
The Australian Short Story: An Anthology from the 1890s to the 1980s edited by Laurie Hergenhan
R.D. FitzGerald edited by Julian Croft
Catherine Helen Spence edited by Helen Thomson
James McAuley edited by Leonie Kramer

In preparation:

Nettie Palmer edited by Vivian Smith
John Shaw Neilson edited by Clifford Hanna
Nineteenth Century Prose edited by Elizabeth Webby
Randolph Stow edited by A. J. Hassall

BARBARA BAYNTON

Bush Studies, other stories, *Human Toll,* verse, essays and letters

Edited by

Sally Krimmer & Alan Lawson

University of Queensland Press
ST LUCIA • LONDON • NEW YORK

First published 1980 by University of Queensland Press
Box 42, St Lucia, Queensland, Australia
Reprinted 1988

Typeset by Press Etching Pty Ltd, Brisbane
Printed in Australia by The Book Printer, Melbourne

Distributed in the UK and Europe by University of Queensland Press
Dunhams Lane, Letchworth, Herts. SG6 1LF England

Distributed in the USA and Canada by University of Queensland Press
250 Commercial Street, Manchester, NH 03101 USA

Cataloguing in Publication Data

National Library of Australia

Baynton, Barbara Janet Ainsleigh, 1862-1929.
Barbara Baynton.

(Australian authors series)
Bibliography.

I. Krimmer, Sally, joint ed. II. Lawson, Alan John, joint ed. III. Title. (Series)

A828'.2

British Library (data available)

Library of Congress (applied for)

ISBN 0 7022 1469 8

Contents

Verse (1897-1919)

Articles and Correspondence (1899-1921)

Acknowledgments

Acknowledgment is made to the editor of *Australian Literary Studies* in which substantial material for the Introduction and Bibliography earlier appeared. This material is largely based on original research by Sally Krimmer for her thesis on Baynton at the University of Queensland (1974). Acknowledgment is also made to Chatto & Windus for permission to use the letter to Melba from *Melba: A Biography* by Agnes Murphy (1909); to Mrs Nancy Gray of Scone, New South Wales for providing some important biographical information; to Mrs A.H. Brigden, a grand-daughter of Baynton for information and clippings about the author; to Ms Margaret O'Hagan, Ms Margaret Brenan, and Ms Marianne Ehrhardt of the Fryer Memorial Library of Australian Literature for help in locating and copying the original materials used in the selection; to Ms Alrene Sykes and Dr Laurie Hergenhan for useful discussions on matters of interpretation and presentation; and for some leads which helped to unearth new material, Ms Brenda Niall, Mr Terence O'Neill, and Mr David Gilbey.

Photograph of Barbara Baynton published in the *British-Australasian*, 21 July 1916 (photograph by courtesy of the State Library of Victoria).

Introduction

Barbara Baynton died on 28 May 1929 leaving one slim volume of short stories, a short novel, and a few poems and stories, some of which have never been collected. On her death her name was linked more closely with the world of fine china and antique furniture than it was with the literary world. Though her literary work has not gone without acknowledgment it is mainly in recent times that Baynton has emerged as an important figure in the history of Australian literature, and in her own right.

Principally a short story writer, writing in the 1890s, Baynton does not belong to the dominating legend which is supposed to have originated in that period. Her contribution to Australian literature is unique although she echoes in her writing much of what Lawson and Paterson felt. Like them, she too rejected the harshness of bush life. In seeking to offset, indeed to invert, the legend, Leon Cantrell[1] argues that the period shows a sense of alienation and loss as a principal literary hallmark. Baynton provides ample evidence for this theory, for nowhere in her stories can be found the characteristics often attributed to Australian literature in the 1890s. There is no nationalistic pride, no love of the bush and no feeling of mateship or affinity between the bush and its inhabitants.

The stark reality of Baynton's stories suggests little of her unromantic origins in the Hunter Valley area of New South Wales. All biographical accounts, presumably provided by Baynton herself, give her birth date as 4 June 1862.[2] In fact she was born on 4 June 1857,[3] making her five years older than she claimed. Not only did she change her birth date, she also disguised the identity of her parents. According to

Baynton she was the daughter of Penelope Ewart and Captain Robert Kilpatrick who met and fell in love on a ship coming out to Australia from Ireland. Her mother at this time was supposedly already married to Robert Ewart but entered into a de facto relationship with Kilpatrick, marrying him only when Robert Ewart died. By this time Penelope and Kilpatrick had had five children.[4]

This was the story that even her grandchildren believed and it would have been perpetuated had not the certificate of her marriage to Thomas Baynton, her second husband, been discovered. There her parents were cited as John Lawrence and Elizabeth Ewart. On further investigation it gradually became clear that she was not born Barbara Kilpatrick, but Barbara Lawrence. On the certificate of marriage to Alexander Frater, the first of her three husbands, the names of her parents are not given but she does give her name as Barbara Lawrence. On the certificate issued when she married Lord Headley (her third husband), Baynton gives her father's name as Robert Lawrence Kilpatrick. The name "Lawrence" appeared, but only as a second name. Various biographical records state that Baynton was born in the country town of Scone, New South Wales. No birth certificate for Barbara Kilpatrick is to be found in the Registrar's Office in Scone but the birth certificate of Barbara Jane Lawrence is held there.[5] Barbara Jane Lawrence's birth date is given as 4 June 1857 and the name accords with that given on the certificate of marriage to Thomas Baynton; day and month of birth are those she customarily gave; only the year of birth is different. To verify the matter further all ship immigration lists were checked since Baynton's grandson, Henry Gullett, states that Baynton's parents Robert Kilpatrick and Penelope Ewart came out to Australia from Ireland.[6] No record of this couple's arrival in Australia could be found, but on 9 November 1840 John and Elizabeth Lawrence arrived at Port Jackson on the "Royal Consort" from Derry, Ireland.[7]

While the mystery of Baynton's "true identity" has been solved, it is still unclear why she chose to circulate a story about her parents that varied so much from the truth. Baynton's alteration of her age is perhaps explicable but her invention for her parents of a de facto relationship is difficult to comprehend in an era when public opinion and social standards made a respectable background so important. It may have been that in some of the bohemian circles in which she later moved her background was acceptable, romantically enviable. On the other hand her claim that her father was a landowner may have seemed more advantageous socially than his real occupation of carpenter.[8] The other parts of the mystery that still remain unsolved are the identity of Robert Kilpatrick, her putative father, and the name Penelope attributed to her mother.[9]

The source of her tale of illegitimacy may be easier to locate. Barbara Baynton was the seventh child of John and Elizabeth Lawrence with Elizabeth, Sarah, John, David, Robert, and Mary Ann preceding her. On 11 November 1860, a further child was born, registered, and given the christian names of James Ewart. The birth certificate shows the child to be illegitimate and it seems that since the child bore the mother's name it was hers. Lawrence, however, is the informant and appears to have brought up the child as part of his family. In this may have lain the genesis of Baynton's own story of her family background.

The early years of Baynton's life were spent in the Scone district of New South Wales where her father worked as a carpenter. In "A Dreamer", the first story in *Bush Studies*, the sound of a bush carpenter working at night on a coffin is an important early clue to the outcome of the story. The Lawrence family moved twenty-five miles further north from Scone to Murrurundi sometime between 1861 and 1866. In 1877–78 Robert Lawrence, one of Baynton's brothers, began work as a blacksmith, while another two brothers established a sawmill at Spring Ridge, Liverpool Plains. There are still today many families named Lawrence living in the Murrurundi-Quirindi area.

While all the male members of her family learnt their trades, Baynton became a governess at Merrylong Park, on the Liverpool Plains in the Quirindi district. It was here that she met the first of her three husbands Alexander Frater, a selector, the son of Alexander and Penelope Hay Frater. Baynton was married at the age of twenty-three in the Tamworth Presbyterian Church on 24 June 1880.[10] The couple had three children: Alexander Hay, Robert Guy, and Penelope. While the children were still very young, however, Baynton's husband left her for one of her cousins.[11]

Baynton moved to Sydney and wasted no time in carving out a life of her own. It is at this time that the "other Barbara" seems to emerge and conflicting stories about her begin. On 4 March 1890, her divorce from Frater was granted and the following day she married Dr Thomas Baynton, describing herself on the marriage certificate as a "widow".

It would be unfair to say that Baynton simply used her marriage to a wealthy, seventy year old doctor as a stepping stone on her way up the social ladder, but the marriage clearly marked a change in her fortune. Barbara and Thomas Baynton had a son whose early death is alluded to in "Goodbye Australia!", a poem Baynton wrote for the *Bulletin* in 1899.[12] "Baby", an unpublished poem of the same year laments the death fulsomely.[13] The fifteen years of this marriage were happier, for Baynton now had someone to help her financially with the expensive task of rearing three young children. She no longer had to sell bibles from door to door in order to secure a living for herself and her young family.[14] Probably more important to her was the fact that she was now mixing with people from all walks of life.

Baynton's social circle by 1903 was a wide one which included many well known identities both in Australia and overseas. She was a friend of Billy Hughes who was at one time Prime Minister of Australia. George Reid, High Commissioner for Australia in London wrote the foreword to *Cobbers*. A letter to Sir Samuel Griffith congratulating him on his appointment as Federal Chief Justice shows that she moved in high society. She was painted in 1903 by Sir John Longstaff, a fashionable Edwardian portrait painter. Her portrait by Spencer Pryse was exhibited in London in 1921 and her daughter Penelope was painted by Tom Roberts. An inscribed copy of *Bush Studies* given to Hallam, Lord Tennyson, son of Alfred Tennyson, gives another indication of her social standing and ambitions as he was Governor General at the time.

Thomas Baynton was a keen reader and a collector of antiques — two pastimes his wife adopted. Not only did she collect fine antiques but she is reputed to have had one of the finest collections of black opals in the world. An auction sale advertisement described her antique collection as impressive — "the most important assemblage of objets d'art ever offered at auction to the Australian public".[15] In 1903 the Bayntons bought "Fairmont" in Charlotte Street, Ashfield, Sydney which was, in Baynton's own words, "one of the show houses of Sydney for interior decoration".[16] It was while married to Thomas Baynton that she began to write. Living in financial security and surrounded by fine furniture and wealthy friends, her childhood days in the bush must have seemed remote. From that early hard existence, however, she was to draw most of the inspiration for her writings. In doing so she avoided the sentimental kind of fiction written by so many of her contemporary Australian women writers.

A.G. Stephens published Baynton's first story in the Christmas edition of the *Bulletin* in 1896. The story at this time was published under the title of "The Tramp", although Baynton did suggest in a letter to Stephens that the title be "What the Curlews Cried".[17] The title was later changed to "The Chosen Vessel" in *Bush Studies* where the episode concerning Peter Hennessey's vision was added. Stephens became Baynton's friend and mentor during this period, also publishing some of her poems. Baynton's letters show that she accepted A.G. Stephens's editorial revisions and derived a great deal of pleasure from his friendship and encouragement. A letter sent to Stephens, after "The Tramp" had been accepted by the *Bulletin*, states "I agree with your opinion as to the omitted portion and have no suggestion to offer concerning the proofs because my experience has been so limited, I really don't understand anything about revision".[18] One manuscript version of "Squeaker's Mate"[19] does show that Stephens changed Baynton's pronouns to nouns, placing more tension on the personal conflicts which form a significant part of the story. The manuscript version goes on to tell of the birth of the new mate's child, and the old mate's death in hospital, comforted by a warmly sympathetic nurse and a pietistic parson. The last lines demonstrate this adequately: "And knowing the hope that nourished her heart, the nurse understood. She laid the woman back, and when the parson came he said she had gone to Him". Whether Stephens was responsible for the omission of this ironically pietistic ending is unknown.[20] Stephens' revisions are also to be found on manuscripts of some of Baynton's poems. For the most part, though, Stephens' corrections were mainly grammatical.

When Baynton had completed *Bush Studies* she tried unsuccessfully to find a publisher in Sydney. She subsequently continued the search in London. In an address to the Writers' and Artists' Union in 1911 [21] Baynton told of the difficulties that this entailed. On arrival in London she went to the Society of Authors, a body set up to help writers get their work published. She received little help there so she sought letters of introduction to some of the chief London publishers from Mr Henry Copeland, the Agent General for New South Wales. Heinemann advised that they would not look at short stories and another firm agreed to take a short story at two guineas a thousand words. It was a chance meeting with Edward Garnett, the critic and publisher's reader, that helped Baynton to success with *Bush Studies*. Liking Baynton's manuscripts very much he persuaded Duckworth & Company of London to publish *Bush Studies* in 1902. The same company later published *Human Toll* in 1907 and *Cobbers* in 1917. Garnett had helped Henry Lawson a few years earlier and had also influenced literary men of the calibre of Galsworthy, Conrad and D.H. Lawrence, so Baynton was more than happy when he recommended her work and put her in contact with a select literary circle in London which included writers such as W.H. Hudson, R. Cunningham Graham and the well known literary historian and critic Edmund Gosse.

When her manuscript was rejected so many times she almost admitted defeat, saying to Vance Palmer (probably in 1905) that she had thought of throwing it in the fire, for

"English readers are only interested in a background they know . . . and Australia to them is more remote than Abyssinia!"[22] Palmer's interest in Baynton's works had earlier been aroused by a chance meeting in Sydney with her son, Robert Frater. In London about nine years later, Palmer published an article on Baynton's work in the *Book Monthly* (October 1914). This elicited a surprised enquiry from Baynton, "Who are you that you know my work so well? Where do you come from? All the time I've been over here I've never had such encouragement. Won't you come and have dinner with me at my club?"[23] Accepting with delight, mixed with embarrassment because of his youth, Palmer met Baynton who still seemed like a bushwoman despite being a member of a fashionable London club.

After Thomas Baynton's death in 1904 Baynton spent much of her time living in London, although she made frequent visits to Australia. Whilst in London with her daughter she stayed either at Claridges or at 64 Great Cumberland Place. Antique collecting took up much of her time but in 1917, two more stories, "Trooper Jim Tasman" and "Toohey's Party" were added to *Bush Studies* to make a new book, *Cobbers*. These stories no doubt arose from Baynton's experiences during World War I. During the war she was in England and both her home in London and her country house in Ugley Green, Essex (about twenty miles south of Cambridge) were "open houses" for soldiers. She was particularly proud of the Australians, although both her sons served with the British and were severely wounded.[24]

Baynton spent most of 1920 in Australia visiting her daughter Penelope, by then the wife of H.S. Gullett, Minister for Trade and Customs. She returned to England in December 1920 and on 11 February 1921 Lord Headley became her third husband at Marylebone Registry Office, London. The wedding was a fashionable affair — "Mrs Baynton wore a beautiful costume (from Jay's) of pale grey cloth, embroidered in the same colour, the long jacket being worn over a tête de nègre satin jumper, worked in gold. Her very becoming hat was also in tête de nègre, with gold threads. She wore opals, and carried a sheaf of wattle, tied with wattle coloured tulle streamers".[25] Luncheon at Claridges followed for the few intimate friends who were present. The marriage, however, did not last very long. Both were independent people and celebrities in their own right. Lord Headley was the 5th Baronet of Little Warley, Essex. He was President of the Muslim Society and made a pilgrimage to Mecca in 1923. He had publications on various subjects including boxing and "Foreshore Protection", a branch of engineering of which he made a special study.[26] He is said to have embraced Islam while building a bridge across the Ganges and it became politic for him to do so.[27] The marriage settlement on his wife included Ardoe House, reputedly one of the most beautiful old places in Ireland, overlooking the lakes of Killarney.[28] In October 1922 Lord Headley sought a judicial separation from Baynton on the grounds of her desertion. After eighteen months of legal negotiation the parties came to terms, all allegations were withdrawn and they agreed, on 28 March 1924, to draw up a deed of judicial separation.[29]

After their separation Baynton divided her time between London and Melbourne. In London she had moved a couple of streets to 6 Connaught Square and while in Melbourne she lived at The Lodge, Moonga Road, Toorak. Both houses bore witness to her passion for antiques and fine furniture. Chippendale furniture crowded the rooms and Persian rugs lined the floors. Baynton also owned a magnificent collection of china which included many rare Chinese pieces as well as china from Dresden and Sèvres.[30]

Even before the death of Dr Baynton, her second husband, she suffered ill-health.[31] Various respiratory ailments frequently interrupted her work. In 1905-06 she went to a Swiss health resort for lengthy treatment, and later had a major operation. From 1922 she spent many periods in nursing homes in London. Although she still travelled frequently between England and Australia her health deteriorated and in her last years a change in personality was noticed by many who knew her.[32]

Always outspoken, Baynton never tolerated fools gladly. It was whilst listening to an elderly journalist discussing the fashionable novel of the day that she called out "Man! why do you waste your brains by troubling to read such stuff? It's not for grown up men and women; it's for poor creatures who just take what's given them by the girl at the library!''[33] Her grandson, H.B. Gullett, recalls that W.M. (Billy) Hughes once said of Baynton, "I used to go a lot to your grandmother's house — a remarkable woman. My God, she used to make me laugh! But you know you never wanted to argue with her. I haven't a very good reputation myself when it comes to verbal disagreement, but Barbara — she was bloody well impossible!''[34]

Her independent viewpoint and social awareness are again evidenced in a scathing article, "Indignity of Domestic Service", written in 1911 and reprinted in this volume, in which she demanded that domestic service be "classed among the high places" and laments the fact that there has never been a concerted earnest movement to make the Eight Hours Act apply to domestic workers. In her address to the Writers' and Artists' Union, Baynton spoke of the need for unionism in the literary profession "to make the rich papers pay decent rates for writers' brains . . . you can claim the last ounce of my strength in support of your union here''.[35] Baynton in another article written about 1911 condemned the deplorable conditions that existed in the Crown Street Women's Hospital, Sydney.[36]

In 1929 Baynton broke her leg, contracted pneumonia, and died at her Melbourne home on 28 May, a few days before her seventy-second birthday. Her funeral at the Fawkner Crematorium in Melbourne was, at her request, a private and unostentatious one, attended only by relatives and a few friends. She asked that her ashes be placed beside those of her second husband, Dr Thomas Baynton.

Baynton was throughout her life a striking woman both in appearance and in personality. Although not tall, her presence commanded respect from all she knew. She was an attractive brunette in her youth and lost none of her good features in old age.

It is always difficult to understand the personality of one who has been dead for some time and the terms used to describe Baynton by those who knew her are always so remarkably extravagant that she has assumed larger than life dimensions. A grand lady with a strong character, she was said to have been "lovable, rash, clever, impulsive, generous . . ., quick to anger, liable to be unjust, but always ready to forgive and to make friends". She was noticeable for "her eloquence, her wit and charm, her taste in dress, her love of jewels, her outspokenness without regard of consequences . . . and her dramatic nature".[37] These traits, especially the last, recur in many of the anecdotes which are told of her, but such descriptions reveal little of the inner woman — indeed they may be obscuring.

Something of her extraordinary nature is reflected in the grim and often shocking stories of *Bush Studies*. They seem to be written almost in revenge, as if provoked by the hardships of the bush. The stories can be seen also as a record of Baynton's quest for reality, expressed through her unifying vision of the bush. Although the six stories are separate, the recurrent themes, imagery and situations help to unify the book. The stories form a composite symbolic narrative to which each contributes a distinctive and memorable part. They are not limited in any way by their setting in the Australian bush: Baynton manages to make her studies reflect general human problems while she examines characteristically Australian bush situations.

Several themes can be seen running throughout *Bush Studies*. The landscape Baynton chose to write about was particularly brutal, as were its inhabitants. It is the brutalizing environment which her contemporary, Henry Lawson, described in "Crime in the Bush". More specifically Baynton shows men lacking in compassion in their attitude towards women. Lawson and even Steele Rudd wrote of a harsh landscape but Baynton studies the psychic effects of that landscape more explicitly. The bush is constantly portrayed as a lonely, hostile place, antagonistic to its inhabitants who depend on it for survival; Squeaker's Mate is felled by a tree, the Dreamer is impeded by water and whipped by the now "hostile" willows her mother had planted, Scrammy 'And is maimed, Billy Skywonkie's friends are deformed, and the landscape turns the chosen vessel into a ghastly parody of the Virgin Mary while offering her no refuge from her rapist and murderer.

Here is found no noble sentiment but rather a savageness man has retained from his beginnings to enable him to cope with his brutal surroundings. But the land takes its toll, its "revenge" as Henry Handel Richardson put it. Always the sun is greedy, sucking any nourishment from the barren land. When man likewise becomes a predatory being, it can be seen that the landscape has moulded him in its own image. In "Scrammy 'And" Baynton writes of the primitiveness of a man who hangs on to life, with a primeval violence his only strategy for survival.

The absolute horror of the bush is introduced in the first story of *Bush Studies*, "A Dreamer", where the trip which the pregnant daughter makes home to her mother belongs almost to the world of nightmare. Nature is depicted in this story in angry human forms: ". . . little Dog-trap Gully was proudly foaming itself hoarse"; the wind yelled at the daughter and a "giant tree's fallen body said 'Thus far' and in vain the athletic furious water rushed and strove to throw her over the barrier". The woman's struggles with a cruel force are portrayed in the violent terms of a murderer fighting his victim. But despite the human qualities given to it in "A Dreamer", the landscape is mostly unfeeling and unresponsive. The "sun-sucked" land in "Bush Church" parallels the arid spiritual life of the inhabitants. For Baynton, as for Lawson, Clarke, Richardson and many other Australian writers, the landscape is seen as having a direct effect on the spiritual and emotional, as well as on the physical, lives of its inhabitants: it is, as Lawson wrote in "The Bush Undertaker", "the nurse and tutor of eccentric minds".

If a malevolent landscape dominates *Bush Studies* so also does the man/woman confrontation where women, without choice, become acquiescent victims of men largely without realizing it. In most of the stories woman is shown as maternal, loving and peaceful while man is portrayed as brutally sexual. Man's natural home is the cruel landscape while woman is instinctively associated with civilization and the town. In "A Dreamer", "Squeaker's Mate", and "Billy Skywonkie", town women arrive in the country and journey towards an inevitable fate. The woman in "The

Chosen Vessel" is never in harmony with the bush, at least partly because of her city origins, and it is certainly from this base that her husband's cruel taunts arise. Knowing her fear he forces her to meet the advancing cow with nothing more than the phallicly parodic stick. The woman's human, and explicitly female, vulnerability is a culmination of Baynton's studies of the bush. Removed from the social security of a town, she is anonymous (like all but one of Baynton's victims) and besieged by hostile predatory forces. In this story the psychological and symbolic rape is made scarifyingly actual. The woman is, from the beginning, a fourfold victim. Her husband's sexual sneer (intensified by being changed into direct speech in Baynton's revision printed here) — "Needn't flatter yerself, he had told her, nobody 'ud want ter run away with yew" — is of course ironic in terms of the plot, but more importantly it is a predatory male imposition of sexual value. Like the woman in "Billy Skywonkie" her sense of her identity is sexually assaulted. Secondly, she is also acutely aware of the vulnerability caused by her isolated situation. In a paragraph added after the story's first publication (in the *Bulletin* in 1896), Baynton draws attention to this in a way which also carries an irony of similar quality: "She was not afraid of horsemen; but swagmen, going to, or worse, coming from the dismal drunken little township, a day's journey beyond, terrified her". The fear of swagmen is, of course, well-founded but her confidence in horsemen is not. Indeed it is this confidence which leads her to run from her house when she hears Hennessey ride by and thus expose herself defencelessly to her attacker. Thirdly, she is also a victim of Peter Hennessey's appalling religious vision. Just as she is taken as a sexual object by the swagman so is she taken as a religious object by Hennessey. The full horror of this conjunction is carried in the fact of his confusing a rape-victim with the Virgin Mary. Her fourth, and most obvious, vulnerability is to the exploiting male predator, the swagman, but this is compounded by the other three and given extra dimensions by her attempts to save herself from her fate. There is no point running to her husband — "in the past, when she had dared to speak of the dangers to which her loneliness had exposed her, he had taunted and sneered at her". The walls of her hut are easily breached and her potential saviour is instead preoccupied with his own spurious spiritual salvation over a political contest. The poverty of her resources is shown when she tries to bargain with the swagman by placing food and her one valuable object on the kitchen table. Her only defence is to bargain with him. Vulnerable when he first called she remains so even given time to assemble all her defences. For the lone woman in the bush there is no escape, no defence, no refuge and no rescue. A victim of man's carnal fervour in the first half of the story, she becomes a sacrifice to man's spiritual fervour in the second half. (This story affords an interesting comparison with Lawson's "The Drover's Wife" in which the woman protagonist is self-sufficient, but at a cost.)

Men are exploitative in all aspects of their activities. Nowhere is this more evident than in "Squeaker's Mate", one of the most powerful stories in *Bush Studies*. Sombre human emotions of greed, violence, fear, anxiety, loneliness and quiet desperation combine to give the story an immediate impact. Here Baynton has written a stark but sympathetic study of a woman lying alone and isolated with a broken back, a woman formerly strong enough to do a man's job. Her previous strength confounded the difference of her sex, but even she finds that once strength is broken, anatomy is destiny. Nameless for most of the story — except as "Squeaker's mate", an appendage — she is identified at the end as "Mary", the archetypal maternal figure after her barrenness has been taunted by her realization of the obvious fertility of Squeaker's new mate. She alone of Baynton's victims is given a name and even hers is both generalized and ironic.

In "Billy Skywonkie" the familiar is inexorably inverted, and perverted. In what is a characteristic Australian pattern, the world is depicted "upside down". Mag and Biddy, for instance, are an obscene parody of the mother/daughter relationship. The landscape is a vivid realization of a wasteland and, as in T.S. Eliot, the landscape becomes an expression of the disunity between love and sex. The woman's role is made obvious through Billy's excessively delicate intonations and his remark that he had "promised ther 'Konk' t' leave 'im 'ave furst squint at yer". The sexual tension becomes more evident as boundary gates close, one after the other. The anonymous woman has no individuality apart from her sex, and remains unnamed throughout the story. Her intellectuality is emphasized in direct contrast to the baseness of the men, and thus implies another aspect of the cultural disjunction between the city and the bush. Her alienation and its effect on her ability to adapt to this new environment is expressed in a paragraph which is central to Baynton's vision of life in the bush. It is also remarkably close here, and on other occasions, to Lawson's. Like the old man in "Scrammy 'And", the denizens of "Bush Church", or Lawson's "Bush Undertaker", her perception of reality is distorted; her "normal" reactions inhibited:

> A giddy unreality took the sting from everything, even from her desire to beseech him to turn back to the siding, and leave her there to wait for the train to take her back to civilization. She felt she had lost her mental balance. Little matters became distorted, and the greater shrivelled.

That final sentence prepares us for the following story, the grim meaninglessness of "Bush Church". The final image in "Billy Skywonkie", that of the sheep ready for the slaughter, prefigures the meaningless sacrifice of the woman in the last story, "The Chosen Vessel". The woman in "Billy Skywonkie", suffering from the compound disadvantages of age, race, sex, and background is an unresponsive victim, an object, like the lamb, to satisfy man's hunger. Unlike Baynton's other victims she is away from secure surroundings. The others suffer in their homes and the fragility of that security is emphasized. This woman has not even that. Her isolation is complete.

Baynton approached the basic situation of "Billy Skywonkie" again in a later story, here printed in book form for the first time. Published in an English weekly in 1921, "Her Bush Sweetheart" also combines the elements of a city woman whose youth is passing, a station-owner looking for a wife, and the Chinese. This time her view is less stark, there are fewer grotesques, but there is also less sympathy. The woman is predatory in a small but desperate way, the man limited and uninteresting, and the Chinese hostile. The bush is depicted with some sympathy but from a distance, and a poverty of circumstances and spirit takes its toll. Caroline Bell "was one who expected no friendship from women because she gave none to them".

The traditional bush values of mateship, hospitality and compassion are largely absent from the landscape of Baynton's stories. The bush community of "Billy Skywonkie" lacks humanity towards an " 'alf chow", traditional bush hospitality is mocked at the beginning of "Bush Church" ("The hospitality of the bush never extends to the loan of a good horse to an inexperienced horseman") and at the end when food is withheld from those who have none. Squeaker's mate receives little sympathy from the other bush women — she had been "a woman with no leisure for yarning" — and her "uncompromising independence" becomes their excuse for indifference.

In contrast to the pervading vision of moral chaos and cruelty Baynton's images of motherhood emerge as a hope for humanity. Just as Baynton is aware of the inevitability of death, so is she keenly aware of the inevitability of birth, which ensures a continuity of life, and gives it meaning. In "A Dreamer" the daughter's own impending motherhood induces her to return home and know once more a mother's love. Amongst all of the destructive, environmental forces against which the daughter is doing battle, motherhood is the one creative element. The watchful mother bird's warning call gives security, just as "loving arms" and "a mother's sacred kisses" give a feeling of warmth and protection to the frightened, lost daughter as she imagines how her meeting with her mother will be. The daughter is anxious; she quickens her pace, but "did not run — motherhood is instinct in women". The supreme example of woman's instinctive desire to protect her young is found in "The Chosen Vessel", where motherhood is presented as being the one quality which cannot be overwhelmed. The terrified mother constantly forgets her own safety in an effort to protect her child. When she calls for help, she does so in the baby's name, and her protectiveness continues even beyond her death: the boundary rider who finds her body has to cut the still-living child's gown from the persistent grasp of the dead mother.

As well as seeing an inherent goodness in maternity Baynton sees a value in the loyalty of the dog to its owner as Lawson does. Human loyalty between men and women may be non-existent but canine loyalty is present in several of the stories. Only the dog recognizes the returning daughter in "A Dreamer" and it is the dog which is the true mate in "Squeaker's Mate". The dog has the qualities of humanity found lacking in Squeaker and it is this that Baynton constantly stresses against the greed and violence of Squeaker. The best example of devotion is perhaps found in ''Scrammy 'And'' where ''Warderloo'' is endowed with practically human qualities — Baynton achieves this effect by giving the dog answers to the man's questions and remembering past conversations, while the old man is silent. Even the dog's bark was "terribly human". The women in "Billy Skywonkie" and "The Chosen Vessel" are each without this loyalty and protection and so their vulnerability is correspondingly increased.

Religion on the other hand offers no such protection or succour. The bush society which Baynton depicts is one with no real use for it; in the class politics, and in the personal plight in "The Chosen Vessel" its interference is disastrous. In "Bush Church" religion comes under particular attack, as Baynton depicts the ineffectual relevance of a parson to the lives of people living in a land which offers scope only for the practical, and none for the spiritual. Throughout the scene depicting the service, Baynton's contempt is directed against the parson's lack of vision rather than at the barbarity of the listeners. Keogh, the government inspector, is a more relevant god figure to these bush people who have little sympathy for a stranger who visits the district once a year, demanding dates of birth from people who live by no calendars, Christian or otherwise. For people who are in continual conflict with the elements of the bush, the fact that the hen lays is more important than the ceremonial baptism of one of the children. The entire incongruity of religion, such as the parson offers, is climaxed in the subtle creation of absolute chaos at the bush service itself, as ten adults and eighteen children restlessly make their presence felt. Fear had been the only operating factor in getting these people to the service, so once the "gentle voice of the parson, and his nervous manner soon convinced them that they had nothing to fear from him" the scene became one of chatter and scrambling children.

Baynton's stories are powerfully expressed and closely unified. Her vision is communicated through a straightforward yet intense style. Each story has a clear, almost single-minded impulse and each contributes to a cumulative effect which is memorable and convincing. Her stories were first published in book form under the title of *Bush Studies* and it is as studies, and not just stories, that they are best understood. Each sets out to investigate a particular situation, to explore a particular emotion, and to develop a particular motif. The characters are slightly developed but it is the situations which are given a symbolic resonance and which become interesting and involving. These qualities have induced critics to call the stories "universal", despite the clear and definitive way in which the stories express and diagnose Australian experiences. Each story has an inexorable progress towards a dire conclusion — death, rape, rejection or some combination of these — and the progress itself is in the form of an ordeal which serves to heighten the victim's (and our) perception of the horror of his or her vulnerability. The terrible logic of each study is increased by recurrent motifs, "light" in "The Chosen Vessel", "death" and "motherhood" in "A Dreamer", "decay from within" in "Squeaker's Mate". A cumulative effect derives from the single-mindedness of each of the component stories, from a consistent style, from a consistent vision, and from a careful ordering of the stories. The last two stories of *Bush Studies* for instance can each be seen to take their direction from "Billy Skywonkie". From its announcement that "little matters became distorted, and the greater shrivelled" we enter the chaotic wasteland of "A Bush Church". From the final horrifying image of meaningless sacrifice in "Billy Skywonkie" — "the sheep lay passive, with its head back till its neck curved in a bow, and . . . the glitter of the knife was reflected in its eye" — we move unerringly towards the final story, "The Chosen Vessel". The two elements of Baynton's vision of the bush — meaninglessness and malice — are finally separated and focused upon. The composite image of the besieged bush hut containing a defenceless, unnamed victim and a predatory, named attacker is created; human goodness is assailed and largely defeated, but a residue of goodness and hope remains, its fragility emphasized.

In 1917 *Bush Studies* was augmented by two new stories, "Trooper Jim Tasman" and "Toohey's Party", both reprinted in this volume. The first of these had appeared the previous year in the *British-Australasian*. The two new stories are of little interest in themselves, but while they lack the powerful impulse of the earlier ones they do offer a useful comparison helping to show where Baynton's strengths and limitations lie. In each she indulges her bent for recording dialect speech and her taste for a rather harsh form of social comedy. The new volume was given the unprepossessing title of *Cobbers* and seems to have been directed at the market composed of Australian soldiers on leave in London. The loose episodes of "Trooper Jim Tasman" derive from their experiences on leave. This story was also revised prior to publication in *Cobbers* and in the revision an interesting reference to Australia was omitted. After referring to the early pioneers she quotes Lord Salisbury (in a personal conversation) as having said "Courage is your inheritance; your forebears possessed it, or they never would have sailed far away to that great and unknown country". More importantly, though, the six earlier stories from *Bush Studies* were revised and it is that revised version which is now brought back into print for the first time in over sixty years. Page proofs of *Cobbers* corrected in Baynton's hand, and now in the National Library of Australia, show these revisions to be hers.

Barbara Baynton's only novel, *Human Toll*, appeared in a single edition, also under the Duckworth imprint in London, in 1907. It has never been reprinted until its appearance in this volume and has become a rare book. Nevertheless it is an important part of her literary output and her achievement cannot be understood without examining it as well as the much more familiar *Bush Studies*.

Like *Bush Studies*, *Human Toll* is based on Baynton's early experiences in the bush. However unlike the stories of *Bush Studies*, the novel lacks a firm plot structure and at times becomes discursive, only occasionally reaching the achievements of *Bush Studies*. Nevertheless *Human Toll* excels in presenting short, compact and realistic scenes typical of bush life. While the stories in *Bush Studies* often refer to nearby bush towns it is only in *Human Toll* that Baynton portrays the life of bush towns in any detail. She seems to regard the small town as a minor civilizing influence (especially on the men) but while this restrains the malevolence it cannot remove the meanness and petty nastiness from people whose lives must be lived in such places. The narrative of the novel is interesting in that Baynton is clearly writing from personal experience, but how much of it is autobiographical is difficult to determine. The heroine of the story, Ursula Ewart, bears Baynton's mother's maiden name and Ursula is the name of one of her grandchildren. On several occasions in *Human Toll* Ursula expresses a desire to write. She feels, though, that she must wait until she moves away from the bush in order to distance herself from her experiences there.

The title *Human Toll*, like that of *Bush Studies*, points to Baynton's basic approach. The earlier book was a collection of "bush studies" not bush stories, the word "studies" implying a more serious observation. Similarly *Human Toll* focuses on the demands made of men and women who live in a harsh bush environment. Working within this framework, Baynton presents the familiar themes of *Bush Studies* again. She is concerned with the vulnerability of woman, the greed of man, the vapidity of religion, the vulgarity and ugliness of social life in the bush — symbolized as it is repeatedly in her work by the isolated bush hut. As with *Bush Studies*, the only positive value to emerge from the malevolence which pervades the book, lies in the powerful and instinctive response to maternity. The story line is a simple one. It follows the life of Ursula Ewart, an orphaned girl in the bush, who on the death of her father is taken away from the care of a reformed convict, Boshy, who adores her. She is brought up by people who lack real love or understanding and at this period of her life Andrew is her only friend. With the death of Ursula's guardian Boshy returns to the girl and she tends him in his last days. Ursula then returns to her former home with Andrew and Mina, a girl who has tricked Andrew into marrying her. Mina has a child and Ursula's attraction to Andrew suffers a further taunt: she is deprived of Andrew and of having his child. When Mina's ill-treatment of the baby culminates in attempted suffocation, Ursula "rescues" it and flees into the bush. The child dies and Ursula becomes delirious and hopelessly lost. On the last page the reader is tantalized with her "rescue" by Andrew and the Aboriginal Nungi, which may well be an hallucination.

Human Toll does not begin well, and the first chapter is confusing. The search for treasure has the appearance of being vital to the story but its significance soon diminishes and it becomes irrelevant to the narrative. This happens with many of the digressions throughout the novel, seeming to have no real function in either the story or the character development. The slow start of the novel may be attributed to Baynton's attempt to recreate the vernacular of the bush. Boshy is talking to his "Little Lovey" and the aborigines in a dialect that, at times, can be difficult to follow, impeding the flow of the action. Sometimes Baynton has to resort to giving a translation of the dialect in brackets, a practice which is intrusive. Yet despite stylistic flaws early in the novel, *Human Toll* has scenes which recall Barbara Baynton's great ability as a short story writer. The bush town scenes, the sabbath at Mrs Irvine's, the drunken dance, and Ursula lost in the bush have a self-contained unity and intensity which echo the achievements of *Bush Studies*.

In Baynton's brilliant description of a Sunday at Mrs Irvine's, Mr Civil the parson is portrayed with the contempt found in *Bush Studies*. The visiting parson is also mocked. His reverberating "rs" and the repetition of key phrases — "The tears must flow — the tears must flow" (p. 160) — parody precisely a parson's evangelistic style, and emphasize the thin line between clergyman and salesman which Baynton contains in the words "alert showman". In contrast to the apathy in "Bush Church" the parishioners here prepare themselves for the church service with solemnity, but nevertheless the service still degenerates into a mere social routine. Ursie is ceremoniously washed, combed, and dressed in a ludicrous black hat and frock. Mrs Irvine's invitation for tea, which she extends to the vicar, is no more than a mark of her social stature. Only those without the social position, and without desire to perpetuate the existing order, such as Fanny, Jim and Boshy, can see Mr Civil for the harsh and hypocritical man that he is.

Whilst the sabbath at Mrs Irvine's is one kind of social event, the drunken dance is another. The male/female confrontation evident in *Bush Studies* again emerges in this scene, where the male once more establishes himself as an aggressive domineering character. Woman's value resides totally in her sexual role. Animal terms describe men as "colts" and "cattle", and women are seen by the men as "pieces of mutton". These terms effectively reduce man to a level of bestiality, appropriate for Baynton's purpose — her attack on man's animality. This can be seen in Hugh Palmer's sexuality, succinctly captured in the image "The bull on Keen's Mustard" (p. 247). Gus Stein's imitation of Hugh as the bull is wholly sexual; "He threw his body forward and sank his neck into his upraised shoulders". The physical nature of the dance is captured in the wine-frenzied faces of the dancers, with Andrew's eyes blazing excitedly. Ironically, the performers and participants in the dance dress for the occasion with the same ceremony as the Irvine household prepare for church. The finery produced for both occasions is juxtaposed derisively with flagrant passions at the dance. Sexual rivalry exists between Ursie and Mina who feels a sense of "malignant triumph" over Ursie when asked to dance by both Andrew and Hugh Palmer.

The last chapter of *Human Toll* is characteristic of

Baynton at her best. Her writing is vibrant as she dramatically shows Ursie, lost in the bush, carrying Mina's dead child. Time and distance are not measured in any ordinary sense, but in terms of Ursie's mental state — she progresses from ignorance to self-knowledge, thereby conquering her fears. Behind Bayton's images lies a horror of universal isolation, of fundamental loneliness. In this last section, after the social battles and the personal confrontations, Ursie's basic conflict is within herself played out through a battle with the land. Her fear springs from her surroundings since "nature was frankly brutal". To her confused mind nature is grotesque — the spider's web becomes an "insidious circle", "trees shivered meaningly" and the sun "sent piercing tongue-shafts, till even the tough trailing vegetation drooped, showing the hot sand beneath". During her journey into madness, while wandering in the bush, Ursie never forgets the child as it was when alive and cares even more for it now that it is dead. Ursula's maternal possessiveness, surging "like the spring sap in a young tree", was the maddening irritant which drove Mina to murder the child — her own infant. Mina is continually described in terms of a serpent — her "venomous eyes" blaze with "green malignity"; she hisses; is "snake-head"; and her hands are "scaly". She is the symbolic embodiment of the evil which Ursula must overcome on her surreal journey through the wasteland.

Ursula's torment is shown by her constant questioning, and her answers, or the absence of answers, mirror the conflict of her internal and external predicaments. Her time in the bush is a struggle towards the light, her nightmare in the bush is a mystical dark night of the soul. Her strict religious upbringing had left her with a warped view of Christianity wherein her God was a God of Wrath and she associated herself with the ancient Israelites who sought guidance in the wilderness. The dead baby, referred to as "the lamb", was indeed her blood sacrifice in expiation for her sins. The traditional characteristics of an archetypal mystical experience are present, too, in her discarding all garments other than a "hair shirt"; in her fasting; and in her beholding a vision while in the wilderness. The sight of the devil (the "gohanna"), and her trip to hell leave her begging for mercy. The vision of Christ in the gum tree, however, brings about her redemption. While she communes with Him she is found by the Aborigine Nungi and Andrew (the dark and fair centurions), and is saved. Ursula's dubious sanity though introduces an ambiguity into the ending. Is she saved, or is "Andree" another hallucination? Earlier incidents point to her being sane, and the punctuation in the last paragraph seems to indicate that this is so. It is here that the stream of consciousness gives way to direct speech.

For many years Baynton's work was largely unknown and unread. In the past decade she has been enthusiastically "discovered" by a large number of readers as a writer of six brilliant and distinctive short stories. Now that her name is relatively well known the time is ripe to make available the whole range of her literary work.

NOTES

1. *The 1890s: Stories, Verse, and Essays*, ed. Leon Cantrell, Portable Australian Authors Series (St.Lucia: University of Queensland Press, 1977), p.xxx.
2. Fred Johns, *Fred Johns's Notable Australians: Who's Who in Australia* (Adelaide: Fred Johns, 1908).
3. Birth Certificate, 4 June 1857, Registrar's Office, Scone.
4. H.B. Gullett, "Memoir of Barbara Baynton", in Barbara Baynton, *Bush Studies* (Sydney: Angus & Robertson, 1965), p.5.
5. To Mrs Nancy Gray of Scone we are indebted for this and other biographical information.
6. Gullett, "Memoir", p. 5.
7. Index to Immigration Lists, Mitchell Library, Sydney.
8. Baynton's father's occupation is listed as landowner on her death certificate, 28 May 1929, but on her birth certificate it is listed as carpenter.
9. The only Kilpatricks that can be associated in any way with Barbara Baynton are Robert Kilpatrick, a coachman, who in 1888 lived at Retford Lodge, Yarrambee Road, Woollahra and also W.W. Kilpatrick who, in 1890, lived at 22 Moncur Street, Woollahra: the Bayntons lived in Woollahra Lodge, Moncur Street, Woollahra from 1890 until September 1903. Clearly no inferences can be drawn from these slender associations — the source of the romantic "Kilpatrick" remains a mystery. The name

Penelope may be linked to that of Penelope Frater, Baynton's first mother-in-law. Penelope was also the name of her only daughter and the child to whom she seems to have been closest.

10. Marriage certificate, Alexander Frater and Barbara Lawrence.
11. Gullett, "Memoir", p.15.
12. B[arbara] B[aynton], "Goodbye Australia!", *Bulletin* (12 August 1899), in "Under the Gum Tree".
13. Barbara Baynton, "Baby", MS, Hayes Collection, Fryer Library, University of Queensland.
14. Mrs A.H. Brigden, Baynton's grand-daughter, in a letter to one of the present authors (1974).
15. Advertisement from the A.G. Stephens Scrapbook, Mitchell Library, N.S.W., n.d.
16. Barbara Baynton, letter to A.G. Stephens (September 1903), Hayes Collection, Fryer Library, University of Queensland.
17. Barbara Baynton, letter to A.G. Stephens (9 November 1896), Hayes Collection, Fryer Library, University of Queensland.
18. Barbara Baynton, letter to A.G. Stephens (10 November 1896), Hayes Collection, Fryer Library, University of Queensland.
19. Barbara Baynton, "Squeaker's Mate", MS, Mitchell Library, N.S.W.
20. For a full discussion of the relation between the Mitchell Library manuscript/typescript, the Fryer Library typescript, and the *Bush Studies* text(and a transcription of the Mitchell copy), see Elizabeth Webby, "Barbara Baynton's Revisions to 'Squeaker's Mate' ", *Southerly* 44 (1984): 455–68.
21. "England and the Australian Writer — Barbara Baynton's Experience", *Sydney Morning Herald* (6 July 1911).
22. Vance Palmer, "Writers I Remember — Barbara Baynton", *Overland* No. 11 (Summer 1958), p.15.
23. Palmer, "Writers I Remember", p.15.
24. Gullett, "Memoir", p. 18.
25. "Wedding: Lord Headley and Mrs Baynton", *British-Australasian* (London: 17 February 1921), p.11.
26. *Who Was Who 1929-1940*, (London: A.& C. Black, 1942).
27. "Lady Headley: Death of Remarkable Personality — Woman of Wide and Varied Interests", Unidentified Newspaper Cutting, held by Mrs A.H. Brigden.
28. "Wedding: Lord Headley and Mrs Baynton", *British-Australasian* (London: 17 February 1921), p.11.
29. Lady Barbara Headley, Papers 1907-38, National Library of Australia, MS3077; *The Times* (28 March 1924), p.5.
30. "Australian and New Zealand Homes in England: No. 7 — The Residence of the Lady Headley, 6 Connaught Square, W.2.", *British-Australasian* (London: 24 November 1921), p.13.
31. Gullett, "Memoir", p.25 refers to her "unvarying good health" but see letters to Stephens, September 1903, 24 January 1906, in Fryer Library; Lady Barbara Headley, Papers 1907-38, National Library of Australia, MS3077; *The Times* (6 June 1924), p.17,

"Court Circular"; *British Australian and New Zealander* (London: 30 May 1929), p.13.

32. "The Late Lady Headley", *British Australian and New Zealander* (London: 30 May 1929), p.13.
33. Palmer, "Writers I Remember", p.16.
34. Gullett, "Memoir", p.18.
35. "England and the Australian Writer — Barbara Baynton's Experience", *Sydney Morning Herald* (6 July 1911).
36. Unidentified newspaper cutting from A. G. Stephens's Scrapbook, Mitchell Library, N.S.W.
37. "The Late Lady Headley", *British Australian and New Zealander.* (London: 30 May 1929), p. 13.

Stories from Bush Studies 1902

Editors' Note

Bush Studies, Baynton's best known (and often her only known) work, was first published in book form in Duckworth's Greenback Library, in London in 1902 at the price of one shilling. It was issued in another edition (with two additional stories) by the same publisher in 1917: this edition was given the title *Cobbers*. Other modern texts of Baynton have chosen to reprint the *Bush Studies* text. However it is believed by the present editors that it is the *Cobbers* version of 1917 which represents the author's final intention and accordingly it is that edition which is followed here. In the Lady Barbara Headley papers in the National Library of Australia, Canberra there are some photocopies of page-proofs of *Cobbers*. On those proofs are corrections in what is recognizably Baynton's own hand. All of her corrections were incorporated into the text of *Cobbers* as it was finally printed. Although Baynton proclaimed her lack of experience with the practices of authorship and publication in a letter to A.G. Stephens in 1896, it is clear that by 1917 she was both confident and competent in these matters. The corrections are detailed and thorough. There is no reason, either aesthetic or bibliographical, for preferring the earlier edition.

The revisions are never drastic but they are careful. Punctuation is altered, syntax is simplified and generally a greater clarity is achieved. "The Chosen Vessel" attracted most attention in her revision, and at the very end of the story she reverts to her original *Bulletin* version by adding the macabre touch of: "But the dog was also guilty". In one place (p.57, 7th paragraph), however, the punctuation of the *Cobbers* text is clearly corrupt and an editorial preference for the 1902 reading is adopted. Otherwise the 1917 edition is the one given here, except for slight changes in punctuation marks and the standardization of "-ise" and "-ize".

Earlier drafts of "Squeaker's Mate" are held in the Fryer and Mitchell Libraries. As Elizabeth Webby has shown (*Southerly* 44 [1984]: 455–68), the Fryer typescript contains all the corrections made by both Baynton and Stephens to the Mitchell typescript/manuscript. In the *Bush Studies* version most of Baynton's original forms survive, but the *Bush Studies* version differs very substantially from either of these earlier versions. Similarly, Stephens' most substantial changes to "The Chosen Vessel" were eventually rejected by Baynton. The textual situation of this story is complex but it would seem that the original version (in the absence of a manuscript) is the one Baynton had privately printed and circulated in Sydney — probably soon before or after the *Bulletin* printing of the emended version of it (12 December 1896) under the title of "The Tramp". Baynton had suggested the alternative title "What the Curlews Cried" but it was not adopted. A.G. Stephens was presumably responsible for the title under which it appeared, just as he was responsible for omitting that section of the story concerned with Peter Hennessey and his vision. The *Bulletin* version, which is occasionally reprinted in anthologies, is entirely concerned with the unequal contest between the lone woman and the tramp (as he is called in that version). For the restoration of that section and other substantial revisions in the *Bush Studies* text we must assume that Baynton was responsible. The version of "Squeaker's Mate" in the typescript differs in many respects from the book version. A good deal of it is "told" by two mates Bill and Jim who, thankfully, disappear in the revision and it has a rather ineffectual postscript in which Squeaker's mate is taken to hospital (accompanied by her dog) and finally dies after being ministered to by an imperceptive parson and a very sympathetic nurse.

Bush Studies was dedicated by Baynton "To Helen McMillen of New South Wales". In the copy presented by her to Lord Tennyson (now held in the National Library) this is corrected in Baynton's hand to "McMillan".

A Dreamer

A SWIRL of wet leaves from the night-hidden trees decorating the little station, beat against the closed doors of the carriages. The porter hurried along holding his blear-eyed lantern to the different windows, and calling the name of the township in language peculiar to porters. There was only one ticket to collect.

Passengers from far up-country towns have importance from their rarity; he turned his lantern full on this one, as he took her ticket. She looked at him too, and listened to the sound of his voice, as he spoke to the guard. Once she had known every hand at the station. The porter knew every one in the district; this traveller was a stranger to him.

If her letter had been received, some one would have been waiting with a buggy. She passed through the station, seeing nothing but an ownerless dog, huddled, wet and shivering, in a corner. More for sound she turned to look up the straggling street of the township. Among the she-oaks, bordering the river she knew so well, the wind made ghostly music, unheeded by the sleeping town. There was no other sound, and she turned to the dog with a feeling of kinship. But perhaps the porter had a message! She went back to the platform. He was locking the office door, but paused as though expecting her to speak.

"Wet night!" he said at length, breaking the silence.

Her question resolved itself into a request for the time, though this she already knew. She hastily left him.

She drew her cloak tightly round her. The wind made her umbrella useless for shelter. Wind and rain and darkness lay before her on the walk of three bush miles to her mother's home. Still it was the home of her girlhood, and she hoped she knew every inch of the way.

As she passed along the sleeping street, she saw no sign of life till near the end, where a light burned in a small shop, and the sound of swift tapping came to her. They work late to-night, she thought, and, remembering their gruesome task, hesitated, half-minded to ask these night workers, for whom they laboured. Was it someone she had known, man or woman, old or young? The long dark walk — she could not — and hastened to lose the sound.

The zigzag course of the railway brought the train again near to her, and this wayfarer stood and watched it tunnelling in the teeth of the wind. Whoof! whoof! its steaming breath hissed at her. She saw the rain spitting viciously at its red mouth. Its speed, as it passed, made her realize the tedious difficulties of her journey, and she quickened her pace. There was the silent tenseness that precedes a storm. From the branch of a tree overhead she heard a watchful mother-bird's warning call, and the twitter of the disturbed nestlings. The tender care of this bird-mother awoke memories of her childhood. What mattered the lonely darkness, when it led to mother? Her forebodings fled, she faced the old track unheedingly, and ever and ever she smiled, as she foretasted their meeting.

"Daughter!"

"Mother!"

She could feel loving arms around her, and a mother's sacred kisses. She thrilled, and in her impatience ran, but the wind was angry and took her breath. Then the child near her heart stirred for the first time. The instincts of motherhood awakened in her. Her elated body quivered, she fell on her knees, lifted her hands, and turned her face to God. A vivid flash of lightning flamed above her head. It dulled her rapture, for the lightning was very near.

She went on, then paused. Was she on the right track? Back, near the bird's nest, were two roads. One led to home, the other was the old bullock-dray road, that the railway had almost usurped. When she should have been careful in her choice, she had been absorbed. It was a long way back to the cross roads, and she dug in her mind for landmarks.

Foremost she recalled the "Bendy Tree", then the "Sisters", whose entwined arms talked, when the wind was from the south. The apple trees on the creek-split flat, where the cows and calves were always to be found. The wrong track, being nearer the river, had clumps of she-oaks and groups of pines in places. An angled line of lightning illumined everything, but the violence of the thunder distracted her.

She stood in uncertainty, near-sighted, with all the horror of the unknown, that this infirmity could bring. Irresolute, she waited for another flash. It served to convince her she was wrong. Through the bush she turned.

The sky seemed to crack with the lightning; the thunder's suddenness shook her. Among some tall pines she stood awed, while the storm raged.

Then again that indefinite fear struck at her. Restlessly she pushed on till she stumbled, and, with hands outstretched, met some object that moved beneath them as she fell. The lightning showed a group of terrified cattle. Tripping and falling, she ran, she knew not where, but keeping her eyes turned towards the cattle. Aimlessly she pushed on, and unconsciously retraced her steps.

She struck the track she was on when her first doubt came. If this were the right way the wheel ruts would show. She groped, but the rain had levelled them. There was nothing to guide her. Suddenly she remembered that the little clump of pines, where the cattle were, lay between the two roads. She had gathered mistletoe berries there in the old days.

She believed, she hoped, she prayed, that she was right. If so, a little further on, she would come to the "Bendy Tree". There long ago a runaway horse had crushed its drunken rider against the bent, distorted trunk. She could recall how in her young years that tree had ever after had a weird fascination for her.

Thankfully she saw its crooked body in the lightning's glare. She was on the right track, yet dreaded to go on. Her childhood's fear came back. In a transient flash she thought she saw a horseman galloping furiously towards her. She placed both her hands protectingly over her heart, and waited. In the dark interval, above the shriek of the wind, she thought she heard a cry, then crash came the thunder, drowning her call of warning. In the next flash she saw nothing but the tree. "Oh, God, protect me!" she prayed, and diverging, with a shrinking heart passed on.

The road dipped to the creek. Louder and louder came the roar of its flooded waters. Even little Dog-trap Gully was proudly foaming itself hoarse. It emptied below where she must cross. But there were others, that swelled it above.

The noise of the rushing creek was borne to her by the wind, still fierce, though the rain had lessened. Perhaps there would be some one to meet her at the bank! Last time she had come, the night had been fine, and though she had been met at the station by a neighbour's son, mother had come to the creek with a lantern and waited for her. She looked eagerly, but there was no light.

The creek was a banker, but the track led to a plank, which, lashed to the willows on either bank, was usually above flood-level. A churning sound showed that the water was over the plank, and she must wade along it. She turned to the sullen sky. There was no gleam of light save in her resolute, white face.

Her mouth grew tender, as she thought of the husband she loved, and of their child. Must she dare! She thought of the grey-haired mother, who was waiting on the other side.

This dwarfed every tie that had parted them. There was atonement in these difficulties and dangers.

Again her face turned heavenward! "Bless, pardon, protect and guide, strengthen and comfort!" Her mother's prayer.

Steadying herself by the long willow branches, ankle deep she began. With every step the water deepened.

Malignantly the wind fought her, driving her back, or snapping the brittle stems from her skinned hands. The water was knee-deep now, and every step more hazardous.

She held with her teeth to a thin limb, while she unfastened her hat and gave it to the greedy wind. From the cloak, a greater danger, she could not in her haste free herself; her numbed fingers had lost their cunning.

Soon the water would be deeper, and the support from the branches less secure. Even if they did reach across, she could not hope for much from their wind-driven, fragile ends.

Still she would not go back. Though the roar of that rushing water was making her giddy, though the deafening wind fought her for every inch, she would not turn back.

Long ago she should have come to her old mother, and her heart gave a bound of savage rapture in thus giving the sweat of her body for the sin of her soul.

Midway the current strengthened. Perhaps if she, deprived of the willows, were swept down, her clothes would keep her afloat. She took firm hold and drew a deep breath to call her child-cry, "Mother!"

The water was deeper and swifter, and from the sparsity of the branches she knew she was nearing the middle. The wind unopposed by the willows was more powerful. Strain as she would, she could reach only the tips of the opposite trees, not hold them.

Despair shook her. With one hand she gripped those that had served her so far, and cautiously drew as many as she could grasp with the other. The wind savagely snapped them, and they lashed her unprotected face. Round and round her bare neck they coiled their stripped fingers. Her mother had planted these willows, and she herself had watched them grow. How could they be so hostile to her!

The creek deepened with every moment she waited. But more dreadful than the giddying water was the distracting noise of the mighty wind, nurtured by the hollows.

The frail twigs of the opposite tree snapped again and again in her hands. She must release her hold of those behind her. If she could make two steps independently, the thicker branches would then be her stay.

"Will you?" yelled the wind. A sudden gust caught her, and, hurling her backwards, swept her down the stream with her cloak for a sail.

She battled instinctively, and her first thought was of the letter-kiss, she had left for the husband she loved. Was it to be his last?

She clutched a floating branch, and was swept down with it. Vainly she fought for either bank.

She opened her lips to call. The wind made a funnel of

her mouth and throat, and a wave of muddy water choked her cry. She struggled desperately, but after a few mouthfuls she ceased. The weird cry from the "Bendy Tree" pierced and conquered the deep throated wind. Then a sweet dream voice whispered "Little Woman!"

Soft, strong arms carried her on. Weakness aroused the melting idea that all had been a mistake, and she had been fighting with friends. The wind even crooned a lullaby. Above the angry waters her face rose untroubled.

A giant tree's fallen body said, "Thus far!" and in vain the athletic furious water rushed and strove to throw her over the barrier. Driven back, it tried to take her with it. But a jagged arm of the tree snagged her cloak and held her.

Bruised and half conscious she was left to her deliverer, and the back-broken water crept tamed under its old foe. The hammer of hope soon awoke her heart. Along the friendly back of the tree she crawled, and among its bared roots rested. But it was only to get her breath, for this was mother's side.

She breasted the rise. Then every horror was of the past and forgotten, for there in the hollow was home.

And there was the light shining its welcome to her.

She quickened her pace, but did not run — motherhood is instinct in woman. The rain had come again, and the wind buffeted her. To breathe was a battle, yet she went on swiftly, for at the sight of the light her nameless fear had left her.

She would tell mother how she had heard her call in the night, and mother would smile her grave smile and stroke her wet hair, call her "Little woman! My little woman!" and tell her she had been dreaming, just dreaming. Ah, but mother herself was a dreamer!

The gate was swollen with rain and difficult to open. It had been opened by mother last time. But plainly her letter had not reached home. Perhaps the bad weather had delayed the mail boy.

There was the light. She was not daunted when the bark of the old dog brought no one to the door. It might not be heard inside, for there was such a torrent of water falling somewhere close. Mechanically her mind located it. The tank near the house, fed by the spouts was running over, cutting channels through the flower beds, and flooding the paths. Why had not mother diverted the spout to the other tank?

Something indefinite held her. Her mind went back to the many times long ago when she had kept alive the light while mother fixed the spout to save the water that the dry summer months made precious. It was not like mother, for such carelessness meant carrying from the creek.

Suddenly she grew cold and her heart trembled. After she had seen mother, she would come out and fix it, but just now she could not wait.

She tapped gently, and called "Mother!"

While she waited she tried to make friends with the dog. Her heart smote her, in that there had been so long an interval since she saw her old home, that the dog had forgotten her voice.

Her teeth chattered as she again tapped softly.

The sudden light dazzled her when a stranger opened the door for her. Steadying herself by the wall, with wild eyes she looked around. Another strange woman stood by the fire, and a child slept on the couch. The child's mother raised it, and the other led the now panting creature to the child's bed. Not a word was spoken, and the movements of these women were like those who fear to awaken a sleeper.

Something warm was held to her lips, for through it all she was conscious of everything, even that the numbing horror in her eyes met answering awe in theirs.

In the light the dog knew her and gave her welcome. But she had none for him now.

When she rose one of the women lighted a candle. She noticed how, if the blazing wood cracked, the women started nervously, how the disturbed child pointed to her bruised face, and whispered softly to its mother, how she who lighted the candle did not strike the match but held it to the fire, and how the light bearer led the way so noiselessly.

She reached her mother's room. Aloft the woman held the candle and turned away her head.

The daughter parted the curtains, and the light fell on the face of the sleeper who would dream no dreams that night.

Squeaker's Mate

THE woman carried the bag with the axe and maul and wedges; the man had the billy and clean tucker bags; the cross-cut saw linked them. She was taller than the man, and the equability of her body contrasting with his indolent slouch accentuated the difference. "Squeaker's mate" the men called her, and these agreed that she was the best long-haired mate that ever stepped in petticoats. The Selectors' wives pretended to challenge her right to womanly garments, but if she knew what they said, it neither turned nor troubled Squeaker's mate.

Nine prospective posts and maybe sixteen rails — she calculated this yellow gum would yield. "Come on," she encouraged the man; "let's tackle it."

From the bag she took the axe, and ring-barked a preparatory circle, while he looked for a shady spot for the billy and tucker bags.

"Come on." She was waiting with the greased saw. He came. The saw rasped through a few inches, then he stopped and looked at the sun.

"It's nigh tucker time," he said, and when she dissented, he exclaimed, with sudden energy, "There's another bee! Wait, you go on with the axe, an' I'll track 'im."

As they came, they had already followed one and located the nest. She could not see the bee he spoke of, though her grey eyes were as keen as a Black's. However she knew the man, and her tolerance was of the mysteries.

She drew out the saw, spat on her hands, and with the axe began weakening the inclining side of the tree.

Long and steadily and in secret the worm had been busy in the heart. Suddenly the axe blade sank softly, the tree's wounded edges closed on it like a vice. There was a "settling" quiver on its top branches, which the woman heard and understood. The man, encouraged by the sounds of the axe, had returned with an armful of sticks for the billy. He shouted gleefully, "It's fallin', look out."

But she waited to free the axe.

With a shivering groan the tree fell, and as she sprang aside, a thick worm-eaten branch snapped at a joint and silently she went down under it.

"I tole yer t' look out," he reminded her, as with a crow-bar, and grunting earnestly, he forced it up. "Now get out quick."

She tried moving her arms and the upper part of her body. Do this; do that, he directed, but she made no movement after the first.

He was impatient, because for once he had actually to use his strength. His share of a heavy lift usually consisted of a make-believe grunt, delivered at a critical moment. Yet he hardly cared to let it again fall on her, though he told her he would, if she "didn't shift".

Near him lay a piece broken short; with his foot he drew it nearer, then gradually worked it into a position, till it acted as a stay to the lever.

He laid her on her back when he drew her out, and waited expecting some acknowledgement of his exertions, but she was silent, and as she did not notice that the axe, she had tried to save, lay with the fallen trunk across it, he told her. She cared almost tenderly for all their possessions and treated them as friends. But the half-buried broken axe did not affect her. He wondered a little, for only last week she had patiently chipped out the old broken head, and put in a new handle.

"Feel bad?" he inquired at length.

"Pipe," she replied with slack lips.

Both pipes lay in the fork of a near tree. He took his, shook out the ashes, filled it, picked up a coal and puffed till it was alight — then he filled hers. Taking a small firestick he handed her the pipe. The hand she raised shook and closed in an uncertain hold, but she managed by a great effort to get it to her mouth. He lost patience with the swaying hand that tried to take the light.

"Quick," he said, "quick, that damn dog's at the tucker."

He thrust it into her hand that dropped helplessly across her chest. The lighted stick falling between her bare arm and the dress slowly roasted the flesh and smouldered the clothes.

He rescued their dinner, pelted his dog out of sight — hers was lying near her head, put on the billy, then came back to her.

The pipe had fallen from her lips; there was blood on the stem.

"Did yer jam yer tongue?" he asked.

She always ignored trifles he knew, therefore he passed her silence.

He told her that her dress was on fire. She took no heed. He put it out, and looked at the burnt arm, then with intentness at her.

Her eyes were turned unblinkingly to the heavens, her lips were grimly apart, and a strange greyness was upon her face, and the sweat-beads were mixing.

"Like a drink er tea? Asleep?"

He broke a green branch from the fallen tree and swished from his face the multitudes of flies that had descended with it.

In a heavy way he wondered why she did sweat, when she was not working? Why did she not keep the flies out of her mouth and eyes? She'd have bungy eyes, if she didn't. If she was asleep, why did she not close them?

But asleep or awake, as the billy began to boil, he left her, made the tea, and ate his dinner.

His dog had disappeared, and as it did not come to his whistle, he threw the pieces to hers, that would not leave her head to reach them.

He whistled tunelessly his one air, beating his own time with a stick on the toe of his blucher, then looked overhead at the sun and calculated that she must have been lying like that for "close up an hour". He noticed that the axe handle was broken in two places, and speculated a little as to whether she would again pick out the back-broken handle or burn it out in his method, which was less trouble, if it did spoil the temper of the blade. He examined the worm-dust in the stump and limbs of the newly-fallen tree; mounted it and looked round the plain. The sheep were straggling in a manner that meant walking work to round them, and he supposed he would have to yard them to-night, if she didn't liven up. He looked down at unenlivened her. This changed his "chune" to a call for his hiding dog.

"Come on, ole feller," he commanded her dog. "Fetch 'em back."

He whistled further instructions, slapping his thigh and pointing to the sheep.

But a brace of wrinkles either side the brute's closed mouth demonstrated determined disobedience. The dog would go if she told him, and by and bye she would.

He lighted his pipe and killed half an hour smoking. With the frugality that hard graft begets, his mate limited both his and her own tobacco, so he must not smoke all afternoon. There was no work to shirk, so time began to drag. Then a goanner crawling up a tree attracted him. He gathered various missiles and tried vainly to hit the seemingly grinning reptile. He came back and sneaked a fill of her tobacco, and while he was smoking, the white tilt of a cart caught his eye. He jumped up. "There's Red Bob goin' t'our place fur th' 'oney," he said; "I'll go an' weigh it an' get the gonz" (money).

He ran for the cart, and kept looking back as if fearing she would follow and thwart him.

Red Bob the dealer was, in a business way, greatly concerned, when he found that Squeaker's mate was "'avin' a sleep out there 'cos a tree fell on her". She was the best honey strainer and boiler that he dealt with. She was straight and square too. There was no water in her honey whether boiled or merely strained, and in every kerosene tin the weight of honey was to an ounce as she said. Besides he was suspicious and diffident of paying the indecently eager Squeaker before he saw the woman. So reluctantly Squeaker led to where she lay. With many fierce oaths Red Bob sent her lawful protector for help, and compassionately poured a little spirits from his flask down her throat, then swished away the flies from her till help came.

Together these men stripped a sheet of bark and laying her with pathetic tenderness upon it, carried her to her hut. Squeaker followed in the rear with the billy and tucker.

Red Bob took his horse from the cart, and went to town for the doctor. Late that night at the back of the old hut (there were two) he and others who had heard that she was hurt, squatted with unlighted pipes in their mouths, waiting to hear the doctor's verdict. After he had given it and gone they discussed in whispers, and with a look seen only on bush faces, the hard luck of that woman who alone had hard-grafted with the best of them for every acre and hoof on that selection. Squeaker would go through it in no time. Why she had allowed it to be taken up in his name, when the money had been her own, was also for them among the mysteries.

Him they called "a nole woman", not because he was hanging round the honey tins, but after man's fashion to eliminate all virtue. They beckoned him, and explaining his mate's injury, cautioned him to keep from her the knowledge that she would be for ever a cripple.

"Jus' th' same, now then fur 'im," pointing to Red Bob, "t' pay me, I'll 'ev t' go t' town."

They told him in whispers what they thought of him, and with a cowardly look towards where she lay, but without a word of parting, like shadows these men made for their homes.

Next day the women came. Squeaker's mate was not a favourite with them — a woman with no leisure for yarning was not likely to be. After the first day they left her severely alone, their plea to their husbands her uncompromising independence. It is in the ordering of things that by degrees most husbands accept their wives' views of other women.

The flour bespattering Squeaker's now neglected clothes spoke eloquently of his clumsy efforts at damper making. The women gave him many a feed, agreeing that it must be miserable for him.

If it were miserable and lonely for his mate, she did not

complain; for her the long, long days would give place to longer nights — those nights with the pregnant bush silence suddenly cleft by a bush voice. However she was not fanciful, and being a bush scholar knew 'twas a dingo, when a long whine came from the scrub on the skirts of which lay the axe under the worm-eaten tree. That quivering wail from the billabong lying murkily mystic towards the East was only the cry of the fearing curlew.

Always her dog — wakeful and watchful as she — patiently waiting for her to be up and about again. That would be soon, she told her complaining mate.

"Yer won't. Yer back's broke," said Squeaker laconically. "That's wot's wrong er yer; injoory t' th' spine. Doctor says that means back's broke, and yer won't never walk no more. No good not t' tell yer, 'cos I can't be doin' everythin'."

A wild look grew on her face, and she tried to sit up.

"Erh," said he, "see! yer carnt, yer jes' ther same as a snake w'en ees back's broke, on'y yer don't bite yerself like a snake does w'en 'e carnt crawl. Yer did bite yer tongue w'en yer fell."

She gasped, and he could hear her heart beating when she let her head fall back a few moments; though she wiped her wet forehead with the back of her hand, and still said that was the doctor's mistake. But day after day she tested her strength, and whatever the result was silent, though white witnesses, halo-wise, gradually circled her brow and temples.

" 'Tisn't as if yer was agoin' t' get better t' morrer, the doctor says yer won't never work no more, an' I can't be cookin' an' workin' an' doin' everythin'!"

He muttered something about "sellin' out", but she firmly refused to think of such a monstrous proposal.

He went into town one Saturday afternoon soon after, and did not return till Monday.

Her supplies, a billy of tea and scraps of salt beef and damper (her dog got the beef), gave out the first day, though that was as nothing to her compared with the bleat of the penned sheep, for it was summer and droughty, and her dog could not unpen them.

Of them and her dog only she spoke when he returned.

He d—d him, and d—d her, and told her to "double up yer ole broke back an' bite yerself". He threw things about, made a long-range feint of kicking her threatening dog, then sat outside in the shade of the old hut, nursing his head till he slept.

She, for many reasons, had when necessary made these trips into town, walking both ways, leading a pack-horse for supplies. She never failed to indulge him in a half-pint — a pipe was her luxury.

The sheep waited till next day, so did she, then for a few days he worked a little in her sight; not much — he never did. It was she who always lifted the heavy end of the log, and carried the tools; he — the billy and tucker.

She wearily watched him idling his time; reminded him that the wire lying near the fence would rust, one could run the wire through easily, and when she got up in a day or so, she would help strain and fasten it. At first he pretended he had done it, later said he wasn't goin' t' go wirin' or nothin' else by 'imself if every other man on the place did.

She spoke of many other things that could be done by one, reserving the great till she was well. Sometimes he whistled while she spoke, often swore, generally went out, and when this was inconvenient, dull as he was, he found the "Go and bite yerself like a snake", would instantly silence her.

At last the work worry ceased to exercise her, and for night to bring him home was a rare thing.

Her dog rounded and yarded the sheep when the sun went down and there was no sign of him, and together they kept watch on their movements till dawn. She was mindful not to speak of this care to him, knowing he would have left it for them to do constantly, and she noticed that what little interest he seemed to share went to the sheep. Why, was soon demonstrated.

Through the cracks her ever watchful eyes one day saw the dust rise out of the plain. Nearer it came till she saw him and a man on horseback rounding and driving the sheep into the yard, and later both left in charge of a little mob. Their "Baa-baas" to her were cries for help; many had been pets. So he was selling her sheep to the town butchers.

In the middle of the next week he came from town with a fresh horse, new saddle and bridle. He wore a flash red shirt, and round his neck a silk handkerchief. On the next occasion she smelt scent, and though he did not try to display the dandy meerschaum, she saw it, and heard the squeak of the new boots, not bluchers. However he was kinder to her this time, offering a fill of his cut tobacco; he had long ceased to keep her supplied. Several of the men who sometimes in passing took a look in would have made up her loss had they known, but no word of complaint passed her lips.

She looked at Squeaker as he filled his pipe from his pouch, but he would not meet her eyes, and, seemingly dreading something, slipped out.

She heard him hammering in the old hut at the back, which served for tools and other things which sunlight and rain did not hurt. Quite briskly he went in and out. She could see him through the cracks carrying a narrow strip of bark, and understood: he was making a bunk. When it was finished he had a smoke, then came to her and fidgeted about; he said this hut was too cold, and that she would never get well in it. She did not feel cold, but submitting to his mood, allowed him to make a fire that would roast a sheep. He took off his hat, and fanning himself, said he was roastin', wasn't she? She was.

He offered to carry her into the other; he would put a new roof on it in a day or two, and it would be better than this one, and she would be up in no time. He stood to say this where she could not see him.

His eagerness had tripped him.

There were months to run before all the Government conditions of residence, etc., in connection with the selection, would be fulfilled, still she thought perhaps he was trying to sell out, and she would not go.

He was away four days that time, and when he returned slept in the new bunk.

She compromised. Would he put a bunk there for himself, keep out of town, and not sell the place! He promised instantly, with additions.

"Try could yer crawl yerself?" he coaxed, looking at her bulk.

Her nostrils quivered with her suppressed breathing, and her lips tightened, but she did not attempt to move.

It was evident some great purpose actuated him. After attempts to carry and drag her, he rolled her on the sheet of bark that had brought her home, and laboriously drew her round.

She asked for a drink, he placed her billy and tin pint besides the bunk, and left her gasping and dazed to her sympathetic dog.

She saw him run up and yard his horse, and though she called him, he would not answer nor come.

When he rode swiftly towards the town, her dog leaped on the bunk, and joined a refrain to her lamentation, but the cat took to the bush.

He came back at dusk next day in a spring cart — not alone — he had another mate. She saw her though he came a roundabout way, trying to keep in front of the new hut.

There were noises of moving many things from the cart to the hut. Finally he came to a crack near where she lay, and whispered the promise of many good things to her if she kept quiet, and that he would set her hut afire if she didn't. She was quiet, he need not have feared, for that time she was past it, she was stunned.

The released horse came stumbling round to the old hut, and thrust its head in the door in a domesticated fashion. Her dog promptly resented this straggler mistaking their hut for a stable. And the dog's angry dissent, together with the shod clatter of the rapidly disappearing intruder, seemed to have a disturbing effect on the pair in the new hut. The settling sounds suddenly ceased, and the cripple heard the stranger close the door, despite Squeaker's assurances that the woman in the old hut could not move from her bunk to save her life, and that her dog would not leave her.

Food, more and better, was placed near her — but, dumb and motionless, she lay with her face turned to the wall, and her dog growled menacingly at the stranger. The new woman was uneasy, and told Squeaker what people might say and do if she died.

He scared his missus at the "do", went into the bush and waited.

She went to the door, not the crack, the face was turned that way, and said she had come to cook and take care of her.

The disabled woman, turning her head slowly, looked steadily at her. She was not much to look at. Her red hair hung in an uncurled bang over her forehead, the lower part of her face had robbed the upper, and her figure evinced imminent motherhood, though it is doubtful if the barren woman, noting this, knew by calculation the paternity was not Squeaker's. She was not learned in these matters, though she understood all about an ewe and lamb.

One circumstance was apparent — ah! bitterest of all bitterness to women — she was younger.

The thick hair that fell from the brow of the woman on the bunk was white now.

Bread-and-butter the woman brought. The cripple looked at it, at her dog, at the woman. Bread-and-butter for a dog! but the stranger did not understand till she saw it offered to the dog. The bread-and-butter was not for the dog. She brought meat.

All next day the man kept hidden. The cripple saw his dog, and knew he was about.

But there was an end of this pretence when at dusk he came back with a show of haste, and a finger of his right hand bound and ostentatiously prominent. His entrance caused great excitement to his new mate. The old mate, who knew this snake-bite trick from its inception, maybe, realized how useless were the terrified stranger's efforts to rouse the snoring man after an empty pint bottle had been flung on the outside heap.

However, what the sick woman thought was not definite, for she kept silent always. Neither was it clear how much she ate, and how much she gave to her dog, though the new mate said to Squeaker one day that she believed that the dog would not take a bite more than its share.

The cripple's silence told on the stranger, especially when alone. She would rather have abuse. Eagerly she counted the days past and to pass. Then back to the town. She told no word of that hope to Squeaker, he had no place in her plans for the future. So if he spoke of what they would do by and bye when his time would be up, and he able to sell out, she listened in uninterested silence.

She did tell him she was afraid of "her", and after the first day would not go within reach, but every morning made a billy of tea, which with bread and beef Squeaker carried to her.

The rubbish heap was adorned, for the first time, with jam and fish tins from the table in the new hut. It seemed to be understood that neither woman nor dog in the old hut required them.

Squeaker's dog sniffed and barked joyfully around them till his licking efforts to bottom a salmon tin sent him careering in a muzzled frenzy, that caused the younger woman's thick lips to part grinningly till he came too close.

The remaining sheep were regularly yarded. His old mate heard him whistle as he did it. Squeaker began to work about a little burning off. So that now, added to the other bush voices, was the call from some untimely falling giant. There is no sound so human as that from the riven souls of these tree people, or the trembling sighs of their upright neighbours whose hands in time will meet over the victim's fallen body.

There was no bunk on the side of the hut to which her eyes turned, but her dog filled that space, and the flash that passed between this back-broken woman and her dog might have been the spirit of these slain tree folk, it was so wondrous ghostly. Still, at times, the practical in her would be dominant, for in a mind so free of fancies, backed by bodily strength, hope died slowly, and forgetful of self she would almost call to Squeaker her fears that certain bees nests were in danger.

He went into town one day and returned, as he had promised, long before sundown, and next day a clothes line bridged the space between two trees near the back of the old hut; and — an equally rare occurrence — Squeaker placed across his shoulders the yoke that his old mate had fashioned for herself, with two kerosene tins attached, and brought them filled with water from the distant creek; but both only partly filled the tub, a new purchase. With utter disregard of the heat and Squeaker's sweating brow, his new mate said, even after another trip, two more now for the blue water. Under her commands he brought them, though sullenly, perhaps contrasting the old mate's methods with the new.

His old mate had periodically carried their washing to the creek, and his mole-skins had been as white as snow without aid of blue.

Towards noon, on the clothes line many strange garments fluttered, suggestive of a taunt to the barren woman. When the sun went down she could have seen the assiduous Squeaker lower the new prop-sticks and considerately stoop to gather the pegs his inconsiderate new mate had dropped. However, after one load of water next morning, on hearing her estimate that three more would put her own things through, Squeaker struck. Nothing he could urge would induce the stranger to trudge to the creek, where thirst-slaked snakes lay waiting for some one to bite. She sulked and pretended to pack up, till a bright idea struck Squeaker. He fastened a cask on a sledge and harnessing the new horse, hitched him to it, and, under the approving eyes of his new mate, led off to the creek, though, when she went inside, he bestrode the spiritless brute.

He had various mishaps, any one of which would have served as an excuse to his old mate, but even babes soon know on whom to impose. With an energy new to him he persevered and filled the cask, but the old horse repudiated such a burden even under Squeaker's unmerciful welts. Almost half was sorrowfully baled out, and under a rain of whacks the horse shifted it a few paces, but the cask tilted and the thirsty earth got its contents. All Squeaker's adjectives over his wasted labour were as unavailing as the cure for spilt milk.

It took skill and patience to rig the cask again. He partly filled it, and just as success seemed probable, the rusty wire fastening the cask to the sledge snapped with the strain, and springing free coiled affectionately round the terrified horse's hocks. Despite the sledge (the cask had been soon disposed of) that old town horse's pace then was his record.

Hours after, on the plain that met the horizon, loomed two specks: the distance between them might be gauged, for the larger was Squeaker.

Anticipating a plentiful supply and lacking in bush caution, the new mate used the half bucket of water to boil the salt mutton. Towards noon she laid this joint and bread on the rough table, then watched anxiously in the wrong direction for Squeaker.

She had drained the new tea-pot earlier, but she placed the spout to her thirsty mouth again.

She continued looking for him for hours.

Had he sneaked off to town, thinking she had not used that water, or not caring whether or no.

She did not trust him; another had left her. Besides she judged Squeaker by his treatment of the woman who was lying in there with wide-open eyes. Anyhow no use to cry with only that silent woman to hear her.

Had she drunk all hers?

She tried to see at long range through the cracks, but the hanging bed clothes hid the billy.

She went to the door, and avoiding the bunk looked at the billy.

It was half full.

Instinctively she knew that the eyes of the woman were upon her. She turned away, and hoped and waited for thirsty minutes that seemed hours.

Desperation drove her back to the door, dared she? No she couldn't.

Getting a long forked propstick, she tried to reach it from the door, but the dog sprang at the stick. She dropped it and ran.

A scraggy growth fringed the edge of the plain. There was the creek. How far? she wondered. Oh, very far, she knew, and besides there were only a few holes where water was, and the snakes; for Squeaker, with a desire to shine in her eyes, was continually telling her of snakes — vicious and many — that daily he did battle with.

She recalled the evening he came from hiding in the scrub with a string round one finger, and said a snake had bitten him. He had drunk the pint of brandy she had brought for her sickness, and then slept till morning. True, although next day he had to dig for the string round the blue swollen finger, yet he was not worse than the many she had seen at the "Shearer's Rest" suffering a recovery, now there was no brandy to cure her if she were bitten.

She cried a little in self pity, then withdrew her eyes, that were getting red, from the outlying creek, and went again to the door. She of the bunk lay with closed eyes.

Was she asleep? The stranger's heart leapt, yet she was hardly in earnest as she tip-toed billy-wards. The dog, crouching with head between two paws, eyed her steadily, but showed no opposition. She made dumb show. "I want to be friends with you, and won't hurt her." Abruptly she looked at her, then at the dog. He was motionless and emotionless. Beside if that dog — certainly watching her — wanted to bite her (her dry mouth opened), it could get her any time.

She rated this dog's intelligence almost human, from many of its actions in omission and commission in connection with this woman.

She regretted the pole, no dog would stand that.

Two more steps.

Now just one more; then, by bending and stretching her arm, she would reach it. Could she now? She tried to encourage herself by remembering how close on the first day she had been to the woman, and how delicious a few mouthfuls would be — swallowing dry mouthfuls.

She measured the space between where she had first stood and the billy. Could she get anything to draw it to her. No, the dog would not stand that, and besides the handle would rattle, and she might hear and open her eyes.

The thought of those sunken eyes suddenly opening made her heart bound. Oh! she must breathe — deep, loud breaths. Her throat clicked noisily. Looking back fearfully, she went swiftly out.

She did not look for Squeaker this time, she had given him up.

While she waited for her breath to steady, to her relief and surprise the dog came out. She made a rush to the new hut, but he passed seemingly oblivious of her, and bounding across the plain began rounding the sheep. Then he must know Squeaker had gone to town.

Stay! Her heart beat violently; was it because she on the bunk slept and did not want him?

She waited till her heart quieted, and again crept to the door.

The head of the woman on the bunk had fallen towards the wall as in deep sleep; it was turned from the billy, to which she must creep so softly.

Slower, from caution and deadly earnestness, she entered.

She was not so advanced as before, and felt fairly secure, for the woman's eyes were still turned to the wall, and so tightly closed, she could not possibly see the intruder.

Well, now she would bend right down, and try and reach it from here.

She bent.

It was so swift and sudden, that she had not time to scream when those bony fingers had gripped the hand that prematurely reached for the billy. She was frozen with horror for a moment, then her screams were piercing. Panting with victory, the prostrate one held her with a hold that the other did not attempt to free herself from.

Down, down the woman drew her prey.

Her lips had drawn back from her teeth, and her breath almost scorched the face that she held so close for the starting eyes to gloat over. Her exultation was so great, that she could only gloat and gasp, and hold with a tension that had stopped the victim's circulation.

As a wounded, robbed tigress might hold and look, she held and looked.

Neither heard the swift steps of the man, and if the tigress saw him enter, she was not daunted. "Take me from 'er," shrieked the terrified one. "Quick, take me from 'er," she repeated it again, nothing else. "Take me from 'er."

He hastily fastened the door and said something that the shrieks drowned, then picked up the pole. It fell with a thud across the arms which the tightening sinews had turned into steel. Once, twice, thrice. Then the one that got the fullest force bent; that side of the victim was free.

The pole had snapped. Another blow with a broken end freed the other side.

Still shrieking "Take me from 'er, take me from 'er," she rushed to and beat on the closed door till reluctantly Squeaker opened it.

Then he had to face and reckon with his old mate's maddened dog, that the closed door had baffled.

The dog suffered the shrieking woman to pass, but though Squeaker, in bitten agony, broke the stick across the dog, he was forced to gave the savage brute best.

"Call 'im orf, Mary, 'e's eating me," he implored. "Oh, corl 'im orf."

But with stony face the woman lay motionless.

"Sool 'im on t' 'er." He indicated his new mate who, as though all the plain led to the desired town, still ran in unreasoning terror.

"It's orl er doin'," he pleaded, springing on the bunk beside his old mate. But when, to rouse her sympathy, he would have laid his hand on her, the dog's teeth fastened in it and pulled him back.

Scrammy 'And *

Along the selvage of the scrub-girt plain the old man looked long and earnestly. His eyes followed an indistinct track that had been cut by the cart, journeying at rare intervals to the distant township. At dawn some weeks back it had creaked across the plain, and at a point where the scrub curved, the husband had stopped the horse while the woman parted the tilt and waved good-bye to the bent, irresponsive old man and his dog. It was her impending motherhood that made them seek the comparative civilization of the township, and the tenderness of her womanhood brought the old man closer to her as they drove away. Every week since that morning had been carefully notched by man and dog, and the last mark, cut three nights past, showed that time was up. Twice this evening he thought he saw the dust rise as he looked, but longer scrutiny showed only the misty evening light.

He turned to where a house stood out from a background of scrub. Beside the calf-pen near it, a cow gave answer and greeting to the penned calf. "No use pennin' up ther calf," he muttered, "when they don't come. Won't do it termorrer night. She was milked dry this mornin'; calf must 'ave got 'is 'ed through ther rails an' sucked 'er. No one else can't 'ave done it. Scrammy's gorn; 'twarn't Scrammy." But he watched anxiously along the scrub, and the gloom of fear settled on his wizened face as he shuffled stiffly towards the sheep yard.

His body jerked; there was a suggestion of the dog in his

* "Scrammy" indicates malformation of the hand.

movements; and in the dog, as he rounded up the sheep, more than a suggestion of his master. He querulously accused the dog of "rushin' 'em, 'stead er allowin' Billy (the leader) to lead 'em".

When they were yarded he found fault with the hurdles. "Some 'un 'ad been meddlin' with 'em." For two pins he would "smash 'em up with ther axe".

The eyes of the sheep reflected the haze-opposed glory of the setting sun. Loyally they stood till a grey quilt swathed them. In their eyes glistened luminous tears materialized from an atmosphere of sighs. The wide plain gauzed into a sea on which the hut floated lonely. Through its open door a fire gleamed like the red steaming mouth of an engine. Beyond the hut a clump of myalls loomed spectral and wraith-like, and round them a gang of crows cawed noisily, irreverent of the great silence.

Inside the hut, the old man, still querulous, talked to the listening dog. He uncovered a cabbage-tree hat — his task of the past year — and laid upside down, on the centre of the crown, a star-shaped button that the absent woman had worked for him.

"It's orl wrong, see!" The dog said he did. "Twon't do!" he shouted with the emphasis of deafness. The dog admitted it would not. "An' she done it like thet, ter spile it on me 'er purpus. She done it outer jealersy, 'cos I was makin' it for 'im. Could 'ave done it better meself, though I'm no 'and at fancy stitchin'. But she can't make a 'at like thet. No woman could. The're no good." The dog neither endorsed nor disputed this condemnation.

"I tole 'er ter put a anker jes' there," he continued. He pointed to the middle of the button which he still held upside down. "Thet's no anker!" The dog subtly indicated that there was another side to the button. "There ain't," shouted the old man. "What do you know about an anker; you never see a real one on a ship in yer life!" There was an inaudible disparaging reference to "imperdent kerloneyals" which seemed to crush the dog. To mollify him the man got on his knees, and bending his neck showed the dog a faded anchor on the top of the cabbage-tree hat on his head. A little resentment would have served the dog, but he was too eager for peace.

Noting this, the old man returned to the button for reminiscences. "An' yet you thort at fust a thing like thet would do." There was a sign of dissent from the dog. "Yer know yer did — Sir. An' wot's more yer don't bark at 'er like yer used ter!"

The dog was uneasy, and intimated that he would prefer to have that past buried.

"None er thet now; yer know yer don't." Bending the button he continued, "They can't never do anythin' right, an' orlways, continerally they gets a man inter trouble."

He had accidentally turned the button the right way, he reversed it looking swiftly at the dog. "Carn't do nothin' with it. A thing like thet! Might as well sling it inter ther fire," putting it carefully away.

"W'ere's 'e now?" he asked abruptly. The dog indicated the route taken by the cart.

"An' 'ow long 'as 'e bin away?" The dog looked at the tally stick hanging on the wall. "Yes, orl thet time! What does 'e care about me an' you, now 'e's got 'er? 'E was fust rate afore 'e got er. Wish I 'ad er gorn down thet time 'e took ther sheep. I'd er seen no woman didn't grab 'im. They're stuck away down there an' us orl alone 'ere by ourselves with only ther sheep. Scrammy wanted me to clear out with 'im to-day, sez 'e wouldn't stay if 'e wus me. See's there any sign er 'em comin' back!"

While the dog was out he hastily tried to fix the button, but failed. "On'y mist, no dust?" he asked, when his messenger returned. "No fear," he growled, " 'e won't come back no more: stay down there an' nuss ther babby. It'll be a gal too, sure to be! Women are orlways 'avin' gals. It'll be a gal sure enough."

He looked sternly at the unagreeing dog. "Yer don't think so! Course yer don't. You on 'er side? Yer are Loo!"

The dog's name was "Warderloo" (Waterloo) and had three abreviations. "Now then, War!" meant mutual understanding and perfect fellowship. "What's thet, Warder?" meant serious business. But "Loo" was ever sorrowfully reminiscent. And accordingly "Loo" was now much affected and disconcerted by the steady accusing eyes of the old man.

"An' wot's more," he continued, "I believe ye'll fool roun', ye'll fool aroun' 'er wusser nor ever w'en she comes back with ther babby." At this grave charge the dog, either from guilt or dignity or injury, was silent. His master, slowly and with some additions, repeated the prophecy, and again the dog gave him only mute attention.

"'Ere she comes with ther babby," he cried, flinging up his arms in clumsy feigned surprise. Loo was not deceived, and stood still.

"Oh, I'm a ole liar, am I? Yit's come ter thet; ez it? Well, better fer I ter be a liar 'n fer you ter lose yer manners, — Sir."

In vain Loo protested. His master turned his back, and when poor Loo faced that way, he drew his feet under him on the bunk and faced the wall. When the distressed Loo, from outside the hut, adroitly caught his eye through the cracks, the old man was forced to blink to stifle remorse at the eloquent dumb appeal in the dog's eyes.

Usually their little differences took some time to evaporate; the master sulked with his silent mate till some daring feat with snake or dingo on the dog's part mollified him. Loo, probably on the look-out for such foes, moved to the end of the hut nearest the sheep. Two hasty squints revealed his departure, but not his whereabouts, to the old man, who coughed and waited, but for once expected too much from poor Loo. His legs grew cramped, still he did not care to make the first move, so it was a godsend when an undemonstrative ewe and demonstrative lamb came in.

Before that ewe he held the whole of her disgraceful past, and under the circumstances, "'er imperdence — 'er blarsted imperdence —" in unceremoniously intruding on his privacy with her blanky blind udder, and more than blanky bastard, was something he could not and would not stand.

"None er yer damn sauce now!" he shouted as he jumped down, and shook his fist at the unashamed, silent mother. "Warder," he shouted, "Warder, put 'em out!"

Warder did so, and when he came back his mollified master explained to him that the thing that "continerally an' orlways" upset him was "thet dam old yew". It was the only sorrow he had or ever would have in life. "She wusn't nat'ral, thet ole yew." There was something in the Bible, he told War, about "yews" with barren udders. "An' 'twarn't as though she didn't know." For that was her third lamb he had had to poddy (hand feed). But not another bite would he give this one, he had made up his mind now, though it had been "worritin' " him all day. "Jes' look at me," showing his lamb-bitten fingers. "Wantin' ter get blood outer a stone!"

He shambled round, covered the cabbage-tree hat and the despised woman-worked button carefully; then his better nature prevailed. "Warder, see 'ere!" and there was that in his voice that indicated a moral victory. He took off the cloth and placed the button right side up and in its proper place. "Will thet do yer?" he asked.

After this surrender his excitement was so great, that the dog shared it. He advised War to lie down "an 'ave a spell", and alone in strong agitation he went round the sheep yard twice, each time stopping to hammer down the hurdles noisily, and calling to War not to "worrit; they's orlright now, an' firm as a rock".

Through these proceedings the ewe and lamb followed him, the lamb — lamb fashion — mixing itself with his legs. He had nothing further to say to the ewe, and from the expression of her eyes she still had an open mind towards him. Both went with him inside the hut. Were they intruders? the dog asked. He coughed and affected not to hear, went to the door, looked out and said the mist was gone, but the dog re-asked. "I think, War, there's some er that orkerd little dam fool's grub lef'," he said, gently extricating the lamb from between his legs. "I wouldn't give it a bite, but it'll on'y waste. Jes' this once an' no more, min' yer, an' then you skiddy addy," he said to the ewe, then carried the lamb outside, for he would not finger-suckle it that night before Waterloo.

From his bunk head he took an axe, cut in two a myall log, and brought in half. He threw it on the fire for a back-log, first scraping the live coals and ashes to a heap for his damper.

He filled and trimmed his slush lamp, and from a series of flat pockets hanging on the wall he took thread, needle, and beeswax. He hung a white cloth in a way that defined the eye of the needle which he held at long range; but vary as he would from short to long the thread remained in one hand, the needle in the other. Needle, thread, light, everything was wrong, he told War. "Es fer me, thenk the Lord, I ken see an' year as well as ever I could. Ehm, War! See any change in me seein' and 'earin'?" War said there had been no change observable to him. "There ain't no change in you neither, War!" he said in gratitude, laying his hand affectionately on the grizzled old dog's head. But he felt that War had been disappointed at his failure, and he promised that he would rise betimes to-morrow and sew on the button by daylight.

"Never mind, War; like ter see 'em after supper?" War would, and pleasure and comradeship was never by speech better demonstrated.

From the middle beam the old man untied two bags: boiled mutton was in one, and the heel of a damper in another.

"No blowey carn't get in there, eh?" the agreeing dog looked at the meat uncritically, but critically noted the resting-place of two disturbed "bloweys".

"No bones!" He had taken great care to omit them. As ever, War took his word; he caught and swallowed instantly several pieces flung to him. At the finish his master's "Eny?" referring to bones. War's grateful eyes twinkled, "Not a one." "Never is neow!" referring to a trouble War had with one long ago.

It was now time for his own supper, but after a few attempts he shirked it. "Blest if I evven fergot t'bile th' billy; funny ef me t' ferget!" He held his head for a moment, then filled the billy, and in a strange uncertainty went towards and from the fire with it, and in the end War thought there was no sense at all in putting it so far from the blaze when it had to boil.

"Tell yer wot, War, w'ile it biles us'll count 'em. Gimme appertite, ehm, War?"

War thought "countin' 'em" was the tonic. Then together they closed the door, spread a kangaroo skin on the floor, and put the slush lamp where the light fell on it. The man sat down, so did War, took off his belt, turned it carefully, tenderly, and opened his knife to cut the stitching. This was a tedious process, for it was wax thread, and had been crossed and recrossed. Then came the chink of the coins falling. The old man counted each as it rolled out, and the dog tallied with a paw.

"No more?" Certainly more, said War. A jerk, tenderly calculated, brought another among the seductive heap.

"All?" no — still the upraised paw. The old man chuckled.

"Ole 'en gets more b' scratchin'." This was the dog's opinion, and a series of little undulations produced another, and after still further shaking yet another.

War was asked with ridiculous insincerity, "All?" and with ridiculous sincerity his solemn eyes and dropped paw said "all". Then there was the honest count straight through, next the side show with its pretence of "disrememberin' ", or doubts as to the number — doubts never laid except by a double count. In the first, so intent was the man, that he forgot his mate; though his relief, in being good friends again, had made him ignore his fear.

But the dog had heard an outside sound, and, moving to the door, waited for certainty; and at this stage the man missed his mate's eyes.

He lay face downward, covering his treasure, when he realized that his friend was uneasy. And as the dog kept watch, he thrust the coins back hurriedly, missing all the pleasure and excitement of a final recount.

With dumb show he asked several anxious questions of his sentinel, and took his answers from the dog's uneasy eyes. Then, when Warder relieved began to walk about, the old man with forced confidence chaffed him. He sought refuge from his own fears by trying to banish the dog's, and suggested that it had been dingoes at the sheep yard, or a "goanner" on the roof. "Well, 'twas 'possum," he said, making a pretence of even then hearing and distinguishing the sound.

But round his waist the belt did not go that night. Only its bulk in his life of solitariness could have conceived its hiding place.

He bustled around as one having many tasks, but these he did aimlessly. With a pretence of unconcern he attempted to hum, but broke off frequently to listen. He was plainly afraid of the dog's keen ears missing something. But his mate's tense body proclaimed him on duty.

"I know who yer thort 'twas, Warder!" They were sitting side by side, yet he spoke very loudly. "Scrammy 'and. Ehm?" He had guessed correctly.

"An' yer thort yer see 'im lars' night!" He was right again.

"An' yer thort 'twas 'im that sucked the cow and 'ad bin ramsakin' the place yesterday, when we was shepherdin'. An' yer thort 't must 'ave bin 'im shook the tommy!" The dog's manner evinced that he had not altered this opinion. The old man's heart beat loudly.

"No fear, Warder! Scrammy's gone, gone 'long ways now, Warder!" But Warder's pricked ears doing double duty showed he was unconvinced. "'Sides, Scrammy wouldn't 'urt er merskeeter," he continued. "Poor ole Scrammy! 'Twarn't 'im shook the tommy, Warder!" The dog seemed to be waiting for the suggestion of another thief having unseen crept into their isolated lives, but his master had none to offer. Both were silent, then the man piled wood on the fire, remarking that he was going to sit up all night. He asked the dog to go with him to the table to feed and trim the slush lamp.

Those quavering shadows along the wall were caused by its sizzling flare flickering in the darkness, the dog explained. "Thort it mighter bin ther blacks outside," the man said. "They ain't so fur away, I know! 'Twar them killed ther lamb down in ther creek." He spoke unusually loudly. He hoped they wouldn't catch "poor ole one-'anded Scrammy". He said how sorry he was for "poor ole Scrammy, 'cos Scrammy wouldn't 'urt no one. He on'y jes' came ter see us 'cos 'e was a ole friend. He was gone a long ways ter look fur work, 'cos 'e was stoney broke after blueing 'is cheque at ther shanty sixty miles away".

"I tole 'im," he continued in an altered voice, "thet I couldn't lend 'im eny 'cos I 'ad sent all my little bit er money (he whispered "money") to ther bank with the boss.

Didn' I?" Emphatically his mate intimated that this was the case. The old man held his head in his shaking hands, and complained to the dog of having "come over dizzy".

He was silent for a few moments, then abruptly raising his voice, he remarked that their master was a better tracker than "Saddle-strap Jimmy", or any of the blacks. He looked at the tally stick, and suddenly announced that he knew for a certainty that the boss and his wife would return that night or early next morning, and that he must see about making them a damper. He got up and began laboriously to mix soda and salt with the flour. He looked at the muddy coloured water in the bucket near the wall, and altered his mind.

"I'll bile it first, War, same as 'er does, 'cos jus' neow an' then t' day I comes over dizzy-like. See th' mist t's evenin'! Two more, then rain — rain, an' them two out in it without no tilt on the cart." He sat down for a moment, even before he dusted his ungoverned floury hands.

"Pint er tea, War, jes' t' warm ther worms an' lif' me 'art, eh!"

Every movement of the dog was in accord with this plan.

His master looked at the billy, and said, "'twarn't bilin' yet", and that a watched pot never boils. He rested a while silently with his floury hands covering his face. He bent his mouth to the dog's ear and whispered. Warder, before replying, listened and reassuringly pointed his ears and raised his head. The relieved old man's hand rested on the dog's neck.

"Tell yer wot, War, w'ile it's bilin' I'll 'ave another go at ther button, 'cos I want ter give 'im ther 'at soon as he comes. S'pose they'll orl come!" He had sat down again, and seemed to whistle his words. "Think they'll orl come, Loo?"

Loo would not commit himself about "orl", not being quite sure of his master's mind.

The old man's mouth twitched, a violent effort jerked him. "Might be a boy arter orl; ain't cocky sure!" His head wagged irresponsibly, and his hat fell off as he rolled into the bunk. He made no effort to replace it, and for once unheeded, the fire flickered on his polished head. Never before had the dog seen its baldness. The change from night-cap to hat had always been effected out of his sight.

"War, ain't cocky sure it'll be a gal?"

The dog, discreetly or modestly, dropped his eyes, but his master had not done with concessions.

"Warder!" Warder looked at him. "Tell yer wot, yer can go every Sunday evenin' an' see it if 'tis a boy!"

Then he turned over on his side, with his face to the wall, and into the gnarled uncontrolled hand swaying over the bunk the dog laid his paw.

When the old man got up, he didn't put on his hat nor even pick it up. Altogether there was an unusualness about him to-night that distressed his mate. He sat up after a few moments, and threw back his head, listening strainingly for outside sounds. The silence soothed him, and he lay down again. Presently a faded look was in his eyes.

"Thort I 'eard bells — church bells," he said to the dog looking up too, but at him. "Couldn't 'ave. No church bells in the bush. Ain't 'eard 'em since I lef' th' ole country," turning his best ear to the fancied sound. For the time he had left his dog and the hut, and was dreaming of shadowy days.

He raised himself from the bunk, and followed the dog's directing eyes to a little smoke-stained bottle on the shelf. "No, no, War!" he expostulated. "Thet's for sickness; mus' be a lot worser'n wot I am!"

Breathing noisily, he went through a list of diseases, among which were palsy, snake-bite, "dropersy", and "suddint death", before he would be justified in taking the last of his pain-killer.

His pipe was in his hidden belt, but he had another in one of those little pockets. He tried it, said "twouldn't draw'r", and very slowly and clumsily stripped the edge of a cabbage-tree frond hanging from the rafter, and tried to push it through the stem, but could not find the opening. He explained to the intent dog that the hole was stopped up, but it didn't matter. He placed it under the bunk where he sat, because first he would " 'ave a swig er tea". His head kept wagging at the billy. No, until the billy boiled he was going to have a little snooze. The dog was to keep quiet until the billy boiled.

Involuntarily he murmured, looking at his mate, "Funny w'ere ther tommy'awk's gone ter!" Then, to his horror, he missed the axe. "My Gord, Warder!" he said, "I lef' the axe outside; clean forgot it!" This discovery alarmed the dog also, and he suggested they should bring it in.

"No, no!" his master said, and his floury face grew ghastly.

He stood still; all his faculties seemed paralyzed for a time, then fell stiffly on his bunk. Quite suddenly he staggered to his feet, rubbed his eyes, and between broken breaths he complained of the bad light, and that the mist had come again.

One thing the dog did when he saw his master's face even by that indifferent light, he barked low, and terribly human.

The old man motioned for silence, "Ah!"

His jaw fell, but only for a moment. Then a steely grimness took possession. He clung to the table and beckoned the dog with one crooked finger. "Scrammy?" cunningly, cautiously, indicating outside, and as subtly the dog replied confirmingly. The old man groped for his bunk, and lay with his eyes fixed on the billy, his mouth open.

He brought his palms together after a while. "'Cline our 'earts ter keep this lawr," he whispered, and for a moment his eyes rested on the hiding-place of his treasure, then turned to the dog.

And though soon after there was a sinister sound outside, which the watchful dog immediately challenged, the man on the bunk lay undisturbed.

Warder growling savagely went along the back wall of the hut, and despite the semi-darkness his eyes scintillating with menace through the cracks, drove from them a crouching figure who turned hastily to grip the axe near the myall logs. He stumbled over the lamb's feeding-pan lying in the hut's shadow and dropped the axe. The moonlight glittering on the blade recalled the menace of the dog's eyes. The man grabbed the weapon swiftly, but even with it he felt the chances were unequal.

But he had planned to fix the dog. He would unpen the

sheep, and the lurking dingoes, coming up from the creek to worry the lambs, would prove work for the dog. He crouched silently to again deceive this man and dog, and crept towards the sheep yard. But the hurdles of the yard faced the hut, and the way those thousand eyes reflected the rising moon was disconcerting. The whole of the night seemed pregnant with eyes.

All the shadows were slanting the wrong way, and facing him was the moon, with its man calmly watching every movement. It would be dawn before it set. He backed from the yard to the myall's scant screen, for they had moulted with age. From under his coat the handle of the axe protruded. His mind worked his body. Hugging the axe, he crept towards some object, straightened himself to reach, then with the hook on his handless arm, drew back an imaginary bolt, and stooping entered. With the axe in readiness he crept to the bunk. Twice he raised it and struck.

It was easy enough out there, yet even in imagination his skin was wet and his mouth was dry, and even if the man slept, there was the dog. He must risk letting out the sheep. He covered the blade of the axe and went in a circuit to the sheep, and got over the yard on the side opposite to the hut. They rushed from him and huddled together, leaving him, although stooping, exposed. He had calculated for this, but not for the effect upon himself. Could they in the hut see him, he would be no match for the dog even with the axe. Heedlessly, fear-driven, he rushed to where he could see the door, regardless of exposing himself. Nothing counted now, but that the dog or the old man should not steal upon him unawares.

The door was still closed. No call for "Warder!" came from it, though the man stood there a conspicuous object. While he watched he saw the old ewe and lamb make for the hut's shelter. He stooped, still watching, and listening, but could hear nothing. He crept forward and loosened the hurdles, and never were they noisier, he was sure. He knew that the sheep would not go through while he was there, so crept away, but although the leader noted the freed exit, he and those he led were creatures of habit. None were hungry, and they were unused to feeding at night, though in the morning came man and dog never so early, they were waiting.

Round the yard and past the gateway he drove them again and again. He began to feel impotently frenzied in the fear that the extraordinary lightness meant that daylight must be near. Every moment he persuaded himself that he could see more plainly. He held out his one hand and was convinced.

He straightened himself, rushed among them, caught one, and ran it kicking through the opening. It came back the moment he freed it. However it served his purpose, for as he crouched there, baffled, he unexpectedly saw them file out. Then they rushed through in an impatient struggling crowd, each fearing to be last with this invader.

When he "barrowed" out the first, he had kept his eyes on the hut, and had seen the old ewe and lamb run to it and bunt the closed door. But if there was any movement inside, the noise of the nearer sheep killed it.

Now they were all round the hut, for above it hung the moon, and they all made for the light. He crept after them, his ears straining for sound, but his head bobbing above them to watch the still closed door.

Inside, long since, the back-log had split with an explosion that scattered the coals near enough to cause the billy to boil, and the blaze showed the old man's eyes set on the billy. The dog looked into them, then laid his head between his paws, and still watching his master's face, beat the ground with his tail. He whined softly and went back to his post at the door, his eyes snapping flintily, his teeth bared. Along his back the hair rose like bristles while he sent an assurance of help to the importunate ewe and lamb. As the sheep neared the hut, he ran to the bunk, raised his head to a level with his master's, and barked softly. He waited, and despite the eager light in his intelligent face, his master and mate did not ask him any questions as to the cause of these calling sheep. Why did he not rise, and with him re-yard them, then gloatingly ask him where was the chinky crow by day, or sneaking dingo by night, that was any match for them, and then demand from his four-footed trusty mate the usual straightforward answer? Was there to be no discussion as to which heard the noise first, nor the final compromise of a dead-heat?

The silence puzzled the man outside sorely; he crouched, watching both door and shutter. The sheep were all round the hut. Man and dog inside must hear them. Why, when a dingo came that night he camped with them, they heard it before it could reach a lamb. If only he had known then what he knew now! His hold on the axe tightened. No one had seen him come; none should see him go! Why didn't that old fellow wake to-night? for now, as he crept nearer the hut, he could hear the whining dog, and understood, he was appealing to his master.

He lay flat on the ground and tried to puzzle it out. The sheep had rushed back disorganized and were again near the hut and yard, and both inside must know. Ah! by God, they were waiting for him. They were preparing for him, and that was why they were letting the dingoes play up with the sheep. That was the reason they did not openly show fight.

Still he would have sacrificed half of the coveted wealth to be absolutely certain of what their silence meant. And now it was surely almost daylight. He spread out the fingers of his one hand; he could see the colour of the blood in the veins. He must act quickly, or he would have to hide about for another day. And the absent man might return. To encourage himself, he tried to imagine the possession of that glittering heap that he had seen them counting on the mat. Yet he had grown cold and dejected, and felt for the first time the weight of the axe. It would be all right if the door would open, the old man come out and send the dog to round up the sheep. It was getting daylight, and soon shelter would be impossible.

He crept towards the hut, and this time he felt the edge of the axe. Right and left the sheep parted. There was nothing to be gained now in crawling, for the hostility of the dog told him that he could be seen. He stood, his body stiffened with determination.

Mechanically he went to the door; he knew the defensive resources of the hut. He had the axe, and the stolen tomahawk was stuck in the fork of those myalls. He had no need for both. The only weapon that the old fellow had was the useless butcher's knife. His eyes protruded, and unconsciously he felt his stiffened beard.

He breathed without movement. There was no sound now from man or dog. In his mind he saw them waiting for him to attack the door; this he did not debate nor alter. He went to the shutter, ran the axe's edge along the hide hinges, pushed it in, then stepped back.

Immediately the dog's head appeared. He growled no protest, but the flinty fire from his eyes and the heat of his suppressed breath, hissing between his bared fangs, revealed to Scrammy that in this contest, despite the axe, his scrammy hand was a serious handicap.

But with the first blow his senses quickened. The slush lamp had gone out and there was no hint of daylight inside. This he noted between his blows at the dog, as he looked for his victim. It was strange the old fellow did not show fight! Where was he hiding? Was it possible that, scenting danger, he had slipped out? He recalled the dog's warning when his master was counting his hoard. The memory of that chinking belt-hidden pile dominated greedily. Had the old man escaped? He would search the hut; what were fifty dogs' teeth? In close quarters he would do for him with one blow.

He was breathing now in deep gasps. The keen edge of the axe severed the hide-hinged door. He rushed it; then stood back swinging the axe in readiness. It did not fall for the bolt still held it. But this was only what a child would consider a barrier. One blow with the axe head smashed the bolt. The door fell across the head of the bunk, the end partly blocking the entrance. He struck a side blow that sent it along the bunk.

The dog was dreadfully distressed, and the bushman outside thought the cause only the fallen door. Face to face they met — determined battle in the dog's eyes met murder in the man's. He brandished an axe circuit, craned his neck, and by the dull light of the fire searched the hut. He saw no one but the dog. Unless his master was under the bunk, he had escaped. The whole plot broke on him quite suddenly!

The cunning old miser, knowing his dog would show his flight by following, had locked him in, and he, Scrammy, had wasted all this time barking up the wrong tree. He would have done the old man to death that minute with fifty brutal blows. He would kill him by day or night.

He ran round the brush sheep yard, kicking and thrusting the axe through the thickest parts. He had not hidden there, nor among the myall clump where he had conceived his bloody plot. The dog stood at the doorway of the hut. He saw this as he passed through the sheep on his way to search the creek. He was half minded to try to invite the dog's confidence and cooperation by yarding them.

He looked at them, and the moonlight's undulating white scales across their shorn backs brought out the fresh tar brand 8, setting him thinking of the links of that convict gang chain long ago. Lord, how light it must be for him to see that!

He held out his hand again. There was no perceptible change in the light. There were hours yet before daylight. He moulded his mind to that.

The creek split the plain, and along it here and there a few she-oak blots defined it. He traversed it with his eyes. There were no likely hiding places among the trees, and it would be useless to search them. Suddenly it struck him that the old man might be creeping along with the sheep — they were so used to him. He ran and headed them, driving them swiftly back to the yard. Before they were in he knew he was wrong. Again he turned and scanned the creek, but felt no impulse to search it. It was half a mile from the hut. It was impossible that the old man could have got there, or that he could have reached the more distant house. Besides, why did the dog stay at the door unless on guard? He ran back to the hut.

The dog was still there, and in no way appeased by the yarding of the sheep. He swore at the threatening brute, and cast about for a gibber to throw, but stones were almost unknown there. A sapling would serve him! Seven or eight myall logs lay near for firewood, but all were too thick to be wielded. There was only the clump of myalls, and the few stunted she-oaks bordering the distant creek. To reach either would mean a dangerous delay. Oh, by God, he had it! These poles keeping down the bark roof. He ran to the back of the hut, cut a step in a slab, and putting his foot in it, hitched the axe on one of the desired poles and was up in a moment. He could hear the cabbage fronds hanging from the rafters shiver with the vibration, but there was no other protest from inside.

He shifted a sheet of rotten bark; part of it crumbled and fell inside on the prostrate door, sounding like the first earth on a coffin, and in a way that the dog particularly resented. Scrammy knelt and carefully eyed the interior. The dog's glittering eyes met his. The door lay as it had fallen along the bunk. The fire was lightless, yet he could see more plainly, but the cause was not manifest, till from the myalls quite close the jackasses chorused. From his post the dog sent them a signal. Quite unaccountably the man's muscles relaxed. "O Christ!" he said, dropping the pole. He sprang up and faced the East, then turned to the traitorous faded moon. The daylight had come.

The sweat stung his quivering body. Slowly, he made an eye circuit round the plain; no human being was in sight. He took a deep breath; all he had to face was a parcel of noisy jackasses and a barking dog, and he would soon silence the dog. He took the pole and made a jab at the evasive brute. One thing he noticed, that if he did get one home, it was only when he worked near the horizontal door. His quickened senses guessed at the reason. He could have shifted the door easily with his pole, yet feared, because, if the old man were under, he would expose himself to two active enemies. He must get to close quarters with the dog, and chop him in two, or brain him with the axe.

He ripped off another sheet of bark, and smashed away a batten that broke his swing. Encircling a rafter with his hooked arm, he lay flat, his feet pressing another just over the bunk, because only there would the dog hold his ground. One blow well directed got home on the dog. He planted his feet firmly, and made another with such tremendous force that his support snapped. He let go the axe and it fell on the door. He gripped with his hand the rafter nearest, but strain as he would he could not balance his body. He hung over the door, and the dog sprang at him and dragged him down. In bitten agony, he dropped on the door that instantly up-ended.

It was daylight, and in that light the power of those open eyes set in that bald head, fixed on the billy beside the dead fireplace, was mightier than the dog. His unmaimed hand had the strength of both. He lifted the door and shielded himself with it as he backed out.

But that was not all the dog wanted. At the doorway he waited to see that the fleeing man had no further designs on the sheep.

It was time they were feeding. Though the hurdles were down, even from the doorway, the dog was their master, and he waited for commands from his, and barked them back till noon.

Several times that day the ewe and lamb came in, looked without speculation at the figure on the bunk, then moved to the dead fireplace. But though the water in the billy was cold, the dog would not allow either to touch it. That was for tea when his master awoke.

There was another circumstance. Those blowflies were welcome to the uncovered mutton. Throughout that day he gave them undisputed right, and they had to be content with it, but never for moment rest on his master.

Next day the ewe and lamb came again. The lamb bunted several irresponsive objects — never its dam's udder — baaing listlessly. The first day the ewe had looked at the bunk, and baaed, she was wiser now, though sheep are slow to learn. Around that dried dish outside the lamb sniffed, baaing faintly. Adroitly the ewe led the way to the creek, and the lamb followed. From the bank the lamb looked at her, then faced round to the hut, and baaing disconsolately, trotted a few paces back. From the water's edge the mother ewe called. The lamb looked at her vacantly, and without interest descended. The ewe bent and drank sparingly, meaningly. The lamb sniffed the water, and unsatisfied, complained. The hut was hidden, but it turned that way. Again the ewe leisurely drank. This time the lamb's lips touched the water, but did not drink. Into its mouth raised to bleat a few drops fell. Hastily the mother's head went to the water; she did not drink, but the lamb did. Higher up, where the creek was dry, they crossed to tender grass in the billabong, then joined the flock for the first time.

Through the thicker mist that afternoon a white tilted cart sailed joltingly, taking its bearings from the various landmarks rather than from the undefined track. It rounded the scrub, and the woman, with her baby, kept watch for the first glimpse of her home beyond the creek. She told her husband that there was no smoke from the nearer shepherd's hut, but despite his uneasiness, he tried to persuade her that the mist absorbed it.

It was past sun-down, yet the struggling unguarded sheep were running in mobs to and from the creek. Both saw the broken roof of the hut, and the man, stopping the horse some distance away, gave the woman the reins and bade her wait. He entered the hut through the broken doorway, but immediately came out to assure himself that his wife had not moved.

The sight inside of that broken-ribbed dog's fight with those buzzing horrors, and the reproach in his wild eyes, was a memory that the man was not willing she should share.

*Billy Skywonkie**

THE line was unfenced, so with due regard to the possibility of the drought-dulled sheep attempting to chew it, the train crept cautiously along, stopping occasionally, without warning, to clear it from the listless starving brutes. In the carriage nearest the cattle-vans, some drovers and scrub-cutters were playing euchre, and spasmodically chorusing the shrill music from an uncertain concertina. When the train stopped, the player thrust his head from the carriage window. From one nearer the engine, a commercial traveller remonstrated with the guard, concerning the snail's pace and the many unnecessary halts.

"Take yer time, old die-ard," yelled the drover to the guard. "Whips er time, — don't bust yerself fer no one. Wot's orl the worl' to a man w'en his wife's a widder?" He laughed noisily and waved his hat at the seething bagman. "Go an' 'ave a snooze. I'll wake yer up ther day after termorrer."

He craned his neck to see into the nearest cattle-van. Four were down, he told his mates, who remarked, with blasphemous emphasis, that they would probably lose half before getting them to the scrub country.

The listening woman passenger in a carriage between the drover and the bagman, heard a thud soon after in the cattle-truck, and added another to the list of the fallen. Before dawn that day the train had stopped at a siding to truck them, and she had watched with painful interest these drought-tamed brutes being driven into the crowded vans.

* "Skywonkie" signifies weather-prophet.

The tireless, greedy sun had swiftly followed the grey dawn, and in the light that even now seemed old and worn, the desolation of the barren shelterless plains, that the night had hidden, appalled her. She realized the sufferings of the emaciated cattle. It was barely noon, yet she had twice emptied the water bottle, "shogging" in the iron bracket.

The train dragged its weary length again, and she closed her eyes from the monotony of the dead plain. Suddenly the engine cleared its throat in shrill welcome to two iron tanks, hoisted twenty feet and blazing like evil eyes from a vanished face.

Beside them it squatted on its hunkers, placed a blackened thumb on its pipe, and hissed through its closed teeth like a snared wild cat, while gulping yards of water. The green slimy odour penetrated to the cattle. The lustiest of these stamped feebly, clashing their horns and bellowing a hollow request.

A long-bearded bushman was standing on the few slabs that formed a siding, with a stockwhip coiled like a snake on his arm. The woman passenger asked him the name of the place.

"This is ther Never-Never, — ther lars' place Gord made," answered one of the drovers who were crowding the windows.

"Better'n ther 'ell-'ole yous come from, any'ow," defended the bushman. "Breakin' ther 'earts, and dyin' from suerside, 'cos they lef' it," he added derisively, pointing to the cattle.

In patriotic anger he passed to the guard-van without answering her question, though she looked anxiously after him. At various intervals during the many halts of the train, she had heard some of the obscene jokes, and with it in motion, snatches of lewd songs from the drovers' carriage. But the language used by this bushman to the guard, as he helped to remove a ton of fencing wire topping his new saddle, made her draw back her head. Near the siding was a spring cart, and she presently saw him throw his flattened saddle into it and drive off. There was no one else in sight, and in nervous fear she asked the bagman if this was Gooriabba siding. It was nine miles further, he told her.

The engine lifted its thumb from its pipe. "Well — well — to — be — sure; well — well — to — be — sure," it puffed, as if in shocked remembrance of its being hours late for its appointment here.

She saw no one on the next siding, but a buggy waited near the slip-rails. It must be for her. According to Sydney arrangements she was to be met here, and driven out twelve miles. A drover inquired as the train left her standing by her portmanteau, "Are yer travellin' on yer lonesome, or on'y goin' somew'ere!" and another flung a twist of paper towards her, brawling unmusically, that it was "A flowwer from me angel mother's ger-rave".

She went towards the buggy, but as she neared it the driver got in and made to drive off. She ran and called, for when he went she would be alone with the bush all round her, and only the sound of the hoarse croaking of the frogs from the swamp near, and the raucous "I'll — 'ave — 'is — eye — out," of the crows.

Yes, he was from Gooriabba Station, and had come to meet a young "piece" from Sydney, who had not come.

She was ghastly with bilious sickness, — the result of an over-fed brain and an under-fed liver. Her face flushed muddily. "Was it a housekeeper?"

He was the rouseabout, wearing his best clothes with awful unusualness. The coat was too long in the sleeve, and wrinkled across the back with his bush slouch. There was that wonderful margin of loose shirt between waistcoat and trouser, which all swagger bushies affect. Subordinate to nothing decorative was the flaring silk handkerchief, drawn into a sailor's knot round his neck.

He got out and fixed the winkers, then put his hands as far as he could reach into his pockets — from the position of his trousers he could not possibly reach bottom. It was apparently some unknown law that suspended them. He thrust forward his lower jaw, elevated his pipe, and squirted a little tobacco juice towards his foot that was tracing semi-circles in the dust. "Damned if I know," he said with a snort, "but there'll be a 'ell of a row somew'ere."

She noticed that the discoloured teeth his bush grin showed so plainly, were worn in the centre, and met at both sides with the pipe between the front. Worn stepping-stones her mind insisted.

She looked away towards the horizon where the smoke of the hidden train showed faintly against a clear sky, and as he was silent, she seemed to herself to be intently listening to the croak of the frogs and the threat of the cows. She knew that, from under the brim of the hat he wore over his eyes, he was looking at her sideways.

Suddenly he withdrew his hands and said again, "Damned if I know. S'pose it's alright! Got any traps? Get up then 'an 'ole the Neddy while I get it." They drove a mile or so in silence; his pipe was still in his mouth though not alight.

She spoke once only. "What a lot of frogs seem to be in that lake!"

He laughed. "That's ther Nine Mile Dam!" He laughed again after a little — an intelligent, complacent laugh.

"It used ter be swarmin' with teal in a good season, but Gord A'mighty knows w'en it's ever goin' ter rain any more! I dunno!" This was an important admission, for he was a great weather prophet. "Lake!" he sniggered and looked sideways at his companion. "Thet's wot thet there bloke, the painter doodle, called it. An' 'e goes ter dror it, an' 'e sez wot 'e 'll give me five bob if I'll run up ther horses, an' keep 'em so's 'e ken put 'em in ther picshure. An' 'e drors ther Dam an' ther trees, puts in thet there ole dead un, an' 'e puts in ther 'orses right clost against ther water w'ere the frogs is. 'E puts them in too, an' damned if 'e don't dror ther 'orses drinkin' ther water with ther frogs, an' ther frogs spit on it! Likely yarn ther 'orses ud drink ther water with ther blanky frogs' spit on it! Fat lot they know about ther bush! Blarsted nannies!"

Presently he inquired as to the place where they kept pictures in Sydney, and she told him, the Art Gallery.

"Well, some of these days I'm goin' down ter Sydney," he continued, "an' I'll collar thet one 'cos it's a good likerness of ther 'orses — you'd know their 'ide on a gum tree — an' that mean mongrel never paid me ther five bob."

Between his closed teeth he hissed a bush tune for some miles, but ceased to look at the sky and remarked, "No sign er rain! No lambin' this season; soon as they're dropt we'll 'ave ter knock 'em all on ther 'ead!" He shouted an oath of hatred at the crows following after the tottering sheep that made in a straggling line for the water. "Look at 'em!" he said, "scoffin' out ther eyes!" He pointed to where the crows hovered over the bogged sheep. "They puttywell lives on eyes! 'Blanky bush Chinkies!' I call 'em. No one carn't tell 'em apart!"

There was silence again, except for a remark that he could spit all the blanky rain they had had in the last nine months.

Away to the left along a side track his eyes travelled searchingly, as they came to a gate. He stood in the buggy and looked again.

"Promised ther 'Konk' t' leave 'im 'ave furst squint at yer," he muttered, "if 'e was 'ere t' open ther gate! But I'm not goin' t' blanky well wait orl day!" He reluctantly got out and opened the gate, and he had just taken his seat when a "Cooee" sounded from his right, heralded by a dusty pillar. He snorted resentfully. "'Ere 'e is; jes' as I got out an' done it!"

The "Konk" cantered to them, his horse's hoofs padded by the dust-cushioned earth. The driver drew back, so as not to impede the newcomer's view. After a moment or two, the "Konk", preferring closer quarters, brought his horse round to the left. Unsophisticated bush wonder in the man's face met the sophisticated in the girl's.

Never had she seen anything so grotesquely monkeyish. And the nose of this little hairy horror, as he slewed his neck to look into her face, blotted the landscape and dwarfed all perspective. She experienced a strange desire to extend her hand. When surprise lessened, her mettle saved her from the impulse to cover her face with both hands, to baffle him.

At last the silence was broken by the driver drawing a match along his leg, and lighting his pipe. The hairy creature safely arranged a pair of emu eggs, slung with bush skill round his neck.

"Ain't yer goin' to part?" inquired the driver, indicating his companion as the recipient.

"Wot are yer givin' us; wot do yer take me fur?" said the "Konk" indignantly, drawing down his knotted veil.

"Well, give 'em ter me fer 'Lizer."

"Will yer 'ave 'em now, or wait till yer get 'em?"

"Goin' ter sit on 'em yerself?" sneered the driver.

"Yes, an' I'll give yer ther first egg ther cock lays," laughed the "Konk".

He turned his horse's head back to the gate. "I say, Billy Skywonkie! Wot price Sally Ah Too, eh?" he asked, his gorilla mouth agape.

Billy Skywonkie uncrossed his legs, took out the whip. He tilted his pipe and shook his head as he prepared to drive, to show that he understood to a fraction the price of Sally Ah Too. The aptness of the question took the sting out of his having had to open the gate. He gave a farewell jerk.

"Goin' ter wash yer neck?" shouted the man with the nose, from the gate.

"Not if I know it."

The "Konk" received the intimation incredulously. "Stinkin' Roger!" he yelled. In bush parlance this was equal to emphatic disbelief.

This was a seemingly final parting, and both started, but suddenly the "Konk" wheeled round.

"Oh, Billy!" he shouted.

Billy stayed his horse and turned expectantly.

"W'en's it goin' ter rain?"

The driver's face darkened. "Your blanky jealersey'll get yer down, an' worry yer yet," he snarled, and slashing his horse he drove rapidly away.

"Mickey ther Konk," he presently remarked to his companion, as he stroked his nose.

This explained her earlier desire to extend her hand. If the "Konk" had been a horse she would have stroked his nose.

"Mob er sheep can camp in the shadder of it," he said.

Boundless scope for shadows on that sun-smitten treeless plain!

"Make a good ploughshere," he continued; "easy plough a cultivation paddock with it!"

At the next gate he seemed in a mind and body conflict.

There were two tracks; he drove along one for a few hundred yards. Then stopping he turned, and finding the "Konk" out of sight abruptly drove across to the other. He continually drew his whip along the horse's back, and haste seemed the object of the movement, though he did not flog the beast.

After a few miles on the new track, a blob glittered dazzlingly through the glare, like a fallen star. It was the iron roof of the wine shanty — the Saturday night and Sunday resort of shearers and rouseabouts for twenty miles around. Most of its spirits was made on the premises from bush recipes, of which bluestone and tobacco were the chief ingredients. Every drop had the reputation of "bitin' orl ther way down".

A sapling studded with broken horse-shoes seemed to connect two lonely crow stone trees. Under their scanty shade groups of dejected fowls stood with beaks agape. Though the buggy wheels almost reached them, they were motionless but for the quivering gills. The ground both sides of the shanty was decorated with tightly pegged kangaroo skins. A dog, apathetically blind and dumb, lay on the verandah, lifeless save for eyelids blinking in antagonism to the besieging flies.

"Jerry can't be far off," said Billy Skywonkie, recognizing the dog. He stood up in the buggy. "By cripes, there 'e is — goosed already, an' 'e on'y got 'is cheque lars' night."

On the chimney side of the shanty a man lay in agitated sleep beside his rifle and swag. There had been a little shade on that side in the morning, and he had been sober enough to select it, and lay his head on his swag. He had emptied the bottle lying at his feet since then. His swag had been thoroughly "gone through", and also his singlet and trouser pockets. The fumes from the shanty-grog baffled the flies. But the scorching sun was conquering; the man groaned, and his hands began to search for his burning head.

Billy Skywonkie explained to his companion that it was "Thet fool, Jerry ther kangaroo-shooter, bluein' 'is cheque fer skins". He took the water bag under the buggy, and poured the contents into the open mouth and over the face of the "dosed" man, and raised him into a sitting posture.

Jerry fought this friendliness vigorously, and, staggering to his feet, picked up his rifle, and took drunken aim at his rescuer, then at the terrified woman in the buggy.

The rouseabout laughed unconcernedly. "'E thinks we're blanky kangaroos," he said to her. "Jerry, ole cock, yer couldn't 'it a woolshed! Yer been taking ther sun!"

He took the rifle and pushed the subdued Jerry into the chimney corner.

He tilted his hat, till, bush fashion, it "'ung on one 'air", and went inside the shanty.

"Mag!" he shouted, thumping the bar (a plank supported by two casks).

The woman in the buggy saw a slatternly girl with doughy hands come from the back, wiping the flour from her face with a kitchen towel. They made some reference to her she knew, as the girl came to the door and gave her close scrutiny. Then, shaking her head till her long brass earrings swung like pendulums, she laughed loudly.

"Eh?" inquired the rouseabout.

"My oath!" "Square dinkum!" she answered, going behind the bar.

He took the silk handkerchief from his neck, and playfully tried to flick the corner into her eye. Mag was used to such delicate attentions and well able to defend herself. With the dirty kitchen towel she succeeded in knocking off his hat, and round and round the house she ran with it, dexterously dodging the skin-pegs. He could neither overtake nor outwit her with any dodge, so he gave in, and ransomed his hat with the "shouts" she demanded.

From the back of the shanty, a bent old woman, almost on all fours, crept towards the man, again prostrate in the corner. She paused, with her ear turned to where the girl and the rouseabout were still at horse-play. With catlike movements she stole on till within reach of Jerry's empty pockets. She turned her terrible face to the woman in the buggy, as if in expectation of sympathy. Keeping wide of the front door, she came to the further side of the buggy. With the fascination of horror the woman looked at this creature, whose mouth and eyes seemed to dishonour her draggled grey hair. She was importuning for something, but the woman in the buggy could not understand till she pointed to her toothless mouth (the mission of which seemed to be, to fill its cavernous depths with the age-loosened skin above and below). A blue bag under each eye aggressively ticked like the gills of the fowls, and the sinews of the neck strained into *bassi relievi*. Alternately she pointed to her mouth, or laid her knotted fingers on the blue bags in pretence of wiping tears. Entrenched behind the absorbed skin-terraces, a stump of purple tongue made efforts at speech. When she held out her claw, the woman understood and felt for her purse. Wolfishly the old hag snatched and put into her mouth the coin, and as the now merry driver, followed by Mag, came, she shook a warning claw at the giver, and flopped whining in the dust, her hands ostentatiously open and wiping dry eyes.

"Ello Biddy, on ther booze again!"

The bottle bulging from his coat pocket made speech with him intelligible, despite the impeding coin.

He placed the bottle in the boot of the buggy, and turning to Mag, said "Give ther poor ole cow a dose!"

"Yes, one in a billy; anything else might make her sick!" said Mag, "I caught 'er jus' now swiggin' away with ther tap in 'er mug!"

He asked his companion would she like a wet. She asked for water, and so great was her need, that, making a barricade of closed lips and teeth to the multitude of apparently wingless mosquitoes thriving in its green tepidity, she moistened her mouth and throat.

"Oh, I say, Billy!" called Mag as he drove off. Her tones suggested her having forgotten an important matter, and he turned eagerly. "W'en's it goin' ter rain?" she shrieked, convulsed in merriment.

"Go an' crawl inter a' oller log!" he shouted angrily.

"No, but truly, Billy." Billy turned again. "Give my love to yaller 'Lizer; thet slues yer!"

They had not gone far before he looked round again. "Gord!" he cried excitedly. "Look at Mag goin' through 'er ole woman!"

Mag had the old woman's head between her knees, dentist-fashion, and seemed to concentrate upon her victim's mouth, whose feeble impotence was soon demonstrated by the operator releasing her, and triumphantly raising her hand.

What the finger and thumb held the woman knew and the other guessed.

"By Gord. Eh! thet's prime, ain't it? No flies on Mag; not a fly!" he said admiringly.

"See me an' 'er?" he asked, as he drove on.

His tone suggested no need to reply, and his listener did not. A giddy unreality took the sting from everything, even from her desire to beseech him to turn back to the siding, and leave her there to wait for the train to take her back to civilization. She felt she had lost her mental balance. Little matters became distorted, and the greater shrivelled.

He was now more communicative, and the oaths and adjectives so freely used were surely coined for such circumstances. "Damned" the wretched, starving, and starved sheep looked and were; "bloody" the beaks of the glutted crows; "blarsted" the whole of the plain they drove through!

Gaping cracks suggested yawning graves, and the skeleton fingers of the drooping myalls seemingly pointed to them.

"See me an' Mag?" he asked again. "No flies on Mag; not a wink 'bout 'er!" He chuckled in tribute. "Ther wus thet damned flash fool, Jimmy Fernatty," he continued; "—— ther blanky fool; 'e never 'ad no show with Mag. An' yet 'e'd go down there! It wus two mile furder this way, yet damned if ther blanky fool wouldn't come this way every time, 'less ther boss 'e wus with 'im, 'stead er goin' ther short cut, — ther way I come this mornin'. An' every time Mag ud make 'im part 'arf a quid. I wus on'y there jus' 'bout five minits meself, an' I stuck up nea'ly 'arf a quid! An' there's four gates" (he flogged the horse and painted them crimson when he remembered them) "this way, more'n on ther way I come this mornin'."

Presently he gave her the reins with instructions to drive through one. It seemed to take a long time to close it, and he had to fix the back of the buggy before he opened it, and after it was closed.

After getting out several times in quick succession to fix the back of the buggy when there was no gate, he seemed to forget the extra distance. He kept his hand on hers when she gave him the reins, and bade her "keep up 'er pecker". "Some one would soon buck up ter 'er if their boss wusn't on." But the boss, it seemed, was a "terrer for young uns. Jimmy Fernatty 'as took up with a yaller piece an' is livin' with 'er. But not me; thet's not me! I'm like ther boss, thet's me! No yaller satin for me!"

He watched for the effect of this degree of taste on her.

Though she had withdrawn her hand, he kept winking at her, and she had to move her feet to the edge of the buggy to prevent his pressing against them. He told her with sudden anger that any red black-gin was as good as a half chow any day, and it was no use gammoning, for he knew what she was.

"If Billy Skywonkie 'ad ter string onter yaller 'Lizer, more 'air on 'is chest fer doin' so" (striking his own). "I ken get as many w'ite gins as I wanter, an' I'd as soon tackle a gin as a chow any day!"

On his next visit to the back of the buggy she heard the crash of glass breaking against a tree, then after a few snatches of song he lighted his pipe, and grew sorrowfully reminiscent.

"Yes, s'elp me, nea'ly 'arf a quid! An' thet coloured ole 'og of a cow of a mother, soon's she's off ther booze, 'll see thet she gets it!" Then he missed his silk handkerchief. "Ghost!" he said breathing heavily, "Mag's snavelled it! 'Lizer'll spot thet's gone soon's we get 'ithin cooee of 'er!"

Against hope he turned and looked along the road; felt every pocket, lifted his feet, and looked under the mat. His companion, in reply, said she had not seen it since his visit to the shanty.

"My Gord!" he said, "Mag's a fair terror!" He was greatly troubled till the braggart in him gave an assertive flicker. "Know wot I'll do ter 'Lizer soon's she begins ter start naggin' at me?" He intended this question as an insoluble conundrum, and waited for no surmises. "Fill 'er mug with this!" and the shut fist he shook was more than a mugful. "'Twouldn't be ther first time I done it, nor ther lars'." But the anticipation seemed little comfort to him.

The rest of the journey was done in silence, and without even a peep at the sky. When they came to the homestead gate he said his throat felt as though a "goanner" had crawled into it and died. He asked her for a pin and clumsily dropped it in his efforts to draw the collar up to his ears, but had better luck with a hairpin.

He appeared suddenly subdued and sober, and as he took his seat after closing the gate, he offered her his hand, and said, hurriedly: "No 'arm done, an' no 'arm meant; an' don't let on ter my missus — thet's 'er on the verander — thet we come be ther shanty."

It was dusk, but through it she saw that the woman was dusky too.

"Boss in, 'Lizer?" There was contrition and propitiation in his voice.

"You've bin a nice blanky time," said his missus, "an' lucky fer you Billy Skywonkie 'e ain't."

With bowed head, his shoulders making kindly efforts to hide his ears, he sat silent and listening respectfully. The woman in the buggy thought that the volubility of the angry half-caste's tongue must be the nearest thing to perpetual motion.

Under her orders both got down, and from a seat under the open window in the little room to which 'Lizer had motioned, she gave respectful attention to the still rapidly flowing tirade. The offence had been some terrible injustice to a respectable married woman, "slavin' an' graftin' an' sweatin' from mornin' ter night, for a slungin', idlin', lazy blaggard". In an indefinable way the woman felt that both of them were guilty, and to hide from her part of the reproof was mean and cowardly. The half-caste from time to time included her, and by degrees she understood that the wasted time of which 'Lizer complained was supposed to have been dissipated in flirtation. Neither the shanty nor Mag had mention.

From the kitchen facing the yard a Chinaman came at intervals, and with that assumption of having mastered the situation in all its bearings through his thorough knowledge of the English tongue, he shook his head in calm, shocked surprise. His sympathies were unmistakably with Lizer, and he many times demonstrated his grip of the grievance by saying, "By Cli', Billy, it's a bloo'y shame!"

Maybe it was a sense of what was in his mind that made the quivering woman hide her face when virtuous Ching Too came to look at her. She was trying to eat when a dog ran into the dining-room, and despite the violent beating of her heart, she heard the rouseabout tell the boss as he unsaddled his horse, "The on'y woman I see was a 'alf chow, an' she ses she's the one, an' she's in ther dinin'-room 'avin' a tuck in."

She was too giddy to stand when the boss entered, but she turned her mournful eyes on him; and, supporting herself by the table, stood and faced him.

He kept on his hat, and she, watching, saw curiosity and surprise change into anger as he looked at her.

"What an infernal cheek *you* had to come! Who sent you?" he asked stormily.

She told him, and added that she had no intention of remaining.

"How old?" She made no reply. His last thrust, as in disgust he strode out, had the effect of a galvanic battery on her dying body.

Her bedroom was reeking with a green heavy scent. Empty powder boxes and rouge pots littered the dressing table, and various other aids of nature evidenced her predecessor's frailty. From a coign in its fastness a black spider eyed her malignantly, and as long as the light lasted she watched it.

The ringing of a bell slung outside in the fork of a tree awoke her before dawn. It was mustering — bush stock-taking — and all the station hands were astir. There was a noise of galloping horses being driven into the stockyard, and the clamour of the men as they caught and saddled them. Above the clatter of plates in the kitchen she could hear the affected drawl of the Chinaman talking to 'Lizer, who trod heavily along the passage, preparing the boss's breakfast. This early meal was soon over, and with the dogs snapping playfully at the horses' heels, all rode off.

Spasmodic bars of "A Bicycle Built for Two" came from the kitchen, "Mayly, Mayly, give me answer do!" There was neither haste nor anxiety in the singer's tones. Before the kitchen fire, oblivious to the heat, stood the Chinaman cook, inert from his morning's opium. It was only nine, but this was well on in the day for Ching, whose morning began at four.

He ceased his song as she entered. "You come Sydiney? Ah! You mally? Ah! Sydiney welly ni' place. This placee welly dly — too muchee no lain — welly dly."

She was watching his dog. On a block lay a flitch of bacon, and across the freshly cut side the dog drew its tongue, then snapped at the flies.

"That dog will eat the bacon," she said.

"No!" answered the cook. "'E no eat 'em — too saw."

It was salt; she had tried it for breakfast.

He began energetically something about, "by-an'-bye me getty mally. By Cli', no 'alf cas' — too muchee longa jlaw." He laughed and shook his head, reminiscent of "las' a-night," and waited for applause. But, fascinated, she still watched the dog, who from time to time continued to take "saw" with his flies.

"Go ou' si', Sir," said the cook in a spirit of rivalry. The dog stood and snapped. "Go ou' si', I say!" No notice from the dog. "Go ou' si', I tella you!" stamping his slippered feet and taking a fire stick. The dog leisurely sat down and looked at his master with mild reproof. "Go insi' then, any bloo'y si' you li'!" but pointing to their joint bedroom with the lighted stick. The dog went to the greasy door, saw that the hens sitting on the bed were quietly laying eggs to go with the bacon, and came back.

She asked him where was the rouseabout who had driven her in yesterday.

"Oh, Billy Skywonkie, 'e mally alri'! 'Lizer 'im missie!" He went on to hint that affection there was misplaced, but that he himself was unattached.

She saw the rouseabout rattle into the yard in a spring cart. He let down the backboard and dumped three sheep under a light gallows. Their two front feet were strapped to one behind.

He seemed breathless with haste. "Oh, I say!" he called out to her. "Ther boss 'e tole me this mornin' thet I wus ter tell you, you wis ter sling yer 'ook. To do a get," he explained. "So bundle yer duds tergether quick an' lively! 'Lizer's down at ther tank, washin'. Le's get away afore she sees us, or she'll make yer swaller yer chewers." Lowering his voice, he continued: "I wanter go ter ther shanty — on'y ter get me 'ankercher."

He bent and strained back a sheep's neck, drew the knife and steel from his belt, and skilfully danced an edge on the knife.

She noticed that the sheep lay passive, with its head back, till its neck curved in a bow, and that the glitter of the knife was reflected in its eye.

Bush Church

I

THE hospitality of the bush never extends to the loan of a good horse to an inexperienced rider. The parson bumping along on old Rosey, who had smelt the water of the "Circler Dam", was powerless to keep the cunning experienced brute from diverting from the track. With the bit in her teeth, her pace kept him fully occupied to hold his seat. At the edge of the Dam old Rosey, to avoid the treacherous mud, began, with humped back and hoofs close together, to walk along the plank, that pierwise extended to the deeper water. The parson's protests ended in his slipping over the arched neck of the wilful brute, on to the few inches of plank that she considerately left for him. The old mare drank leisurely, then backed off with the same precaution, and stood switching the flies with her stunted tail. The parson followed her and thankfully grabbed the reins. After several attempts to get up, on the wrong side, he led the exacting animal to a log. He removed the veil he wore as a protection from the sticky eye-eating flies, so that Rosey might recognize him as her erstwhile rider. It was at this stage that "flash" Ned Stennard, always with time to kill and a tongue specially designed for the purpose, rode up and gave him lurid instructions and a leg-up.

He had come to their remoteness, he told Ned, as they rode along, to hold a service at a grazier's homestead some miles distant. Under Ned's sympathetic guidance he pulled up at the sliprails of a cockey's selection to announce these tidings. It was Ned's brother's place, but Ned, who was not on speaking terms with his sister-in-law, rode on and waited.

A group of half-naked children lay entangled among several kangaroo pups, in a make-believe of shade from a sickly gum tree. A canvas bag, with a saddle strap defining its long neck, hung from a bough, and the pups were yelping mildly at its contents, and licking the few drops of blood that fell. The parson saw the children rub the swarming flies from their eyes and turn to look at him. An older girl, bare-footed and dressed in a petticoat and old hat, was standing near a fire before the wide opening that served as a doorway to the humpy. She had a long stick, and was employed in permitting an aged billy-goat to bring his nose within an inch of the simmering water in the bucket slung over the fire.

"Are your parents in?" he asked.

"You ain't ole Keogh? " said the girl.

When he admitted that he wasn't, he saw her interest in his personality was gone. "Are your mother and father in?"

The thirsty billy was sneaking up again to the water, and she let him advance the prescribed limit before she made the jab that she enjoyed so thoroughly. "Mum's gorn ter Tilly Lumber's ter see t' ther kid, and ther rester them's gorn ter the Circler Dam."

He made known his mission to the girl, but she didn't divide her attention. The water would soon be too hot for the billy to drink, and there was no fun to be got out of the pups. For when she took the salt pork out of the canvas bag and put it in the bucket, they wouldn't try to get it out of boiling water.

Doubtful of his success, the parson rejoined Ned, and along the dusty track they jogged. The parson's part in the dialogue was chiefly remonstrative as to the necessity of Ned's variegated adjectives. And he had frequently to assure the bushman that it would be useless for him to search in his clerical pockets for tobacco, as he didn't smoke.

At the Horse Shoe bend they overtook hairy Paddy Woods of eighteen withering summers. Paddy was punching and blaspheming a nine-mile day out of his bullocks. These were straining their load along with heads bent close to the dust-padded track, silent, for all the whip weals, but for a cough to free their mouths and nostrils from dust. Old Rosey, an inveterate yarner, pulled up abruptly; but Paddy, who had his day's work cut out to a minute, gave a voiceless side-long nod in recognition of the parson's greeting, and went on driving his team. Probably his share of the conversation, mainly catechismal, would have been yea and nay nods, but for catching Ned's eye when the parson asked if he were married. Paddy struck an attitude of aged responsibility, and, tipping Ned an intelligent wink, made a pretence of searching through a dusty past, and replied that he thought he was. The parson, giving him the benefit of the doubt, inquired if there were any children for Baptism. Paddy, still with an eye on Ned, reckoned that the number of his offspring was uncertain, but promised that as soon as he delivered his load of wool he would have a day's "musterin' an' draftin' an' countin' an' earmarkin' " and send him the returns. Ned's loud laugh and "Good old Paddy!" had not the effect on its young-old recipient's well-filled tobacco pouch that he had hoped. The disgusted parson was trying to urge Rosey onward, but Rosey refused to leave her pleasant company till Ned brought his switch across her back.

Ned stayed with Paddy long enough to tell him that, in his opinion, the black-coated parson was "nothin' but a sneakin' Inspector, pokin' an' prowlin' roun' fur ole Keogh" — the lessee of the run, and their common enemy. He added that the green veil he wore over his eyes was a "mast" (mask), but that it didn't deceive him. Tobaccoless Ned tried further to arouse practical admiration from pouchful Paddy, by adding that he would ride after this disguised Inspector, "pump 'im dry as a blow'd bladder, an' then 'ammer 'ell outer 'im". But even this serious threat against the parson's stock-in-trade had no fruitful result, and putting his empty pipe back he galloped after his companion.

As they rode along, the parson in admiration watched the wiry little bushman dexterously winking both eyes to the confusion of the flies, and listened to the substitutions of words of his own coinage dropped red hot into the conversation in place of the sulphurous adjectives. Soon there was but little unknown to Ned's listener of the inner history — and with such additions as contrasted unfavourably with his own — of every selector on this sun-sucked run. In order of infamy Ned placed the lessee first; a good second came the land agent in the little township whence this pilgrim parson had come. But this fact was made clear to him: that, were the lessee ten times richer, the land agent ten times more unscrupulous, were "dummy" selectors occupying every acre, Ned was more than a match for them all.

At a later stage of their journey, when he turned again to the narratives of his cockey brethren, another circumstance stood out. It was only when Ned had exhausted the certainty, probability, and possibility of increase among the mares, cows, ewes and nannies of his and the other cockeys' flocks and herds, that he would descend to the human statistics, and the parson found that impending probability and possibility entered largely into Ned's computation of these.

From time to time they sighted the cockeys' humpies, but Ned, intent on making the most of his amazed listener, kept him on the track to his destination by promising to call at all the selections on his way back, and tell them that there was to be a service to-morrow morning. To emphasize his thoroughness, he added, with a wink of bush freemasonry, that he would "on'y tell two sorts — them wot arsts me, an' them wot don't". And this clerical brother, newly initiated into the mysteries of bush craft, could not have found a better messenger. But the wonder expressed in his eyes, as he watched this new labourer in the vineyard cantering briskly away to bear the glad tidings, would have changed to awe could he have heard the varied versions Ned gave to the scattered families as to the need of their being at the grazier's homestead the first thing next day. Moreover, most of the conversation related by Ned as having taken place between the parson and him would have been as new to the former as it was to Ned's audience. For the adjectives with which he flavoured the parson's share proved him to have readily and fluently mastered the lurid bush tongue.

It was shearing time, and being also the middle of the week, most of the men were away. Those who were at home left their dinners, and came outside to talk to him. A visitor at meal times is always met outside the humpy, and the host, drawing a hand across a greasy mouth, leads the way to the nearest log. The women of the bush have little to share, and nursing the belief that how they live is quite unknown to one another, they have no inclination to entertain a caller. Two of the daily meals consist mainly of sliced damper dipped in a pan of fat, that always hangs over the fire. Mutton at shearing time is a rarity, as the men feed at the sheds. Wild pigs caught and killed by the women make the chief flesh food; but these are often scarce in the dry season.

And in addition Ned was no favourite among the women. This was partly from his being "flash", but more from his reputation for flogging his missus. Ned, moreover, had tried to force his example on the male community by impressing upon them his philosophy, that it was the proper thing to hit a woman every time you met her, since she must either be coming from mischief or going to it. As to his flashness, he considered he had something to be flash about. He had been twice to Sydney; and not only could he spell by ear, but, given an uncertain number of favouring circumstances, he could use a pen to the extent of putting his name to a cheque. Certainly, before he would attempt this, Liz, his missus, had to pen up the goats, shut the hut, and, with the dogs and the kids, drive the fowls a mile from the house, and keep them there till Ned fired a gun. Left to himself, Ned would tear out a cheque, lay it on the table, place a block of wood on the bottom edge of the paper, to keep his hand from travelling off it to the table below. Then he had to tie his wrist to the left side of his belt — he was left-handed — in such a manner that his hand could not stray to the foreign region above the cheque, ink the pen with his right hand, and place it in the left. But even then the task was often unaccomplished. Sometimes he would be so intent on trying to keep the EDWARD on the line, that it would run to the end of the paper, excluding the STENNARD; and, despite Ned's protests anent insufficient space, the bank did not approve of part of the signature being placed on the back of the cheque.

When he tried to write small and straight, the result generally seemed satisfactory till a careful analysis showed a letter or so missing. Or, just as success seemed probable, his cheque-book would give out, or his pen break. It was bad for Liz and her own boy Joey when either of these accidents occurred, for he would fire no gun, and, despite all the perspiring activity of Liz, the kids, and the dogs, some of the fowls would make their way home to roost on the hut when night came. For allowing him to be disturbed "jes as I wus gettin' me 'and in" he would "take it outer" Liz, or, what was worse to her, "outer" Joey.

But on this occasion Ned, ever resourceful and now hungry, refused to be led to a log. His reputation for startling discoveries was against him, but he knew that many of them must have seen him riding past with a black-coated stranger, and he trusted to that to support the story his ingenious imagination had ready for them. Authoritatively he demanded in each case to see the missus. They came ungraciously, but after his dark, bodeful hints as to the necessity of their attending service at the grazier's homestead next day, he was invited inside and a place was cleared for him at the table. Quite recklessly they plied him with pints of tea and damper and dip, sprinkled with salt, and in some extravagant instances with pepper. And Ned took these favours as his due, though he knew he was no favourite.

Flogging and flashness were lost sight of by these anxious women, as they listened to all he had to say. They coaxed him to wait while they searched among the few spare clothes in the gin cases with hide-hinged lids, for land receipts, marriage lines, letter from Government Departments, registered cattle brands, sheep ear-marks, and every other equipment that protects the poor cockey from a spiteful and revengeful Government, whose sole aim was "ter ketch 'em winkin' " and then forfeit the selection. All of these documents Ned inspected upside down or otherwise, and pronounced with unlegal directness that "a squint et them 'ud fix 'im if thet's wot 'e's smellin' after".

He told them to bring them next day. Those of the men who had swapped horses with passing drovers, without the exchange of receipts, were busy all afternoon trumping up witnesses.

II

NEXT morning the minister was sitting in the rocking chair on the verandah of the grazier's house. He had a prayer book in one hand and a handkerchief in the other, with which he lazily disputed the right of the flies to roost on his veil. This gave an undulating motion to the chair which was very soothing after old Rosey's bumping. He saw a pair of brown hands part the awning enclosing the verandah. Then a black head, held in the position of a butting animal, came in view. Free of the screen, the head craned upwards. He saw a flat, shrewd face, with black beady eyes set either side of a bridgeless nose. A wisp of dried grass hung from the wide mouth.

"Sis wants er ride in thet ther cock 'orse yer in," said the mouth, ejecting the grass with considerable force in his direction.

Sis had worked her head in by this. She was fair, with nondescript hair and eyes, and she was "chawrin' ".

"Wer's ther cock 'orse, Jinny?" she asked, for the chair was not rocking.

"Ridey it an' let 'er see it; an' undo this," commanded Jinny.

"Come round to the front," said the minister mildly, and pointing to the opening opposite the door.

They came in and walked up to him, with hoods hanging by the strings down their backs.

"Have you come alone?"

"The ether uns er comin'. Me an' Sis giv' 'em ther slip; we didn' wanter 'ump ther dash kid."

"How far have you walked?"

"Yer parst our place yesserday mornin'. Didn' yer see me an' ther billy? Gosh, we nigh bust oursels at ther way yer legs stuck out. Fust I thort yer wus ole Keogh. Yer rides jes' like er Chinymun." The dark one did all the talking.

"Our Sis wants er ride in this," she continued. She gave the chair a lurch that sent the parson's feet in the air. To avoid the threatened repetition he gripped both sides and planted his feet firmly on the boards.

The younger one poked a stem of dried grass from her mouth through the mesh of the veil in a line with his left ear. Thoroughly routed, he sprang up, and the elder child leapt in.

"'Ere they cum, Jinny," warned Sis.

Jinny peeped through the awning. "So they is. You gammon ter them we ain't cum, w'en they arsts yer," she said to the parson, "an' we'll sneak roun' ther back. Eh, Sis?"

Mammy and Daddy — commonly called "Jyne" and "Alick" even by their offspring — came in with four children, all younger than Jinny and Sis. Jyne carried the youngest "straddled" across her hip.

The most pronounced feature of Jyne's face was her mouth, and it seemed proud of its teeth, especially of the top row. Without any apparent effort, the last tooth there was always visible. She was a great power in the bush, being styled by the folk themselves "Rabbit Ketcher", which, translated, means midwife. And the airs Jyne gave herself were justifiable, for she was the only "Rabbit Ketcher" this side of the township. To bring a qualified midwife from civilization would have represented a crippling expenditure to these cockies. Jyne's moderate fees were usually four-legged.

"D'y ter yous," said Alick, blinking his bungy eyes, and smiling good-naturedly at the parson and at the grazier and his wife. He sat down without removing his hat. Jyne's teeth saluted them but without any good-nature. Jinny and Sis sneaked in behind their mother.

"You young tinkers," cried Jyne, "tyke this chile this minute." Her voice, despite the size of her mouth, came through her nose. She put the baby on the floor, and, taking off her hood, mopped her face with the inside of her print dress.

"We wus lookin' fer you an' Alick," said Jinny to her mother, and winking at the parson.

"Yes, you wus, — with ther 'ook," answered Jyne.

Without further introduction she slewed her head to one side, shut one eye knowingly, and said to the staring minister, "Ther ain't a wink about Jinny."

The unblinking daughter instantly offered an illustration of her wakefulness. "Yer orter seen me an' gran'dad th' ether morning. He wus milkin' ther nannies, an' ther billy you seen 'e wus jes' close agen 'im. I sneaks up to ther billy an' gives 'im er jab. Lawr' ter see 'im rush et ole Alex an' bunt 'im! 'E'd er killed th' ole feller on'y fer me. Wou'dn' 'e, mum?"

"Yer a bol' gal," said mum in a proud voice.

The bewildered minister, to turn the conversation, took a vase of wild flowers.

"They belong to the lily tribe, I think," said the hostess. "They are bulbous."

"Wile hunyions," sniffed Jyne, making no attempt to conceal her contempt for this cur of a woman, who thought so much of herself that she always brought a nurse from town.

Then came Alick's brother, "Flash" Ned; they were as unlike as brothers sometimes are. Ned greeted the parson with bush familiarity. He had his hat on one side, and was wearing a silk Sydney coat that reached to his heels. He was followed by Liz with their family of five. Joey stayed outside, and from time to time dexterously located his step-father. He was Liz's child by an early marriage — at least, she always said she had been married.

Perched on Liz's head was a draggled hat that a month ago had been snow white. This also was one of Ned's Sydney purchases. It was the first time Liz had worn it, but she and the children had overhauled it many times and tried it on. This privilege had been extended to all the women whose curiosity and envy had brought them to Liz's place. Jinny had called on her way to church, and the missing end of the white feather, after being licked of its ticklesomeness, was now in her safe keeping.

Jyne, catching sight of Joey, invited him inside. But the

boy, at a warning glance from his mother, slunk further back. He had run in the wrong horse for his step-father that morning, and was evading a threatened hiding that was to remove both skin and hair. Liz would gladly have taken the hiding herself in place of Joey,but her interference, as she knew to her cost, would mean one for herself without saving the boy.

But for all this Liz thought she was fairly happy. For it was not every day that Ned tried to sign a cheque or that the sheep got boxed, or that his horse refused to be caught. Nor did it always rain when he wanted it fine. Things did not go wrong every day, and he did not beat her or Joey unless they did. A pound of lollies for her and the kids from a dealer's cart when one came round, would make her think him the best husband in the world.

There was between Jyne and Ned the opposition that is instinctive between commanding spirits. Liz yielded obedience first to Ned then to Jyne.

"Ow's Polly?" inquired Liz, her countenance showing the gravity of the question.

"Arst 'im," snarled Jyne, baring her fangs and looking at uneasy shuffling Alick. "Makin' 'er dror three casts er worter ten mile, an' 'er thet way. Wil' pigs eatin' 'er as I cum along."

"No!" said Liz, though she had known it all yesterday. News of such catastrophes soon spread in the bush.

"Better corl me a liar at onct," snapped Jyne.

Next to arrive were Jyne's mother and Alick's father, both of whom lived with Jyne. The old woman rode on a horse astride a man's saddle. The old man led it. She had Jyne's mouth, or rather Jyne had hers, but the teeth were gone. The old man greeted the parson reverently, blew with his breath on the seat, and wiped it carefully with the handkerchief he had taken from his hat. Even then before sitting he raised the tails of the coat he had been married in so long ago. Until Ned's Sydney purchase his had been the only decorative coat in the district.

Tilly and Jim Lumber, with their ten days-old baby, followed. Jim was the champion concertina player and bullock driver in the district. He came as the representative of the several families across the creek, whom energetic Ned had rounded up the day before. He had been chosen by them for his size and strength to do battle on their behalf. Ned's effort to frighten those women whose husbands were away shearing into the necessity of attending service had over-reached itself, and they had been afraid to come. But they had entrusted their precious documents to Jim's powerful keeping. He had his own registered brand tied up in a spotted handkerchief. This he dropped with a clank beside him as he sat sheepishly and gingerly on the edge of a chair. He was over six feet, but he sat with his head almost between his knees, till he resembled a quadruped. His shirt front bulged like a wallet with his clients' papers. He slyly took stock of those assembled. Spry little Tilly got the credit of having done all the courting. Even after marriage she had always done his share of the talking.

"Ow's ther kiddy, maroo?" said Alick to Jim, lisping from the size of the plug he had just bitten. He had a fatherly interest in all Jyne's "rabbit ketchin' ".

Jim, who never used his voice except to drive his bullocks, answered with a subterranean laugh.

"Noo bit er flesh," said Ned, nodding at the baby.

"'Ow's Polly this mornin'?" gravely inquired Tilly, as she took a seat near Jyne.

"Ah, poor Polly," quavered Jyne's mother, and sparing Jyne by telling of Polly's untimely end.

"Well, I'm blest; what a lorse!" said the sympathetic Tilly. She repeated a well-known story of the bu'stin' of a poley cow last year.

Jyne took the baby, and began to rate the mother mildly for "walkin' seven mile ser soon", but Jyne's mother interposed with a recital of "wot I dun w'en Jun (John) wur two days old". John was present, fully six feet of him, grinning with a mouth bigger than Jyne's, but mercifully hidden by a straggled moustache.

However, Jyne was not to be outdone even by her own mother, and the narrative of her last, assisted in many minor details by Jinny, aged eleven, left little to be desired in the way of hardihood.

Liz kept her teething baby respectfully silent by

industriously rubbing its lower gum with a dirty thumb. She expressed her surprise at Jyne's phenomenal endurance by little clicks of the tongue, shakes of the head, and other signs indicative of admiration and astonishment. When Jyne finished, she began eagerly on an experience of her own. "Well, w'en I wus took with Drary (short for Adrarian), think I could fin' ther sissers?"

Jyne, who knew that the recital of a daring feat was coming, inquired, "W'en yer wus took with Joey?"

"No," said Liz, stopping short with a nervous click in her voice, and looking at Ned.

The next item was ventriloquizing by Jyne per medium of Tilly's uneasy baby. "My mammy, she sez, yer dot me all o'a hoo, she sez. No wunny, she sez, me can't keep goody, she sez, 'ith me cosey all o'a hoo, she sez." She had been examining the baby's undergear, and at this stage her tone of baby banter suddenly changed to one of professional horror. "My Gawd, Tilly!" she cried, the drooping corners of her mouth nearly covering her upper teeth. "Look w'er' 'er little belly-bands is — nearly un'er 'er arms," she explained, probably to the company, but looking directly at the clergyman. And, with true professional acumen, she intimated that had she not been on the spot, an intricate part of the little one's anatomy in another minute would "'a bust out a bleedin' an' not all ther doctors in ther worl' couldn' 'a' stopt it".

The minister was very busy, meanwhile, blushing and getting his books in order, and with this congregation of ten adults and eighteen children he began, "Dearly beloved brethren——"

Jim Lumber gripped his bullock brand, took a swift look at him and turned to Tilly. It had been settled between them that she was to do the talking. Alick, who, despite his father's efforts to enlighten him as to the nature of a church service, and encouraged by Jyne's remark that "they'd eat nothin' ", had also brought his valuable documents in his shirt front, thrust in a groping hand.

For a few minutes the adults listened and watched intently, but the gentle voice of the parson, and his nervous manner, soon convinced them that they had nothing to fear from him. Ned had been "pokin' borak" at them again; they added it to the long score they owed him.

The children wandered about the room. Jinny and Sis invited their little sister to "cum an' see ther pooty picters in the man's book", and they assisted the minister to turn over the leaves of his Bible.

Alick's father, who was from the North of Ireland, and, for all his forty years in the bush, had not lost his reverence for the cloth, bade his grand-daughters beseechingly to "quet", whereupon Jinny showed him quite two inches of inky tongue. Ink was a commodity unknown in Jinny's home, and all the unknown is edible to the bush child.

"Woman!" he said, appealing to Jinny's mother, "whybut you bid 'er to quet?"

"You orter be in er glars' ban' box w'er' ther' ain't no children; thet's w'er' you orter be," answered Jyne.

He beckoned to one straggler, a girl of six, with Alick's face, who came to him promptly and sat on his knee.

Presently her brown hand stroked his old cheek. "Gran'dad," she said.

"Choot, darlin'," he whispered reverently.

The child looked at him wonderingly. "I says you's a gran'dad," she repeated, "not ole Alick."

He laid his white head on hers.

"Gran'dad, ole Tommy Tolbit's dead."

Turning his glistening face to Liz in momentary forgetfulness, he said solemnly, "The knowledge of this chile!"

"Ole Talbert" had been dead for two years, and the knowledgable child had been surprising him so, at least twice a week.

"We have erred and strayed from Thy ways like lost sheep," murmured the minister.

The smaller children wandered in and out of the bedrooms, carrying their spoils with them. But Jinny and Sis had drawn the now disabled rocking chair up to the window, and were busy poking faces at two of Liz's children, who were standing on the couch inside. One of these made a vicious smack with a hair-brush at Jinny's tongue, flattened against the glass. The ensuing crash stopped even the parson for a moment.

Bravely he began again, and paused occasionally for a sudden subterranean laugh to cease or to put one book after another on the shelf behind him out of the children's reach. Just as he read the last line of the *Te Deum*, "O Lord, in Thee have I trusted: let me never be confounded", one of Liz's children tugged at his trousers, with a muzzled request that his teeth might be freed from a square of pink soap. Another offered to the baby Liz was nursing a pincushion she brought from the bedroom.

"Jyne," called Jinny from the verandah, "'Ere cums young Tommy Tolbit by 'isself. You wus right, Jyne; she ain't cummin'!"

Even Jyne's gums gleamed; she looked triumphantly at Alick her husband, at Liz, then at all but Ned.

In shambled Tommy, moist and panting. He had been a drover, and had recently taken up a selection on the run. He was a bridegroom of a month's standing. His missus had been a servant at one of the hotels in the township.

"Made a start!" he remarked. His voice gave the impression that he did not mind their not waiting for him.

"Missus ain't comin'!" inquired Alick, trying to atone to Jyne for overloading Polly.

"Not ter day," said the bridegroom, but his voice intimated that in all probability she would have been able to come to-morrow.

"No!" said Jyne, putting him under fire, and trying to keep the crow out of her voice. "Ain't very well, is she! Didn' eat a very 'earty breakfuss this mornin'!"

And a further remark suggested that even if the meal had been hearty, the usual process of assimilation had not taken place.

"'Ow's Polly!" he inquired.

"Cooked," said Jyne, instantly diverted.

"Go on!" said the bridegroom, with well-feigned astonishment. His breathless and perspiring state had been caused by his "going on" to capture one of the wild suckers that had been eating Polly.

"Let us pray," said the minister. His host, hostess, and Alick's father knelt, but the rest sat as usual.

The knowledgable child, considering the grandfather's position an invitation to mount, climbed on his back. Making a bridle of the handkerchief round the old fellow's neck, and digging two heels into his sides, she talked horse to him. The protesting old man bucked vigorously, but it was no easy task to throw her.

The clergyman gave out his text, and the sermon began.

Jyne's children commenced to complain of being "'ungery" and a fair-sized damper was taken from a pillow-slip. This, together with two tin tots and a bottle of goat's milk, was given to Jinny and she was told to do "ther sharin' ".

The hostess asked Jyne in a whisper to send them to the verandah, and for a time there was comparative quiet. Such interruptions as "Jinny won't gimme nun, Arnie" (Auntie) from Liz's children being checked by Jyne with "Go an' play an' doan' 'ave ser much gab, like yer father."

"Thet greedy wretch uv er Jinny is guzzlin' all ther milk inter 'er, Jyne" from her own children, was appeased by her promise to "break ther young faggit's back w'en I get 'ome".

There was a wail of anguished hunger from Liz's empty children that aroused paternal sympathy in Ned. "Se'p me Gord," he said "some wimmen is like cows. They'll give ther own calf a suck, but if any one else's calf cums a-nigh 'em they lif' their leg an' kick it ter blazes."

Jyne tossed her head and, with a derisive laugh, expressed the opinion that "it 'ed fit sum people better if ther munny wasted in buyin' flash coats an' rediclus 'ats wus spent in flour-bags".

For a short space only the voice of the preacher sounded, as, in studied stoicism, he pursued his thankless task. Occasionally they looked at him to see "'oo 'e wus speakin' ter", but finding nothing directly personal, even this attention ceased.

Liz leant across to Tilly Lumber and asked, "Fowl layin'!"

"Ketch 'em er layin' et Chrissermus."

Ned told how he had brought home a number of law

books from Sydney, and that he and an old man he had picked up "wus readin' 'em". It was his intention to absorb such an amount of knowledge that all he would have to do with the lessee of the run — an ex-barrister — would be to put him in a bail. What would follow was graphically illustrated by Ned's dropping his head, gripping an imaginary bucket between his knees, and opening and shutting his hands in rhythmic up and down movements. Some of his audience, remembering his threats and warning against the parson, thought this pantomime must have an ominous meaning for the preacher.

But sceptical Jyne was not impressed. "Upon me soul," she said, "sum people is the biggest lyin' blowers that ever cocked er lip."

Alick, always for peace, stepped into the breach. "Comin' along jes' now," he said, shifting his plug of tobacco from one side to the other, and aiming at the flies in the fireplace with the juice, "we 'as a yarn with Mick Byrnes. 'E 'as ther luck of er lousy calf. 'E sez 'e got eightpence orl roun' fer 'ees kangaroo skins. Damned if I can."

"Now a good plan 'ed be," said Ned, "ter get a good lot, sen' 'em down ter them Sydney blokes. Slip down yerself, go ter ther sale, don' let on 'oo yer are, an' run 'em up like blazes. Thet's wot I'll do with my wool nex' year."

This plan seemed commendable to Alick. "By Goey," he said, his mild eyes blinking.

Jyne never, on any occasion, showed the slightest interest or attention when Ned was speaking, unless to sniff and lay bare her bottom teeth, but here she remarked, "Sum people 'ud keep runnin' ter Sydney till 'e 'asen' er penny ter fly with."

"If sum people with ser much jawr, an' 'er mouth 'es big 'es 'er torn pocket, belonged ter me," said Ned, "I'd smash 'er ugly jawr."

Jyne slewed hers to an awful angle in his direction. "I'd like ter see yer try it."

A look of agony came into the eyes of the grazier's wife as she heard the door of the dining-room open. The children were so quiet that she knew they were up to mischief.

She heard Jinny's hoarse whisper: "Orl of yez wait 'an I'll bring yer sumsin'." On the dining-room table was the cold food prepared for the clergyman's dinner. She looked across at her husband with dumb entreaty. He, with eyes devoutly on the carpet, was listening intently to Ned's account of how he nearly made the squatter take a "sugar doodle" (back somersault) when he heard that he had been to Sydney.

" 'Day, Keogh,' sez I.

" 'Oo 'ave I ther 'oner of speakin' ter!' sez 'e.

" 'Mr Stennard,' I sez.

" 'Oh indeed,' 'e sez, 'very 'appy ter make yer acquaintance, Mr Stennard, Esquire,' 'e sez.

" 'Never mind no blarsted acquaintance,' I sez, 'w'en are yer goin' ter take yer flamin' jumbucks orf my lan'!' I sez.

" 'Your lan',' 'e sez, 'I didn' know you 'ad any lan' about 'ere,' 'e sez.

" 'Oh, didn' yer,' I sez, 'you ner ther bloody white-livered lan' agent won't frighten me orf,' I sez, 'gammonin' I'm on er reserve,' sez I; 'I've paid me deposit, an' I've been ter Sydney,' I sez; 'I put me name ter a cheque,' sez I, 'an'——' "

Jyne ceased sniffing, to laugh long and loudly. "Gawd, eh!" she said, with her eyes on the ceiling and apparently appealing to the flies. "Wot 'erbout sech game-cocks plantin' under ther dray w'en old Keogh kem bullyin' w'en we fust kem out 'ere!"

Ned went hastily out at the front door, pretending "ter squint at ther jumbucks", three miles away. Joey, who had been peering round that door, now appeared at the back.

"Come in, Joey," snorted Jyne. "No one ain't game ter 'it yer w'en I'm 'ere."

The minister still preached, but he had only old Alick for a listener.

Even the hostess's mental picture of Jinny "sharin" her dinner for three among that voracious brood was distracted. Only the fear of suffering in the clergyman's mind as one of "them" kept her to her seat. She could give the sermon no attention, but listened to Sis licking her fingers, and wondered if it was the vinegar or the wine that caused Jinny's cough. Presently Jinny set that doubt at rest by coming in odorous, and with the front of her dress wine-stained.

"Little 'un snoozin!" Jinny remarked, lurching giddily towards her to merrily twirl her fist in the snoozer. The snoozer's mother wondered if they had shut the dining-room door. But soon the noise of the fowls scattering the crockery told her they had not.

"Them busted fowls is eatin' orl yer dinner," said Jinny dreamily.

"'Unt 'em out an' shet ther door," said sympathetic Jyne.

"You go, Sis, I'm tired." Jinny laid her giddy head on the floor, and went to sleep.

"Liz," said Jyne maliciously, for she immediately grudged Sis's efforts to chase the fowls out of the dining-room. "Wot's thet there flower?" pointing to the vase.

"Wild huniyon," said Liz, promptly.

"Er, is it? Thet's orl yew know. Thet's a bulbers, thet is. Thet's ther noo name she give it." She looked at the grazier's wife and laughed ironically.

"Bulbers! yer goat," said Liz, laughing dutifully.

The sermon was over, and the worried minister began the christening.

Naming the hostess's baby was plain sailing. He then drew towards him a child of about two years, and asked, "What is this child's name?"

"Adrarian," said Liz. An old shepherd reading to her a love story had so pronounced the hero's name. It staggered the minister, until his hostess spelt "Adrian".

"What is its age!"

"About two year."

This was too vague for him, and he pressed for dates. But for these dwellers in the bush the calendar had no significance. The mother thought it might be in November. "'Cos it wus shearin', an' I'd ter keep Teddy at 'ome ter do ther work." Teddy was "about ten".

From these uncertainties the clergyman had to supply the dates for his official returns to the Government.

"But, Lawd," as Jyne remarked to ease his perplexity,

"wot did it matter fer a brat of a boy!" She had a family of six, and all were girls.

There was much the same difficulty with all the others, an exception being Tilly Lumber's baby of under a fortnight. A cowardly look came into the minister's eyes as he turned to this grotesque atom already in the short-coat stage. He remembered Jyne's awful discovery of a little while back, and shirked the duty of holding it even for a moment.

The christening was a matter that had some personal interest for the elders, and they grouped round the minister. Bridegroom Tommy, striking the mossy back of Alick's old father, suggested that he and Jyne's mother should get spliced, and he expressed the opinion of the fruitfulness of such union within record time as a set-off dig at Jyne.

She instantly balanced matters between herself and the incautiously smiling Liz and the laughing unfilial Ned. "Stop scratchin' yer 'ed, miss; anyone 'ud think there wus anythink in it," she said to Liz's eldest girl, who was brushing the christening water from her hair. Ned's stepson she invited to come nearer, and tell her who had blackened his poor eye. She advised the silent lad "ter get a waddy ther nex' time anyone bigger'n yer goes ter 'it yer". And she gave him directions by twirling an imaginary waddy swiftly, its circuit suddenly diverting in a line with Ned's skull.

It was long past noon when the ceremony was ended. The minister drained his glass of water, mopped his face, and heaved a deep sigh. As the whole congregation still sat on, he gave them a hint that "church" was out, and their presence no longer required. He spoke with a show of concern of how very hot they would find the walk home, and to further emphasize his meaning, he shook hands with all the adults, and walked to the verandah. Without the slightest concern they sat on, listening intently to the sounds the hostess made in trying to scrape together a meal for the clergyman. Apparently they all meant to stay the day.

The grazier's wife appeared for a moment to beckon him to go round the house into the dining-room, and he sat down to the remains of the dinner the children had left.

At that moment Jinny, who had been awakened for the christening, looked round the door. "Our Sis wants ter know w'en 'er supper's goin' ter be!" she said.

This perhaps was an acknowledgment that Sis had already dined.

The Chosen Vessel

SHE laid the stick and her baby on the grass while she untied the rope that tethered the calf. The length of the rope separated them. The cow was near the calf, and both were lying down. Feed along the creek was plentiful, and every day she found a fresh place to tether it, since tether it she must, for if she did not, it would stray with the cow out on the plain. She had plenty of time to go after it, but then there was her baby; and if the cow turned on her out on the plain, and she with her baby, — she had been a town girl and was afraid of the cow, but she did not want the cow to know it. She used to run at first when it bellowed its protest against the penning up of its calf. This satisfied the cow, also the calf, but the woman's husband was angry, and called her — the noun was cur. It was he who forced her to run and meet the advancing cow, brandishing a stick, and uttering threatening words till the enemy turned and ran. "That's the way!" the man said, laughing at her white face. In many things he was worse than the cow, and she wondered if the same rule would apply to the man, but she was not one to provoke skirmishes even with the cow.

It was early for the calf to go to "bed" — nearly an hour earlier than usual; but she had felt so restless all day. Partly because it was Monday, and the end of the week that would bring her and the baby the companionship of his father, was so far off. He was a shearer, and had gone to his shed before daylight that morning. Fifteen miles as the crow flies separated them.

There was a track in front of the house, for it had once been a wine shanty, and a few travellers passed along at intervals. She was not afraid of horsemen; but swagmen, going to, or worse coming from, the dismal, drunken little township, a day's journey beyond, terrified her. One had called at the house to-day, and asked for tucker.

That was why she had penned up the calf so early. She feared more from the look of his eyes, and the gleam of his teeth, as he watched her newly awakened baby beat its impatient fists upon her covered breasts, than from the knife that was sheathed in the belt at his waist.

She had given him bread and meat. Her husband she told him was sick. She always said that when she was alone and a swagman came; and she had gone in from the kitchen to the bedroom, and asked questions and replied to them in the best man's voice she could assume. Then he had asked to go into the kitchen to boil his billy, but instead she gave him tea, and he drank it on the wood heap. He had walked round and round the house, and there were cracks in some places, and after the last time he had asked for tobacco. She had none to give him, and he had grinned, because there was a broken clay pipe near the wood heap where he stood, and if there were a man inside, there ought to have been tobacco. Then he asked for money, but women in the bush never have money.

At last he had gone, and she, watching through the cracks, saw him when about a quarter of a mile away, turn and look back at the house. He had stood so for some moments with a pretence of fixing his swag, and then, apparently satisfied, moved to the left towards the creek. The creek made a bow round the house, and when he came to the bend she lost sight of him. Hours after, watching intently for signs of smoke, she saw the man's dog chasing some sheep that had gone to the creek for water, and saw it slink back suddenly, as if it had been called by some one.

More than once she thought of taking her baby and going to her husband. But in the past, when she had dared to speak of the dangers to which her loneliness exposed her, he had taunted and sneered at her. "Needn't flatter yerself," he had told her, "nobody 'ud want ter run away with yew."

Long before nightfall she placed food on the kitchen table, and beside it laid the big brooch that had been her mother's. It was the only thing of value that she had. And she left the kitchen door wide open.

The doors inside she securely fastened. Beside the bolt in the back one she drove in the steel and scissors; against it she piled the table and the stools. Underneath the lock of the front door she forced the handle of the spade, and the blade between the cracks in the flooring boards. Then the prop-stick, cut into lengths, held the top, as the spade held the middle. The windows were little more than portholes; she had nothing to fear through them.

She ate a few mouthfuls of food and drank a cup of milk. But she lighted no fire, and when night came, no candle, but crept with her baby to bed.

What woke her? The wonder was that she had slept — she had not meant to. But she was young, very young. Perhaps the shrinking of the galvanized roof — hardly though, since that was so usual. Yet something had set her heart beating wildly; but she lay quite still, only she put her arm over her baby. Then she had both round it, and she prayed, "Little baby, little baby, don't wake!"

The moon's rays shone on the front of the house, and she saw one of the open cracks, quite close to where she lay, darken with a shadow. Then a protesting growl reached her; and she could fancy she heard the man turn hastily. She plainly heard the thud of something striking the dog's ribs, and the long flying strides of the animal as it howled and ran. Still watching, she saw the shadow darken every crack along the wall. She knew by the sounds that the man was trying every standpoint that might help him to see in; but how much he saw she could not tell. She thought of many things she might do to deceive him into the idea that she was not alone. But the sound of her voice would wake baby, and she dreaded that as though it were the only danger that threatened her. So she prayed, "Little baby, don't wake, don't cry!"

Stealthily the man crept about. She knew he had his boots off, because of the vibration that his feet caused as he walked along the verandah to gauge the width of the little window in her room, and the resistance of the front door.

Then he went to the other end, and the uncertainty of

what he was doing became unendurable. She had felt safer, far safer, while he was close, and she could watch and listen. She felt she must watch, but the great fear of wakening her baby again assailed her. She suddenly recalled that one of the slabs on that side of the house had shrunk in length as well as in width, and had once fallen out. It was held in position only by a wedge of wood underneath. What if he should discover that? The uncertainty increased her terror. She prayed as she gently raised herself with her little one in her arms, held tightly to her breast.

She thought of the knife, and shielded its body with her hands and arms. Even the little feet she covered with its white gown, and the baby never murmured — it liked to be held so. Noiselessly she crossed to the other side, and stood where she could see and hear, but not be seen. He was trying every slab, and was very near to that with the wedge under it. Then she saw him find it; and heard the sound of the knife as bit by bit he began to cut away the wooden support.

She waited motionless, with her baby pressed tightly to her, though she knew that in another few minutes this man with the cruel eyes, lascivious mouth, and gleaming knife, would enter. One side of the slab tilted; he had only to cut away the remaining little end, when the slab, unless he held it, would fall outside.

She heard his jerked breathing as it kept time with the cuts of the knife, and the brush of his clothes as he rubbed the wall in his movements, for she was so still and quite, that she did not even tremble. She knew when he ceased, and wondered why, being so well concealed; for he could not see her, and would not fear if he did, yet she heard him move cautiously away. Perhaps he expected the slab to fall — his motive puzzled her, and she moved even closer, and bent her body the better to listen. Ah! what sound was that? "Listen! Listen!" she bade her heart — her heart that had kept so still, but now bounded with tumultuous throbs that dulled her ears. Nearer and nearer came the sounds, till the welcome thud of a horse's hoof rang out clearly.

"O God! O God! O God!" she panted, for they were very close before she could make sure. She rushed to the door, and with her baby in her arms tore frantically at its bolts and bars.

Out she darted at last, and running madly along, saw the horseman beyond her in the distance. She called to him in Christ's Name, in her babe's name, still flying like the wind with the speed that deadly peril gives. But the distance grew greater and greater between them, and when she reached the creek her prayers turned to wild shrieks, for there crouched the man she feared, with outstretched arms that caught her as she fell. She knew he was offering terms if she ceased to struggle and cry for help, though louder and louder did she cry for it, but it was only when the man's hand gripped her throat, that the cry of "Murder" came from her lips. And when she ceased, the startled curlews took up the awful sound, and flew wailing "Murder! Murder!" over the horseman's head.

"By God!" said the boundary rider, "it's been a dingo right enough! Eight killed up here, and there's more down in the creek — a ewe and a lamb, I'll bet; and the lamb's alive!" He shut out the sky with his hand, and watched the crows that were circling round and round, nearing the earth one moment, and the next shooting skywards. By that he knew the lamb must be alive; even a dingo will spare a lamb sometimes.

Yes, the lamb was alive, and after the manner of lambs of its kind did not know its mother when the light came. It had sucked the still warm breasts, and laid its little head on her bosom, and slept till the morn. Then, when it looked at the swollen disfigured face, it wept and would have crept away, but for the hand that still clutched its little gown. Sleep was nodding its golden head and swaying its small body, and the crows were close, so close, to the mother's wide-open eyes, when the boundary rider galloped down.

"Jesus Christ!" he said, covering his eyes. He told afterwards how the little child held out its arms to him, and how he was forced to cut its gown that the dead hand held.

•

It was election time, and as usual the priest had selected a candidate. His choice was so obviously in the interests of the squatter, that Peter Hennessey's reason, for once in his life, had over-ridden superstition, and he had dared promise his vote to another. Yet he was uneasy, and every time he woke in the night (and it was often), he heard the murmur of his mother's voice. It came through the partition, or under the door. If through the partition, he knew she was praying in her bed; but when the sounds came under the door, she was on her knees before the little Altar in the corner that enshrined the statue of the Blessed Virgin and Child.

"Mary, Mother of Christ! save my son! Save him!" prayed she in the dairy as she strained and set the evening's milking. "Sweet Mary! for the love of Christ, save him!" The grief in her old face made the morning meal so bitter, that to avoid her he came late to his dinner. It made him so cowardly, that he could not say good-bye to her, and when night fell on the eve of the election day, he rode off secretly.

He had thirty miles to ride to the township to record his vote. He cantered briskly along the great stretch of plain that had nothing but stunted cotton bush to play shadow to the full moon, which glorified a sky of earliest spring. The bruised incense of the flowering clover rose up to him, and the glory of the night appealed vaguely to his imagination, but he was preoccupied with his present act of revolt.

Vividly he saw his mother's agony when she would find him gone. Even at that moment, he felt sure, she was praying.

"Mary! Mother of Christ!" He repeated the invocation, half unconsciously, when suddenly to him, out of the stillness, came Christ's Name — called loudly in despairing accents.

"For Christ's sake! Christ's sake! Christ's sake!" called the voice. Good Catholic that he had been, he crossed himself before he dared to look back. Gliding across a ghostly patch of pipe-clay, he saw a white-robed figure with a babe clasped to her bosom.

All the superstitious awe of his race and religion swayed his brain. The moonlight on the gleaming clay was a "heavenly light" to him, and he knew the white figure not for flesh and blood, but for the Virgin and Child of his mother's prayers. Then, good Catholic that once more he was, he put spurs to his horse's sides and galloped madly away.

His mother's prayers were answered, for Hennessey was the first to record his vote — for the priest's candidate. Then he sought the priest at home, but found that he was out rallying the voters. Still, under the influence of his blessed vision, Hennessey would not go near the public-houses, but wandered about the outskirts of the town for hours, keeping apart from the towns-people, and fasting as penance. He was subdued and mildly estactic, feeling as a repentant chastened child, who awaits only the kiss of peace.

And at last, as he stood in the graveyard crossing himself with reverent awe, he heard in the gathering twilight the roar of many voices crying the name of the victor at the election. It was well with the priest.

Again Hennessey sought him. He was at home, the housekeeper said, and led him into the dimly lighted study. His seat was immediately opposite a large picture, and as the housekeeper turned up the lamp, once more the face of the Madonna and Child looked down on him, but this time silently, peacefully. The half-parted lips of the Virgin were smiling with compassionate tenderness; her eyes seemed to beam with the forgiveness of an earthly mother for her erring but beloved child.

He fell on his knees in adoration. Transfixed, the wondering priest stood, for mingled with the adoration, "My Lord and my God!" was the exaltation, "And hast Thou chosen me?"

"What is it, Peter?" said the priest.

"Father," he answered reverently; and with loosened tongue he poured forth the story of his vision.

"Great God!" shouted the priest, "and you did not stop to save her! Do you not know? Have you not heard?"

●

Many miles further down the creek a man kept throwing an old cap into a water-hole. The dog would bring it out and lay it on the opposite side to where the man stood, but would not allow the man to catch him, though it was only to wash the blood of the sheep from his mouth and throat, for the sight of blood made the man tremble. But the dog also was guilty.

Later Stories
1916-1921

Editors' Note

When Duckworth published *Bush Studies* in a new edition with the new title *Cobbers* in 1917, two new stories by Baynton were added. "Trooper Jim Tasman" opened the volume and "Toohey's Party" concluded it, providing a rather odd frame for the earlier stories. "Trooper Jim Tasman" had appeared in the *British-Australasian* in the Summer Number for 1916 (21 July); "Toohey's Party" is known only in its *Cobbers* version. The *Cobbers* text of "Trooper Jim Tasman" is reprinted here as it contains several revisions which we can confidently presume are Baynton's. Most of the revisions are minor, usually directed at registering Jim's speech more realistically, but a few are more substantial. The sentence about a mother's grief in the fourth paragraph is an addition, and an interesting observation on courage is omitted from the paragraph beginning "He went on talking . . .". It read:

> The late Lord Salisbury once said to me, commenting on our boys' fighting qualities, even in the Boer War:
>
> "Courage is your inheritance; your forebears possessed it, or they never would have sailed far away to that great and unknown country."

Barbara Baynton included the following dedication in *Cobbers*: "To my cobbers of the past, the present, and the future admiringly and gratefully."

The last story in this section, "Her Bush Sweetheart", was published in the Summer Number of the *British-Australasian* (September 1921) and is reprinted here for the first time.

Trooper Jim Tasman

"FUNNY thing! we can be larfin' an' torkin' an' chiackin' all about our tarts we've left behind, which was ther prettiest, an' which was ther best, an' we can be arguin' about which col'ny is ther best, or which company done ther best, till we're ready to lay one another out. Yer know, ther funniest thing is, ther minute we get ther order to get ready ter charge we're all the best of pals — brothers even."

There were three others, and a flash of more than comradeship illumined each face.

Jim was reminiscent for a few moments, and then in a different key, he said—

"An' another funny thing is that every blessed one of us at ther very last minute when we do charge, ther very last thing we think about is mother. Yer see, if we're wiped out it's all over in two ticks, but she goes on greevin' for ever."

And again there was a glistening confirmation of Jim's "funny" fact.

Jim continued—

"Not ther ole pot, mind yer, but ther ole pan yet my old pot — Lord, 'e could mag. 'E was all agin me enlistin' — too young, 'e said. I was oney sixteen," he added confidentially. "Reckoned I didn't know enough; kept maggin' away at first one thing, then another, till I wound 'im up. 'Very well, then,' I said, 'I'll do a bolt ter Sydney an' enlist there.' 'E give in then, an' when I came 'ome from enlistin' 'e was all ther other way, said it was quite right ter go an' fight, an' if he'd been young enough 'e'd a' been at it. Awful old blower, the ole pot, till I shut 'im up with: 'Why didn't yer go ter the Boer War, yer were young enough then?' That fetched 'im, an' 'e tried to land me one in ther ear, but I sloped off ter me granny's."

"And what did your mother say?" I inquired.

"Nuthin'," he answered promptly, "not a blarny word; just see'd ter me clobber, an' sewed on all me buttons. Ghost! she did sew 'em on, that's why I've got 'em all on now. Me sister, she reckoned I'd come back with one of those flash French tarts. Yer see, we all thought we was all going ter France, not ther Peninsula."

He lowered his head and wailed a weird, wild tune that wafted me back thousands of miles, and, it seemed, thousands of years. His words were a tribute to never-forgetting "Australia" and the good "gurls" left behind. And, as ever, his sentiments were shiningly endorsed by his comrades. Then even Jim's lips closed with a grimness, for we were all spell-bound in the fellowship of loneliness and longing for our own land.

"But your mother said nothing?" I asked again.

"Not a blarny word. Yer see, if she'd made a 'ole in 'er face she'd a' been gone a million; bowled me over meself, p'r'aps, front me cobbers."

He went on talking, but he had conjured a picture for me of his speechless mother that blotted out all else. I saw those silent bush women. Early pioneers, who had left father and mother, and sister and brother and friends, to face the great unknown as mate to their man, and of their silent courage had bred these Anzac heroes.

I know that these bereft mothers will take their sorrows silently, though what these stalwart sons were to them, who have little else, I, as a Bush woman, know. Time and again I have watched for some comment on their sacrificing heroism, but I have never seen it. Maybe because it is not understood, for, happen what will to the European mother, she has at least companionship. "Misery loves company." The Bush mother must tell her grief to Nature, her only outlet. It is not that her man does not sympathize or feel the loss in his way equally with her, but from instinct a man feels helpless in great grief, and, therefore, avoids all possible contact with it.

Jim had three honourable scars — all narrow squeaks —

one, a bayonet wound in his side, got in an encounter with a Turk, bordering on the miraculous.

"That was the biggest fright you ever had, Jim," I ventured.

"No," he said decisively. "Ther bonza fright I ever 'ad in ther course ov me whole natural was when I was about fourteen. Yer know, I was a trapper?"

I did, for Ernie had told me how Jim had been at it from his overgrown eighth year, living alone in the trapping haunts, but for weekly visits from his father coming for scalps and skins, and bringing Jim supplies.

"I'd been out all night trappin'," Jim went on, "an' about three o'clock in ther mornin' — it was bright moonlight — just as I got to ther 'ead ov ther gully where me tent was, I see somethin' all in white at ther tent door. I took aim in a tick. My God! I dunno now what stopped me, for she never spoke. It was me mother. Ghost! I was white for a week afterwards," he said, turning away, his face ashen then.

"Tell me something about Gallipoli, Jim," I said, to divert him, for by common consent Jim was the spokesman of the party.

"Oh, Johnnie Turk wasn't too far up ther pole," was all Jim had to say, although he had been in five of the greatest fights, and the clothes he wore had gory stains, all of different dates.

"But you went through terrible times there?" I encouraged. Jim sniffed ironically.

"Yet a Johnnie from (naming another country), at Trafalgar Square the other day, said ter me, 'You Australians think yer done some fightin' in ther Peninsula; but yer oughter been at ther retreat from Loos.' "

"What did you say?" said I.

"We wouldn't 'ave retreated!" he replied laconically.

(This story has been told before, nevertheless it is Jim's.)

"You liked the Turks, didn't you?"

"Yes, an' they liked us when they found we wasn't cannibals. They're great snipers," he added admiringly. "As cunnin' as a wagon-load of monkeys."

"Jim found one ov their burrows, though," said Roy.

"Tell me about it, Jim," I implored.

"Nothin' ter tell," he said. "Any one 'ud know by ther withered leaves. We pulled 'em away, an' after a while we found a 'ole just big enough ter work into by yer feet. Just about eight feet under we found a cell; blarny! nigh as big as this room. Lord! there was ammanition, an' one of our chap's duds, an' grub enough for three months — everything but cigarettes, ther very thing we wanted. We groped round, an' right agen one wall we see a blanket 'anging. I went to pull it aside" — stretching out his left hand — "an' I got it there," showing a scar through the palm, "but we had our rifles, and we banged into 'im with our rights," illustrating their aim. "We scooped up plenty of smokes and eleven quid. We gave ther colonel 'is rifle."

He smiled complacently at the remembrance, showing the gaps where his teeth had gone, in tribute to the "buttered brick". Then, groping in his pockets, he handed me a metal appendage from the sniper's belt.

I have many Australian war trophies, but this was my most cherished possession up to yesterday, when another of our boys gave me a fir cone from the Lone Pine. Despite the bloodily, memorable onslaught during the day, he had seen three fir cones on that vanished, but immortal, tree, and at the risk of life, late at night, he crept out and got them. His mother has one, his sister the other, and by the time this is in print he will be back in the trenches, or somewhere, with his brave face turned to the foe. Whatever befalls you, my dear countryman, the daring glory and sentimental grace of your courage will shine through my life.

Looking at Jim, one could readily conceive that the natural observation of our boys has played a prominent part in their valorous fighting.

Jim's ears pricked to a point; eyebrows elevated in a line with them; his keen eyes and resolute mouth shewed that every sense he possessed were taut and tensioned for any emergency, and every action of his long and alert body demonstrated the intellectual and swift union of both. He was the quickened embodiment of instructive intake.

Yes, in the game of observation Trooper Jim Tasman was a match for Johnnie Turk. And with this living example before me an early conviction awoke in me, and I realized in this supreme struggle the utter valuelessness of technical learning. I wished anew that it would be evermore where it is now, uncut and shelved in the encyclopaedia. Some of Jim's comrades had occasionally given him a lesson so that he might write home, and in a month we had him quite competent, if a little unconventional, to write to his people.

Jim and his companions stayed with me for about seven weeks. At night, under their graphic tuition, I rapidly rose to top-notch at nap, poker, two-up, and burnished afresh my early euchre. Sometimes we slashed the country life with a week-end in town, visiting music-halls, theatres, and various places of amusement. Jim came with me to a fashionable resort one Saturday afternoon.

"What do you think of it all, Jim?" I asked.

"Ther tea's prime, and ther music's like the wazzas."

"And the dancing?" I inquired.

A cynical smile widened his large mouth.

"Reminds me ov ther yarns me grandad used ter spit out about ther blacks. Ther ole bucks took all ther young gins for their lubras (wives), an' give all ther young black fellers ther old 'uns. 'Ere," waving his hand to include the dancers, "ther old coves is dancin' with ther young tarts, an' all ther ole tarts is dancin' with ther young cocks. Funny, ain't it?

"An' lots o' these rare old tarts with the wattle-coloured 'air is marryin' our chaps. Chicken stealin', we call it. Funny, ain't it?"

I was not in accord with Jim's adjective, though I bowed the knee to the truth of his observation.

Yet it was only as an onlooker that Jim was safe, for at close quarters with duplicity his guilelessness was pathetic, and in ten days Jim the cute had been taken down for his £70. But that was when he was up against the city human, or rather inhuman, element.

Now he is back in Egypt. I had a long letter from him just lately. I notice he has almost discarded the use of the little alphabet; but then one expects capitals from him. With him the traditional postscript holds the gem — "x x x x x x x", seven kisses, which I have the right to receive and he to send.

It happened at Claridge's. An American came up to him

and asked was he alone. Jim looked round and located me with his eye and hand.

"That's me mother," he said.

Then he came hastily to me, his eyes gleaming, his face flushed.

"Yer don't mind?" he said contritely.

For answer I put my arm proudly through his, and, so linked, mother and son passed down Brook Street.

Toohey's Party

THE capture of "The Comet", a noted bushranger, gained Sergeant Toohey his promotion together with the reward of £500. His first purchase for the Missus was a grand piano, ignoring such details as the outlay of half his capital and that neither he nor his Missus could play. Certainly at first there were varied one-finger performances by the Sergeant containing an occasional note of *Barney O'Hea*. But even his reputation for bravery, linked to the mysterious influence inseparable from the uniform, did not insure him from the chiacking applause of the little town's incorrigibles. Some would readily accompany him, and loud requests would be given for "Give us ther toon tha ole cow died on, for a change", or even the inflammable *Boyne Water* would be suggested. But when the Sergeant went on "dooty", and his son and heir, Joseph Aloysius Michael, "tooned up" after his father's precedent, weird cat-calls and stones on the roof might have stood for encores; however, when the novelty wore off the piano became as mute as the harp in Tara's halls. To keep marauding mice from exploiting its internals, a wire-netting guard was tacked round it, and eventually Mrs Toohey used it for an ironing table.

But now, by the recent coming of Anty Jo (and her nephew), the Sergeant's unmarried sister, from Ireland, all was changed. Joseph Aloysius Michael (shortened into "Jam" at school), who had been sent to the Sacred Heart school in a railway town, had come home for his holidays, and in his honour Anty Jo was giving a party. Of all the Sergeant's family, Joseph Aloysius Michael, with his brag and boast, was the light and love of her ambitious heart.

She, being a good Catholic, loved her Protestant brethren, as they being good Protestants loved her; but when Jam told her that his list of invitations had embraced Jim and myself she loyally submitted.

At this time suitable society for the Tooheys, owing to the Sergeant's promotion and prosperity, was rather limited.

Therefore all Mrs Toohey's relations and friends after the advent of Anty Jo were excluded, and, heart-burnings here or there, invitations to Jam Toohey's party were only for the children whose homes as Toohey's now "did a servant".

Dressed in my Sunday black dress, worn one year and guaranteed to fit for still another, I looked anything but festive. However, I detached purple strings from my mother's best bonnet, and these around my waist, however incongruous, were a joy and solace. Jim had sneaked our big brother's watch and chain, and he too was well content. And my mother's white gloves on my hands were a delicate attention which Anty Jo thoroughly appreciated, being the only gloves worn.

Little Mrs Toohey sat in a corner nursing what, from its regularity, the local paper facetiously called "Toohey's Last Annual". Though it was sound asleep she kept mechanically rocking, and looking without interest or speech at the assembling guests.

The big Sergeant, his countenance aglow, stood with his back to the mantelpiece, and the rest sat round in expectancy, for the party was to open with a pianoforte solo, or rather duet, by Josephine Teresa Joanna, entitled *Nelly Bly*, with Anty Jo as vocalist and conductor.

"What d'ye think of thet for yer neow?" said the proud father as, after many attempts tearful and trembling, Josephine Teresa Joanna lamely and haltingly accompanied Anty Jo's vocalization to—

Nil-lee Bloiy, Nil-lie Ber-loy,
Brir-ring therr bur-room a-long.

"Nill — Nill," she still encouraged the scared child. But the insistence on an encore was generously waived by the applauding father and company when little Mrs Toohey and the now awake Last Annual mingled tears and sobs with the unwilling performer.

Diplomatic Anty Jo, to distract attention from this untoward finale, bawled loudly for "Nixt Achtor", though Jam, ready and willing, was by her side.

"Joseph Aloyishus Michael, me de-ar, tork Frinch," she said tenderly.

Jam bowed in a manner suggesting a sense of security in his audience, then began—

"Parley vu frongsie, sher tray beang, jer trey beang parley vu frongsie sher trey bu parley frongsie, sher parley."

And the burst of laughter with which the father applauded his blushing son's efforts in French were mainly responsible for his repetitions, the monotony of these being broken by transposition.

The Sergeant held his aching sides till tears came into his eyes, composed of admiration for his son and mirthful contempt for the ignorance of the French nation, who could expect decent people to understand "sich gatherin' gibberish". His delight and pride Anty Jo shared to the full, though the idiosyncrasies of the French tongue did not appeal to her.

"Me de-ar, neow dance yer kerdrille," she said, striking a conducting attitude.

"Funna na nun nar na na nun narna," she lilted, clapping time, and the Sergeant clanking it with his heel on the firestone. But just as Jam gave a preliminary bow to an imaginary partner, and began the opening caper of the first set, the "gurrl" brought in Father Tierney.

Host, hostess and conductor received him with reverent warmness. Then he was led to a chair near to me, while my heart-beats increased insistently, lest it be discovered by this shepherd that Jim and I were stragglers in this flock and fold, and as such be banished from these pleasant pastures. However, creed mattered little to the genial Father, who, with a burst of laughter, demanded a continuance of the programme.

But actor Jam had disappeared. And when our Jim and Willy Dalton, after a long search, dragged him in, he slouched into a corner; and neither coaxing from Anty Jo, nor exasperated threats from his father, could induce him to "tork Frinch" nor finish his "kerdrille" before his Riverence.

However, Anty Jo had one more arrow in her quiver, a "racitement" by little Francis Dooley of *The Wearing of the Green*, a performance which little Dooley made memorable by endeavouring to recite the whole piece without once drawing breath: the strenuousness of his efforts being well defined by the volume of sound produced when nature bested him.

The night was still young when Anty Jo, who never once sat down, discovered that another musical item was due from her niece.

She looked round for Josephine Teresa Joanna, and discovered the child in hiding as she imagined because part of her mother's skirt covered her head.

"Josephine Teresa Joanna, come neow and plaay agin for his Riverince." The child's head bent to the mother's knee, but being in hiding she did not speak. The mother laid a tamely protecting hand on the covered head, but inexorable Anty Jo went to bring her to the piano. The unchecked tears quickly rolling down from Mrs Toohey's eyes and the resisting wail from the child were so distressing that the priest interfered.

"Wait now, and I'll bring Dinny Hogan wid his fiddle; I will, so I will. I'll be going now with the Sergeant. Sure it's back in Ould Ireland you'll think you are, Miss Toohey, win yer hear him," he said seductively.

Duty had begun again for the Sergeant, and he left with the priest after an invitation to another room, to look at something.

Old Dinny Hogan, at the priest's request, left his daily and nightly cobbling, put on his long-tailed coat green with age, and fiddle in hand joined the party. Doubtless his beloved tunes were as old to him as the coat he wore, and both were older than Dinny. But he, with lean left cheek resting lovingly on the fiddle, his eyes turned upwards and his toothless mouth ecstatically agape, was a rare subject for a sculptor.

To most of us, however, the tunes were new and were

part of the rapture-filled face of the old man, feeding his heart through his ears in *Killarney* or *The Meeting of the Waters*. The quiet of his children audience at its close brought him back to the present and duty. Then his thin long face corrugated smilingly from his mouth to his eyes at their appreciation of his spirited rendering of *Green grow the Rushes — oh!*

It was so inspiring that all those whose feet touched the floor accompanied him. Anty Jo, though, at no time was enthusiastic. Dinny Hogan for all his national music was but Dinny Hogan the cobbler, to her. Haughtily she went to see to the supper. With her disappearance Mrs Toohey brightened visibly, and even little Josie uncovered her head and ventured to look and listen.

Jam sat near the front door, and in response to a tap opened it.

"Is ower pup 'ere, Mary?" inquired Patsie M'Grath, one of Mrs Toohey's little brothers.

"I dunno, Patsie," gently said his scared looking sister. The whereabouts of the pup, however, seemed to be of no importance to the boy, who unconcernedly took the priest's seat. He had no coat on, but had a decorative saddle strap round his waist in addition to his first pair of braces. His bluchers were freshly greased and his old Granny had herself oiled and combed his curly red hair.

He was scarcely seated when a tap came on the window just behind Patsie's head outlined on the blind. He opened the window and Jerry M'Grath slid through. He was bare-footed, and the absence of either braces or strap showed that the elder brother had forced him to feel the penalties attached to the yoke of youth.

"Is our Patsie 'ere, Mary?" he asked, dutiful to Granny's instructions, but rendering a reply unnecessary by making a grab at his strap round Patsie's waist. There was a scuffle between them that dislodged Anty Jo's piece of sea-coral adorning the window sill. Its crash brought in Anty Jo, and her entrance was the signal for immediate calm; but this tribute to her presence had no softening effect on herself. She turned her wrathful crimson countenance on her white-faced sister-in-law, who had risen and was standing helplessly, open-mouthed but silent, in the middle of the room.

"Turrn thim disgrasheful young blaggards eout this insthint moment," she commanded.

"Yous boys better go 'ome like good boys," said their sister, a weak plea in her voice. The boy with the bluchers again sat down and planted them firmly on the floor, and the boy without did likewise and curled his bare feet round the legs of his chair, and gripped the seat with the look of a determined buckjumper who does not mean to be ousted. Both turned stormily with mutinous eyes on Anty Jo. There was a lull in active hostilities in which both sides seem to be gauging the situation. Anty Jo grasped it. She crossed over to Jam, and said something in a whisper to him; then came back and faced the intruders, while Jam communicated the whisper to the other boy guests by a series of masonic signs lost by the invaders through their eyes being fixed on Anty Jo. There was a concerted movement by the boys towards the supper-room, a like whisper to Anastasia Nolan sent the girls following, till only Anty Jo, Mrs Toohey, the baby and little Josephine Teresa Joanna and the two intruders were left.

"Faith, thin, I wish yer j'y of yer kimpany, Mary M'Grath," said Anty Jo to her sister-in-law, as she with head thrown back entered and closed the door of the supper-room to carve the potted meat, "paches" pie and other delicacies in season and reason.

The clatter of plates, popping of ginger-beer and lemonade corks, soon made clear to hungry Pat and Jerry that Granny's plan to get them a good feed had failed. Jerry sank all party feeling between himself and Patsy, and in their common cause waged war. Putting his head out of the open window he shouted, "Granny, Granny, listen to them greedy pigs, all eatin' and guzzlin' down all the grub, and me and Patsy locked out in 'ere, starvin'."

It was plain to the listening Anty Jo that the old woman reconnoitring outside was about to enter by the window, so she rushed in and slammed it just as the old woman reached it.

"Jerry, Patsy, w'ere arr yers?" she yelled.

"'Ere, Granny! all be ourselves, and thim all locked up, these hours an' hours, eatin' everythin'."

Mrs Toohey ceased trembling to say again: "Yous boys better go 'ome, like good boys." Then she lowered her voice and added imploringly: "An' to morrow mornin' I'll come round an' bring yous a good feed of lollies, and bring yous pence apiece."

"An' listen to our Mary tryin' to 'unt us 'ome, Granny, without nothin'."

Mary's standing form was plainly outlined on the window blind outside. She heard an ominous growl of rage and disgust from her Granny, and knew there was a threat of speedy vengeance on herself. She went whiter and trembled even more, but stood where she was. Then there was the dramatic silence that always preludes some big event, then crash through the window came a brick which struck her on the elbow. From among the débris of glass Anty Jo picked up the baby the mother had dropped, and immediately the room was filled with all the guests, whose curiosity had overcome their manners and even their appetites. Mrs Toohey was still standing — only, most unusual for her, she was doing three things at once: quietly crying, rubbing her elbow, and listening to old Granny. Granny's head and hands, full weaponed with two gibbers, were well in evidence through the broken window. Doubtless it was due to the fact that even from outside Granny had proved herself a good shot, that she now had unopposed opportunity to pour out the family history to the indecently interested guests.

"Oh dear, but it's a fine party yer havin' in big splay-footed Joey Toohey's grand 'ome; an' oh but it's the brave gintleman that 'e is, to be sure! The great Sargint Toohey snakin' up wid his loaded revolver to the pooer 'armless Comet, an' lettin' daylight true 'im, and grabbin' all the pooer bushranger's 'ard 'earnings, an' 'e fasht ashleep, the pooer cratur. The Lord have mercy on 'im.

"An' is it the loikes of you — you, Joanna Toohey, that 'd be 'untin' an' starvin' two boys of a dacent, dead mother? Miss Joanna Toohey to be sure, indade; faith it's *Miss* you are, right enough, but it's 'ow is your nephew I'd be after askin'; an' I'm thinkin' that if it's only your nephew 'e is, it's knowin' it he would be long before this, though God 'elp the pooer cratur, it's dotty it's well known that 'e is with your bad usage, God 'elp 'im. I nodis 'e's not 'ere among yers this even. Oh, yer mane cratur, you; Mary, you mane crawler that you arre that daresn't raise yer voice in yer own 'ouse an' 'ome an' that'd be after turnin' out yer own two motherless brothers. Oh, God forgive yer, for a pooer weak crooil crathur that you arre."

Little Mrs Toohey cried louder, and stopped rubbing her elbow, and it was plain to see that her distress touched old Granny, who turned again to Anty Jo; but at that moment there was the clinking sound of the "Sargint's" return. In an instant Granny withdrew her head. "Patsy, Jerry", and immediately they were through the window and off with her.

The party was over. Little Joanna crept up to her mother. "Mummy don't yer like parties?"

"No, I don't like parties," answered Mrs Toohey without hesitation.

"Don't yer like me Granny?" said the child in puzzled wistful fellowship.

Mrs Toohey stopped crying to think. "Yes, Josey, I like me Granny, but I wish I never seen 'er," she said passionlessly.

Her Bush Sweetheart

THE joss-house gleamed garishly in the afternoon sun. From a hill it looked down on the straggling settlement of a tin-mining town, whose chief inhabitants were Chinese. Principally for the flowers which girt it on all sides, Caroline Bell wandered towards it. Her lips curled as she saw the priest's ever-watchful boy scurry in to warn the priest of her coming. He was ready to receive her, though breathless from his efforts in changing his working-clothes for his best.

"Ah!" he gasped, "me welly glad you come again to see my joss." With uninterested eyes she looked at the priest, his joss, and the two boys kneeling before him.

The gaudy tinsel surroundings did away with any suggestion of reverence. But she had no reverence for anything, except for ease and luxury, and little of these fell to her share.

From the joss-house they wandered out to the gardens. The finest blooms, regardless of their "keep it seed" command, were plucked for her. She was not fond of flowers, but they were a tribute, and even from a Chinaman a tribute was acceptable.

They returned to the joss-house, and again she stood looking at the idol, waiting till the priest returned with her bound bouquet.

A tall, sunburnt man suddenly appeared from where he had been taking a back view of the joss. He had wide, clear eyes, and very white teeth. She took him in at a glance, and instantly returned his amused smile.

"So that's his botanic majesty," he said. The "botanic" irritated her. "He's got a soft job, hasn't he?"

She agreed with him, and when the dismayed priest returned they were having a brisk conversation.

"You blother?" he asked anxiously. She said "No," curtly, without looking at the priest, and she made no attempt to take the flowers.

"You mally man?" he questioned.

"No such luck, Johnnie."

"My joss no likee sclange man come in joss-house."

"Then why do you keep the door open?" the stranger said, unperturbed. "Well, I can't do any harm in the garden, anyway, and I like flowers. You've got some beauties."

The enraged priest grew livid when he saw Caroline lead the way outside. He followed them, muttering in his own tongue.

Quite oblivious of him or his rage was Caroline. This new-found stalwart protector radiated security. But in the end she mentally cursed the priest, for she wanted, in the shortest possible time, to get this stranger's social standing, ways and means. Already she had gleaned that he was a squatter, and had come to this little town to truck a mob of his sheep for the city markets. And that particular city was the one to which she was returning on the morrow.

"Let's sit down," said Robert Ingall. "Here's a seat, if it isn't preserved."

The misused word jarred her nerves. But all her lifetime she had never once got just what she wanted, and she had made up her mind that she never would. At any rate he was single, and her chances might be better than her present position — typist to a married man.

The jealous priest was now beside himself. He had dropped the flowers. His top lip was lifted in a snarl that made his yellow, fang-like teeth look as ferocious as those of a hungry wolf.

"Which of us are you grinning at?" tormented Robert.

In an instant there was no doubt which. He plucked forth the knife hidden in his coat, but the wary bushman had dealt with many a Chinaman, and had bent and blent them to his own will. His ju-jitsu grip on the priest's wrists soon caused the foaming wretch to drop the knife, which Caroline seized and flung on to the joss-house roof. Picking up the flowers, they left the gibbering priest and went townwards.

There was much in him she admired — his height, his free, easy walk, and the supple strength he had displayed in the recent encounter. Then, as ever, she returned to his worldly prospects. He had a station beyond Bourke, which to her, town-bred and town-loving, seemed the Never Never Land. Moreover, an occasional slip in his grammar instantly brought her harsh nature to the surface. But, as she thought bitterly, never in her life had she obtained her full heart's desire, and he at least was single, which was something on which to build. She knew while she was ruminating that he was taking her in, and she mentally smiled at his scrutiny, which was confined to her exterior.

"Didn't you get any education?" she asked bluntly, and she felt a savage satisfaction in seeing his face and even his neck flame.

"Well, I had a fair education, if I'd made the most of it; but I hated school and I loved the bush. When I first went out there among the boys, the way they spoke pretty well got on my nerves, as I do on yours. At first I tried to correct them, and, finding that no good, I drifted into their ways of speech."

"Do you read books?"

"No time," he said, laconically.

"Is it all work?" she asked, in horror.

"Pretty much," he said.

She looked at his brown hands, and noted they were not coarsened by his work.

"How old are you?"

"Thirty-two," he said promptly. Then he looked enquiringly at her for a like frankness. She understood, but age was a sore subject with her — though she looked younger than her years — and he was not enlightened.

She enquired about his household. His sister kept house for him, and the servants were mostly Chinese or half-castes, which appalled her.

As they walked along they heard the tom-tom from the joss-house, and realized that the priest was invoking the joss's aid for vengeance. They looked at one another and smiled. The scene altogether pleased her at that moment. She was not in love with her employer, yet she wished that he had been there, solely from a spirit of rivalry.

Robert Ingall's station was twenty-three miles from any town. "How lonely!" she said, shuddering. He laughed.

"I'm never lonely in the bush, though I was pretty lonely here this afternoon till I struck you". She agreed that this was "a beastly little hole", and he took courage to ask her if she lived here.

She never told anything more about herself than was absolutely necessary. She merely remarked that she was a private secretary, and was there only on business, and returned on the morrow to Sydney. He was going to Sydney, too, only he was off to-night. They agreed to meet there, but she gave him only her business address, stipulating that he must write, not call.

In the city they met often, and as often as they met he pleaded his cause. She hung back. The life he lived nauseated her. The flowers that gave him such pleasure for themselves gave her none. She simply used them as an aid to her own appearance. Besides, wild flowers withered she told him, and more quickly than garden flowers. His eyes widened in amazement as she made this statement.

"Why," he said, "the bush is always in bloom. All on its own, too."

Perhaps some day he might sell out, she suggested. "No fear. I've put too much hard graft into Eulandri," he said, determinedly. "And besides, it's not the biggest, but it's the best, station, and the best run station in that part."

If he sold out, he could buy a big business in town. He laughed outright at this.

"Oh, yes. I can see myself behind the counter, weighing three penn'orth of sugar and six penn'orth of tea!" He wasn't looking at her, and it was just as well.

There was little variety in any interview between them. He was wasting his time, he told her, valuable time. He had sold his sheep, the object of his visit, and the net sum made her mouth water. Her annual holidays were imminent. She would give him no definite decision. She was constantly pitting her present circumstances against his bush home, which, obstinately, he would not change; and at their parting she said, very decidedly, "Well, I can just as readily see myself turn into a bush hermit as you into a townsman."

She packed up and left next day for a little township in the Blue Mountains, without a word to her sister Margaret as to her purpose.

The church bells gave her an idle impulse to enter one of the usual ugly little chapels. She was shown into a seat, and placing her fur coat over the back of an empty seat in front of her, set her marvelling why Margaret had not asked her how she had come by such an expensive article, and involuntarily her thin lips curled contemptuously — Margaret, always smiling and happy as long as her canary sang and her handiwork sold, darning the holes in the overworn carpet, thrilling with enthusiasm over her success as a stallholder in a church bazaar, sleepless the night before the Sunday school picnic! She dismissed Margaret for the time. The local preacher was the township's saddler, and rumour had it that he had been insolvent so often and so successfully that he had virtually built the little chapel.

Stutteringly he gave out the hymn, and she found the place, and while they sang, independently of each other, she recalled the scene of the joss-house.

The wheezy blare of the harmonium distracted her. Apparently it was suffering severely from asthma. Oh, if only it could have been a grand organ, rolling forth the Wedding March, while she, bedizened with the finery she loved and longed for, walked in triumph on the arm of some titled father-in-law!

The prayer that followed the hymn was over. So was the first reading of "God's Word". From curiosity she waited to hear the text. The saddler was suffering with a cold in his head. He raised a forefinger and bade his congregation "Now listen to this". The "this" at that moment was a prodigious sniff. Then followed the text: "He that cometh unto Me I will in no wise cast out." She rose, with a half-smile of derision about her lips unceremoniously walked out of the church.

Near it there was a small graveyard. She entered it, and went about reading with cool scorn the maudlin epitaphs.

Sitting on a bench in the corner, she watched the congregation file out, "all in their Sunday clothes," she thought. Heavens! what clothes, what boots, what home-trimmed hats! How she hated poverty. Her dead father had been unmercifully cruel to her dead mother, who, like Margaret, was content with little things. Caroline's one grudge against him was that he had squandered all her mother's money, and had left only a legacy of poverty and debts to his two daughters.

Her sordid home rose before her. She loathed it, too, but she did nothing to remedy it, and Margaret's best efforts to improve things were at times grotesque. She wondered if Margaret would ever marry, and decided not while she was useful to her, and while comfort could be extorted from her cheerful ministrations. Caroline was by nature as luxurious as a cat, and as indolent.

She spent a fortnight in a mood of despondency and dissatisfaction. There were only three other women in the small boarding-house, but she was one who expected no friendship from women, because she gave none to them.

Quite suddenly she came to a decision. She would write to him, as she had promised. No; still better, she decided. She would return on the morrow by an early train, have lunch in town, and take a boat to Manly. He always went there on Monday afternoons, giving stray children chocolates and donkey rides. She never doubted for one moment, but that he would wait for her return. His concurrence or otherwise was nothing to her. She wondered how much he knew about women. She tossed her head. What would that matter, once they were married?

She landed from the ferry boat and walked along the straggling street to the other side of the beach. Her first thought when she saw the broad expanse of the ocean was that she would get him to take a voyage to Europe. She really began to applaud his decision. He had plenty of money, which she would control entirely, as she meant to control him.

There he was, as usual, treating the little stragglers, after filling them with chocolates, to donkey rides. He saw her, nearly as soon as she saw him, and a flaming face met hers, condescendingly smiling. Hat in hand, he advanced to meet her. She was puzzled at his expression, and before he could explain a woman sitting near in a white dress, her face quite concealed by a white parasol, rose and came towards them. She merely glanced at the figure, then in a flash she recognized her.

"You! You!" she almost shrieked. "Margaret!"

"He came to the house for your address," said Margaret, half-apologetically. "You've said 'No' to him many times," she added, with trembling lips, her face aflame, and her eyes dewy with tears.

Human Toll
a novel
1907

Editors' Note

Baynton's only novel, *Human Toll*, was published in London in 1907. A Colonial Edition was issued (a practice common among English publishers at the time) for distribution in India and the British Colonies (including the ex-colonies like Australia). *Human Toll* was never reprinted or republished. The Colonial Edition has been used as copy-text for this volume and is printed in full. The spelling and punctuation of the original have been retained to preserve Baynton's attempts to render dialect; the copy-text's treatment of hyphenation (excessive by present standards) has also been retained and line-endings have been checked to ensure consistency in this. Minor inconsistencies in accidentals have been silently corrected.

The date of composition is unknown but there are a few possible clues. Baynton refers to the proofs of *Human Toll* lying about her in a letter to A.G. Stephens from Switzerland in January 1906: she seems to have had them for some time. This novel may also be the "long story" she mentions in another letter to Stephens, in February 1903.

Barbara Baynton dedicated the novel "to Boshy's Lovey and mine".

DUCKWORTH'S COLONIAL LIBRARY

HUMAN TOLL

BY

BARBARA BAYNTON

Author of "Bush Studies"

LONDON

DUCKWORTH & CO.

3 HENRIETTA STREET, COVENT GARDEN, W.C

1907.

1

WHAT was this blocking the tallow-scoop? Boshy, secretly styled "The Lag", or "One Eye", bent to see. Leisurely he thrust down a groping hand and drew up, but not out, a fat-clogged basil-belt. Hastily his other hand clawed it conferringly, then with both he forced it back again into its greasy hiding-place of past long years. Cautiously his one eye went from door to window, then he rolled the fat-can with its mouth to the wall, and, going out, he took a sweeping survey. The sky and plain still drowsed dreamily, and neither the sick Boss's home, nor Nungi the half-caste's hut on the other side of the river-split plain, showed sign of smoke. The only gleam of life was a breath-misted string of cows filing leisurely but lovingly to their penned calves.

Boshy entered the hut and shut and bolted both door and window, then rolled the precious casket, a rusty nail-keg, before the door, and to further insure his sense of security sat on it. He made no attempt to examine his treasure. He was certain the contents of that gold-lined belt were old Miser Baldy's hoard. For a few moments he sat quivering, gloating greedily. Musingly his one eye roamed all over the hut. Not a splinter in the walls that he, and many others, had not probed as with a tooth-pick, for this coveted "plant"; not a crack or mortised joint in the roof; not a mouse-hole but had been tunnelled to the bitter end, for tenant above or below. Nor had the search stopped at the hut, for had not a night-ghouling Chinaman, in his hunt for this hoard, gone the dauntless but fruitless length of disinterring and stripping poor old Baldy? And now just by a fluke he had struck it. Could it be true? Was he only dreaming? And again he thrust in a confirming hand. "Gord A'mighty!" burst from him as his felt certainty electrified him.

When Nungi came in the spring cart an hour later to shift him, all his personal and furnishing belongings were in their accustomed places, except the belt. Though this was now round his waist, he sat shivering beside the fire, and one quick glance at his drawn face showed the half-caste the unusual had happened.

"Tucked up, Boshy? Got the Barcoo?" (a sudden sickness). "Boss is goin' t' peg out."

"I'm nut a-goin' t' shift t'-day; nut till t'-morrer."

"W'y ther blazes did yer le' me 'arness up, then?" asked Nungi resentfully, as he took out the horse, and on it shogged back, leaving the cart to await to-morrow's duty.

Boshy watched his every movement from the window, then with an effort he roused himself and went after him, but at the river he turned back. Into the frying-pan he hurriedly scraped the fat that earlier he had scooped from the oilcan, and when it melted he carefully poured it into the keg, then speedily crossed to the house.

There was no moon that night, yet he waited till it was well spent, then almost on all fours crept to the graves beneath the myalls close to his hut; with infinite care he tunnelled into the aforetime desecrated grave till he could feel the end of the coffin, then with all his strength he drove the pick beneath, and upending it, kept it atilt with the pick.

He got up, watched and listened, but though his cautiousness had magnified all sounds, he knew from his distance he was secure. Laboriously he tunnelled for a couple of feet below the coffin, then from two wallets strapped across his back he took out several sealed pickle-bottles and thrust them well into their gruesome nest; then, as before, he listened and watched, and, as before, was assured.

He did not shift camp for a week, by then the earth on the disturbed graves, which day and night he had watched, was again normal, and he again outwardly composed. But often during his duties day or night his one eye sought anxiously the hiding-spot of his treasure, till gradually he realized that it was safe; for from superstitious awe the blacks would not molest the dead, and the whites had long since abandoned hope.

Yellow tongues from the slush lamp-light had spluttered through the gridiron slabs of the Boss's bedroom for several nights. Towards the end of one Boshy drew the pillow from beneath the head and the cover over the face of the man on the bed, scrutinized the child sleeping on the one opposite, then, for him, noiselessly took the lamp into the outer room.

The darkened window was the signal for a prolonged lamentation from an old dog, partially blind and deaf, chained outside.

Then from the blacks' camp on the fringe of the scrub the lean dogs, dozing beside the meagre dying fire, yelped back a semicivilized echo, and almost simultaneously the blacks ran about their camp, like disturbed, molested ants.

Boshy, coming out to harangue the chained dog, heard the tintin jangling of their billies and pannikins in their hasty, unorganized flight. The gins, burdened with pickaninnies and camp-gear, were whimpering well in the rear, but above all rose the angry, impotent lamentations and execrations of "Tumbledown Jimmy". Many wintry moons had almost disabled Jimmy, stiffened his joints and tightened his sinews, bending his body on one side like a boomerang, so his callous kinsmen only too gladly left him as hostage for the dreaded Debbil-debbil now among them.

Boshy's mouth shaped into an ecstatic circle. "Hor, hor, hor!" he snorted in lonely mirth. He was tempted to give chase, shouting, "Ketch 'em, Debbil-debbil! ketch 'em, Debbil-debbil!" but for the sleeping child and a heavy task, awaiting him inside.

Carefully he prised up the table-leaf, greasing the nails with the lamp-fat to prevent creaking. His back was to the door between the two rooms, as noiselessly opening as the gap in the table. Simultaneously and correspondingly wide grew Gin Queeby's eyes watching this door through an outside crack, though, in a nightmare of fear, she stood dumb and motionless.

Through a few inches of door space the little girl squeezed, and, unseen by Boshy, laid her hand on him.

"Ghos' A'mighty!" yelled he, voicing his thoughts and dropping the hammer, and instantly the cry of an ill-used child who sees its mother gushed from Queeby.

"Lovey, Lovey, Queeby wanter come ter yer. Me wanter come ter yer," waggling her black fingers directingly through the cracks.

A silencing clod flung by Nungi hiding between two myall logs, rebounded and struck the chimney, increasing the confusion.

"Oh!" whispered the child, "you'll all wake me father. Naughty, naughty, bad things, all of yous — and you, too, Queeby," catching sight of the hand still at the crack. "Stop you, Queeby, an' come in."

Queeby rushed in noisily tearful, and caught up the child.

"Hish!" with her nightgown wiping Queeby's face, "don't wake me father, Queeby."

Queeby had no fear of doing that, but the name of the dead man calmed her.

"Don't wake me father, 'less I'll beat you, Queeby. Oo's been beating you?" threatened and inquired the child.

"Boshy," said Queeby promptly.

"Well," said he, aghast, "if lies would choke yer, yer lyin'—"

But now from her elevation the child looked down on the wrecked table.

"Oh you bad, bad Boshy, t' break up the table! Me father'll give it to you!"

"Iden broke up, Lovey. Yer daddy tole me ter make er — er — thingy-me-callum outer ther top."

"To do w'at with?"

"Eh?" he evaded. "Wot's ther time, Lovey? Mornin' time, I think."

Walking to the window, he turned his ear to the well out on the plain, hidden by a band of trees that, in seeming boldness, had left the scrub and stood like sentinel outposts. From one a magpie, partly tamed, flew to the window-ledge on Boshy's blind side, startling him with her discordant imitation of cock-crow, then squawked for food.

"Yer bole faggit, a-crowin' in me very face, like a cock! Go an' look fer worms."

Angrily he attempted to sweep her off, but the magpie flew to the chimney-top, from there crowing arrogantly, till an ambitious cockerel, mistaking hers for his sire's dawn heralding, imitated huskily and incipiently. The magpie derisively mocked, then swooped and beaked its legitimate prey, the early worm. Reascending, it again raised its head, and from bird-throat never issued a more mellifluous grace after meat. Such a requiem should console the worm and justify its Maker.

It was the youth of a plenteous spring, and from the scrub flanking the back of the house came a concerted twittering of newly-awakened birdlings, increasing till the air seemed filled with dewy-throated sky-crickets.

"Listen to th' birdies," said the child, raising her radiant face to the roof, and at the supreme moment accompanying them in perfect mimicry.

"Sweet-pretty-little creasures, sweet-pretty-little-creasures. Tha's wot they says all the time. They's been asleep like me," yawning, "and they's jus' waked up like me now," explained Lovey.

"An' they're arstin' fer their liddle breakfusses," supplemented Boshy, taking her in his arms to the window. "An', Lovey dear, lis'en to ther poor liddle lambs a-arstin' an' a-beggin' an' a-prayin' fer theirs too, Lovey. Thet lazy wretch ov a Nungi's gorn this long time, an' ain't bin a-nex', nur a-nigh, nur a-near 'em. Isen't 'e a lazy wretch ov a Nungi, Lovey, eh?"

"Ways 'e?" she asked.

"Lord above knows, I don't. Make 'er dress yer, Lovey, an' le's go an' see."

"'N," she agreed, looking at distressed Queeby.

"Get 'er clo'es an' dress 'er, yer gapin' phil garlic yer!" said Boshy.

Queeby's tears began afresh.

"Me father can't see you. 'E's sleepin' little with the clothes over his face," Lovey said. Then addressing Boshy: "W'a's 'e doin' like that way for?"

"'Cos 'e's better, Lovey."

"Is this the day w'en 'e'll get up, then?"

"No, ter-morrer. Lovey, you get yer clo'es yer own self. This useless animal" — shaking a warning fist at Queeby — "is frightened; on'y thet 'er'll wake 'im," he added cautiously.

The child tiptoed in and returned with her clothes.

"Now you bad Boshy, too, as well, too. Ways me going t' be put w'en me father's goin' t' lace up me boots?" she asked.

The despoiler of the table drew his head from the window.

"Poor liddle lambs, Lovey! Thet lazy, idle wretch ov a Nungi ain't gi' 'em a sup of water. 'E's been gorn this over an hour, an' ain't bin a-nex', nur a-near, nur a-nigh ther well. Ain't 'e a bad, wicked Nungi, Lovey?"

Lovey nodded.

"Ways 'e?"

"Git yer boots an' socks orn now, Lovey, an' le's go an' see."

Queeby, mindful of the dead man's past duty, would have laced the child's boots.

"No, no, not you," Lovey said; "me father will. Boshy," she said angrily, noticing the boots he was wearing, "you jus' take my father's boots on orf of your feet."

"'E as'ed me to stretch 'em for 'im, Lovey. Poor liddle lambs! a-famishin' an' a-faintin' an' a-perishin' for a drink, Lovey. Come on t' we find Nungi."

He took down the stockwhip hanging on the wall, and taking the dressed child's hand, went first into the kitchen.

"Make 'er kin'le a fire."

"Not kin'le; light," corrected the little girl.

"Light," said he humbly.

He pushed Queeby towards the fireplace but she followed him out.

"Go wi' 'er, Lovey dear, an' I'll see kin I fin' Nungi be meself," he said, shaking the stockwhip.

There was no need to search, for Nungi, anticipating a betrayal from Queeby, instantly revealed himself, standing between the logs, his arms encircling Tumbledown Jimmy eagle fashion, who, to fit the simile, drooped lamb-like.

"Somethin' gorn wrong er ther well-wim; water won't come up, Boshy. An' this lazy ole grub-chawrer an' 'oney waterer, ez you call im, won't come an' gi' me a 'and B——ole black feller say Debbil-debbil sit down in ther bottom ov ther well-water, dam ole fool!"

Nungi laughed mirthlessly, and kicked the prey he had dropped, who lay with his face on the ground.

Untwirling, thereby entangling the stockwhip, Boshy advanced; but Nungi speedily increased the distance between them.

"Es Gord 's me Jedge, Nungi," declared Boshy,

advancing, "ef yer don' go this instant minit——" both hands fumbling longingly to twirl the whip.

Nungi danced in simulated excitement, and, pointing to the raised platform of the house, said:

"Big feller goanna crawl in onder there, eat all ther 'en eggs, me go in arfter 'im, rip 'im open, take out ther eggs." Boshy still advanced. "Black feller snake too; pretty quick me catchem, that feller b—— whirroo!" grabbing an imaginary snake, and twirling it round, as Boshy would have liked to have handled the stockwhip.

"Yer lie! yer lying dorg! Yer see no snakes an' no go'annas in under ther 'ouse," said Boshy, weakening his assertiveness by going on his knees and looking under.

"Urgh!" grunted Nungi, now at a safe distance from whip or even missile. "Fat lot you can see, ole Bungy-Blinkey-eye, ole one-eye! Couldn' see er butterfly nur anythin' else, yur ole blather skyte! 'Oo cares fur you? Nut me!"

This sudden outburt shocked and surprised Boshy into fatal weakening, and he stood for parley.

"N-N-Nungi," he stammered, "w'ats come over yer ter go orn like thet? Nungi," coaxingly, "look 'ere now, ole man, yer know well w'at I gut ter do ter day. Go orn now an' get ter yer work an' water them yeos an' lambs, like ther w'ite man w'at yer are."

"Not be meself," said Nungi, but less aggressively, till, turning to take a look at the well, and catching sight of the rising sun, he grew at once savagely and cunningly courageous.

Boshy's discomfiture increased.

"Go on now, Nungi; don't be a slinker on a day like this."

"Nut fer you nur no one like yer, b—— old blinky Boshy, ole splay-foot! Lars night I collared a bag er yer wool, an' ter smornin' I'll take it into Tambo, sell it, an' git on ther plurry spree, sneak back ter night, plenty matches me," drawing one from his trouser-pocket and striking it along the bare sole of his foot. "Budgeree fire that feller, cobbon fire that feller," pointing to the house. "See ole plurry one-eye Boshy burnin' like blazes! See old splay-foot runnin' 'ell for leather!"

With an aboriginal yell he bounded into the air, and coming down on his feet reproduced to perfection the stiffened run and general gait of Boshy.

Nungi's noisy revolt had a reviving effect on Tumbledown Jimmy. From his perch now on the logs he ceased food importuning to burst into appreciative laughter. Boshy made a rush for him.

"Ye'd larf at me, would yer? Lemme on'y ketch yer doin' ov it again, an' I'll kick ther beggin' belly out ov yer!"

Jimmy, who had instantly ceased, began to beg and count the moons that had whitened his head; then, as Boshy advanced, he slid from the logs, and burrowing a hip into the ground, resolved into a rapidly revolving four-spoked wheel, his hands and feet actively protecting his threatened hub.

"Blanky ole One-eye, jes' tech 'im!" shouted Nungi, seizing a shank-bone and taking steady aim at Boshy. "Jes' lay a finger orn 'im, thet's all."

"Nungi," pleaded Boshy, "w'at's wrong wi' you? You're a-goin on like az if you've been pea-eatin', or a-swankin' ov ther kerosene, or the pain-killer. W'at's kranked yer?"

Nungi's reply was another aboriginal bound and yell that brought out the child and Queeby.

"W'a's the matter?" asked the child.

"Oh, Lovey, jes' you 'ear w'at e' sez, ther yeller an' w'ite savage; see w'at 'e's goin' ter do — set fire ter ther 'ouse, an' burn me an' you an' yer 'elpless dead daddy alive. Me an' you too," repeated Boshy, individually classifying the relative importance of Nungi's threats.

"Would yer, Nungi?" shouted the disbelieving child, going across to him.

"No, Lovey," retracted Nungi. "Carn't believe a word thet old cursed ole liar sez, ole splay-foot!"

"Nungi wouldn't," she said, "you see" — turning resentfully to Boshy.

"I see I'm mistook," thankfully agreed Boshy; "but 'e sez 'e won't water ther poor liddle lambs, Lovey, an' them a-dyin' ov———"

"Yer will water ther ewes an' lambs, won't yer, Nungi?"

"Nut be me owen self, Lovey — carn't. No one ter watch w'at comes up in ther bucket," said Nungi, determined not to assist the Debbil-debbil to land even in daylight. "No one ter talk ter," he added, to disguise his cowardice.

"I'll come, Nungi."

"Giandidilliwong!" delightedly yelled he, bounding high and coming down on all fours. "Git on me back, an' I'll carry yer all ther ways, Lovey" (joyfully) "an' arter gi' yer a ride on Billy all round ther well. An' arter we'll shin inter ther scrub an' git wattle-gum. I know wur ther's a lump ez big ez thet" (a shut fist), "an' geebungs, an' five-corners. Come on, Lovey," coaxed he, continuing to buck progressively.

"Tell me father I'm gone t' water th' ewes an' lambs w'en 'e wakes up for his breakfuss," she importantly commanded Boshy.

"Git yer bunnet fust, Lovey," stipulated Boshy. "Nungi," he said inducively, "come beck wi' 'er soon ez yer water 'em."

"Urh!" snorted Nungi, "w'at'll yer gimme?"

"I'll nut say black's ther w'ite ov yer eye."

"Urh!" unappeased. "W'at'll yer gimme ter eat?"

"A box ov sardines."

"Ter me own cheek? an' out 'ere nigh ole Jimmy?"

"In 'ell if yer like," curtly agreed the vanquished new master.

He watched the half-caste hoist the child on his shoulder and trot briskly away to the well. To govern his kingdom did not appear so easy, and a half-defeated sense irritated him. He shook a clenched fist at the oblivious half-caste.

Tumbledown Jimmy immediately raised his black hand towards his half-caste brother and did the same.

"Plurry rogue that pfeller Nungi; good pfeller Boshy. Cobbon budgeree pfeller Boshy" (whining); "poor pfeller me, 'ungry poor pfeller ole Jimmy. Plurry long time now, Boss baal gib it black pfeller baccy."

"Lie down, yer black dorg yer, lie down, or I'll sen' me foot through yer black beggin' paunch!"

Jimmy again spun round, till Boshy disappeared.

Queeby had returned to the kitchen, where, beside the fireplace, partly shrouded in a cloud of breath-blown ashes and smoke, he found her. Her now vigorous eye-service was obvious and stung him, but his recent defeat disinclined him even for an easy victory. In silence he lifted a nail-keg improvised into a bucket, and slung it on to the lowest crook in the chain over the fire, now blazing through Queeby's lusty efforts. She rose and made way for him. His eye travelled from her black curly hair, powdered white with the myall ashes, to her equally disguised boots, his recent gift. He had intended to ask, "Comfor'able?" as a spurring reminder; instead burst from him:

"Ghos', w'at a infernal mess ter get them into already!"

Queeby grabbed the kitchen towel and dusted them vigorously, then stood anxiously watching Boshy, her twitching toes, showing through their leather environments, sharing her uneasiness.

"Better ter weer 'em 'en ter sling 'em onter ther roof for spiders t' lay eggs in, iden it?" he said, suddenly peaceful.

"Sling on ther kettle an' set ther breakfuss for all 'an's out 'ere; an' lemme know wen this boils," pointing to the bucket. "We must gi'e 'im," indicating the dead, "a wash."

"I ain't be 'arf done a-rootin' an' a-runtin' about in theere yit. Terbaccer b' ther barrer-load, an' a 'ole keg ov rum up in ther loft — in under the bed," he substituted, to lessen detection. "On'y let's git our work done, then us'll ev a bust up; so fust, Queeby, put orn ther kittle for breakfuss," he repeated.

He carried the leaves of the table-top to his tool-house and workshop. Reappearing, tape-measure in hand, he went into the bedroom and took slow and accurate measurements, whistling delightedly to find that his pre-mortem theoretical calculations and post-mortem practical measurements hardly varied.

In the workshop he took off his hat, knotted the four corners of his red handkerchief and sized it to his head; then, utterly oblivious to all but his work, he lifted up his voice to the accompaniment of either saw or plane, and sang in tone outside all emotion: "Oh say, did yer ever know sorrer lik-er this?"

Queeby had finished all her appointed tasks, save the information Boshy wanted about the water in the bucket. Remembering its feared purpose, she ignored his orders, and when, by boiling over, it threatened to put out the fire, she raised it to a crook higher in the chain, then squatted outside by the old dog. She selected the dog, for the brute, though appreciative of her company, would be undemonstrative, save for quivering body and wagging tail; but old Jimmy's begging mania would soon betray her.

Close to the dog she watched for the coming of the child and Nungi, for she knew that by now their labour must have ceased.

The little girl's eye-service had been thorough and earnest. Long before he could sight the filled bucket, she, either sitting or leaning over the dark, cavernous well, would strain her eyes then announce: "No, nothin' in it, Nungi," which statement, though inaccurate, comforted Nungi. Moreover, should Debbil-debbil be in the bucket, cowardly though it might be, her outpost proximity gave him a sense of security.

Now in gratitude he, with her, was hunting among the wattle-scrub for the promised abnormal lump of gum, atoning for its deficiency with handfuls of geebungs and five-corner berries. And from this unexpected quarter, with the flower-decked child on his shoulder, her teeth tightly locked with the gluey wattle-gum, and her arms full of its chenille tassels, he bore down on old Jimmy. Still lock-jawed, the little girl, motioning back Queeby, poured the contents of her pinafore into Jimmy's eager palms; then, with her flowers, went softly in to her father. Child-trouble widened her brown eyes as she turned them on the shrouded figure stiffly outlined by the sheet, now partly screened by the mosquito-net. Noiselessly she laid the clematis and wattle on her bed, then stood near the covered face, and, looking down at her untied bootlaces, sighed an impatient sigh always well known and understood by this now unresponsive father. She waited till she worked her teeth free, then from there listened to Boshy's vocalizing, with intermission for change of tools or to tap the shavings from the plane.

"Wonder Boshy's noise doesn't wake father!" she thought.

"Father," softly, for she was hardly justified in wakening him to lace and tie her boots. "Father," louder, "I've been waterin' th' ewes an' lambs, an' one ewe won't 'ave she's little lamb, an' she's lamb's cryin' like anything — poor liddle lamb!" she added, in Boshy's diction and tones.

Neither sound nor movement from the bed. Behind compressed lips she groaned disappointedly.

"It's a long time," she sighed, moving her restless feet; "you've been a too ———"

"Lovey," said hunger-driven Nungi, putting his eye and mouth to a crack near her, "w'at about me box ov sardines? I feel like's if me throat was cut frum ear ter ear fer a month er Sundees! Arst 'im," taking his hand from his stomach and waving towards the workshop.

"Boshy, is this the day w'en me father gets up?"

"W'y, Lovey dear, yer comes a-sneakin' in, an' a-crawlin' in, an' a-creepin' in, an' I never see yer, an' yer frightens ten years' growth out ov me!"

"W'at you got on you 'ead?" looking at Boshy's improvised cap, the flap from one corner overhanging his eyeless socket.

"This's a kep, a kerpinter's kep, Lovey."

"It's a long time," she complained, looking towards the bedroom.

"W'eere yer bin this long, long time, Lovey?" said Boshy, alert to distract her.

"You know," picking the gum from her teeth.

"Ah! a-wattle-gum 'untin'."

"Yes; an' w'at else?"

"Geebun's."

"Geebungs," corrected she.

"An' fi'-corners."

"Five-corners," counting her fingers.

"Look et yer dear liddle 'ands! They's nut a meal for a merskeeter." He stroked them admiringly.

"Mosquitoes been biting my father, Boshy?"

He knew from this she had been in the dead man's room. He nodded affirmatively, then lowered his voice:

"Gosh me! w'at a mornin' you've 'ad!" Then, suddenly earnest, "Way's Nungi?" he asked.

"Outside, an' wants 'is tin o' sardines."

"Wi' Jimmy, is 'e?"

She nodded.

"Le's all go an' get breakfuss in ther kitchen."

"W'at's me father goin' t' have for ees breakfuss?" asked Lovey, looking at the table set for four.

Boshy readjusted his cap divertingly, but the child re-asked.

"Lovey dear, 'e's 'ad 'is breakfuss."

"W'en?"

"W'en you was gone."

"W'at did 'e have?"

"Eggs an'———"

"Boiled?"

"No, fried," said Boshy, suspecting a pitfall and supplying one.

Looking round the fireplace:

"Urgh!" she sniffed incredulously, "w'ere's the egg-shells, then?"

"W'at hell-sheggs?" transposed Boshy in his agitation, and looking both sides of the fireplace also.

"Now look 'ere, Lovey dear, me nur Gord won't love you if you keep on a-ketchin' an' a-snarin' an' a-trippin' ov poor ole Boshy up so."

The child's eyes were fastened on his face:

"W'y am I?"

"By allus an' continerally a-astin' ov questions. Arsk no questions, Lovey, an' I'll tell yer no lies," he bargained, looking at her contritely. "Up wi' yer neow, Lovey, inter yer liddle cheer, an' at yer breakfuss yer goes like one o'clock. Yer know thet ole yeller-belly goanner wot's always a-pokin' an' a-prowlin' an' a-poachin' after ther eggs?"

She nodded, the light of new interest in her eyes.

"Well, w'en 'er" — indicating Queeby, who ceased pouring the tea wonderingly to listen to incidents new to her — "were gettin' your sop ready, if 'e didn' waller right in 'ere, an' 'as a try ter snatch ther tot out ov 'er 'ands, yer tin tot ov sop."

"My tot?" from Lovey indignantly.

"Yes, your very tot; but me an' 'er," frenziedly trying to lessen Queeby's surprise by including her, "grabs 'im be ther scruff ov ther neck an' ther tip ov ther tail, makes er whistlin' stock-whip outer 'im, an' slings 'im fair inter ther middle ov nex' week. Cheek ov 'im ter want your breakfuss."

"Ern," Lovey agreed, guarding against a recurrence by quickly gobbling the disliked bread-and-milk sop. "But," she said, wiping her mouth, "it's the last time Ill 'ave nasty sop, then 'e wont come after it."

After breakfast, astride the piebald pony, his long legs nearly touching the ground, Nungi, well fed and docile as a pet cat, rode off to tell and bring help from Cameron, their nearest neighbour.

Boshy went back to his work, and despite Queeby's pleading eyes, the child yielding to his tempting inducements, went with him. He sat her on the corner of the carpenter's bench, and parried or diverted her questions about her father, and the desirability of wakening him by handing her the long curled shavings; and when these palled, he whiled her on by the impossible task of teaching him her version of the "Three Golden Balls", a blank-verse poem, but rhythmically intoned, which he had taught her.

"They wors three girls wot was orlways a-kiddin' an' a-coaxing their fathers ter buy them three goldin balls, an' any of the three of them wot lostes theys goldin balls was to be 'ung———"

"Like ther mangy pup was," was an explanatory interruption that cost the narrator her grip.

"An' then w'at they do?"

"Begin at the startment over again afore they was 'ung," advised Boshy, unintentionally furnishing the thread she seized.

"So one of 'em losed 'er goldin ball, so she was to be 'ung. 'Oh, 'angman, 'angman, stop the rope. I think I see me dear mother comin———' "

"A-comin'," corrected Boshy.

"A-comin' a-with me goldin ball. W'at's she's mother says?"

"No, I 'aven't gut," supplied Boshy, incautiously interested.

"No, I haven't got yer goldin ball. Nor I haven't come t' set yer free. But I 'ave come t' see yer 'ung upon this iron gallers tree."

It was a long list, and should have been a lasting lesson on the futility of expecting anything from relations or connections. For all came in Indian file, and sometimes announced by the reciter in the wrong order, but all from morbidity, though of each the girl with the rope round her neck asked the same question.

"Oh, dear brother" (or other), "'ave yer gut me goldin ball?" and promptly received the answer, facile from much repetition, therefore delivered with a steep incline: "No, — I — 'aven' — gut — yer — goldin — ball, — nor — I — 'aven' — come — ter — set — yer — free, — but — I — 'ave — come — ter — see — yer — 'ung — upon — this — iron — gallers — tree."

However, it was a splendid and seized opportunity for the "terue" lover who turns up at the end of the list. Familiar and oft-repeated as was the legend, the little girl broke it to ask:

"W'at's a true lover?"

Boshy's one eye grew reminiscent with unbidden long-slumbering sentiment.

"Terue lover? Well, Lovey," he explained, gruffly reluctant, "'e iden a feller wot goes a-smellin' an' a-sniffin' an' a-sneezin' roun' after every rag orn every bush, an' a-pickin' an' a-pluckin' an- a-choosin' ov none." And by the way of more lucidity, he added: "Nor one wot goes all through the woods, an' then comes out wi' a crooked stick an' " (contritely) "on'y one eye — leastways, one long-sighted eye." For to no one did Boshy admit that he could not see with both.

The child was looking at the empty socket.

"Come here and bend down."

She stood, and covering his seeing eye with one hand, held the other before the quivering muscle.

"Count now — how many fingers I got?"

"Five," promptly from Boshy.

"They's all story liars, 'cause yer can see, Boshy, right enough. But," she said, slowly shaking a puzzled head at the withered eye, "you can see my two eyes, Boshy, but I can on'y see your on'y one eye."

Boshy looked at the perturbed brow, then chanted:

"I think I see me terue lover a-comin' wi' me a-goldin ball," with planing accompaniment.

"W'at's a true lover," re-asked Lovey, ignoring past explanations.

"Terue lover, Lovey. Well, it's this ways. An' nandsome young feller fancies some good-lookin' young woman; well, then, Lovey, Gord nur ther devil nur no one won't keep 'em apart, an' they never rests till they gets spliced — thet's they ties a knot wi' their tongues wot they can't undo wi' their teeth. Married, thet is, an' then they 'as a liddle girl like you."

"Boshy, was my father an' my mother — w'at's gone up to Mr Gord's 'ouse — married?"

"Dunno, Lovey," slowly, "an' nut knowin' can't say." Then gravely, "Lovey, did yer daddy never tell yer, you 'e's own flesh an' blood, w'ether 'e was married or nut?"

"No," said she, shaking her head solemnly, "not yet, but w'en me father wakes———"

"Thet's orlright, Lovey, but if 'e wouldn't tell you, Lovey, tain't likely 'e'd a-told me. I reelly can't say, ez neither ov 'em ever said word ov mouth ter me ez they was. I on'y know 'e picked 'er up in some towen, w'en 'e went down wi' some sheep, an' w'en they come 'ere I arst no questions, so's they tell me no lies, fer she'd an eye in 'er 'ead thet 'ud coax a duck — a nole duck — off ov the water. I see nothin' wrong wi' 'er frum ther day 'er come to ther day she died, an' I made 'er coffin — same uz 'is," tapping the boards.

"Whose?" said the child sharply.

"Oh, Lovey dear," entreated perturbed Boshy, unprepared with a substitute, "don't be always a-ketchin' an' a-snarin' an' a-trippin' ov me up wi' yer liddle staggerin' questions w'en I'm a-thinkin' fer yer good."

"Wot yer say?"

"Jes this: Gord in 'eaven 'elp you if they wusn't married, for nut one acre, nur one 'oof orn this 'ere place ken yer claim or touch."

"W'at place can't I touch?"

"This place — Merrigulandri."

"Uh!" she sniffed incredulously.

"An' even s'posin' they was married, an' you a gal, blest if I think you could touch it."

"Uh!" she sniffed again; but Boshy was deep in the issues of entail, early English, all he had known.

The child with both hands demonstrated her sense and power to touch, while listening to him in silence. He raised his foot in a stool, and, leaning his elbow on his knee, held his head with his palm.

"W'y can't I touch it?" asked the child, still working her pliant fingers.

"'Cos bein' a gal."

"Who can stop me?"

"Ther crown ov Englan', weere I come from. Or maybe ther Gov'ment 'ere 'll step in an' claim, az they's ther nex'-in-kin, an' swaller ther 'ole damn lot in one gulp — the greedy, guzzelin', plunderin' crew!" He was greatly excited. "Thet it may bust 'em if they do!"

"Clover busted poor ole Strawberry," interposed Lovey.

As excited Boshy ignored this one glint of comprehension, she added:

"I can touch everythin' I want t'," rousing Boshy by verifying this on him.

"They's the smallest and ther lovliest liddle 'an's on this 'ere yearth," kissing them. "An' yer the innercentest liddle lamb, too," stroking her tousled wattle-perfumed hair.

"I'm a big girl, Boshy."

"Yes," sorrowfully as to the sex; "an' fer oncet I wish ter Christ yer wuzn't a girl, Lovey."

It was too dark a mood to hold the child.

"Oh, you make your box, Boshy. I," shaking her head, "don't want no more goldin balls. I want me father. 'E's a long time waking up," fretfully shaping her face for tears, and twisting her body impatiently.

"Yer gettin' sleepy-tired, Lovey ov mine. Yer bin up long agen daybreak. Come," sitting swaying his knees like a cradle, "to I sing yer ter bye-bye."

"An' w'en I go to bye-bye, w'ere'll yer put me t' sleep?"

"Side ov yer daddy," promised Boshy, not looking at her.

She came to his arms and instantly shut both eyes. He, looking down at her tightly closed lids and mouth, was not deceived, as tensely still in his arms she lay.

"Dont' shet yer eyes a-puppus, Lovey. Keep 'em open," he pleaded, "an' wait to I sing yer ter bye-bye reely."

"Sing quick, then, less I will."

Yielding to the sentimental, he began:

Oh, it wus all in ther month ov May,
  When green birds wus swellin',
A young man on his death-bed lay
  Fer ther love ov Barbary Ellen,
  Fer ther love———

"No, no, not that one," she interrupted impatiently.

"W'at now, Lovey?"

She was thoughtful.

"Liddle more cider?" Boshy prompted.

She nodded, and he broke out jauntily:

A liddle more cider for Miss Dinah,
  A liddle more cider too a-hoo,
A liddle more cider for Miss Dinah,
  A liddle more cider too a-hoo.

She suffered this for a time, because the motion of his rapidly jerking foot-beats interfered with her speech. However, she stopped him with her hand on his mouth. Boshy looked into her sleepless eyes, with their strange, lonely expression, and began another with equally vigorous foot movement:

Blow, bellers, blow; blow, bellers, below.
Knock away, boys, for er nour er so,
An' its double shuffle on we the re ro rady oh,
An' its double shuffle on we the re ro ray,
An' its double shuffle on we the re ro rady oh,
An' its double shuffle on we the re ro ray———

Wide-open eyes looked up at him when he paused for breath, and again he returned to the sentimental:

Oh, me preetty, pretty bird,
An' me well-feathered bird,
Don't crow until it be day,
An' yer comb it shall be of the yeller beaten gold,
An' yer wings of the silver so grey.

But the bird it was false,
And very, very false,
An' it crowed an hour too soon,
An' she thought it was day,
An' she sent 'er love away,
An' 'twas only the light of the moon.

She seemed too deeply interested for sleep.

"Sing more again."

So, changing his programme, behind closed teeth he crooned with insinuating dreaminess his unfailing cat's slumber song:

Crowin-aogies-gone-t'-Sligie
T'-marry-a-wife-for-Donal'-Magibbie.
Good-e-love-er-good-e-give-er.
Everything-to-chicken-liver.
Blow-high-ye-winds-they'll-live-together.
Blow-low-ye-winds-they'll-live-for-ever.
From-chimbly-tops-ye'll-shift-em-never.
Zoo-morigan-za-morigan-zam-zam-zee.

She yawned, and with renewed hope and earnestness Boshy went on, till she suddenly requested:

"Sing pretty, pretty bird again. No, no! crow, Boshy," suddenly.

"Ur, Lovey," reproachfully; "nut crow, Lovey," disapprovingly, for no sleep that way. "Jim Crow, Lovey, d'ye mean?" hopefully.

"No, no;" but stroking his face coaxingly: "Crow like nice, good cock-a-doo, what made she's love wake up an' go away."

"Ah, Lovey! carn't go asleep along ov me a-crowin'. Thet cock-a-doo oughtn't t' 'ave crowed."

"Well, you crow, an' I'll go t' sleep then," she promised.

Boshy gave an incipient crow.

"Tha's on'y like little cock-a-doo. Stand up," she said, slipping down between his knees, "an' clap yer wings, like w'at they do, an' crow big — *b-i-g*, like big cock-a-doo," she said breathlessly.

Boshy's best efforts failed to stimulate the roosters, which seemed to him to be the child's desire, for she listened intently for outside sound.

"Laugh like laughin' jackasses," she commanded abruptly, changing her tactics, a grim intent about her mouth.

"Wot oh! you bol' jackasses a-larfin' so loud," chanted Boshy, uncertain about laughing mimicry. "Thet right, Lovey?"

"Laugh like w'at they do."

Boshy did nobly.

"Laugh louder 'n w'at they do," she exacted.

Boshy tip-toed, raised his head towards the roof, and made a supreme effort. The old dog growled disapprovingly, and dozing Jimmy laughed unintelligently. Boshy grinned at both tributes.

"Laugh more agen, Boshy; go on, go on!" said the child, tip-toeing in her eagerness.

Boshy, elated, improvised a series of unbirdlike notes, startlingly loud, and new to all feathered folk.

"W'at about thet lot, Lovey?" he asked, hungry for her approval and disappointed, for she had turned towards the door.

She looked back at him, a look on her face new to him.

"Now, let's see; didn't that wake me father?"

Boshy raised his hands.

"Oh, Lovey! O Gord A'mighty, Lovey! You to play a trick like thet on poor me!" gasped he, aghast, undone by her ruse.

2

FIFTY miles parted the dead man's property and Cameron Cameron, and it was not till the afternoon of the next day that he with his daughter Margaret drove up.

Boshy, with Lovey beside him, was watching for them. Margaret held out her arms for the little orphan, but she shrank from them closer to Boshy, who gripped her hand. Cameron Cameron bared his head, and noiselessly they entered the house. Boshy, leading Lovey, came out a little later to the kitchen and bade Queeby "take Lovey for a ta-ta in the scrub", while he, Cameron Cameron, and Margaret discussed things inside.

Queeby instead went to Jimmy, still lying or squatting between the myall logs, and greedily begging from an uninterested horse grazing near, for as a food beggar Jimmy was ceaseless; even in his sleep his hands went out.

"Cobban Master (God) spillum flour-bag (frost) las' night on poor Jimmy. Plurry cole," he complained to the child. "W'ite pfeller frost las' night."

She understood and covered him with a bag. Laying his hands on his moon-whitened head, he continued:

"Yulegrin (hungry). Poor pfeller me, Tumbledown Jimmy — poor pfeller me!" was a further demand for food. Then angrily: "That pfeller," pointing out on the plain to Nungi, "been eatem big pfeller breakfuss; baal gib it poor pfeller Jimmy enny breakfuss!" he squeaked harshly in self-pity, pointing from his mouth to his stomach, whining, "Yulegrin! yulegrin!"

His hungry importunity was no more to the child than the magpie's, for in that respect the magpie was his superior. The methods of both were strangely alike, and had long since palled on her, and this afternoon she hardly saw him. Leaving Queeby with him, she went noiselessly round to the widest crack in the bedroom and looked through.

Still that silent sleeping father. She put her mouth to a crack and directed a deep sigh to his ear. The net and sheet fluttered, and the child's heart beat audibly.

"Father," she whispered, tremulous with hope; but neither motion nor sound answered her. Child though she was, the sense of the mysterious fell upon her, and her mouth set maturely as she turned away.

"Sweet, pretty little creature," the birds, her old friends, twittered to her. She turned from them and the scrub with its lurking shadows, and looked across the plain. The ewes and lambs were again round the empty troughs surrounding the well. She climbed on the butcher's block near the meat room; from this coign she could see the graves. One end of the palisading was down, and she saw the dirt being flung up under the myall clump by two of Cameron's men.

Since the coming of Margaret Cameron and her father, Lovey had ceased to ask questions, but had followed their every movement with widely questioning eyes. She went now to the chimney corner, and applied her eye to a well-known crack: Margaret sat beside her father on a stool, and Boshy stood facing them and herself, his left arm extended, his thumb holding down the two middle fingers. His whole hand shook whenever he spoke, but too impartially for emphasis.

"Her father wrote to me just before he died about taking her — and the child must be schooled," said Cameron Cameron.

"Git me the books; I'll school her. Town," sniffed Boshy — "towns' no place fer a chile like 'er. Nothin' in 'em but a lyin' an' a-swearin' an' a-Sabbath-breakin,' a-drinkin' an' a-forgin' an' a———" Boshy looked at Margaret and ceased abruptly. "I don't say sech a awful thing 'ud 'appen ter Lovey ez thet. But I see" — Boshy's jaw set — "no good in towns, nur schoolin' neither," he said sullenly.

Cameron began, but Boshy stopped him.

"Mr Cameron, sur, I knows ter ther full you means well ter Lovey alright. They" (giving a backward jerk towards the bedroom and uniting it by a handwave with a grave now being lengthened under the myalls) "may 'ave been married or they may nut 'ave been."

"Of course they were, Boshy. I've got their marriage lines here with these papers," said Cameron.

"Oh! you've a-snavelled 'ees papers, then," said Boshy suspiciously, who had been too distressfully absorbed watching Margaret pack the child's clothes to notice this.

Boshy paused, and after a visible struggle went on with a matter even nearer his heart.

"Well, married or nut, it'll be all ther same t' Lovey in ther long run, you understan'."

Neither did.

"Well, it's this way: I've bin 'ere, young man an' ole — leastways middle age, for though me 'ead may be a bit greyish outside, it's no-ways greyish inside. Serpose you don't think I've bin 'ere fer ther love ov it, jest stuck 'ere in this one-eyed country w'ere no one comes, so ther dorgs don't 'ave ter bark at strangers, jest for the run ov me knife an' pannikin."

"No?" remarked Cameron, in tones inviting further confidences.

"Yer right theere; theere's bin bad seasons, and theere's bin good, but I've bin asleep with one eye open, good or bad."

Boshy paused, but his hearers were again bushed as to his drift. He saw this, and in an effort to enlighten them, said slowly:

"Her'll want for nothin'."

He put both hands in his pockets, and looked from the nubbly carbuncles there outlined to the two. Still both failed to understand, or no one appeared to; withdrawing his hands impatiently, he reluctantly said slowly, dropping his voice:

"P'r'aps you 'ave nodiced they's nut many ole emp'y pickle bottles knockin' about"; then considering this alarmingly explicit, he changed the subject hastily. "I sez nothin' about 'er a-goin' wi' this 'ere young woman fer a day or so, t' we gits 'im laid by. Same time, she'd be jest as well, if nut better, in ther scrub 'ere wi' Queeby a berry-huntin' as she is now; an' at ther time w'en all's ready, w'en 'er comes back an' 'er sees 'im gone, I can easy chalk 'er off be tellin' 'er 'e's gone up to Mr Gord's 'ouse, as 'er calls it, ter see 'er mammy. Trust me fer thet," said Boshy, grinning egotistically.

But the hearts of his hearers were still cold in his cause. Cameron was for closing the discussion as useless and ununderstandable.

Boshy, mistaking the silence, winked, and looked insinuatingly from one to the other, and in gratitude further entrenched on his secretiveness.

"An' I may say, furthermore, seein' thet I'm a-talkin' ter w'ite people, thet them ole emp'y pickle bottles is w'eere no crows wi' colds on their chests will mistake them bottles' insides fer yeller cough lozengers," he went on, without pausing to elucidate the, to him, obviousness of his meaning. "Now, w'at d'yer serpose I make out ov a damn one-eyed 'ole like this? Thet is, annerly or yearly, take season wi' season all roun'."

He paused to look for commercial freemasonry from Cameron.

"I couldn't say, Boshy. What do you make now?"

"Yer wouldn't believe me, no, nut if I took me oath."

"Try me now," induced Cameron.

Boshy looked round the room, then under the safe and sofa. Beside them only the cat by the fire. He opened the back door wide enough for the cat's exit, then, taking his cap from his head, he beat her out with it, and closed the door carefully.

Backing into a corner furthest from Margaret, he beckoned to Cameron, who bent, while Boshy, tiptoeing, whispered in his ear.

"No, it couldn't be done in the time," incredulously pretended Cameron.

"I told yer yer'd doubt me word; but Gord may strike me dead if I lie," challenged and confirmed the testator. He added immediately: "But thet confession 'as never been mouthed be me afore, nut even t' 'im," pointing to the bedroom with one hand, and letting in the importuning cat with the other.

All Boshy's past history was pure conjecture; from himself nothing had ever been gleaned, though many had pumped.

"How did you come out here, Boshy?" insinuated Cameron, intent on more confidences.

"That's neither 'ere nur theere, an' yer gut no business ter try t' git me on ther raw, Mr Cameron," said Boshy resentfully.

There was an audible breathing-space between the two men, then Margaret said:

"Father meant out here, Boshy — Merrigulandri."

"Oh," he said, relieved. "Well, I'd 'ad me bellyfull of towns, so I took a look roun' fer a careful sort ov mate, an', be 'eavens! I gut more then I wanted, fer I struck one as mean as cats' meat. Pat the Jew, as 'e was called, soon giv' ther bush best, an' I 'ear now that 'e is landed proprietor ov the Court 'Ouse Hotel, and quite the juicy cockroach."

He paused, and allowed a smile to form and slowly fade at his mental picture of his old mate as a Boniface, and reminiscence hazed his one eye and relaxed his mouth.

"We camped one evening at Narrangidgery Creek, close b' a cocky's 'umstead. We was clean dead-beat, an' 'adn't tasted a bite ov fresh meat fer some time, an' w'en we sees a cupple ov wimin a-roundin' up and a-runnin' in some cattle, tired as we was, we bucks up and gi'es 'em an nand. Well, in less 'an no time, the ole woman she brings out ther gun and pops one off fust go. After thet me an' Pat rolls in an' skins an' dresses it. But, be 'eavens! the ole woman was a standin' by, an' nut even so much as a lick at the blood would 'er le' our two dorgs sneak, an' them as dead-beat as we wuz. By and by the two wimin starts a-runnin' of ther" — looking at Margaret — "ther — intrils, but the two of 'em wuz at the same time a-beatin' and a-beltin' and a-bashin' of both dorgs' back. We tried t' coax ther skirts an' liver out ov 'er. 'I gi'e away nothin',' she said. An' be 'eavens! thet wus all we did git, so we christened the place 'Gi'-Away-Nothin' 'All'."

"Now," said Cameron, "we must buck up; it's getting late. Now about the child, Boshy: she must come with us, you see."

"I see nuthin' ov ther sort," replied Boshy, surprised. "Oo's gut ther best right to 'er — strangers or them ez weaned 'er? Yes, s'elp me Gord, weaned er!" he added fiercely, looking from one to the other. Then, suddenly softening: "Mr Cameron, an' you, young woman," his pleading mouth working tremulously, "'twas I ez weaned 'er from 'er mother a'most, an' " — red spots glowing on his cheek-bones — "Gord's me Judge, to kid 'er even from playin' wi' the fowls, I used ter take 'er inter me workshop an' turn meself inter a blarsted ole rooster, a-curlin' ov, an' a-crowin' ov, an' a-clappin' ov me wings like — like b-beggary!"

Boshy had turned his one eye on Cameron during this confession. Its cost, though it might have missed the man, drew toll from the woman.

"Kind, kind Boshy! But, you see, it's for the child's good. She could not stay now."

"She must be schooled — can't grow up like a wild animal," interposed Cameron.

"They's nut much wile animal about Lovey; an' if all comes ter all, isen' ther bush ther proper place for a wile animal? Town's all very well for a ornery child, but, Mr Cameron and this young woman 'ere, Lovey ain't be no means a ornery child. She's gut ways be no ways ornery. In fac' 'er were born wi' em, an' thet's w'y 'er's gut ther 'ole ov them under 'er thumb — Nungi an' Queeby, an' ole Jimmy, an' — an' —" after a bashful pause — "the 'ole damn lot ov us!"

This avowal begot another.

"S'elp me Gord, sur, ter tell yer the truth, if 'er were took away I'd feel no better nur a 'ole" — after a pause — "rooster w'at's lorst 'er one chick!"

Then again brick-red spots glowed on the old man's high cheek-bones, and his one eye glistened. He cleared his throat shamefacedly, then proceeded, solely addressing Cameron:

"Mr Cameron, sur, 't were I ez poddied [spoon-fed] thet child w'en 'er mammy fust weaned 'er. W'y, w'en 'er wuz liddle, an' they wuz a-tryin' ter wean 'er, nut bite nor sup could they get inter 'er liddle inside till I tackled 'er like this" — looking round; then, for lack of illustrative matter, improvising with his hands. "I grabs up a lot ov bread-an'-milk sop, an' makes outside wi' it. 'Come along, cock-a-doodle-doo; come along, chooky 'en an' chicks, eat up all Lovey's sop,' sez I. 'W'at!' sez I, 'you greedy chooks, nut leave none fer poor liddle baby Lovey!' sez I, a-spillin' ov it out, an' a-gammunin' az they 'ad gobbled ov it all up out ov me 'ands. Lord Gord! ter see thet liddle child, the spirit ov 'er, the pluck ov 'er, a-fightin' wi' 'er liddle, liddle 'ands wi' them fowls! Game 'er is an' always wuz, an' always will be — game az a liddle ant!"

Boshy wiped the admiring moisture from his eye with the red ear of his handkerchief cap hanging conveniently near it, then ventured on further memories connected with the child that he, like Mary, had "pondered in his heart".

"'Oly Ghost!" said he, inadvertently but appropriately invoking the Pentecostal Bestower of tongues — "'Oly Ghost! 'er could talk long afore 'er could walk, an' plain az you an' me, too. I'll allow az 'er were slow about walkin', an' 'er is ter this day if 'er can be carried. Now, so 'elp me Gord! this is az true as Gospel. This is the dodge 'er gut me up t' try and wake up 'er dead daddy."

He told of the crowing in his workshop, and he seemed to be gaining his cause, for Cameron's Bush-worn face had grown fatherly and Margaret wept; but he suddenly cut him short with:

"Boshy, we know you have been good and kind to the child, but she must come with us for the time, then go to town to my sister to be educated. Why, my boy Andrew is there," he added, to reassure Boshy.

"I've more rights ter ther child than any ov you strangers," said Boshy determinedly. "A nice time 'er'll give you strangers, or anyone else oo wants to tie 'er liddle boots even! Nut me, even if I wuz to put me two eyes out on sticks, will 'er let touch 'em. 'Me father will lace 'em, 'er says continerally. An' theere 'er is, a-waitin' az 'er is, fer 'im as'll wake no more, to wake an' lace 'em up." He paused dramatically. "But soon's 'er knows 'e's dead an' gorn it'll be, 'Boshy, you can lace 'em up,' an' 'Boshy, you can do this, an' do thet, an' ther other thing.' To tell yer ther reel truth, I wuz a-thinkin', az I wuz a-makin' ov 'e's coffin, thet I wouldn' be surprised if 'er didn' take to a-daddyin' ov me — poor liddle motherless, fatherless lamb thet 'er is."

Cameron Cameron moved towards the door.

"We must take the child," he said; "she must be schooled. Suppose you could do everything else for her, you'll allow you couldn't school her, Boshy?"

"Boshy'll allow nothin' at all ov ther sort! Wait, he

earnestly commanded, as Cameron's hand went to the door, and something in his tones caused the man to obey.

In the pregnant pause the cat rose from the fireplace and stretched in a strained, listening attitude, with its eyes on Boshy.

"Get out ov this, yer listenin' tinker yer!"

He aimed a kick at her, and, again opening the door, drove her out.

"There's nut one in the 'ole ov this districk but w'at thinks I come out to this country fer ther good ov me delicate constitootion." (Everyone in that district thought differently.) "Also az well, thet I can't write."

He went slowly to the topless table, and along its dusty frame laboriously traced with his forefinger "Hugh Palmer". He raised his suddenly shrunken, withered face to Margaret's, that had as suddenly crimsoned.

"If so be az I were sent out, an' altered my name, yer may know, young woman, I'm nut ther on'y one. 'Yerhoo Pormer' thet young blade calls 'isself, but Hug Pal-mer he's true name is, fer I see a letter as a-cum to 'im from 'ome; in fac', ther mail-boy lef' it wi' me ter give it ter 'im. 'This fer you?' sez I. 'E takes it, looks at it. 'Yerhoo Pormer,' 'e sez, thinkin' I couldn't read. 'Hug Pal-mer,' sez I to 'im. An' if that young man 'ad a-owned to it theere an' then, an' w'y 'e were sent out, to me, I'd a-tole 'im w'y I come, an' said no more to one on yearth. There's more'n me in ther same boat, yer see, Mr Cameron an' young woman; an' my name is no more Boshy 'n w'at thet young man is Yerhoo Pormer. 'Good ov me 'Ealth' 's my name fer ther cause ov my voy'ge. 'Kerlonial Egsperience' is Mr Yerhoo Pormer's."

Boshy's attempts at the English drawl of Margaret's lover, together with his wrongly bracketing him with himself as a convict, caused a burst of laughter from her father.

"My word! plenty worse than you out of gaol, Boshy, old man," he said, slapping him on the back.

"An' you know w'eere to find 'em!" said Boshy, stung by his noisy mirth; for it was to him a bitter confession, justifiable only by the greatness of the occasion — one that had induced him to uncover his two most hidden secrets.

Cameron Cameron jerked his head at his daughter, and again went to the door.

"I've no wish to put atween you an' thet young man, miss. Gord knows, a conspriricy sent me 'ere, an' mebbe 'e were sent out fer very liddle. Yes, no doubt so were 'e, an' I'd rather yer didn' name it to 'im, fer I never be word ov mouth spoke about it afore," he said, in agitated uncertainty following close after Margaret.

"I won't, Boshy," she promised, too tender for Boshy's coming trial to enlighten him, even if she could.

To his further dismay, the child met them outside, her eyes unnaturally open, her mouth unusually indrawn, and unnaturally and unusually silent.

Cameron's man harnessed the horses and brought the buggy round to the front-door. Old Jimmy immediately sidled up to the horses' heads, and, in his disability to attract the bipeds, importuned the quadrupeds for bacca and tucker.

Margaret Cameron, with Lovey in her arms, went into the bedroom, turned back the sheet from the brow, and held the child's immovable lips to it, then pressed her own, and went to the buggy. All the household were now round it, as she placed the girl on the seat and got in.

Boshy stood near, palsied, speechless.

The child drew away from Margaret's sheltering arms and shuffled to the seat's edge near Boshy. She placed one foot over the side and moved it meaningly towards him. He rushed and with trembling fingers laced it, then the other.

"Lovey," he said brokenly, holding both feet firmly, "Lovey — this — is — a — er — conspriricy — a put-up thing to part us! Jes' yer wait, Lovey ov mine — jes' wait an' see can it be done. Wait, Lovey———"

His lips were disobedient, but his jaw worked strenuously for the love of his heart.

"Long ago a — er — conspriricy parted me from me — mother. This is another conspriricy to part us."

He mouthed silently for some moments.

"Wait, Lovey — er — mine — an' see can it be done. Jes' wait, Lov———"

"Poor pfeller me!" importuned Jimmy as they drove off; "poor pfeller me! Poor Tumbledown Jimmy!" as ever his hand rose and fell.

3

ALL week long the puffing and panting throat of the flour-mill belched vapour-columned arches, which, telescoping airily, spanned the river from bank to bank, as if purposefully linking the mill with Fireman Foreman's dwelling on the opposite side. Fireman Foreman — a godly member of the Methodist chapel — shrouded by dawn or by vapour, on his way to the mill to get up steam, was therefore seldom seen to cross. Some little ones, superstitiously awed by the mill's funnel belchings, credited him with crossing this waterway by the aerial arches. But now, in the unillusioned light and broody quiet of a Sabbath morn, the cold, silent mill, shorn of its nebulous halo, looked old and worn — an aged actor off the stage. The same unsparing realism foreshortened the river's width, and directed those sentimental children's eyes to the mundane stepping-stones from Foreman's to the mill. On the flat behind the mill, dawn-rising Chinamen shogged with nimble bare feet under their yoke-linked watering-cans. These busy brethren, meeting sometimes on the same narrow track, would pause, ant-like, seemingly to dumbly regard one another and their burdens, then, still ant-like, pass silently to their work.

No schoolboys lingered round Bob Robertson's (yclept Roberson's) blacksmith shop, for this sleepy day no lusty throat bellowed attention to the flaming tongues fanned from its bloodily blazing teeth; no luminous stars flinted from the clanking anvil. The lips of its wide-mouthed door were closed, and a cruelly prosaic touch were the Scotch twill shirt and moleskin trousers hanging across the fence. Their owner, George, the blacksmith's apprentice, always wore his Sunday suit on Saturday night, while Granny Foreman as regularly sluiced through his week-day gear.

The front doors of Pat the Jew's Courthouse Hotel and its less successful rival, the Royal, were closed. Old Moore the pound-keeper, Dinnie Donahoe the shoemaker, Tambaroora Phil the chemist, Fry the tailor, and other thirsty back-door compatriots, viewed this inhospitable restriction with equanimity.

Inside the National School the dusty emptiness, surrounding the ink-stained, knife-mutilated forms, was eloquent of relaxation. Dickey, the schoolmaster's old pony, roamed in solitary dejection all round the bare school-ground. The untrodden nibblings under the fence were dry and dusty, and from the quest of these he would raise his head, and thrusting it over the bars, eye up and down the empty street, then whinny gregariously — whether for the schoolboys who had surreptitiously plucked every hair from his mane and tail, or for his work-day acquaintances, the butcher and the baker's old horses, was not clear even perhaps to him.

As she entered the main street, still empty but for her, Eliza Hickson, commonly called "Lizarixin", milk-girl from "up the river", crossed her leg and sat genteely sideways on her milk saddle-bags — flour-sacks ingeniously partitioned into pint or half-pint receptacles. When she passed the schoolhouse, Dickey raised his head over the rails and dropped some of his dry gleanings in his whinnied greeting to 'Liza's old horse. But neither 'Liza nor her mount responded. Unguided, he turned round the corner of the school enclosure, to Sergeant Toohey, their first customer, across the river. The hollow resonance of her horse's hoofs crossing the bridge filled the vacuous morning unduly, rousing old Granny Foreman, whose nightcapped head appeared through the small bedroom window.

"'Liza dear, do 'ee like a good girl, 'and I in George's clo'es: 'twill save I goin' out."

But Granny bought no milk, so her double sentiment of hiding the limited extent of her grandson's wardrobe and observing the sanctity of the Sabbath appearance did not appeal to 'Liza. She turned her expressionless eyes on the old woman, and with, "Oo was yer servant larst year?" went undelayed up the hillside to the gaol. She meant to finish her milk delivery in time to attend morning Sunday-school, for, notwithstanding her double milk duties on the Sabbath, she topped the list for regular and punctual attendance.

Her next service would be the home of Widow Irvine, the well-to-do sister of Cameron Cameron. The house was on the flank of the "gravelly hill", and as 'Liza topped this, she saw with surprise that apparently all there still slept.

And as Granny McGrath's river-going geese waddled their way through the paddock next to this house, they too paused to joyfully comment on the unusual spectacle of an old and relentless dog foe still on the chain. They were not of the order that take their pleasures silently, so shrill laughter was in their gladsome beaked communings. But it was even more galling to the fettered dog when rank and file came in a united line, and through the space beneath the lower rail, slowly and steadily regarded him. It was a relief when a chorus of triumphant "Queg, queg, quegs!" burst from them. Now only the fence and the chained dog divided them and the long coveted grass in the home paddock. An old mother goose was for immediate action, but her less martial spouse hung back for a further futile exhibition from the dog to burst his bonds, then, as became a cautious general, he waddled under and led the way, proscribing a safe limit.

Among the dewy grass they zigzagged their destructive bills, and after each swallowing pause they craned their long necks towards the impotent dog, and the aggressive, arrogant mocking of their "Queg, queg, quegs!" in varied keys under his very nose was maddening.

To add to his humiliation, old mare Cushla on the other side of the fence ceased licking her newly-foaled offspring to gallop up from the flat. She stretched over the fence her head, with extended pricked ears and questioning eyes. Then she, with equine eloquence, whinnied for an explanation from the dog of his lack of hostility to these despoilers of her foal's domain.

Tightening every sinew and muscle, he gave a silent but violent exhibition of his inability to reach or disconcert these invaders; yet unappeased, she still demanded the same duty. Her want of ordinary horse sense to grasp the situation almost scattered his extraordinary dog sense of Sabbath sanctity. He rose, and, inflating his sides, panted with mortified rage. Yet again he slackened his chain to the last loop, then, with concentrated, soundless energy, he bounded with an impetus that turned him tail end to them.

When he reversed, he found that Cushla's eyes had added contempt to complaint, and that Daddy Gander was leading a whole orchestra of amused "Queg, quegs!" He turned his eyes to his dilatory master's room, and, raising his head to the heavens, sent up a prolonged howl that was utterly free from secularism. The startled geese flew incontinently, a change of expression in their "Quegs", and their falling feathers showed their imaginations were anticipating.

Neither parsonage nor rectory kept the sanctity of the Sabbath more sacredly than this household, for Mrs Irvine was a strict Wesleyan. Her home on week-days was often honoured by the presence of the parson, and every Sunday at dinner. Indeed, it seemed to the culprit dog that he and his canine companions had to take on the subdued Sabbath atmosphere with the silence of the mill on Saturday afternoons. His fault now was therefore the more heinous, and guiltily he sent sidelong looks to the room of his master, Jim, man of all work — but thankfully he saw the still closed door.

It was not the contented sense of a week well spent that had prolonged Jim's sleep, but the fact that the night before had been his monthly pay-night. There was no variety in Jim's personal mode of celebrating these occasions, but much in his gifts to Fanny, maid of all work, his fellow-servant, for in the first hour of their meeting Jim's eyes had eagerly sought the third finger on both her work-wealed hands. From their unadorned simplicity he instantly made up his mind to wed her some day, and although passing years, chiefly of an autumnal tend, demanded an undue deciduous toll from Fanny's meagre locks and ample gums, Jim, to his credit, remained faithful.

It was to this home Cameron Cameron's daughter, now Margaret Palmer, had some weeks back sent the child Lovey to be educated. There was little need for Margaret, tender soul, to write to her brother Andrew to bespeak his care for the orphan girl. Instinctively from the first this silent lad took the brown-eyed Bush-girl in his charge; otherwise it was a cold home for her. For there was little love in the barren widow's buxom body for any child save Andrew, whose silence was his strength, radiating security even to the inexperienced Lovey. Quickly she learned to know that a word from "Andree" meant more than a speech from the others. The night before, under his tuition, his own savings had been supplemented by Jim, who had pared down his gift to Fanny, to assist Andrew in the purchase of a doll, much coveted by the unsophisticated child, despite its fearful and wonderful shape. There would be a heavy reckoning when Fanny found that instead of four yards of flannel for a petticoat Jim had purchased only two.

Andrew knew this, and dreading her discovery, slept lightly, and consequently was awakened by the dog's howl. Hastily freeing the now repentant brute and impatiently noisy fowls, he took the milk-jug from the kitchen window-ledge and placed it on the gate-post. Lizarixin, ambling down-hill to fill the waiting jug, was almost shocked into a standstill by the dog's howl; but later catching sight of Andrew, she prodded her old Neddy into a hasty jog-trot. Quite unconsciously, this youth had impressed her maiden fancy, and she had a little plan ready for delivery at Sunday-school this very afternoon.

Liza filled the milk-jug, rather ostensibly draining the quart-bottle.

"Good measure, Anderer," she said to him, demonstrating that not one drop dripped from the inverted bottle. Most customers had accused her of a tendency to short measure by retention.

"Yers," he said, hurriedly taking the jug and turning away.

"Anderer," she called.

"Want me?" he asked, looking at her foolishly-grinning mouth; but she only prodded her heels into her horse's ribs. She had meant her plan to mature at Sunday-school that afternoon, but though she realized that this was a more favourable opportunity, it took time for her slow, determined brain to make the transference.

"Know yer lessins, Anderer?"

He nodded.

"Find ther text?"

"Nuh."

"It's in ther fourth———"

"Mus'n't tell," from him checked her.

"I'm orlways ther first at mornin' an' evenin Sundee-schule, an' ther most reglerestest," said Liza, making this announcement as an offset to his display of righteousness.

"Better be goin' on now or you'll be late this mornin'," he advised, turning away.

"Anderer," decidedly.

"Wot?" impatiently.

She took from the saddle-pocket a soiled pink wad.

"Ketch," she said, but it hit him on the chest.

He picked it up.

"Thanks," he grunted, unrolling and pocketing the acid-drop, and allowing the sentiment on its kiss-paper covering to flutter away unread, until her strategic—

"Oh, ain't yer goin' ter read wot's on ther kiss-paper? It's about you," appealed to his egotism and he took up the paper and read:

If I see thy head on another's knee,
Then I'll knock saucepans out of thee;

then ungallantly he put the lolly and its love-proxy on the gatepost.

"I didn' give it ter yer; I throwed it at yer. Know w'y?"

"No."

"'Cause I throwed me rubbish ware I throwed me love," simpered sex-sophisticated Liza, her sunburnt face flooded with a mulberry hue.

"Don't be a fool;" and he turned away his disgusted face.

"I ain't." As a guarantee she called, "Anderer, you be my sweet'eart, and I'll be yours."

"Urh you! Get on with yer milk-bags," he snorted, hastening into the haven of Jim's room. Ignoring Jim's hazy invitation "t' give it er name," he sobered Jim's "shouting" hospitality by drenching him with the contents of the tin jug.

Jim sat up and tried to moisten his palate with his dry tongue.

"W'a's er time?" he asked.

As if in answer, the cracked bell of the little Scotch

church, first to begin and last to cease, clanged its "first bell" announcement.

"That's the last bell; an' aunt's up this hour." Both were immorally effective statements.

"'Oly Ghost! w'y didn' wake me afore?" reproachfully asked Jim, staggering up.

The bells of the rival churches were swift to follow their despised leader, and the combined clamour awoke the little girl.

"Look," said Fanny to Andrew, as he with studied diplomacy went to get the first, therefore the brunt, of her anger. "Look at them pertaters."

In this Sabbath-keeping household all Sunday duties possible were performed on the preceding day; therefore Andrew, in consideration for Fanny curling the child's hair, had overnight pared the potatoes for Sunday's dinner. Fanny's observation was very limited, and not till this morning did she find that the whole dish of potatoes so thickly shorn by Andrew in record time, now lay in the bottom of a small dipper. Then in addition she enlarged on her real grievance, her just share expended on Ursie's doll; but her tirade was cut short by an unearthly wail from the child's room.

Usula felt her curl-carbuncled head; the papers were all in; she got up to look for her doll. Finding in her sleep contortions she had broken off a leg, she gave Rachel's cry which the boy never forgot. Its poignancy startled even Fanny, who went speedily to the room; but her resentment rekindled when she found the cause to be the maimed doll. "Serves ther both er yer rights," snarled she. But Andrew soon partially assuaged the tearful child's maternal grief; he could easily mend this doll, and later he and Jim would get her a better.

And now the longed-for Sunday had come. Washed, uncurled, and dressed in a grotesquely long black frock, and gloves, which to keep on she had to shut her hands, Ursie was ready for church service at nine o'clock, all but her hat. Her first hat lay in a bandbox in her aunt's room, under the widow's new black bonnet, and the little girl's impatient feet many times went to and from the shut door. Andrew ventured at last to knock, then to intrude his head, and, discreetly augmenting the time, made a demand for the hat. The bandbox was produced, and Ursie was called, and joyfully elevated her eager little face for this large hat, mushroom in shape. Wide strings tied under the chin drew it down till the back brim grazed on the child's shoulders. It was the style of hat worn when the aunt was a child, and though forty years stood between their ages, she saw nothing incongruous about it; and the wilderness had stood between the child and all hats, so she was ignorantly content.

Andrew was sent to invite a visiting minister to dinner, and Ursie commanded to wait on the veranda. The bells had started anew, apparently refreshed by breakfast. Sunday — church — new dress — gloves and hat: Ursula's heart bounded; she would be good on Sunday. A buzzing hornet plied mud-laden between the river and his nest in the chimney corner, above the honeysuckle. Working at his nest on Sunday! She was shocked. Wicked twittering swallows were likewise disregarding and desecrating this holy day. She rather feared the hornet, but she vigorously "shooed" the naughty swallows till both her gloves fell off; but persisted in her devout efforts till the hornet, apparently disapproving of her interference, circled above her head, buzzing ominously. Despite the righteousness of her cause, she was vanquished. Retreating, she watched these uninfluenced sinners fly riverwards for more mud; and as the result of the past few weeks' teaching, meditated on the judgment sure to overtake them.

In their garden just beneath her, and separated from her aunt's paddock only by a gully, the Chinamen still laboured. They were bigger than the hornets or birds, therefore wickeder. Her little heart beat faster at the sight of these grown-up Sabbath desecrators, till their offence was absorbed by a greater. Her aunt's fence ran along the river-bank, and on the top rail of this several boys laboriously but adroitly balanced their progress up the river: towels round their necks made clear their purpose. In varied ways all were intent on attracting the Chinamen, for the purpose of demonstrating the superiority of the white over the coloured races. Some shouted offensive orders, others, variegated Chinky-chows or Ching-chongs. The watching child got her first lesson in the gesticulative boy language of contempt, supplied by thrust-out tongues, "Bacon that fat", and other indications of scornful disgust, but for her mercifully confined to sight, not sound. However, it seemed all in the day's work to the apparently oblivious gardeners. But the limit to the horrified child's endurance was reached, when she saw these boys make a hasty raid on the unripe peaches of a laden tree growing in the corner between, and overhanging, both gardens.

With a bursting heart she ran to Fanny.

"Fanny", she gasped, "naughty, wicked boys goin' to' bogey [bathe] on Sunday are stealin' Aunt's peaches!"

Fanny, after making good the quantity of potatoes that Andrew's prodigality of paring necessitated, was now ungraciously preparing a salad — an extra order for the visitor parson.

"Let 'em bogey till they bust!"

"But, Fanny, they're stealin', an' it's Sunday."

The child was tensely pallid.

"Sunday me eye an' Betty Martin!" retorted Fanny, blinking her eyes, and in tones harmonizing with her radish-scraping.

"W'at Betty Martin?" asked the chilled child, looking at both Fanny's eyes, and hoping for a more sympathetic guide and counsellor in historical Betty Martin.

"Any fool knows!" said equally puzzled Fanny; and at the moment Jim came hastily in with the day's wood, a duty ignored in the excitement of the night before. The sight of him recalled to Ursula her maimed doll.

"Jim," she said, her lips twitching tremulously, "my doll's leg fall off in the bed last night, an' naughty, wicked boys is stealin' an' — an' going to go bogeyin' on Sunday."

Sharp and not short was Fanny's lecture to Jim anent the shortage in her flannel length, and emphatic her disbelief in Jim's assertion that "ole Brooks" the draper had "took" him in. The price of the doll was the true explanation, and at the child's reference to it Jim agitatedly buried his head in the dipper, and, blind to the potatoes at the bottom, rapidly drained them, then went quickly out.

Disconcerted, Ursie went back to the veranda. Below the front of the house, in the hollow that the boundary fence separated from the Chinese gardens, numberless crickets "filed their saws" with impartial, unsectarian opposition to the again clanging bells. Jim had told her it was sure to rain when these earthhiding creatures "cricked". No church for her, then; and, as if in answer to their spiteful request, goose-coloured clouds began to gather in the west. However, across one cloud the end of a rainbow trailed fadingly. Ursula eyed it with a meaning born of the day. "A little bit of Mrs God's sash." But the grey soon covered it. The child's heart was leaden, for it might rain before church. Vague discontent with this holy home stirred her, and indefinitely she longed for some place where there was neither God to offend or devil to fear.

When Andrew joined her she was wiping her eyes with her gloves.

"Wot's up, Ursie?"

"Andree," she said, in reverent tones, "just now, up in the sky, I saw a little bit of Mrs God's sash, but she's gone now."

He looked down at her, as she thought, in disbelief, so she described it.

"That was a rainbow, Ursie; there's no Mrs God."

"Is she dead too, Andree, like my father?"

The boy looked at her wonderingly. It was her father's death that had brought her to this loveless home, but she had not spoken of it before. He led her to the end of the veranda, and pointed to the Sunday-decked folk, then she brightened instantly, putting on her gloves, in a fever to be off that moment.

However, they had not long to wait, for the widow was never late for church. She took a coldly critical survey of the orphan and her clothes — a replica, save for bonnet and gloves, of herself. And for all her Sabbath emotion, the heart of this child of inexperienced Bush years, noted enviously the dangling beads from the bonnet and the tight kid-gloves of her aunt.

The last bell was still clanging as they went in. Mr Civil, the local parson, was a listener to-day, and sat in the widow's pew, next to her. He rose to receive them, and Andrew engineered and followed Ursie to a seat near the end.

The moment the bell ceased a fair, thick-set man adorned the pulpit, sent a pair of calculating eyes all over the building, then gave out a hymn.

By the strenuous medium of Bella Watson's feet and fingers, the inharmonious harmonium's preliminary was a challenge to cracked bell and saw-filing crickets.

Andrew found the place, and Ursie, standing on the seat, felt a due sense of importance in holding half his hymn-book. If there was individuality in the time and tune of many of the brothers and sisters, none were too critical, church being no place for the critical.

The long prayer following the singing, despite its originality and brogue, was very trying to the kneeling, restless child.

More singing followed, and then came an opportunity of studying the preacher, as he, with suggestive unctuousness and double meaning, read a selection from the various Gospels of Christ's healing the blind, the sick, the lame — every miracle performed by the Saviour but that of raising the dead. There was a deep and double significance in the finishing passage, in which Jesus endows certain of His disciples with the power to likewise heal — a significance accentuated by the preacher's solemn, slow repetition of it as a text to his sermon.

According to a custom instituted by Mr Civil, the collection should precede the sermon, as many often made the length of his a pretext for leaving, and so dodging the plate. Anticipatory Andrew slipped his usual small coin into Ursie's palm that she might experience the blessedness of giving. Plate-bearers, Brothers Foreman and Weldon, conscious of the dignity of their high office, stiffened into willing readiness. But to-day this visiting brother parson, though duly apprised, ignored the rule in favour of one of his own. Vainly the true shepherd sought to guide the collectors by directing, impatient eyes; for he of the pulpit had been swift of action and had begun his sermon. Both Brothers thereupon relaxed into flabby ordinariness, till the unorthodoxy of the parson held even them. This preacher was rapidly becoming notorious for his compound of soul and body curing, with the emphasis on the body. He was ever most careful to explain that he had been studying for a physician when he received his call to go and labour in the Lord's vineyard. And if the pay for the soul services was generally in the smaller coin, there were whispers in his many and unduly-changed circuits, that his body ministrations were much more profitable. This circumstance quickly awoke virtuous resentment in the ranks of the many orthodox, and therefore impecunious, labourers. Complaining reports had been made to headquarters; but though remonstrances had been made, the parson, wherever he got the chance, continued to work his double cure. His sermons were mainly anecdotes of his experiences in this dual capacity, differing only from the advertised quack cures by suppressed signature and locality. Nothing more definite than, "I remember w'en I was on the diggings", or "I wuz sent for-r once to visit a supposed-to-be dying brother-r or sister-r that all the doctors had given up. Well, after-r riding day and night for-r forrty-eight hours I kem to the place." A graphic description would follow of the body and soul conditions of the patient, the ever-varying complaints breaking the monotony of the never-varying happy endings.

Accidents and diseases had no separate place in Ursie's mind. Her mother she could not remember; neither had she any fixed idea of her father's death. "He stayed in bed a lot of days, an' then Margaret says 'e died, an' then we come away an' left Boshy, an' stayed a long time till I came here." She found it impossible to localize, or indeed realize any of these graphic anecdotes, with their miraculous cures by the impassioned preacher. Suddenly she remembered poor old Tumbledown Jimmy, who could walk only a few yards and then fall down, and who was always hungry. Now, if he could be cured! Eagerly she wanted to tell Andrew all about it, but he gave a sidelong look at the aunt and grimaced Ursie into silence.

Her hat limited her view to the pulpit and its immediate surroundings. She sighed heavily and drew up her dangling feet, for even Andrew's hymn-book she was not allowed to play with, nor to take off her strange hat, and while nursing it give it closer examination.

She speculated uninterestedly as to the purpose of that little fence round the pulpit, till she suddenly saw the white-spread Communion-table, then swiftly took in the outline of the cloth-crowned "cruet-stand". Rather a small table for such a lot of people; but they, so near the front, would be certain to get some dinner. Her gratified heart shone in her eyes and flushed face, as, sidling up to Andrew, she whispered softly, "Wen's the dinner goin' to be, Andree?"

He took a hasty look at the other end of the pew.

"It's not dinner, Urse," he whispered. She would have climbed to her knees on the seat to be able to show him the convincing cruet but for his restraint. He explained, "It's not for us, Urse — on'y for big people."

She made doubly sure.

"Won't we get any?"

He shook his head.

She immediately divined the purpose of that yard round the little table: to keep poor hungry little children, who ate only a mouthful of breakfast, from getting anything to eat. She was on her knees with her arms round Andrew's neck before he could prevent her. Her eyes were tearfully agleam, as, audibly reckless, she sobbed:

"W'y don't all the people go home, Andree? Tell 'im not to talk to 'em any more."

Andrew got up to take out the child clinging to him, but the aunt placed a firm hand on her and drew her between the frowning parson and herself.

Subdued and magnetized into submission, Ursula sat turning her tearful eyes from one uncompromising face to the other; but their attention was soon diverted to another weeper.

The parson was recounting a most wonderful cure of a cancer that had eaten half the face, and the complete restoration of the affected part by "er bottle er medicine", the properties known only to the narrator. Old Granny Foreman's husband, long past the Biblical limit of three score and ten, had died lately of this disease. "'E could a bin saved! 'E were cut off in his prime!" sobbed Granny, her grief an eloquent testimony to the harmony of their half-century of wedlock and to the moving ability of the parson.

Fireman Foreman's loose-lipped mouth widened in a filial grin, dentally interesting. Grabbing his hat, he nudged his weeping and likewise preparing parent; but the reverend story-teller anticipated him.

"Sit still, brother-r and sister-r. You'll not distur-rb me. The tears must flow — the tears must flow. Jesus wept," he added brokenly, as a precedent for shrouding his own twinkling dry orbs.

Like other lawful emotions, licensed grief is generally short-lived. Beside, Granny fully expected and wanted the distinction of being led out. In the critical interval following she was resentfully silent. The wary waresman in the pulpit saw her, as she wiped her eyes, thrust in her consolatory peppermint, pass it from one cheek to the other, then glare at him.

Unbaulked, the alert showman instantly shifted scene and subject, and though these he varied often, the qualities of his brother in the Lord sitting directly under him had no place in the discourse, neither had church debt nor stipend fund. According to every known precedent, the text of a visiting parson should be the great virtue of the leader of the loaned flock, until, in modest self-deprecation, the recipient of these clerical posters would be forced to shake his bowed head divers times and oft.

It was beyond the local parson to remain passive while this spiritual cuckoo pulled to pieces this little nest of his victim's weary upbuilding. He passed his hand several times over his bald head, cleared his throat, intimating so his disapproval of the unorthodoxy of this sermon. But his palpable restlessness and disapproval had no effect upon the flush-faced orator. The majority were with him, for he knew his book of life, and was adroitly shifting the responsibility of their spiritual shortcomings and bodily ailments to the shoulders of their shepherd.

Suddenly the victim filled the accusatory pause with a violent cough. The preacher waited in sympathetic silence till his reverend sufferer ceased, then asked, with heavy emphasis, "But how can a poo-er-r mistaken mortal-l think of your-r immortal-l soul-l, when-n his-s own poor-r body is racked and tormented-d with disease?"

The widow turned her usually unemotional face to the cougher, and the concern on her countenance showed that the innuendo of the reverend alarmist had reached even her. But the organist's pretty eyes had forestalled her, and the glance she sent to the cougher said plainly: "You want my care and attention."

Dimly even the child knew. She sat near the object of attention, and upturned her wondering eyes to the sympathized one. He glared back at her; but as she had wasted no sympathy, she looked away unaffected, and clicked her heels to break the monotony. The aunt, now limiting her attention to the pew, laid a reproving hand on her. She sat motionless for, to her, a fearfully long time, with her feet extended stiffly, not daring to allow them to fall in relaxation.

The preacher was nearing the close, and intimating to those sick in body or mind that he might be consulted on both matters at the end of this service.

A stealthy glance before and to right and left revealed to Mr Civil that to sit tight was legible on the faces of many, who throughout had audibly demonstrated their faith in the cure of the orator by their "Praise God!" "Bless God!" The rightful shepherd's countenance grew a grey green, realizing that the concluding sentence of this spiritual physician's exhortation, "Ho! everyone that thirsteth, come ye to the waters, without money and without price", though only Scripturally figurative, would have a disastrous effect upon the collection surely now to follow.

The word money reminded Ursie of her possession, and she took a hasty peep at the coin in her palm, which did not escape the notice of Mr Civil.

But now, for the first time in Church history, the collection seemed to have no place in the programme, for the preacher introduced a closing innovation. Before sitting down and without mentioning that "The usual collection will now be taken up", he gave out the hymn. Both the Brother plate-bearers had been thrown out of routine by the postponement. Collector Brother Weldon's big feet stirred nervously as he looked behind for a cue from Brother Foreman; but he was no leader. It was an agonizing few moments for Mr Civil, and he spent them in locking and unlocking his fingers. However, the widow, clear-headed and practical, came to the rescue. She drew from her gloved palm her offering and extended it towards Brother Weldon, who with unclerical haste and noise took the office.

The little girl looked round at the Brothers working their way right and left upward, and very quickly she took in the fact that the object of these plates was for giving, not getting, and her hand closed over her coin determinedly. The plate came to their pew, and the parson, with his eyes turned upward, held it under her hat. The widow gave her fat mite, then passed it to Andrew, who made pretence of a donation. Eagerly Mr Civil again took the plate and again held it down for Ursie's church money. This time he looked at her and she at him, and her mouth tightened in sympathetic tension with her hand. He placed the plate between them on the seat, and seizing the child's hand, forced it open; then into the plate went her only hope and solace for a cruelly long and disappointing morning.

There was a momentary pause, filled with strenuous silence, as with wide, mutinous eyes she looked up at this leader of lambs, looking down at her with the insolence of victory. She raised her face till her hat fell back, then venomously thrust her tongue at him, till her sharp lower teeth sawed the under sinews. Given time she would not have failed to reproduce accurately the "Long-nose-bacon-that-fat" antics of those naughty boys that very morning, albeit it was her first lesson. Savagely the parson knocked up her chin, and with a snarl akin to Jim's dog she fastened her teeth in his coat-sleeve. But Andrew managed to distract his aunt, with his schoolboy trick of nose-bleeding at critical exam. moments, and with handkerchief to nose, passed the furious child. This immediately bespoke her sympathy. Imagining him to have been the victim of their aunt, she flashed her defiant face on her, and taking his free hand, unopposed went out.

"Andree, Andree, wot'll you do to 'im soon as you grow up a big man?"

In silence the boy looked into her eyes blazing at him. He hated tears, but, for choice, he would have seen her weeping rather than this passionate distortion.

"Tell me wot'll you do to 'im?"

He went through a list of injuries.

"An' will that kill 'im up dead like anything?" savagely asked the bloodthirsty maiden.

He thought there could be no doubt. She laughed exultingly, and the boy felt cold and strangely troubled.

"Won't that serve 'im right?" she gloated; "won't it, Andree?"

"Let's run home," said he, to lessen the tension of her fingers round his, and to get away from an indefinite sensation.

"Wot d'yer say yer done?" asked incredulous Fanny.

"Poked me tongue out at nasty ole Civil. Didn't I, Andree?"

He confirmed her without enthusiasm, remembering the reckoning.

Fanny showed slow approval.

"Good on yer!" she said admiringly.

Even Jim nodded satisfaction, and so encouraged, the child gave an illustration.

"An' look w'ere 'e made me bite meself," showing her bitten tongue.

"Knocked yer chin, chin-chopper?" inquired Fanny.

The new expression appealed to Ursie, and she nodded "Chin-chopper".

"Ther crool crawlin' cur," said Jim, "might tackle someun 'is own size."

"I'll tell 'im wot I think ov 'im," promised Fanny, who had never been known to even answer back.

"Get her something to eat," said the boy.

"I will, for if she done a thing like that she deserves a real good crockroach," said Fanny, groping in the sugar-basin for a lump.

Ursula had barely finished when the click of the gate foretold the coming of the judgment.

"Ursula!" called her aunt.

Led by Andrew, she went to her trial.

The parson cited his case: Making a noise in God's house; keeping back His fee; and, yet more heinous, her tongue thrust out at him. But the child, held by the unusual hue of the widow's stolid face, did not even look at him.

"Did you poke out your tongue at Mr Civil?" demanded the purple-faced woman.

The child nodded her head.

"Answer me, miss!" stormed her aunt.

She replied, vigorously nodding her head, influenced by the widow's vibrating with anger.

"You wicked, bold girl! You — you———"

"Limb of the devil," added the minister.

In the momentous pause the child drew the back of her hand across her forehead, puzzled and perplexed over the different views held by the two women of this house. Remembering Fanny's indignation over her bitten tongue, she opened her mouth and again thrust it out.

"An' 'e made me go chin-chopper to I bite me tongue to it bleeded," she defended.

"Hold your tongue!" said the widow. "I don't know what to do with her," she said feebly, almost appealingly, to the parson.

"Punish her severely, then shut her up fasting for the day," said the shepherd. "Flog her severely," he repeated, noting the effect on Andrew.

"She won't be flogged. No one will touch her," vowed Andrew, moving nearer Ursula.

The widow's surprised eyes had gone mechanically to his face as he spoke.

"Don't you interfere," snarled the parson. "What's it got to do with you?"

For answer the boy's bravely challenging eyes met his blinking vindictively.

"I think to shut her up for the afternoon alone, and not allow her to go to Sunday-school, will punish her," the widow said to him.

"Fasting," stipulated he eagerly.

She hesitated, for to her fasting would have been the heavier penalty; but her adviser pressed the point.

"Fasting," she pronounced, cowardly looking away from the child, whose eyes had not wandered from her face.

The gratified shepherd sat back, made a Gothic arch of his long fingers, and over it looked for distress from the sentenced sinner, yet unmoved, still watching her aunt.

"No dinner; to be shut up all afternoon by yourself; no Sunday-school, and no nice tickets," he added. But she would not look at him; nor did her face show any emotion. She had enough service for one day. Andrew would hit anyone who hit her; he also would get her doll for her, so she would not be alone; and thanks to Fanny, she did not want any dinner.

"Will I go now, aunt?"

"At once — go at once," said the widow sternly, for the parson was now appeased.

"Lock her in, Andrew," she commanded.

"And bring the key to your aunt, young impudence," ordered the parson, shaking the right side of the severed Gothic arch at him.

Her prison was the enclosed end of the veranda, and the boy shut and locked the glass door on the child, who, according to his whispered orders, stood in the centre, watching the skylight above the door till the dinner-bell rang. But the watchful parson, intent on the carrying out of the solitary confinement clause of the sentence, had shadowed the surly Andrew, and made him repeat his Sunday-school lessons while dinner awaited the much-overdue visiting parson, evidently doing a brisk business. Consequently it was a weary wait for the impatient doll-mother, and at last it was hastily-instructed Jim's towering length that darkened the window; and his long arm dropped the promised doll through the skylight into the waiting hands, then vanished.

The troubled time of the true shepherd of this wayward flock did not end with the morning, though he was now in his stronghold, fortified by an unspoken engagement with its owner. Even here this visiting brother in the Lord was tactful and steady to his purpose of disposing of his stock of medicine, charging, he said, only for the best drugs, bottles, and corks. Such moderate terms appealed to the widow, who, woman-like, loved a bargain. If she could get a few bottles of medicine that would insure her safety in eating and drinking as much of what she liked at every meal without fear of gouty rheumatism, she would, despite the sniffing, snarling irritability of her customary shepherd. Ordering a good supply, she then demonstrated both frailty and belief by partaking with her comfortable adviser of an equal share of the second quart of porter. In righteous wrath, Mr Civil left the dinner table to walk off his bottled anger on the front veranda.

Down in the swamps of Widgiewa—
    By-by, baby.
(Awesomely) All the big, bitey, black snakes are—
    By-by, baby.
(Reassuringly) But our Tom'll eat off all their heads,
(Revengefully) An' ole Civil's too;
    An' Andree 'll—

The parson had sneaked to the door and looked through. On a box, with her back to the light, sat the swaying singer, with her doll held tightly to her breast. But though he made no sound and stood back to trap her into a finish of Andrew's onslaught, her quick senses had felt his shadow, and she turned quickly round.

She quite understood his vehement finger movements were for her to drop her doll; instead, her hold tightened.

He thrust his jaundiced face round the door of the dining-room.

"Bring the key and follow me. Only you, please," with solemn portent he commanded the well-fed widow, guiding her to the prison.

"This is her repentance," he said, "playing with idols and singing songs on the Sabbath."

"Where did you get that from?" pointing to the doll, asked the surprised aunt.

"Out of church money. She, like another not very far away, would rob the church," supplied the clergyman, from his many injustices anxious to kick the nearest dog. "Take it from her; pull it from her; make her put it down!" he gasped.

The childless woman, who had been a doll-less child, took this one from the now unresisting girl. Under the widow's loose hold its sole garment, a towel swaddling it, fell off.

"A nice play-toy that for a respectable girl," said the shocked parson, his lean fingers indicating the naked, maimed doll and its unabashed mother.

"You'll have trouble with her, mark me," he prophesied; and as he went out his hostess followed and closed the door.

The child stood, when they left her, unnaturally still, her mind skirting mature ideas, unwieldy from her immaturity. Footsteps along the veranda past her prison and the click of the little gate at the side brought her mind to externals. They were going to Sunday-school — Andrew too, and she shut up here.

A hornet had entered with the other despoilers of her peace and pleasure, and, as though it recognized it had been trapped, it buzzed distressfully from skylight to window. She looked round, and with sense of comradeship saw it bunting and bruising itself in futile efforts for freedom. Much as she had feared it that morning, she was fearless now. Evidently the hornet had regarded her as some inanimate object, and her movements in watching it dispelled this illusion, and brought it in a threatening circle over her head. She welcomed without emotion the hostility of this foe, for with its dreadful sting it was one worthy of her mood. Her lower lip relaxed, and the sense of coming battle radiated grimly from her set face, as she picked up the towel that a little before she had draped with loving maternity round her doll.

"Shut up!" she commanded, twirling the towel preparatory to making a bring-down onslaught. Majestically showing the advantage of wings, it rose above her reach, and from, for her, an unattainable height it seemed to buzz a taunt at her diminutiveness. Its noise attracted its outside mate, and the child gloried in its buzzing butts to get in.

"Suizz, suizz!" she hissed in mad mockery at both.

Making a ball of the towel, she flung with an effect that increased with practice, scornfully rejoicing at the cowardly discomfiture of a drowsing blowfly that one of her towel flights had disturbed. Its clumsy attempts to escape seemed to inculcate the same desire in many of the lesser species, which swarmed round it satellite-wise. She hailed any opposing force warmly, but concentrated her fight for the time on the again descending hornet, suffering it to come quite near, then making a vicious, well-calculated slap at it with the towel that sent it partially stunned to the side of the room. For swift victory she could have ended the conflict then, but she allowed it to revive and fly for a breathing spell to the dried bush, acting as a fly refuge, in the centre, rousing it to another attack, destined from its monotony to end the battle. Pinioning its extremities with the edge of the towel, she crushed off its offensive and defensive weapons with a splinter from the wall. The blowfly was her next victim, but an unexciting one. Pulling off its legs, she placed it with the hornet, and both lay side by side unprotestingly.

She brushed back her hair and went from door to window. The insistent "Kirr, kirr, kirr" of the crickets seemed to be the only sound of life outside, and inside the little flies had settled again, so the room was quiet. Both hornet and fly she had considered completely disabled, but when she turned to them they had disappeared. The hornet had flown to a dark corner, but the fly had unwisely soared again to the light. She captured both, and, sitting down, pulled off their wings.

"Ah! what do yer do that for, Ursie?" was a protest from Andrew, looking through the skylight.

"Cos now I know ware they are" — defiantly. "I'll make them stay."

"Poor brutes!"

"I'll kill 'em all up!" she snapped savagely at him.

There was silence till the boy asked:

"Where's your doll, Ursie?"

She softened in a moment.

"Oh, Andree, that nasty ole Civil made her take it from me."

"Wonder where she put it."

She shook her head, intimating that she also wondered.

"Where are they?"

"Still in Sunday-school. My nose bled again an' I had to come out. Look out, Urse, an' I'll jump down."

He opened the skylight, and swinging with one hand on the ledge, dropped into the room.

Hornet and fly, alive, but feigning death, were still in her lap. He took them to the fireplace and killed them outright with his boot.

"Put them out of their misery," he explained.

Ursie's eyes widened and mouth tightened, but she was silent.

Later, when the boy's brow was moist with his earnest efforts to make a satisfactory doll out of a bottle by filing a groove round its neck, she, from a sense of her own shortcomings, began to talk of the failings of others.

With a preliminary sobbing sigh, peculiar to childhood, she began, her hand on his knee:

"Andree, you know wot that Gus Stein done?"

"No, Urse."

"Pelted a stone at a poor cat, and hitted it" (sigh) "like anything."

Andrew expressed a contempt for boys generally, albeit it was he who, just before the advent of this little girl, had been to a boys' party.

"Wuz they any girls there?" asked Jim, an avowed admirer of the sex.

"Girls? girls, Jim, at a respectable place like that?"

"An' Mina, too, know wot she done, too, as well?" for Ursie did not choose to be the sole representative of a cruel sex. "She took Mary Wood's poor little doll and swinged it roun' an' roun' be the legs till the sawdust all come out. Andree" — with a quavering sigh — "that was worse en — en — en doin' that to them," jerking her head, but not looking at the murdered insects in the fireplace.

Andrew agreed, and contrition was the outcome.

"Did it hurt 'em, Andree?"

"Same as t' pull off your arms and legs, Ursie."

She put her arms tightly round his neck.

"Andree," she said brokenly, "I won't do it any, any more," her shaking head burrowing deeply into his neck in emphasis.

Shortly after there was the signalling click of the gate, and the boy was up and out of the skylight instantly. The aunt had both clergymen with her.

These were the days of the sovereignty of Moody and Sankey's hymns, and presently the vigorous voice of the stranger parson sounded meaningly in "Scatter Seeds of Kindness".

Mr Civil was acrimoniously disputing the orthodoxy of this visiting brother's intention to sing this from the pulpit at the close of the evening sermon. In all matters of theological discussion the widow took no part; being a worker, she had little to say, but she listened to both impartially.

Then there was a call for Andrew, and the boy, self-briefed to obtain Ursie's release, was prompt to appear. He was to go to the visitors' quarters for Moody and Sankey's hymn-book. He first made his request in an undertone to his aunt, and it was granted in the same key.

While he, fleet of foot, sped on his message, the child wandered in search of Fanny or Jim. The kitchen looked coldly deserted, for on the Sabbath afternoon Fanny, according to immemorial custom, was out walking with lady friends of like occupation, whose relaxation on their Sundays was a weekly synopsis of the shortcomings of the various "shes" they served.

Ursula found Jim, fully dressed in his Sunday best, sound asleep in his little room, near the brick oven, at the back of the kitchen. His red necktie had slipped above his collar, and its knot, twisted under the left ear, looked like a halter that had crimsoned in doing its work. Jim's sleep contortions had left a wide skin margin between the bottom of his trousers and the top of his elastic-sided boots, so the little girl credited his tightly fitting Sunday boots with the feat of having swallowed his socks, after the manner of her own shoes. She left him and wandered disconsolately about.

Frogs from the river now seemed to croak bass to the

crickets' shrill orchestra, but otherwise there was a stagnant atmospheric stillness that boded well for the sky's leaden greyness.

But as though they anticipated nothing from the overcast heavens, the Chinese gardeners still laboured. Ursie supposed the boys on their return from bathing, and she in church, had stripped the peach-tree, and hidden by the gully, she went down to see. A limb covered with unripe fruit bridged the gully over her head. Digging her hands and feet into the crumbling bank, then gripping the branch, she hung on to it with one hand, and stripped off a shower of peaches with the other. From the rosy side of most she took a bite; then, from a sense of mischievous revenge, she repeated the stripping, till the limb snapped in her struggles to reach those on the highest parts. She came down under it, and then the shock begot by her fall increased to terror at the sight of a Chinaman on the bank of the gully jabbering threats at her, and brandishing a pitchfork. The fruit overhung their ground, and mock them at a safe distance the boys might, yet not one of them had dared openly to touch this limb.

"Oh, mister man, don't kill me!" she pleaded. But he thrust at her with the pitchfork, then made as if to jump down. The gully tunnelled through to the river, and she ran in frenzy that way till she came to the mill; creeping behind a pile of firewood, she crouched, almost paralyzed, draining in her terror the cruellest of Nature's cruelties — unreasoning child fear.

The river zigzagged through the little town, and from where she lay presently she heard a woman's voice raised in weird lament.

Rising cautiously, she stood on a billet of wood, and saw old Granny McGrath running along the river-bank. Her feet and head were bare, and her grey hair was straggling in unusual disorder.

"Arroo, 'Enery! arroo, arroo!" she shrieked piercingly as she flung up her arms to the leaden sky, then breathlessly beat her breasts, and the weird cry she seemed to strike from them awed the child indefinitely. Two other old women, with the sympathetic bond of race and creed were with her, and when their efforts to comfort her failed, they joined her in their national cry:

"Arroo, 'Enery! arroo, arroo!"

The child, for protection, ran to them.

"Poor granny!" she said, catching her skirt.

"W'at's the matter, poor granny?"

"Oh, me bye — me darlint drownded! 'Enery, arroo, arroo!" beating her breasts. "Oh, Mary, Mother o' Christ, pity me!"

A tongue of forked lightning illumined the sullen heavens, and after a swift interval the rumbling thunder followed. As they turned along a bend of the river, men, two abreast, parted from those in the rear by a burden borne on their shoulders, came in view. At the sight of them the women's cries increased.

The men stopped, and, placing the door on the ground, allowed old Granny to take into her arms the dead body of her grandson, Henry, the light and love of her lonely life. His eyes were wide open, and the tensely-strung child quickly recognized him as one of the boys foremost in trespassing on God and man that morning, trespasses all of which she had committed, but in this boy's case so quickly followed by a righteous revenge. As if to assert omnipotent omnipresence, a flash of lightning splintered a tree on the flat near, and the noise of the thunder terrified the child into immediate flight; but this time she ran homeward.

White and recklessly wild with fear, she ran into the parlour, and with starting eyes looked from the surprise of her aunt to Mr Civil's unrelenting countenance.

"Oh, aunt, w'at's that?" she gasped, for the vibration of a sudden clap of thunder had rattled the crystal pendants of the lustre vases decorating the mantelpiece.

"The voice of an angry God," said God's servant, extending his forefinger at her, apparently as an index to his Master.

She was not safe here; frantically she rushed out.

"Andree, Andree!" she screamed, catching sight of the boy, who had been seeking her. "Andree, Andree, plant me, plant me! God's after me; He's after me! Plant me in the brick oven!"

He ran with her in his arms, and to comfort her let her creep into this refuge; then putting up the lid, stood there till the violence of the deluging rain silenced heaven's flash and fire.

4

URSULA'S church experience tempered her expectation of pleasure from school. The aristocratic master and mistress had failed in every other exploit in life, and sad and sour to the childless mistress must have been the elementary teaching of these often ill-kept little ones. Favouritism was so well understood that it provoked no protest: no matter how flagrant the offence, an excuse from the favourites cancelled the penalty, as even the most natural request had to be preferred through them. These were selected ever from the girl ranks of the prosperous, and therefore better dressed. Personal qualities or ability were with the mistress unconsidered ciphers, unless accompanied by the numerals of outward prosperity.

Ursie, weird of face, her diminutive body dressed in misfitting clothes, was from the onset a target. An unconscious smile would be styled an insolent grimace, and as such chastised; the following soberly ordered countenance was a sullenness equally punished, by inexhaustible quince sticks, as an example to the school. Justice or injustice grew into the impotent routine of daily life. But, despite the teacher's inefficiency, omnipotent knowledge sent illuminating shafts through the child's active brain, and rapidly she ripened into a reader. On Saturday nights Andrew usually read to the kitchen audience the "Multum-in-parvo" column of the local paper, which but for this column might have been called *Cuttings and Clippings*; but instead it blossomed once a week as the *World-wide Advertiser*. Trained so by the vivid personal atmosphere of the "Multum-in-parvo" column, even the most elementary school fiction took on locality and individuality for Ursula.

"Can it be Pat or Sam?" laboriously spelled by Mary Woods from the primary reading tablet on the wall, referred to the difficulty the short-sighted master felt in knowing which was which of Pat or Sam Toohey. Though when Mina Stein — who had been in the same class for months — glibly droned to an apathetic audience, "Ned-'as-broke-'es-arm", Ursula was puzzled. The only

Ned she knew sat near her industriously designing and drawing a horse freaked generally and with figure fours for hoofs.

Gradually soaring above the limit of the weekly paper, she examined the few books on the parlour table. From familiarity, *Pilgrim's Progress* she disdained to inspect; Fanny, who could not read a word of it, had been given one for a Sunday-school prize. The *History of Jerusalem*, though in red covers, was heavy and unenticing. The volumes of the Old and New Testaments, standing one on the other in the centre, were uninteresting because of their titles. Shakespeare, coverless and shabby, though not from much reading, had pictures certainly, but one illustrating Lear as a man convinced her that it was not worth perusal. Leah was a girl's name, for didn't she know Leah Cohen? Such a glaring mistake was the books' condemnation, and she tore out the leaf picture to show it to Leah. The list closed with hymn-books and another little book — *Maria Monk*. Maria! her aunt's name was Maria, and even the preface of this wieldy little book owned that Maria was a girl. Lying on the sloping river-bank, hidden from the household, she spent hours daily absorbing the, to her, absorbable in Maria's ugly story. Summing up her facts and fancies finally, she was convinced that her aunt had been poor Maria, and earnestly she hoped that those in search of her very visible and incautious aunt would never succeed in kidnapping her. Lest they should, from that moment she constituted herself her aunt's body-guard, and she went home instantly to duty. She found her in the dining-room with Ann Foster, the little dressmaker, who was endeavouring to scissors through the right side of her underlip with her teeth as proof that the compiling of a list of requisites was no tax to her. Ursula noticed that her aunt was standing when she might have sat, and that her eyes were wider open than usual; also she breathed quickly and kept picking up and laying down various of Ann's craft on the table.

The child's face grew grave, but with wonderful patience she stood watching the widow.

"You're to go a message," said her aunt, embarrassed by

her steadfast scrutiny, and handing her the list.

It was the first time she had been so trusted, and she felt the importance as she walked swiftly with the commission held securely, to the little store styled the "Commercial Exchange". She stood undecided in the middle of the entrance, then advanced and handed the order to the grocer, and he gave it his amused attention, then took it across to the drapery side. After steady perusal the draper remarked to the grocer:

"Things are rather hot for this time of the weather."

"Bit sultry," agreed the grocer.

"Pleasant morn' this," the draper remarked to the girl to lessen her keen attention.

"Think it will be wet if it rains?" asked the grocer.

She was silent; intuition told her they were mocking because she was little, and their frivolity flattened her sense of importance. Her eyes darkened, but, controlling the will of her lips to tremble, she said:

"I'll tell me aunt you won't give me the message that I came for. Give me that message," she excitedly demanded, reaching up her tiny hand to grasp the paper.

"Sit down, miss," said the grocer, hastily bringing forward a chair, "an' in two shakes ov a lamb's tail you'll be served. Presto, pass quick an' begone, sir!" he commanded the draper, who so adjured double vaulted the counters hastily, in his flight striking the grocer across the back with the feather duster.

Again he consulted the list, and producing a box of silk reels, remarked:

"Nice-lookin' young lady that you've got in ther kitchen over there, miss."

The child knew he was talking to lessen his previous offence, so she only glared at him till his next remark.

"Fine head of hair she must have, to be sure."

"Who?" she inquired, wonder costing her her silent dignity, for Fanny was nearly bald.

"Miss Fanny," supplied the grocer. "It's me she comes to see, isn't it, miss — not him?"

"Yuh!" snorted the draper; "you're no Weserleyan. Was it your book she looked on with the other night? She's a fine scholar, miss, isn't she? Why, she can read my book upside down. Did she write this?" tapping the order.

"No," said Ursie shortly.

"No? Not Mrs Irvine?"

Ursie shook her head.

"Not aunt."

"You did then," he guessed, bending his head condescendingly down.

She hesitated; then, not having seen the writing, truth conquered.

"Andrew?" was another wrong venture.

"Not me, an' not Andrew, an' not Jim wrote it, so there now," she said, triumphant in his assumed curious distress, till he, being no artist, overdid it by pretending to faint with bewilderment.

"Give me my message."

"Don't be trifled with, miss," advised the grocer.

"Go on you," ordered the draper, pointing to another customer. "Give that young gentleman his ha'porth of specked fruit, an' not too many water-melons."

Not one melon could the little girl see, though she stood on her chair the better to inspect. In angry silence she waited till the parcel and order was handed to her, then she, much disconcerted, went home.

But Fanny's interest in her description of the contents of her first commission was most soothing and gratifying.

"Notice everything was w'ite?" Fanny remarked, winking vigorously.

Ursula promptly assented that it had struck her; then waited for further enlightenment, which, however, came that Saturday night from the "Multum-in-parvo" columns, which Andrew, as usual, read.

" 'They say a certain buxom widow will not be so much longer.' " Without pause or comment, Andrew united it to its suggestive follower: " 'They say a certain lean shepherd is about to take unto himself a long-haired mate.' "

Fanny instantly called a halt.

"I know who they mean; see it you?" she asked Jim exultingly.

"See w'at?"

"Certainly not — catch you see anythin' you can't eat."

"Well, I'd better eat you, then," with cannibalistic gallantry offered Jim.

"Can't you see it," turning to Andrew, "and it stickin' out a foot?"

"I can see that you are a fool." He was suddenly violently angry.

Fanny looked at Ursula.

"Of course you're too young and senserless to see it, though you done the shoppin' for it this mornin'."

Ursula flared into precocity under her scorn.

"I'm not young, and I can see it," she declared.

"I dessay you ken," agreed Fanny. "The babe unborn could see it; a suckin' dove could. I see it meself from the very first jump."

"So did I too, as well too," declared the child, her face crimsoning in her efforts to maintain her perspicuity.

"That'll do fer another lie. You wuzn't 'ere et first," grunted Fanny.

"I was. Wasn't I, Andree?"

"Wuz she 'ere w'en Mr Civil first come after yer aunt?" appealed Fanny, enlightening Jim.

Andrew crushed the paper noisily, his face white with disgust and anger.

"Fanny shut up! Go to bed, Ursie," he said curtly — a curtness that for once the child, anxious to escape from her bewildering surroundings, did not resent.

The *World-wide Advertiser*'s bald statements were soon verified, but the installation of Mr Civil as a member of the family made no great change. One night, soon as Andrew had gone out, Jim hinted to Fanny that he and some others were going to tinkettle some pair whose identity puzzled Ursula. When next morning she said her aunt did not want two cups and saucers on her breakfast tray, Fanny turned to Andrew with a slow grin.

"Remember 'er gamminin' she knew all along."

"One good thing, you'll soon get your walking ticket," said he, in a white heat.

He pointedly avoided his aunt for days, and when Ursie, who watched both, would have told him what she saw,

"Don't, don't, Ursie!" he pleaded so earnestly that she ceased, and, touched by some subtlety, she refrained from talking about them, even to Fanny.

But *Maria Monk* lay neglected on Fanny's bedroom table, for "Ole Civil" was aunt's guard now, and Ursie regretted her violent sympathy. And the parson, true to the shepherding instincts, soon began to extend his vigilance to every member of his domestic fold. It seemed to Ursie that his mission was to either catch her bootlaces untied or a not untiable knot in them. She, Fanny, Jim, all but Andrew, submitted and bent under the yoke of his economical reform. Even his wife — tuned to obedience — ate her cold dinner on Sunday without porter.

"It is not seemly for Andrew and Ursula to be continuously together."

"Why?" challenged the boy, in tones that surprised Ursie and startled her aunt.

"Nor for James to be in the kitchen with Fanny," piped the parson, ignoring Andrew.

"Hur! You to preach propriety," came like a blast from the boy's throat, and defiant glints of fire sparkled from his clear eyes flashing scornfully on the parson's shifty orbs.

Ursie observed, too, that now Andrew was taller than this guardian of morality. Yes, how tall and strong Andrew had suddenly grown! She felt a sense of security when she looked at him as he, in open disgust, stood towering over the perturbed ex-parson. Then a strange thought troubled her: was Andrew growing away from her? for she assuredly was very little.

That afternoon, when, with Mina Stein, they were coming from school through Stein's paddock, she stood on a log to gauge their heights, but even tiptoeing did not equalize Andrew and her. She lay on the grass, vaguely troubled, for when Mina stood on the log to measure, her head was level with Andrew's.

"Sit down! get off!" said Ursula, suddenly storm-swept.

Mina laughed, and in pretence of falling, put her fat arms round Andrew's neck. But her watching mother called her harshly, and in wonder Ursie got up.

"Urzie, oh, you there, id's allrighd," said Mrs Stein, "but I want Mina to stdir the pig's bloodt."

"We are goin' to kill our pig, and she wants me to stir the blood for the black puddin's. Come and see," invited Mina.

"I can't go, and don't you — Ursie, you'd better not," advised Andrew.

"I will. I want to," and in her perversity she went.

Mr Stein's foot, pressed into the pig's flank, was levering the last blood and breath through its gashed throat into a dish held under it by Mrs Stein. Gus was attending to the boiler of scalding water.

"Run, gedt a spoon, Mina," said her mother.

As she returned with it, "Take this", handing the dish, "andt mindt you dondt let it thicken, lazypones."

The pig to be scalded had to be raised to the trestles, and Ursula was terrified that it might not be dead.

"Come, Mina!" all called.

"You stir while I go," said Mina, handing Ursie the spoon. Involuntarily Ursie drew back.

"I couldn't," she said, with white lips.

Mina let the spoon fall into the dish and ran to help.

When she returned she dived for the disappeared spoon, and went on with her work, alternating the movement from right hand to left, taking the same occasion to slip a lolly into her mouth from her apron pocket.

In sullent discontent Ursie stood, for why should Mina be taller and stronger than she? Her brown eyes darkened and her bloodless lips, though trembling, wealed into a determined line.

"Now I'll stir," she offered.

"Sit here, then, an' min' always ter keep it goin' the one way. See, this way."

"I see," said Ursula, and looking away, took the spoon.

Round and round it went, and when it clicked against the tin dish Ursie felt an electric shock. Her brows, eyelashes, and eyes showed definitely hard on her colourless face. Her nostrils, filled with the steaming odour, dilated ominously.

Soon her movements became spasmodic, and a few splashes stood out like crimson beauty spots on her bleached face. Still round, though slower, went the spoon. Suddenly it dropped, but her hand stirred space, till blindly lurching forward, with an inward heave, she plunged both hands into the warm blood. Partially conscious, she knew someone laid her on her back, and she, a willing sacrifice, turned, so that, like the pig, the blood might be pumped thoroughly from her side. Quite reasonably, she considered the cold water thrown over her useless for scalding her. Ah, but someone was raising her, so they were going to lay her on the trestles, and she not dead. She opened her eyes, took a deep breath, then limply and contritely placed both arms round Andrew's neck.

5

In the autumn, that melancholy avenue to the dreaded winter, the subtle shadow of the infinite enthralled this Bush-girl; for the South was in her blood, and she loved the sun, and sighed regretfully as daily it sank earlier to lighten God's fireside. Bravely she did battle against the deciduous fate of her fuchsia, sheltering it in a warm corner where no wind could come. But inexorably the season demanded its toll, till the plant was leafless and bare, then she, with an inward shiver, laid it aside for its frozen, sapless sleep.

In solitary mood she would wander to the gloomy hills. At this season the dismantling wind, in its greedy intent to disrobe the Bush, seemed to have designs even on the impregnable evergreens. She would watch this bluff, invisible shepherd winnow a variegated leaf flock, garner it assiduously, then drive it on before, whither she in sympathy would almost as speedily follow, only to see it, by this capricious captor, cruelly scattered.

Ah, but she knew the wind's master — those hill-set rocks. Let it blow and beat against them as it might, there they stood, unaffected, unafraid. But how she feared them! One, "The Flat Rock", lay like a vault, and under it, buried in its sudden fall, were said to be a mob of blacks. Suppose they were not killed, and were merely hiding, waiting to catch some unprotected one, preferably a little girl. With ears straining and starting eyes she would hover near it. Her fear peopled and animated even the steep upright rocks, and from their pinnacles and turrets and towers, faces with shaggy brows, hiding malignant eyes, looked down frowningly at hers, turned in magnetic awe up to them. At such times a falling leaf (for the wind in league now was still) meant a lurking human danger to her. A bird's sudden flight signified such discovery, its silence being akin to hers, for since the Sunday of the storm she had met all dangers silently. Even the waving grass betokened the stealthy steal of a snake. Yet often, very often, she braved them — all but one — the noiseless creeping of the cold shadows of winter's sunset: never must that lifeless shroud fall on her. Seeing her fleeing wildly from it, her face, white with fear, turned over her shoulder, watching the pursuing shadow. One galloped swiftly after her, calling reassuringly. She saw and heard, but, undeterred, she fled the faster, as though from double danger in double fear.

"God! to see her run, and from nothing that I could see," he said.

These wintry nights, if she turned from the fire and the beguilement of Jim's songs, to shudderingly look outside at the frosty moonlit world, Andrew's prediction that their waiting pints of water would be all ice in the morning was often a little consolation. But there were other nights, wild and stormy, when the moon had gone to another town and every star was dark side down, and when the wind, while she slept, had left the she-oaks by the river to moan forebodingly round the house. Waking, she would for comfort light her candle; but it was only a feeble flame, wind-driven in the blustering darkness. Nor could covering her head keep out the sound of the humanly howling tempest. Andrew she wanted, and he, though uncalled, almost as often came, lessening by his presence her fear of the outer violence, and comforting her with the assurance that the deluging rain meant an earlier spring, which prematurely she watched for.

"Spring'll soon be 'ere now, Ursie," one day said Jim, after the consolatory manner of Andrew. "I see a cat-an'-dorg flower upon the 'ills to-day."

"Where? What hill, Jim?" she demanded eagerly.

He gave a comprehensive sweep that took in the world's circle. But she, of great faith, sought earnestly, and none were more surprised when he, when, after many days' search, she returned with a precocious specimen of those tiny orchids. Joyfully, yet tenderly, she had gathered this solitary harbinger of spring, well knowing that the cold hillside would in a few weeks be carpeted with them.

With the spring she had brighter moods that carried her to the side of some flower-flecked slope. Among the blossoms she would lie content but for vying with them for the honey kiss of the transitory butterfly, busy garnering the wild-flower seeds for God. Then the distant rock-garrisoned hills became castles — homes for angels. From their breath, the clouds, she peopled the sky — for to hold her there must be a human strain. The bluebell's mission was to summon the flower folk to church; gently swaying it, she would assemble her perfumed flock, and in whispers soft as the breezes tell them of duty Divine. So, imbued and resolute for righteousness, she would go homeward.

One afternoon passing Granny Foreman's cottage, she stopped to watch her thriftily gathering seed from balsam, stock and four-o'clock.

"The butterflies gather the wild-flower seeds for God, Granny."

"'Deed they doesn't. They fills their bellies wi' ther 'oney," bleated Granny blastingly.

Partially disillusioned, Ursula stood regarding the prosaic old woman thoughtfully till the intermittent blare of Ashton's circus rumbling down the hilly roads caught her ear. She ran and joined the mob who had turned out to honour its coming. The tinkling cymbal and sounding brass of its itinerant band stirred her strangely. Heedless of everything, she followed with the barefooted, bareheaded children of the street, till it disappeared into the capacious back-yard of "Pat the Jew's" livery stable.

"Wait," said Nellie Lewis, the shoemaker's big-mouthed daughter, points of light blinking from her porcine eyes — "wait and yous 'll all see 'em pitchin' their tent over on the flat."

Obediently Ursie waited, and a gratified thrill widened her eyes and warmed her heart when, among the great actors about to pitch the tent, she recognized Jim. An exalted flush tingled over her body as he, no way puffed up by his artistic employment, recognized and beckoned her with one long, dirty finger to come within whispering distance.

"See Fanny, Ursie, an' tell 'er ter come an' 'ang roun' about 'ere ter-night, an' I'll git 'er in."

"Me too, Jim?"

"Yerz," promised he.

Never would the girl forget that night, with its tinselled and spangled glories. She had never danced a step in her life, but that experienced girl capering with circus grace in the

Highland fling would, she knew, be as nothing to her given such inspiriting music. Were she but the daring equestrienne jumping through the flaming hoops, little it would matter to her if her gauzy skirts did catch. Death before the wonder-held eyes of such a throng would be painlessly sweet. She had been astride old Cushla led by Jim, and a mild trot had been an ideal; but she felt that the maddest freaks of those circling horses could not unseat her now, if the band played while she dared. She sighed heavily, for, alas! her wonderful potentialities were known only to herself. Lucky, lucky Kate Ashton to enjoy this triumph, and she so big and tall, yet, as the bill-posters said, only seven. But, of course, living always with such clever people, how could she help being big and clever for seven? Never for a moment could she be sad, with the clown continually saying such funny things or cutting such curious capers.

Her mind tragically focused the cruel contrast between the morrow Sabbath's programme for the bespangled circus girl and herself. She, seated between her aunt and Mr Civil (now retired from the ministry on a pension), listening to the wind (for it was autumn) howling vengefully round the porch; while this envied, bedight girl eating her manifold chocolate gifts, would merrily go forth to further triumphs, laughing at the clown, so philosophically funny, despite the cruel ringmaster's whip cuts. Ah, to be of them! Tears shrouded her sleepless eyes, and her introspection made her oblivious to the fact that the circus arena was emptying of the actors. Jim, seeing and misinterpreting her evident sorrow, remarked that, "The old cirkis company is a roguin' lot ov robbers; it's on'y a little after ten, an' 'ere's the b—s pullin' down the tent about our ears, cuttin' it short because ov its bein' on'y their one night."

It was even so, for with indecent haste and indifference to the vehemently disapproving, waiting audience, the circus men began to untie the ropes, and amongst the last Ursie went out sorrowfully in the rear of Fanny. But not the circumstances of the unduly ended performance, dismantled pole, nor Jim's loud assertion, "S'ep me Gord! I've see a better cirkis among the blacks on the Warrego", could take the ambitious taste from Ursie's unsatiated mouth.

Oh, to be one of them, with the clown, merry, smiling, and whip-oblivious, for an uncle, instead of Mr Civil!

She sighed hopelessly, for difficulties great and unconquerable stood between her and these light-hearted folk of the tinsel and spangles.

At dawn next morning she climbed on her bedroom roof to verify that the glories she saw on the night before had not been dreamed. Like dutiful Lot (unremembered but for his daring wife), she saw a cloudy mist going up to heaven — nothing else! Her mighty had flown, but they had taken her heart with them to that great world beyond these hills and near the sea. Soon as opportunity was hers, she took from the sitting-room shelf a shell, and placing it against her ear, she listened to its sea call to her. The river suited best this mood (for it led to the sea), and thither she went; nor could she be found that morn for church.

Fasting, she crouched, in hiding even from Andrew, beneath the she-oaks bordering the bottomless hole that had trapped Henry McGrath. But the oaks' dirging melody no longer moaned for him; to-day she caught her own sad reflex in their shivering lament. Gratefully she crooned with them, so inimitably that old Christine Inglis, on her way to early Mass, vowed the girl was fey. Hopelessly her eyes flitted from point to point that in brighter days and moods had given her distraction, if not pleasure. To-day, in accord with her, they were suitably, sombrely shrouded. They, of course, would change, but not again could she; henceforth no music for her in the Bush birds' minstrelsy, no pleasure in rivalry with buttercups for the butterflies' kiss. They and the flowers might all go, die, anything, even before their mutually hated winter came; all seasons would now be alike to her widowed heart.

6

PAT the Jew, Boshy's first mate, stood with his broad back supported by the bottle shelf. He was smiling, and the satisfaction stretching his thin lips and twinkling from his squinny eyes seemed to illumine the complacency overspreading his broad face. The Quarter Sessions were now on, and His Honour the Judge — "the Jidge" to and from Pat — had, for the first time, put up at the Court House Hotel, thereby justifying its name, and discrediting its older and more select rival, the Royal.

Pat, after parting with Boshy, had drifted back to town possessed of two horses. These and himself he hired to the improvident landlady of the Court House Hotel, and gradually, steadily he worked upward. A driver so careful of beast and vehicle is always to be trusted and tipped, even in his own way.

"I'll pay for a drink for you, Pat."

"If 'tis orl the same t'yer, sur, I'll take the dry sixpence," begot him "Pat the Dry Sixpence".

Slowly but surely he drove his feckless landlady into an inescapable corner, then made a hard loan bargain. Prosperous Paddy's thoughts then turned to matrimony, but not towards the much-curled and beribboned maids of the Court House Hotel.

In all his wanderings he had met but one woman whose thrift matched his own, that was the widow mistress of "Gi' Away Nothin' 'All". With a load of merchandise suitable for the Bush folk Pat started a-wooing, and it was while on this quest his keen business propensities begot his first cognomen, "Pat the Jew".

Pat found subject and scene of his wooing unaltered, but all his specious blandishments could not induce the matured matron of "Gi' Away Nothin' 'All" to join fortunes, though his perseverance would have delighted Bruce's spider. But in the end Pat, acting on the mother's suggestion, had sorrowfully to shift his affections to the red-haired, speckled-faced daughter. With her he came again to the town and opened a livery stable. Shortly after a business announcement came out in the local paper with surprising suddenness — the Court House Hotel was for sale. For a thin cracker of horsehair a schoolboy chalked on the door of Pat the Jew's livery stable, from his dictation, "Back after the sail"; and when Pat came back he was the proud proprietor of the Court House Hotel.

The townsfolk, dwelt long and seriously on the moral aspect of the "dry sixpence" dodge; but, fortunately for its author, the dryness of the subject was its refutation.

Jim (now styled the Swigger), for the run of his knife and fork and tips from customers, was, he said, groom at the Court House Hotel; but Fanny called him "Wood-an'-water Joey for Pat the Jew an' 'ees crew".

Jim, dressed in his "other clothes", had just driven the well-lunched Judge back uphill to the Court House.

"'E," jerking thumb and head toward the Court House, "'e sez t' gim me a wet."

"Hiz Honour the Jidge?"

"Yerz."

"Thin I'd 'ave ye min' yer manners, sir, an' be afther namin' 'im so," snarled the landlord, taking up a smeary glass, holding it at long range from the tap, and filling it partially with beer but brimful of froth. Jim would have allowed it visibly to settle but for the "Now thin!" of the landlord, and in two gulps it was down Jim's throat. While he went back to duty, the landlord, in lettering and figuring absolutely his own, proceeded to chalk up another item to the Judge's score.

Then again he smiled, till a dusty swagsman dumped down his heavy swag beside the bar, and fixed his seeing eye steadfastly on the rotund proprietor, then greeted, "Day, mate."

Pat's squinny eyes rested for an unwelcome moment on the wanderer, then he turned his back on him.

"Don't yer reckernize me?" inquired Boshy, as his salutation was not returned.

"Yor got the idvantige ov me," distantly replied Boniface, still with his back turned and industriously intent on polishing Jim's tumbler.

"Well I knoo you at once," said Boshy. But still Pat was not affected. "Reckerlec' Ulundri Creek, an' me an' you a-campin', an' us a doin' of a perish there op'osite 'Gi' Away Nothing' 'All'?"

"Noa," said Pat harshly, and noisily rearranging the bottles on the shelf.

"Look at me," almost pleaded Boshy the lonely. "D'yer mean to tell me that yer carn't reckernize me?"

"Noa," decidedly, but without looking.

"An' yer don't reckerlec' me an' you 'umpin' our Blueys an' Redman's outer this very towen, nur our campin' at Pinchgut Creek, op'osite 'Gi' Away Nothin' 'All'?" Only angry silence from the landlord. "Nur ther owed woman an' the girl wi' ther majenter 'air an' ther turkey-egg complexion?" inquired Boshy, eager for comradeship. But the landlord only rattled the bottles on the shelf till the door behind him swung back. For a moment Boshy thought his senses were playing up with him, for there in the door entrance stood the identical girl — the same turkey-egg complexion, stubby nose, and her red hair only changed from unkempt to kempt. "Squinny eyes mus' be catchin'," thought Boshy, for with increasing wonder he saw that now she possessed a pair like Pat's.

"Pa," she said complainingly.

"Yis, dea-er," replied Pat.

"That Jim won't saddle me pony t' 'e eats 'is dinner, 'e says."

"Sen' 'im ter me, an' it's me that'll dale wid 'im," promised pa.

Then to Boshy, mouthing in solent wonder:

"Wud yourself be afther shiftin' yerself an' yer swag? The gintleman from ther Coort will be comin' in jis now this minit."

"Ther Lan' Coort?" asked Boshy, in hopeful adaptation.

"Sure what's ther differ to you anny way what Coort, or ther likes ov yer?"

"My Gord! thet from you to me," said Boshy tragically — "you thet till I took up wi' yer was too slow t' trap maggots."

In white heat the publican stood glaring with his cross eyes and tasting a dry mouth.

"Git outer this orr———"

A waving bottle finished the sentence. But, as a customer entered, he put it down hastily, and stood glaring through his misleading cross eyes.

"May the Lord look down on me cross-eyed if I can tell w'ich ov us ur you a-lookin' at!" shouted Boshy, covered by the newcomer, and comforted by his grin, dodging out.

The run of Jim's knife and fork was often strategically delayed till two meals ran into one. He came round to the front entrance with the saddled pony, and from him Boshy inquired the whereabouts of Mrs Irvine, keeper of "me liddle Lovey".

Jim's last glass, however small, had risen from his empty stomach into his head, thereby loosening the hinges of his usually rusty tongue.

"Yer'll get nothin' there," advised he. "She's spliced to a parson chap. If he'd pay me wot's owe to me I could stan' me groun', 'stead er bein' wood-and-water Joey in this 'ungery 'ole," he growled.

"I'm a-wantin', an' awaitin', an' a-wishin' fer nothin' from man ur mortal, thenks be ter Gord Almighty," explained Boshy proudly. "I've come fer ther chile Lovey."

Jim, with a customary side look, took in the abnormal size of Boshy's bulging swag.

"Bin graftin' long?"

"Forty-seven 'ears," informed Boshy.

"Niver bin lambed down, nur run through, nur dosed?"

"Never," said Boshy, "an' ain't likely to so be."

"Be Ghos! if ole yallar lugs the parson gets wind that yer got a sprat 'e'll try an' work yer," cautioned Jim.

"Think so?" said Boshy, with offensive security.

"Know so," from Jim curtly; "that's w'y I've got such a 'ell of a down on 'im ther way 'e razzle-dazzled me for all I wuz worth for 'e's blastid church."

"Yer doan mean yer bits er savin's?" inquired Boshy sympathetically.

"Yerz, me bits er savin's fer forty-seven years — forty-seven years 'ard graft. That's w'y I carn't arst yer ter 'ave a wet, an' no one 'ere won't ast me the way t' my mouth, though I'm d——d well as dry as a emp'y bottle."

"Fine cheek 'e mus' 'ave; but 'ow did 'e git 'em outer yer?" said Boshy anxiously, ignoring Jim's hint.

"Oh, arst me somethin' easy w'ile yer about it," said Jim irritably, having nothing ready.

The resentment and injury in Jim's tone made Boshy uncomfortable. He listened respectfully, and Jim went on:

"'Ow d'e git it outer me? W'y, I know for a reel fac' that a little chap swallered a thrippence. Orl ther doctors went a-fishin' after it, but 'ad ter giv' it up. 'Sen' fur Mr Civil,' says ther boy; "e'll soon git it outer me.' "

Jim's laugh brought the landlord to the door but he drew in his head when he saw Boshy.

"Mick," he called to a brother in blue.

Michael came to his bidding and stood in solemn, speechless wonder at the spectacle of the landlord about to shout.

He took the gratuitous glass of swanky, but suspicion conquered.

"What's wrong?" he inquired.

"Down with it, mann," said Pat, swallowing a small dose himself, in token of safety and fellowship.

"D'ye see thon?" he asked, coming straight to the point, as the policeman put down his empty glass.

"Is't they swaggie beyant?"

"Yis, that same."

"I do; what ov 'im?"

"Thin, Micky, do be afther givin' 'im ther roight about."

"I'll do that same."

But when Bobby came out, Boshy, ignoring the foot-bridge across the river, was making a bee-line for Lovey's home.

But now Lovey was indeed lonely, for under the new régime Jim and Fanny had gone, and Andrew was at school in a distant town. All this afternoon Ursula was down by the river feeding her discontent with stories supplied by the new maid. On that same bank Maria Monk first told stumblingly her tragic tale to Ursie. She knew better now, for Fanny's successor was an up-to-date maid, who nightly burned low her tallow candle reading of lovely Muriels, Daphnes, and Gladys, with their titled, but snubbed suitors.

When she came to the scene where the haughty and pedantic Princess Machuski bids the coachman to "Repair to the equine establishment, dismissing him with an imperious wave of her snowy, shapely hand———" Ursie closed the book. The contrast was too cruel, the matter hopeless. Her aunt's hand, if she ever did wave it, was but a blob of red fat. Nor ever, Ursie felt sure, could her aunt be got to call their little stable the equine establishment; and if she did, lame Tommy, Jim's successor, would not understand. Sighing sadly, Ursie came up the gully leading from the river to the house, as unlike the coveted castle of the Princess as everything else.

As she neared it she saw a swagsman making for the side-gate, and the multi-coloured patches on his faded clothes reminded her instantly of the clown in Ashton's circus. Nestling close to the screening grape-vine, she waited. Mr Civil was reclining on the veranda, waiting to insure good measure from Lizarixin; for, like himself, Liza did not allow religion to interfere with profitable business.

The little gate insuring that privacy indicative of a front entrance swung back noisily.

Boshy stood, as he sighted Mr Civil and — to use his own description — "me 'art began to kick ther wind out ov me w'en I see 'im, a cross between a crow an' a Chinyman."

The minister's well-trained eyes soon sized the swagsman.

"What are you seeking?" he asked coldly.

"Ur — ur — khur, missis in?" asked Boshy throatily.

"There will be a meeting next week at the schoolroom respecting the relief of the poor. Call there if you are in need of clothes."

"Me in want!" said Boshy indignantly. "I like thet. W'y, man alive" — tapping his swag — "thet's orl clo'es 'cep a few 'undred kengeroo an' dingo scalps, an' a couple o' bottles ov goanna ile fer boots. I've saved over fo'teen shillin' in kerridge alone, a-luggin' an' a-lumpin' ov 'em down me own self."

He looked, but there was no surprise from the parson.

"Mebbe me meself ull gi' 'em one or two little things for ther pooer," yielded Boshy coaxingly.

"Don't trouble," said the parson distantly, unmoved by the bepatched swagsman's splendid offer.

"Money perhaps more suitabler?" Boshy faltered, and had his reward in a darting gleam of interest from Mr Civil's close-set eyes.

"Where have you come from?" he asked.

"Merrigulandri," promptly replied Boshy, relieved that his terrible expedient had not been instantly snapped at.

"Merrigulandri," repeated Mrs Civil, emboldened by the familiar name to join the interview.

"Are you Mrs Irvine?"

"I was," she said.

"Cameron Cameron's sister?" asked Boshy eagerly.

"Yes."

"I'm Boshy, jis come from theere," extending his hand. "I've come fer Lovey, Mrs Irvine," he said, relaxing his intense grip.

"For Ursula?" she asked incredulously.

"Lovey, ther liddle un az you gut from Cameron's six 'ears come nex' November."

"What's all this? What's all this?" broke in the parson impatiently.

"Ursula," suggested Mrs Civil to Boshy.

"Lovey t' me," he said grimly, the light of battle on his face.

"Come, come! stop this fooling, my good man, and get about your business."

"Thet's my business, Mr — Mr — Wat's-yur-name. Thet's w'at I've padded ther 'oof an' 'umped me swag fer the lars' week fer — fer the chile Lovey."

Unprecedentedly Mrs Civil's curiosity conquered her lord and master's attempts to silence her with an acrimonious, "Maria, go inside".

Then the appearance of Ursie aided her distraction to his commands.

Listening Ursie's attuned senses saw but one solution: a clown — not the one familiar, nevertheless welcome — had come for her.

"You've come for me?" she asked eagerly, revealing

herself, her eyes excitedly blazing, her face crimson. Her fearlessness struck the parson dumb.

"Nut you," replied Boshy, slowly swallowing, and regarding this big girl with his troubled, uncertain eye, the empty socket quivering sympathetically.

"You never see me afore? Yer carn't reckernize me?" he broke a long silence to ask.

She nodded affirmation diffidently but determinedly.

Then, with trembling lips, "Wat's me name?"

"Boshy," she answered glibly.

"You're nut me liddle Lovey, shooly nut? Yur carn't be."

"I'm Ursie," sorrowfully admitted the girl.

Boshy's eye, staring into hers, seemed set.

"Show me yur 'ands."

She held out the left — she had the book under her right arm. His eye went from it again to her eyes. Suddenly his face grew ghastly, then shrivelled, and his swag seemed voluntarily to slide from his shrunken body. Weakly his aimless hands went to his bewildered head, but did not reach it, while his eye never left hers, nor hers his. At the bidding of his beating throat his mouth opened helplessly, but for a time his tongue clicked inarticulately against his dry palate.

"Christ Gord! yur gut yur mother's eyes," he gasped, as he fell with his hands outstretched to reach her.

7

HUGH PALMER, now husband of Margaret Cameron, came into the town on business soon after the advent of Boshy. In maudlin confidence brewed at the Court House Hotel, he told Mr Civil that Boshy, in addition to his forty-seven years' "'ard scrapin's", was credited in the Bush with having discovered the dead shepherd's hidden hoard. Thenceforth the tender, patient attention of the ex-parson was at least interesting, and stay with them Boshy must; so Boshy did, and accepted these attentions and all others, paying only by diplomacy. To Ursula he explained that he knew for a real fact that Cameron had paid enough for her keep to feed them both. He effectually dodged all forms of present contributions with hints of big bequests; neither would he borrow nor lend. However narrow the rule, the close study he had made of the borrowing devices of the few men met in the Bush served him in good stead for those in town.

"As fer ez money's concerned, I wudn't trus' me right 'and wi' wot belongs to me left," was his advice to Ursula. But to Mr Civil, "On'y wait t' I'm safe in ther arms ov Jeesis."

"But God bless my soul, Boshy! you are hale and hearty. You may see us all out," was Mr Civil's remonstrance.

"Ah, thet's all you know, ur any ov you. It'll nut be long now. I'll never scratch a grey 'ead," shaking it in a manner suggesting a sinister foreknowledge. "On'y a few mo-er tri-uls, on'y a few mo-er tee-urs," he disconcertingly bellowed into the keen face, indecently searching his for indications of coming dissolution. There was no way for the ex-parson, but to wait, patiently or otherwise.

Therefrom Boshy's saving propensities, being but the idiosyncrasies of the rich, were mercifully endured and spoken of by Mr Civil. Even his amazing miserliness was passed over acceptedly, for of such are the kingdom of shepherd millionaires. But one, alone, in that town stood apart from Boshy's coveted acquaintance. The prosperous landlord of the Court House Hotel "wud 'ave nather thruck nor dale wid 'im at all, at all". And Boshy, after the manner of all victors, unsatiated with homage, troubled incessantly how to make Pat the Jew, Pat the Dry Sixpence, bow the knee.

"Kerry cows 'ave long 'or-rns and far-r off fiel's do be green," Pat would remark when talk of Boshy's wealth went round the bar-room, Pat, who knew his Bush, would demand: "Shure now, an' where ud 'e git it? Say now for-r ar-rgimen's sake thet Boshy found an' grabbled ould Baldy's plant: I'd arsk yez 'ow much ud it be — orl himself an' Baldy could put together the whole ov thir nat'ral loives graftin' in ther Bush? Shure, the Lor-rd help yez an' your great forchunes. Shure, wouldn' some ov yez git 'im till tell yez, what bank houlds it? Faith, I'm thinkin' tis the riverbank." And Pat's squinny eyes would twinkle time to his harsh laugh.

That was also the ex-parson's perplexity. Where did Boshy keep it? or was it safe in such keeping? In solemn anxiety Mr Civil sought for this information, likewise, by pressing into his service the lawless element among them to instil fear into Boshy. But Boshy's one eye winked security to friend and foe.

"Don't fret, Mr Civil; me bits ov savin's is weer no crows won't be a-takin' me yaller boys fer cough lozengers, nor me fifty-pun notes fer pocket-'ankerchers", was the nearest location or clue he could get from Boshy.

Vainly the ex-parson preached eloquently on the Hidden Talents, and spoke of profitable interest to be obtained under various speculations; beside, to keep money hidden in a napkin (Boshy would smile) was sinful, wilful waste, and instead, many and varied alluring investments were suggested.

"I'll tell yer w'at," said Boshy one day, after another lengthy investment sermon — "I'll tell yer w'at: I'll buy the Court 'Ouse 'Otel if you'll run it fer me."

Incongruous it might be; nevertheless, the ex-parson took a week to come to a decision. Even then Boshy considered that he owed his escape to Bella Watson.

Bella's disappointed resentment against the union of the parson and widow Irvine had gradually disappeared. She was now a very frequent visitor at the Civils', though

Boshy soon discovered, and said, that she received "on'y a lopsided welcome".

"Before you came she used always to come here to dinner on Sundays, then after dinner they'd go into the parlour, and Bella played the harmonium; but aunt went into her room and shut herself up," informed Ursie.

"To be a-snoozin' or a-sulkin'?" questioned Boshy.

"No; it was the porter. She drinks two big bottles on Sunday, and it makes her sleepy. Haven't you noticed?"

"Yes, 'er drinks be 'arf too much porter. You could crack a flea on 'er face, fer she's jus' a-breakin', an' a-bustin', an' a-bulgin' wi nourishment," he said in sudden heat. "Git 'er ter knock it orf or 'er'll crack up. Tell 'er so, Lovey. 'Er ain't a bad sort for a female."

Boshy was thoughtful for a few moments. "Yes, sure's Gord made liddle apples, 'er'll crack up, an' seems ter me thet would soot some people to a nicety. Git 'er t' knock it orf be jinin' ther Band ov 'ope."

"Oh, I couldn't! I daren't speak of it to her. It's Mr Civil's fault. At first when he came he would not let her have any, and now he makes her take more than she wants sometimes," said Ursula.

"I see," said Boshy, knocking the ashes out of his pipe. "An' ther Lord 'elp 'er, fer 'er doesn't wunt much makin'!"

It was Sunday night, but neither Boshy nor Ursie stayed for the prayer-meeting for Mrs Civil was sick. Both were sitting outside on a stool in a shadow cast by the house, near the sick woman's bedroom.

"Rum yarn thet et church t'-night about them couple or more knowin' ole virgins, Lovey." Boshy's remark referred to the parable of the Wise and Foolish Virgins.

"Don't you think now, Boshy, that the wise ones might have either wakened, or given a little of their oil to, the other poor late things?" asked Ursie.

Boshy sent a disparaging grunt through his nose.

"Nut on'y thet, Lovey, but the way ther greedy beggars crowed over 'em," was his comment.

In silence his mind went away to "Gi' Away Nothin' 'All", and as a similar case he told Ursie the story.

"But Lord, Lovey, 'ow in ther name of Gord them fools

over theere," indicating the chapel, "can be kidded ter fill up thet money-plate reg'lar beats me. They mus' git it easy — thet's all I gut t' say. Seems you've on'y t' git up in the box an' make out thet on'y for you a-bein' sich a sheep-dorg a-busnackin', an' a-blatherin', an' a-barkin' roun' 'urdles day an' night wi'out meat an' drink an' sleep, thet Gord A'mighty 'ud be a-snoozin'; then like a dingo, ther devil 'ud be over ther 'urdles a-woolin', an' a-worritin, an' a-woundin' ov ther yeos an' lambs. An' " — with a laugh — "s'ep me Gord! ther d—d ole yeos an' wethers seem t' be ther wustest, an' ther frightenest. Right enuff t' go t' 'ave a go at ther songs, same 'uz I do. I enj'y ther songs an' toons."

Then to his own tune and time he sang some as an example.

For though Boshy was a regular attendant at church services and prayer-meetings, his sole offering was discordantly vocal. Moody and Sankey had sung their way into every dissentient chapel, and Boshy appreciated their words thoroughly, and sang them to a wrong tune incessantly.

"Ther's no mistake, them songs an' toons of them coves 'as gut me be ther wool proper," was his excuse for bawling them night and day.

"Why doesn't aunt tell Bella Watson she doesn't——"

"Lis'en, Lovey," Boshy interrupted her. "W'at's that they're a-singin' ov now—'Safe in ther arms ov Jeesis'?"

"No; 'Dare to be a Daniel'," Ursie informed him.

" 'Dare t' be er Den-e-i-al'," intoned he softly, mindful of the sick woman. "Nut much go in among 'em over theere wi'out me," he broke in to remark. "An' moosic seems t' gi'e me twice ther wind. I tell yer w'at, Lovey: you mus' begin t' learn chunes on the memorium. It's a-been on me mind fer some time, but the egspense pulled me up. Learn you must, then us'll 'oist me Lady Bella outer both inside 'eere an' out ov ther church over theere. You'll play ther 'ymns, an' I'll start ther singin' meself."

"Here they come," said Lovey, indicating two figures descending the hill.

Boshy looked.

"Arm acrook, too, a-thinkin' thet in ther dark all cats is

grey. Sit still t' us sees 'ow they sez their 'Gord be wi yer t' us meets agin,' " advised he.

But there was no leave-taking between the parson and Bella: Mr Civil came hastily to the house, leaving her in the shadow of the tree. He would have passed without seeing the pair on the stool but for Boshy solemnly chanting his best attempt at "Sound the loud timbrel" — " 'Ole P'aro is dead, but I'll never, wot never, no never, go back into Egyp' agin' " — to the tune of "St Patrick's Day in the Morning".

"Oh, ur, you Boshy?" blustered Mr Civil; "looking at the moon?"

"No, a-lookin' at Miss Wetson; 'er seems to 'ave loss somethin'."

"Oh no; she's waiting for me to bring out her music-book."

"Jis so," said Boshy, much implied in his tones.

The parson went hurriedly inside, and Bella, who had seen the meeting, came down to Boshy and Ursie.

"I was thirsty, so Mr Civil said he would bring me out a drink," explained Bella.

Neither Ursula nor Boshy commented.

"Peculiar how thirsty singing makes you."

"Very pecoorial," agreed Boshy.

Mr Civil appeared with, Ursie perceived, the wrong book.

"I found your book," he said, tapping it.

"I told Boshy and Ursie," bleated Bella confusedly, "I wanted a drink."

"Ov porter — a cupple ov bottles?" Boshy inquired.

"No; water," said Bella lamely.

"Certainly, certainly; I forgot."

Mr Civil went in hurriedly to make good his forgetfulness.

" 'Ho, everyone w'at thurstieth, come to ther water,' " chanted Boshy, to encourage Bella to take more than sacramental sips. "W'en Lovey 'ere wus a liddle girl I cured 'er completely ov a-arstin' fer a drink w'en 'er didn' wunt it, be a-making' ov 'er drink it all up — poor chile! — w'ether or no. It's putty 'ard t' drink w'en yer nut dry. Ain't it, Miss Wetson?"

Bella heroically gulped several mouthfuls; then, handing back the glass to the silent shepherd, began fumbling for her handkerchief.

"Strange — igh — you always — igh — want to wipe your mouth after drinking anything; but being so thirsty, I must — igh — Isn't it peculiar?"

"Very pecoorial," assented Boshy. "An' you've come a long step out ov yur way 'ome fer a drink."

"Yes, indeed, and I must be getting back," she agreed, including Mr Civil in her farewells.

"That was not Bella's music-book Mr Civil had, Boshy. It was aunt's *Sunday at Home*."

"Well, it's gorn abroad now, Lovey."

"Well, why did he say it was Bella's book, and why did she say she wanted a drink when she didn't?" asked Ursie.

Boshy's pipe had been out for some time, but he slowly and carefully tested it, then put it into his pocket.

"Why does she?" repeated Ursula.

"It seems t' me, Lovey, that these lambs ov Gord in this towen must play putty well ther same games as ther lambs in ther Bush."

8

"LOVEY, no mistake, yer mus' learn t' play ther memorium," gravely Boshy repeated next morning. "Be 'ook or be crook, yer mus' learn t' play. If I could but fine out w'at Cameron Cameron is a-payin' fer yer 'ere I'd know 'ow 't ack; but if I 'ints t' either ov 'em any sich question, both ov 'em buttons their lips thet insten' minute. I mus' git out o' this, for I'm beginnin' t' get full up ov bluffin' ole yeller lugs about a-leavin' 'im me money, an' it's time I was earnin' more. So onct more agen I'll be 'umpin' me Bluey, but afore I go I mus' get on to Andrer w'en 'e comes 'ome t' root in among ther parson's papers, an' fine out wut they gut from Cameron fer you; me an' you keepin' ov 'em on ther string w'ile 'e does ov it."

"Oh, Andrew wouldn't touch their papers," said Ursula.

"Nut if you wus t' ast 'im?"

She shook her head decisively, and Boshy mumbled disparagingly about Andrew and youth generally, then suddenly broke out:

"But Lord Gord! yer carn't expec' t' put a nole 'ead on young shoulders. W'y, Lovey, w'en I think ov the chance I 'ad to root an' a-rummage among yer dead daddy's papers afore Cameron come thet time — w'y, I 'ad all one night, an' best part ov nex' day. Se'p me Gord! I wus so honest thet I never so much ez laid a fing-er on 'em, fer I never giv' it a thort t' I see Cameron 'ad a-snavelled ov 'em." The muscles in his maimed eye quivered regretfully. "W'en I'm abed an' begins t' think over it, I turns quick on me other side t' distrack me 'eart away from sich thoughts, t' think w'at a fool I was. Bought sense is the best of sense if yer don't pay too dear, as ther sayin' is, an' don't lose yer receipt. I allus paid putty dear fer mine." He was smilingly silent, then added slowly and softly, "Cep' oncet", and again he paused and pondered, then suddenly: "Tech wood, Lovey! tech wood, t' stop bad luck!" he said excitedly, jumping up and tapping and making her touch the seat. "Me a-boastin' an' a-blatherin' like thet, a-knowin' pride goes afore a fall"; and he grew strangely disturbed and troubled.

Then, under pretence of being reassured by this touch-wood charm, he spoke of a subject that continually appeared to be in his mind — the doings of Pat the Jew; for though Boshy did not again enter the Court House Hotel, some magnetic influence continually caused him to pass the bar. His mood was always indicative of Pat's trade, for if the rapacious publican happened to be in the bar alone, Boshy's one eye would take a steady, disconcerting inside survey. To Lovey he would joyfully prophesy that Pat the Jew's day was done. "Nut a soul a-nex', nur a-nigh, nur a-near the place; everyone's a-droppin' down t' 'is terbaccer-juice. I've cooked 'is goose." In justice to Boshy's prediction, this was a culinary kindness that he lost no opportunity of attempting.

Several times Boshy passed and repassed one afternoon, gloatingly noting that only the discomfited landlord loomed gloomily with his back to the empty fireplace, gnawing his thin moustache, or, as Boshy said, to as many as he could intercept, "a-champin', an' a-chawrin', an' a-chewin' ov ther terbaccer — us knows wot fer."

But next time the insatiable Boshy saw that Pat's daughter, named by her admiring parents "Vi'let", but nicknamed by the Philistines "The Fuchsia", had joined "Pa". They stood each end of the mantelpiece, and between them on it rested a large canvas labelled "Topical Birds at Home", the lack in etymology being equalled by the ornithology of the subjects, these being seven large tropical parrots "at home" on a spray of asparagus. Boshy needed no index to the artist, for the knowledge that The Fuchsia was learning to paint pictures was common to the whole town.

"It's a potygrap. I'll take me oath thet's wut it is," he declared to Ursula. Nor was he comforted by her assurance that it could not be a photograph, because of the fragile impossibility of the perch of those gaudy, well-fed perchers.

"Could you paint one, then, wi' them a-roostin' on a rose-bush, Lovey?" sentimentally he inquired with eagerness.

She, sorrowful for his apparent disappointment, admitted that even The Fuchsia's achievement was beyond her.

"Then don't be jealous, Lovey," he snapped irritably.

"But se'p me Gord! if I gut t' go barefoot you'll go t' learn," he said as he disappeared.

Nothing the ex-parson could say against the expense could dissuade him from this decision. Even the girl's own opposition he beat back, resolutely meeting her unwillingness to part from him with the news that he was about to return to the Bush on important business. Andrew also, by his father's command, was going back to the station.

"I wouldn't leave you 'ere, Lovey, wi'out Anderer." Waving away the suggestion, "No, you can't come wi' me this trip, Lovey ov mine" — whispering — "but please Gord you will nex' time. An' us'll take a memorium wi' us. But Lord, us'll stay no time up theere."

Perhaps it was the over-zealous opposition of Mr Civil that strengthened Boshy's rash resolve, for even when the initial expenses multiplied from pence into shillings and progressed into pounds, he would neither waver nor retreat. Certainly to enforce the shopkeeper's respectful wonder he paid all silver outlays in copper, and pounds in silver, and all with a painfully slow reluctance; yet in the end the girl was, all circumstances considered, fairly equipped for this venture.

The memorable morning found Boshy and Andrew and her beside her boxes on the veranda, awaiting the preliminary horn blast of Jimmy Nancarron's night-journeying coach.

If Boshy's mind had dwelt on the parting, the strenuousness of many other ordeals had suppressed mention. But now as Jimmy's team topped the gravelly hill, he raised his horn, and proudly blew his annuniatory too-tooly-oo-too, too-tooly-oo-too, too-tooly-too-tooly, too, too, too, then he noisily tooled his team to the gate.

It shook the girl distressingly, but she made no sign; only she took one swift look at Andrew, and noted that he had suddenly changed from a boy into a man, with a brave, grave face.

Boshy began to tremble violently.

"Me ole mother called ther ship as I a-sailed in out 'ere

Ther 'Earse, en now all of a instan' minute I begin t' feel ther same," he said, turning to silent Andrew.

"Boshy, I won't go," said Ursula earnestly.

"My Gord! an' them expensie boxes, an' more'n expensie duds wuts in 'em, a-lyin' orl aroun'. Up wi' yer, Lovey, inter yer gran' box seat," he said in the coaxing tones of her childhood. "A box seat's egstra egspense, but I wunt all in ther towen t' see yer. I'm orlright, Lovey, so's Anderer," he encouraged, looking at immovable Andrew; "us is both orlright w'en us thinks on ther picksurs you'll paint and ther toons you'll play when us orl meets again."

9

EVEN in the first little school every lesson subject but reading baffled Ursula, and it was so in this more pretentious establishment. Arithmetic, geography, grammar — strive as ardently as she could, the girl could not get an enlightening glimmer even into their elementary principles. With music, unless she knew the tune, the teacher's efforts were wasted. But on wet days, when the attendance of day scholars was few and the lessons were confined to poetry and history, save for dates, then Ursula shone; and though aided by the ruler she could not draw a straight line, her colour sense was wonderful. Teachers are never students of the scholars, and none of Ursula's gifts were calculated to score in that absolute, but unfortunately not obsolete institution, examinations. Disheartened by continual failure, gradually she made no effort to improve, consoling herself when she reflected on the peculiar protégés that Nature selected, for from the mistress downward these learned spinsters had little of what was lovely to the girl. But when Boshy's ill-spelt, hopeful letters came, her heart charged her unsparingly, though her carefully school-dictated replies to him were destined to contain no hint of failure. Then, one day, came her first letter from Andrew, telling his aunt was very sick; he thought Ursula should come to her. Where, wondered Ursula, had he got all the money he enclosed for her fare? as she excitedly began her preparations for her return journey by train, for during these school years trains had usurped the place of Jimmy Nancarron's coach.

In the early dawn as the train slackened speed she saw Andrew waiting for her on the platform. Despite his added height she knew him instantly, for his steadfast, unchanged eyes shone, and had also sighted her. Eagerly Ursula thrust her hand through the window in greeting to him, but his was by then busy opening the carriage door. Her heart shrank and her face crimsoned as she stepped past him on to the platform; his whitened, and almost in silence they went homeward.

That afternoon they stood at the foot of Mrs Civil's bed. She was propped up by pillows, and through the little window looking westward the afternoon sun blazed unsparingly on the discoloured face of the sick woman, speechlessly rigid. Ursie stood, her eyes going from her aunt's bloated face to her swollen body, outlined and augmented by the white covering. Andrew, intently watching the girl, saw no understood sign of sorrow. Her mouth had set into a straight line, but her eyes were dry and staring. So she had left them all years ago — Boshy, he, all she knew — dry-eyed and almost silent. A sullen, laboured grief against her seized him, and as he stood there he felt without analyzing that not years but the world had rolled between him and her.

"Sit — in — the — light," said the patient to Ursie that night.

The girl moved, and Andrew raised the lamp to the shelf, so that its rays fell on Ursie's face.

"You — have — your father's brow — and — chin, and — your — mother's — mouth — and — eyes, but your — grandmother's — hands. They — were — painted — by——. She had fine-hands——"

Ursie's eyes, intent on the gravely shaking head, gleamed expectantly, but the woman's face turned to Andrew.

"Andrew!"

"Yes, aunt."

"Merri — gu — lan — dri."

"Now, now," stormed Mr Civil, noisily pushing in the door. "Is this keeping quiet? Out of this, out of this, both of you."

"I — want — to — talk — to them," said Mrs Civil, raising her hand imploringly.

"Another time, when you are better, my dear; plenty of time. Come out — come out, Andrew; come out, you, miss."

Mrs Civil's hand fell back heavily, and she closed her eyes.

"Another — time — Andrew," she panted.

"I hear, that before I came," Andrew told Ursula, "if Civil went out, that Bella Watson would come on guard, till one night aunt threw the lamp at her, then took a fit. Bella has not been near her since I came. But he is always upsetting her by taking her death for granted, so I am constantly on the watch. Listen," whispered Andrew, "what's he reading now?"

Both moved close to the patient's window.

" 'For as in Adam all die, even so in Christ shall all be made alive.' "

Solemnly the ex-parson read some verses from St Paul's mournful masterpiece, then, kneeling by the bed, prayed for the soul of one surely in the Valley of the Shadow of Death. And like a muffled drum the stertorous breathing of the woman on the bed beat time to the service. Looking through the window, they saw him rise from his knees, raise the lamp, and holding it close to his wife, peer keenly into her face. She lay with her eyes half closed, taking short laboured breaths through her open mouth. He put down the lamp, then harshly partly chanted and intoned—

If Thou shouldst call me to resign
What most I prize, it ne'er was mine;
I only yield Thee what was Thine,
  Thy will be done.
Thy——

Andrew's broad hand closed over the vocalist's mouth, the other had him by the neck. Ursie held the door wide open and before the startled man could openly protest, Andrew had flung him into a corner of Ursula's one-time prison and shot the outside bolt. From some cause the ex-parson accepted this violence in silence. Waiting his opportunity, he tapped at the window as the servant passed, and she, in unquestioning surprise, freed him.

His shadow fell across the window only once during Andrew's and Ursie's night-watch by the aunt's bed. Baffled by the blind, he crept softly to the closed bedroom door, but hastily as he opened it, Andrew's angry countenance went more than half way to meet his livid visage.

Towards midnight the mill, now working overtime, ceased. After this it seemed to Ursula that the sick woman's pants grew more feeble and irregular. Unblinkingly the girl kept her first vigil. Andrew, looking into those sleepless eyes, thought they alone, through the wonderful change — transfiguring her from gawky girlhood into supple womanhood — had not changed.

The woman on the bed gave no sign of their presence. Her mouth had fallen apart; round it a white weal threw into high relief the stagnant purple hue of the lips and cheeks. Her eyes were partially closed. If only she would wake and close her mouth, mentally prayed the outwardly unflinching girl. Later the doctor came, and sheltered by his presence the sick woman's husband stood in the doorway. Nothing must be done to close that open mouth, but Ursie might, at set times, moisten the breath-dried tongue and throat. Soon after the doctor's departure a woman who "laid out" came and stood at the bed-foot in steady contemplation. "About dawn", she said to them, and went out.

They heard her rouse the sleeping servant, and with her enter the kitchen; then the noise of a fire being lighted and the fountain being filled came to the watchers.

The sick woman's breathing became more fitful. Her head fell aside, and the liquid Ursie would have poured down her throat oozed back.

"No more," whispered Andrew, taking the spoon from Ursie. They were each side of the bed, watching the sick woman.

Gradually the power of the lamplight appeared to be limited to a blurred circle.

There was a long unbroken quiet, seemingly blank from its intensity, till with horrible suddenness a cock crew. The girl and youth had risen, and their hands simultaneously outstretched met across the body, now limp and motionless.

Dissolution did not beautify Mrs Civil. Her great body lay shrouded in stiffly bulging outlines, and in deference to an old custom a plate of salt, to arrest swelling, lay with significant immovability on the stomach. Ann Foster's scissors had perforated elaborately a linen face-spread, which rested as still as the salt. The white curtains and blind screening the window hung lifelessly; white drapes and covers and flowers were everywhere; and a stifling scented stillness filled the room with an intolerable odorous heaviness.

As ever an unreality girt and governed the girl's normal senses — surely this bed-scene must be familiar. An indefinable impulse seized her to go outside, find, then softly sigh through a crack, but low down — she wanted it almost level with the bed.

Dazed, deathly white, but dry-eyed, she followed Andrew outside. There they parted without a word, he going swiftly up the hill, anywhere away to lose sight of her, she purposely watching him.

She felt that he had failed her, why and how was not clear, nor how much it mattered. How tall and strong he had grown, but she would not think about him, so mentally she fell apart from her old mate. Thank God, she was sure of Boshy.

From the kitchen came the smell and clatter of food being prepared for breakfast. Mercy! how could any one eat? She went to her room.

In the afternoon the maid came saying somebody wanted her. Outside, partly screened by the paling fence, Ursula found Fanny, who anxiously inquired the whereabouts of Mr Civil. Ursula assured her that he was in his room, and it was quite safe for her to come in. But another purpose also kept her outside, waiting for Jim, who had promised to bring her some flowers to decorate the dead woman. Jim came downhill hastily to them, a few flowers of many hues in one hand, the other holding something under his coat. Fanny instantly complained of the colour and paucity of the blossoms displayed, whereupon Jim produced from beneath his coat a dilapidated porcelain wreath, which Fanny scorned, declaring that she knew it well — that it was off old Shiel's grave; but Jim swore that he had bought them at great expense. Then they bandied:

"Grave-robber! Pat the Jew's loplolly boy!"

"Old raddle-cheeks! 'Oppy-go-fetch-it."

Till the grotesquely angry scene was interrupted by the arrival of Mina, who came asking for Andrew. With her, from a sense of duty, Ursie went again into the silence with its sickening scents.

"Can I see her?" asked Mina, with orthodox interest and intent, groping for her handkerchief. Ann Foster was in charge, and ostentatiously withdrew her work of art face-cover. Mina bent and kissed the partly open mouth.

"Poor Mrs Civil, don't she look peaceful an' nice?" she whimpered, dabbing her dry eyes.

"Very," agreed Ann, replacing the face-cover, then resuming her seat with an ordered, solemn countenance.

Andrew continually disappeared, on pretext of duty, and Mr Civil, as became a disconsolate mourner, kept himself and his grief in his room. Mina stayed for tea, and with disconcerting wonder Ursula watched the food pass through the lips that had so lately kissed the dead woman's, for to Ursula even here the cold presence of death seemed to penetrate.

"Why don't you eat? Isn't Andrew gone?" asked Mina suspiciously.

"Come outside," ordered Ursula, with scant ceremony rising and forcing out her unsatisfied guest. There in the twilight they sat on a seat that Boshy had built in the recess facing the hill. From the trees crowning it, magnified, pinnacled shadows fell towards them. Below in the river valley a belated bird called plaintively to its mate. Ursula listened to it for a moment, then her eyes again sought the impelling shadows.

Down the hillside came two men bearing the last solemn symbol on their shoulders. Ursula rose, then stood in a line with the bearers, motionless as though waiting for inexorable fate. She suffered the grotesquely and inhumanly lengthened shadow from the men and their burden to fall on her.

"Mina, Mina! Oh, God!"

Ursula's arms went round her irresponsive friend, and her surprised tears deluged and embarrassed her.

"Lord, Urs, what's the matter with you?"

"Mina, Mina!" She sank on her knees, then she fell face downward, blind with tears and grief for an undefinable sorrow.

It was nothing to her that in the ghastly details of the following days Mina seemed to have usurped her place. A waiting quiet possessed her, but she felt alone, though even this was, or appeared to be, of her choice.

Lessons in life are seldom as moral as they should be, and Mrs Civil's will left all her personal and real estate to her dear husband. Her beloved nephew Andrew Cameron of Cameron and her ward Ursula Ewart were unnamed in it. Boshy had hoped otherwise, but Ursula had given it no thought, even when she wrote to him — her only friend.

After due delay Boshy wrote saying he was "a-comin' down at once", and for Andrew to wait till he came. With veiled hostility to Andrew, the widower suffered him to await Boshy's coming. Ursula saw that now Bella Watson's chance meetings with him had to be strategically and singly planned by Bella, whose wifely attentions to the bereaved man were markedly meaning. But those prophets of the past were surprised by the coldness and palpable annoyance of the recipient. Even in the first week his manner to Ursula, without being fatherly, had changed to the tender solicitude of a watchful guardian. He consulted her continuously on all subjects, not even excepting the indelicacy of Bella's unwelcome visits, discountenanced by him now, because of Ursula's and his adored dead wife's dislike to her. Ursula felt like a trapped animal forced to feed from her hated captor's hand. But till Boshy came she would keep her mind in abeyance. Again and again the girl wrote, earnestly importuning his speedy return, but unaccountably he still tarried. Andrew, man-like, saw only Ursula's discontent from being with them, and a moody constraint was always upon and between them. Mina, after the manner of her sex, saw much, but, unlike them, said nothing. She came very often, considering that her parents had now added "accommodation" to their wine business.

Weeks, leaden for Ursula, went by, bringing only messages from Boshy, still on his way down. Mr Civil's kindness daily increased to her, and but for Andrew's open hostilities would have reached him.

Then widower Hugh Palmer came down from Merrigulandri, his wife Margaret having paid the toll of motherhood; and from him Ursula heard that Boshy had been camped on a far-away creek, waiting for the season of the birdling Galahs.

"He told me to tell you that he is up to his eyes a-ketchin' an' a-snarin' an' a-takin' of 'em into Coolabadarin, an' a-sellin' of 'em, but that he would soon be down now."

Andrew was now to go back in Hugh Palmer's place, and Mina began to crochet a red-and-purple necktie as a parting gift. Hugh Palmer commented privately to Ursula on the harmonious blend, but said openly with mimic tragedy that it would cause bloodshed between Andrew and him.

The outward and visible signs of moral ethics likewise were strong points with this learned Englishman. To him, despite the housekeeper, there was an impropriety in Ursula, the elderly ex-parson, and Andrew living under the one roof — a matter that, for all his aforetime vigilance, had escaped Mr Civil.

Mina's mother agreed emphatically with Palmer, too emphatically for her English

"She gan goom mit you, Misder Pommer; dare is room in Mina's room for doo bets."

"For doo bedts plendee room," was emphasis to an inaudible objection from Mr Stein, who, as Palmer disappeared, added:

"But vot erpout Mina? Keep off der krass, den, for Mina ant Pommer."

Mrs Stein's mouth pursed scornfully.

"Oh, ant so is to-morror to-morror," she said with an air of finality.

"Vaid, den, ant ve shall see," prophesied Mr Stein.

"Alvays you growel, or yap-yap 'Vaid — vaid'. I go do my vork," she said meaningly, pinning up her skirts and taking up a broom.

"Orh, a damt lodd you do, dond you? You ant your vork. Ven somesbodies——"

"Orh, somesbodies will dare ees shirt," sneered Mrs Stein.

"Urzler's nod so kreen as hers kabbidge lookin'. It vill be all up for Mina mit Pommer. Then you mit a long mout'."

"Shust you ged vork," said Mina's mother, slamming the door.

But Ursula would make no movement without Boshy, though she longed earnestly to lose the attention of her self-constituted guardian.

On her solitary bush wanderings one afternoon she had come to a felled wild apple-tree. There it lay, denuded by time of leaf and branch and even bark; yet still clinging with parasitical tenacity was the bunch of mistletoe that had brought about its downfall years ago, because its impregnable fruit and height had taunted her. Jim, importuned, had come with his axe and at her wish had felled it with the fruited but unripe mistletoe. She recalled everything as she stood there. Mr Civil, warned and guided by distant axe-whangs, had found them, and had been unsparing in his condemnation of Jim's stupid waste of time in coming an unnecessary mile to chop down a tree uselessly far away.

"She kidded me to," was Jim's defence, and she recollected that then she had none. Nor could she now define her motive.

Thoughtfully she went over all old haunts that had tempted and terrified her childhood. But they begot little of the old emotion, even when from the coign of a precipitous rock she surveyed the whole of this little town that, to her — bush-born — had once seemed so boundlessly vast. It had been the arena for all she read from *Maria Monk* to *Jesus of Nazareth*. On the hill to her left was the convent, and above it, topping its fellows, stood Mount Murrillo — the exceeding high mountain where Satan had led Christ, to tempt Him with the kingdoms of the earth, such surely for Christ and Satan, as for her then, had been this great town, though now so cruelly shrunken and changed.

The river-flat facing the principal street still kept an encircled space for the crude glories of the passing circus show. But not for a moment even now could she dwell upon that mocking epoch, and she came down hastily.

In a fertile hollow between river and hills were the remains of an aforetime vine-garden, full of old-world fruit and flowers. In its centre still flourished, in native independence, a gigantic tree. Near it a forgotten family vault, gaping and mouldering: as if to hide its neglect, a tangle of rank creepers climbed over and about it. This had been her childhood's Garden of Gethsemane, and this the tree beneath which Christ, lonely, had wept. To-day, through the fullness of years, she stood possessed with the right time and place, still she hallowed the old memories. From the garden a track led along the river to the two graveyards — creed-separated, but only by a stone's-throw; she followed it to them. Every turn and twist, every she-oak and shrub she passed, was reminiscent of some callow illusion that touched her even now. The "snaggy hole", that had been the death-trap of Granny McGrath's darling and of many others, was as treacherously quiet and still; seemingly its only duty was to reflect the heavens. As unchanged were the Chinamen, too, and as mechanically labouring, but their gardens, dotted along the river-flats, had surely shrunken, and all landmarks, even the hills, had come nearer town.

Her aunt was now numbered among these silent sleepers, and in the misty twilight her white headstone gleamed with ghostly effect.

Here, on the tomb of one who had been done to death, and lay still unavenged, was a verse that to her had always read as a threat:

> Before the morning light I'll come, with Magdalen to find,
> With tears and sighs to Jesus' tomb, and there refresh my mind.

Leavened by the old influence, she saw, in the grey dawn of a long-dead day, the tomb from which Christ had risen, and Mary, that picturesque sinner, coming with spices and sweet perfume to the tomb — empty, for Christ had gone. In the ages that had passed there had been no sympathy for Mary — Mary, not His mother, but another Mary, who had waited through the long night, then "very early, while yet it was dark", had come: and He, though knowing, was gone.

"Ursula", came like an echo to her, then a well-known "Coo-ee". Instinctively, she fled back into the garden across the river, and from it again to the hills. And not till the darkness governed her mood did she suffer Andrew and Mina to find her.

"Oh, w'at a one you are for sulkin'! We've been 'untin' for you all over the place," complained Mina. "Let's sit down: I'm knocked up."

"Andrew's goin' next week, an' you're to come and stay with us till Boshy comes. Then what are you goin' to do, Ursie?"

"Write a book," she said shortly.

It was a statement that took her by surprise, for till she spoke, her future plans had not been within her mental focus.

Andrew was silent; Mina laughed mockingly.

"I'm sure — I suppose just because you've been down the country to school you've got that in your 'ead. Bah! Boshy's got no money to keep you writin' books."

This also was a new aspect for Ursula.

"Ursula has money of her own, or will have," said Andrew.

"I know, I know," said Mina, resuming her old manner.

"Yuh whur! w'at's bitin' me? Arnts, arnts! We're sittin' on an arnts' bed," she yelled, grabbing her thighs.

Both she and Andrew had an active few minutes, but Ursula stood apparently unmolested.

"None on you?" inquired Mina, after much crushing defeat of her invisible foes.

"No."

"Not one?" Mina re-asked in surprise.

"No," again stormed Ursula, fiercely and unreasonably angry.

"Well, don't bite me 'ead off. They must be sugar arnts, Andrew, to tackle on'y me and you. Yah! there's another. Grab 'im, Andrew, and squeeze him. He's down me back."

As they came down the hillside, they met the full moon rising. By its light Andrew, who had been keenly watching Ursula, saw, among many ants, one crawl towards her ear. He tore it off hastily.

"Let's run downhill," he said; and taking her hand, they speedily outdistanced Mina.

10

WHEN Ursula woke next morning, the once familiar sound of someone's personal washing, outside on Jim's old stool, caused her to peep through the window. For many minutes she stood silently watching Boshy making his morning toilet.

He, with everything else, was cruelly altered. The sparse grey locks he combed were fewer and greyer: and though the accustomed mouth circle was as obdurately set as of old, his head waggled purposelessly: and his hands fumbled stiffly as he folded and replaced his pocket comb. As of old, he took down his portable glass hanging on a nail, and carefully wiping it, replaced it in its case. But instead of sending the water from the basin with a broad, well-directed swirl over the grass, he now poured it carefully into the drain.

The girl, only half dressed, rushed out to him.

"Lovey" — he looked at her steadily — "either you growed up or I've growed down; w'ich is it?" With his eye set on her face, his trembling hands sought hers. "Your dear liddle 'ands. Thenk Gord, your liddle 'an's an' feet's same az ever. Oh, Lovey, but I'm glad t' see you; an' we'll part no more. 'We meet t' paart no mo-ur,' " he sang joyfully.

Now, at the wrong time, she could have wept — wept with the violence of a winter's sudden storm. She drove her tongue to the roof of her mouth, and set her teeth and trembling lips, as she helped the bowed old man put on his coat.

"Learn plenty et schule, Lovey? S'pose you can make the nole memorium in theer all but talk?"

"Boshy," she said, eager to divert him, "everyone says I can't stay here now aunt's dead — everyone but Mr Civil."

"Weer t' go t', then, Lovey, do they say?"

"To Mina's. Mrs Stein says I'll be quite welcome."

"Lovey, they's a nole sayin', an' a terue one, thet fish an' frien'ship stinks in twenty-fower howers. The ole man in theer'es ole enough to be yer gran'father, an' it ud be all right t' you if 'e wasn't. It's ther cracked crockery yer mus' take keer on, nut ther sound, and theere's a good many in this yeer same towen is ser busy a-lookin' after others people's char-racters thet they let their owen go t' blazes. I can un'er'stan' becus ov 'em, thet young ez you are, an' ole ez w'at 'e is, yer couldn' stay 'ere on yer lonesome. But now I'm 'ere——"

"My good Boshy! When did you come? What an unexpected pleasure!"

"Las' night," said Boshy, smiling grimly and taking the widower's outstretched hand. "Sorry t' 'ear ov yer terouble. But we've all got t' face ther same moosic. Funny, though, but I s'pose it's becus it's a sich dead certin thet we don't waste no time a-thinkin' about it."

The widower wiped his little eyes with a black-bordered perfumed handkerchief, and shook his head as one impressed.

"'Ear about 'er a-goin' t' go t' Steins's?" asked Boshy at the breakfast table.

Mr Civil's side jerked.

"No, I did not," he answered. "There's no necessity for Ursula to leave here. Mrs Stein is a deep, designing woman."

"For onct I agree wi' yer, parson: theere's nut ther slightest needcesity," said Boshy with blunt honesty. "Ole mother Stein didn't come down in ther last shower." He shook his head impressively. "Though 'er's gut a 'ard inside, 'er knows wut side to bite a bun. W'y, w'en they kep' ther wine-shanty at Widgiewa there wuz a sayin' thet 'er could dose any man till 'e ud be deaf an' dumb an' blin' fer a month ov Sundees. An' Lord! 'er ud skin a flea fer its 'ide an' taller — nut thet thet's anythin' ag'inst 'er fer bein' savin'."

"She's still a deep, designing woman," repeated Mr Civil fiercely.

"Well, let 'er be deep an' — ther other thing. I think me an' you's 'er match, don't you?" inquired Boshy jocularly.

Mr Civil did not appear so sanguine; but with the coming of Boshy Mrs Stein stayed her hand.

At first it seemed sufficient for Boshy to be near his Lovey, but gradually he began to probe for her accomplishments. Chiefest to him was her music, and in this, of all, she shone least. The grief proprieties in connection with her aunt's death helped Ursula to stave Boshy's knowledge of this inefficiency; but though she clambered through the Sunday-school window to practise, it came. Sore was his disappointment to find that after three — to quote him — "abnormous egspensie 'ears", Ursie could not play nearly as well as Bella Watson.

"Lord, Lovey! I thart ez yer'd a licked 'er inter a cockt 'at in less en no time. Lovey" — gravely — "yer mus' a bin a-spongin' and a-slungin' ov yer time, fer yer gut more brains 'n any of 'em, an' yer liddle 'an's nut a-stretchin' far enough is on'y a egscuse."

He would listen in sad silence to her slow, laboured efforts to play even a simple hymn.

"Lord! ther way I been a-blowin' an' a-boastin' an' a-blatherin' about yer moosic. Oh Lord! rattle into it, Lovey, and makes believe es w'at yer wuz on'y a-gammonin' ez yer couldn't."

"Then the notes would be wrong, Boshy," she said brokenly, for she felt his disappointment keenly.

"I wouldn't know, no more would none ov 'em know, if they wuz wrong, Lovey, if yer could make a bellerin', thundrin' n'ise," he assured her.

To console him she set her mouth, and battered from the wheezy old organ a spirited effect of discords.

"Christ! if they wuz on'y right w'at 'd I give," was his fervent comment. But his daily request for a repetition of her improvization filled her with a nauseating dread. Yet he met any hostile remark about her loyally with "How can yer expec' 'er, wi' 'er liddle 'an's, t' kick up ther same row ez you wi' your lanky triantelopes? W'y, look at 'er 'an's — no more 'en a muskeeter meal," was his offensive defence to Mina. "I never trus' a woman wi' long 'an's" — looking at hers — "and a liddle mouth full ov teeth like a cross-cut saw. I find they're jist about as warm-'earted."

Daily Ursula would hear him muttering the sum total of her school cost that Cameron and he had sent. Then he took to morning rambles in the Bush by himself, coming back at irregular hours, always weary, but in varying moods.

"Nothin' t' be gut er made in this one-eyed 'ole," with a

smokeless afternoon, displayed one mood. "Things isen ez good ez they might be; still" — between pipe-puffs — "they could be wurser 'n w'at they is," was the other.

The girl instinctively felt that he told as much as he cared to, and forbode to question. She filled in every moment of his absence with strenuous, determined efforts at the organ in the Sunday-school.

"Come and listen, Boshy."

It was one of his self-denial afternoons.

"Listen to w'at?" he asked sulkily, for he had long ceased to ask her for music.

"Come on."

Taking him by the arm coaxingly, she led him into the sitting-room and gave him a time-varied rendering of one of his old favourite hymns; then, to her own setting, "My pretty, pretty bird".

"But thet's nut correc', out ov yer book," was his despondent comment. "I mean the 'ymn chunes ain't."

"Yes, they are, every note of the hymn, and I made the other tune."

He sat down heavily.

"Oh, Lord Gord! but I'm thenkful," he said solemnly. "Lovey, I'll 'unt no mo-ore fer shenk-bones, nur 'orse'air, nur 'orns, nur nothin'. I've bin a-goin' ov, an' a-getherin' ov, an' a-gittin' ov 'em fer months past, ter sen' yer back t' learn proper; fer it's a abnormous egspense, and I brought but a few poun's wi' me, a-thinkin' as 'er would 'ave lef' us both somethin'. Se'p me Gord, Lovey! I'd ruther then a fi'-pun note thet yu ken play proper. Ho! ho! I gut ther larf ov 'em now. Shooly t' goodness I hev. Lovey ov mine, ye'll break out yet; I allus knowed yer would. Gi' me me pipe t' I smoke off me shakes. Gi' me me pipe; I'm all o' a shake. See" — holding out his trembling hands — "but it's in real downright j'y," he explained, as she soothingly held and stroked them, and it meant as much to her that he was content.

Then passed a period in the girl's life when the present held in abeyance all thought for her future. The high-flown love scenes of her precocious reading had grafted into her mind certain ideals of both sexes, fortunately lifeless in law, though still alive in literature. Comparing those about her with such high-faluting heroines, she thought the only emotion she possessed was pity. She had this even for a snake being done to death, but immeasurably for this old man who loved her only.

For Boshy was daily becoming more bent and breathless, and occasionally he had vacant intervals. Always after these he ignored the years that had passed, and would startle her by wild, ambitious plans for their future — when she would be grown up. Then he would take her to London.

"Lunnon's ther on'y place fer your brains, Lovey. Yer nut a-goin' t' be no pot-wolloper, Lovey ov mine, fer none ov 'em. No! no! nut be long chalks. But us must wait t' yer grow up — yer on'y a liddle girl yet, Lovey."

He would lie back, muttering his plans for her brilliant future, then doze till roused by his falling pipe. She learned to watch and at the right moment catch it, but the dread of its setting fire to him or the surroundings, some time in her absence, used to fill her with sickening fear. Was it this same dread, she wondered, that caused his heart to beat with such violent breathlessness when he woke from his momentary slumbers? and why did he lift his arms above his head so often? To get her breath she had to raise hers even while wondering.

"Are you sick, Boshy?"

"Me, Lovey? Wut's put thet nonsense inter yer liddle 'ed — yer preddy liddle 'ed? Never wuz better in me life nur stronger, but fer a liddle bit ov cole on me ches'."

He paused breathlessly, and she, watching keenly and uneasily, noted the fluttering pulsations from the hollows of his sunken throat.

"O Lord, Lovey! w'at a nole woman yer wanter turn me inter, wi' yer a-rubbin' and a-rootin' and a-runtin' ther tuppentine inter me ole ches' like this 'ere way. It wouldn' take much t' rub them liddle mouses of 'an's away. An', Lovey, from wen yur wus in long clo'es you've ed a breath like ther smell ov ther scenty stock flowers w'at used t' grow in me old granny's garden at Englan'. Some used t' call 'em gilly-flowers," he explained, "but sweet-scenty stocks wuz the right name. Now, don't rub off them liddle 'an's."

But he opposed her treatment mildly, for he loved the feel of her hands.

"They's no mistake, Lovey ov mine, but yer take some beatin', take yer all roun'," he said, looking with fatuous eye at the glow on her face from this exertion. "None ov 'em 'ere can see your dust, Lovey; an' theere's no mistake, but I'm ridiculous fond ov yer, an' allus was, an' allus will be. W'en I wuz young, wi' two eyes in me 'ead for a likely gel, fust I'd look at 'er feet, then 'er 'an's, then 'er ears — an' I mus' say at 'ome or abroad I never see the ekal ov yourn — then, by 'ook or by crook, I'd menage t' git a sniff ov 'er breath. But" — after a pause — "w'at's Andrer say about yer?"

"Nothing, Boshy."

"Nothin'?" incredulously.

"No."

"Nut even about yer 'an's?"

"No."

"Ur! 'im ther idjut. W'at's it matter? W'en us goes t' London, us'll see who ye'll get. Anderer!" — scornfully — "Anderer! 'e's in no pursition t' marry, w'ich ever way it goes. One comfort, yer'll want fer nothin', thenk Gord."

He was now breathlessly angry and lay back panting, yet vowing disgusted threats against Andrew for a few days.

After a short time she scarcely left him except for sleep, and even then she took on some of his conditions, and the smothered beating of her own overtaxed heart would waken her again and again through the night. Softly stealing to him, she would often find him, if awake, muttering some pleasant plans for their future; but always first they had to go back, for some obscure purpose, to the Bush.

Then one night she found him wandering about in terrible agitation, moist with an agony of fear, straining with eye and ear to discover someone outside with pick and shovel that he heard. For a time she could not soothe nor convince him that it was fancy. He was off that moment to protect something far away in danger.

"Oh, my Gord, Lovey!" he would gasp, "if anyone finds it an' snavels it, w'at would you do? w'at would become ov you? It'd soon cook me, but w'at would become ov you?

No, no, you must not stop me; I must be off."

"Why? Would you leave me alone?"

"No" — weakly — "I wouldn't leave yer, Lovey. Mee-et t' paa'art no mo-ore", he droned, diverted, tremulously clutching her. But he would not go back to bed, and again his fear returned. To convince she led him to the window, and together they looked out on the tranquil, empty night. He thrust his head forward, listening fearfully.

"Try — can you 'ear anyone?" he pleaded.

To humour him she obeyed, and her face grew ghastly, for above the thuds of his excited heart audibly pounding into the night's stillness, she heard footsteps guardedly enter the house.

"W'at's it, Lovey?" confidingly.

How could she tell him? For answer she put her arms round him and drew him back, then spoke hopefully of Andrew to him till he slept.

But gradually his sleep day or night was fear-haunted by a near enemy with a pick and shovel. He muttered guardedly about this dread at first, but sometimes he shrieked it in uncontrollable agony.

"Lovey, w'at woke you? Was it the n'ise ov someun wi' a pick and shovel?"

All night she had sat outside his door listening to him moaning or muttering or coughing.

"No, Boshy. You coughed."

"Certain sure it wuzn't nothin' else? Yer wouldn't deceive me?"

She was quite sure, kissing his moist brow, and she wouldn't deceive him.

"No, thenk Gord, I can trus' you," he said, relieved.

He was feverishly excited, but after a while he yielded, and to please her lay down.

"Go you ter bed, Lovey ov mine," stroking her face with his shaking hands. "Go and get yer beauty sleep. Lovey, go w'en I tell yer," imperiously; and, as ever, she obeyed his old command.

Her rest had been broken for weeks, but now she felt no inclination to sleep. Wide awake, she was lying on her bed, when distinctly she heard the front door stealthily opened.

Boshy had not stirred, she knew, for his harsh cough now, though it disturbed, did not break his sleep of exhaustion. Again she heard the noise from outside, also footsteps. She sat up and listened breathlessly. "Clank, clank", metallically came from outside the wall near Boshy's bunk-head. She rushed into his room. He was sitting up, his eyes protruding and his mouth helplessly open. He raised his arms above his head, then they fell uselessly by his side; but instantly she had hers round him, and wildly as his heart beat her own dulled his.

"Lovey," he panted.

"Hush, Boshy dear! Wait till you are better," she coaxed evasively.

"You 'eerd — thet — time — don't deny — it," he pressed, for she was silent. "You — 'eerd? Lovey, own up."

"Yes."

"W'at?" he gasped, eagerly.

"I don't know, Boshy; perhaps it was some stray dog or cat."

"No dorgs or cats 'ere, Lovey."

"You keep still, Boshy, and I'll look out."

She opened the window. There by the wall near his head lay a pick and shovel. She instantly closed the window, and, conquering her horror, said calmly:

"There's nobody, Boshy, not a soul; and it's nearly morning."

"Yes, theer's ther cocks a-crowin'," he agreed, "an' I'm fair winded," he panted, lying down, for the dawn seemed to reassure him. "An', Lovey, us'll 'ave some breakfuss, an' thet'll pick us up. Soon as I pick up a bit we'll be out ov this. Thet sort ov thing's been a-goin' on fer some time." Again he listened for outside sounds. "Our name 'll soon be Walker, won't it?"

"Very soon," she soothingly assured him. "Sleep now, while I get your breakfast," she suggested, straightening his bed, and bathing his worn face that showed his unfitness to rise. When he dozed she went into the kitchen to make tea for him, going first to where she had seen the pick and shovel — but they were gone.

Later he made several brave attempts to rise and walk

about, and when overcome by breathlessness made light of the cause.

He wanted no doctor's medicine. "Every dose is a nail in yur coffin an', wut's worse, a pound in the doctor's pocket." This view he shared in common with the ex-parson, who daily recounted instances of speedy and inexpensive recoveries, without skilled aid and the reverse with it. Against both the girl's gentle demands were powerless; besides, the fears of the young lift easily, and Ursula knew nothing of sickness.

Gradually, and not without a great fight, Boshy gave up his pipe. But he instructed her to put his tobacco carefully into his pickle bottle, with a cut potato to keep it from undue dryness — "agin' I git meself again, Lovey."

Shaving that morning he had gashed his cheek with the razor.

"Somethin' bumped me elbow," he said. "Come, now," reassuringly, "you look an' see, Lovey: me 'an's as stiddy as th' Rock o' Ages." He made a brave but futile effort to steady his extended hand. "It's not as stiddy 's it might be," he sadly admitted, as she took the razor from his shaking, uncertain hand.

"Drink this. It will do you good, Boshy."

But his hands seemed scarcely able to hold the cup.

"Nut yet — I'm nut thirsty — but by-and-by, w'en I stiddy up a bit," he promised, turning his face away, wishful to hide its trouble and his disability.

"Boshy, let me feed you, like you used to feed me long ago," she coaxed, understanding.

He smiled with grim bravery, and thinking to humour her, gave her the spoon.

When she had finished, "S'ep me goodness, Lovey," kissing her hands, "but yer a-poddyin' ov me, an' me a full-tooth weaner," he bantered, adding with a flicker of his old manner: "I allus knowed them liddle lambs wuz well able ter feed 'emselves, but they jis wanted t' 'ave someun az they was fond ov a-foolin' roun', an' (after a cough) in that respec' I'm no better un them."

He was silent for a while, with an introspective aloofness on his face, which seemed grey and drawn when he spoke.

"Lovey, ez true ez Gord, I've see an' known a wile dingo act ther tame dorg, t' 'e fooled ther rest ov ther dorgs an' me; then all of a sudden one night, my Gord! ter see ther way 'e mangled them poor unfort'nit lambs. Nex' mornin' t' see ther way them poor ole mother yeos looked et me, much ez t' say, 'If they'd bin yer owen flesh an' blood, yer wouldn' a-risked it.' Fer frum fust t' last they never trusted ther dingo, an' I know now in me 'art I never trusted 'im neither."

He was very excited and exhausted, and the perspiration gathered and ran on his forehead.

"Lovey, I often see yer mother's eyes a-lookin' et me ther same."

Ursula laid her cheek on his tremulous mouth.

"Oh, Boshy! My mother could not — she could not. You have been mother and father to me — both, both," she said brokenly.

"I dunno; Lovey, but I oughter tell yer all I know, an' I will some day, please God, I will, an' thet afore long."

This resolution soothed him, and he went to sleep.

Next day, after a breakfast which Boshy made a determined but vain attempt to eat, the two were sitting silently in his room when Mr Civil came in. His manner to Ursula of late had undergone an indeterminate change: courtesy had almost become familiarity. His "my dear" gave her a convulsive shiver; still, she made no spoken sign of aversion, for already she was experiencing the inequality of her struggle to alter the thing that is. But though she acknowledged the personality of his "my dear", she never looked at him.

To-day when he left the room, she followed him.

"Boshy is very ill"; and now she looked at him steadily as she spoke.

"Not worse than usual, I hope?"

He didn't look at her.

"Much worse. What about a doctor? I'll go across and tell him."

There was a challenge in her tones.

"I'll go myself — I'll go at once," he promised, and a little later she saw him leave.

When she went back, Boshy was again lying down.

"Lovey, yer ortn't t' go a-giddin' an' a-gaddin' about wen I want yer," he complained huskily.

She covered his gnarled blue hands, then wiped the tears of lonely grief from his cheeks, kissing him again and again, till in penitence he said:

"S'ep me goodness! if yer out ov me sight fer a moment, I think yer bin gone fer hours an' hours, an' thet I'll never see yer agen."

"I'm going to stay with you all day, Boshy."

"That's ther talk, but git yer stitchin', Lovey, an' doan be a-idlin' of yer time. But I forgot: yer not one ov ther stitchin' sort, are yer, Lovey? An' them deear liddle 'an's wur never made fer work; but," condolingly, "never mind, I'm kintent wi' yer. They's none ov 'em, wi' all their fancy stitchin', I'd a swop or change yer fer. W'at's Anderer say about 'em, Lovey? — I mean ther liddleness ov yer 'ands."

"Nothing, Boshy."

He grew irritable at once.

"Well, 'e's gut no money, ennyways. No, 'e's gut no money."

He ceased speaking, but Ursula saw that he was distressfully deep in thought.

"But, Lovey, make no mistake. Anderer's gut no money now, but 'e will ev it — 'e's (cough) old man Cameron Cameron's cunninger then any dingo. 'E gut off wi' yur daddy's papers, an' no doubt all 'is money thet time (cough) w'en 'e cum fer you. But, Lovey, wait t' yer comes' ov age an' us'll show 'im us——"

He lay back panting and coughing.

After a painful effort he swallowed a mouthful that she held to his lips, and, despite her entreaties, began again:

"W'at does Anderer tork t' yer about?"

"He hardly speaks to me, Boshy."

"Ah, Lovey, yer oughtn't ter tell me wut's nut true. I often see 'im a-lookin' at yer; 'e would if yer encouraged 'im. Yer know, 'e's nut ther torkin' sort."

He was bitterly disappointed, but he waved her into silence when she sought to explain.

"Yer see (cough), I carn't expec' t' live fer yever an' yever, an' surposin' I wur gorn, w'at then?"

Again he motioned her not to interrupt.

"I'm 'ale an' 'earty at present, but, Lovey ov mine, I'm a good ten 'ears older en w'at any ov 'em knows. S'pose, fer argimen's sake, anythin' 'appened t' me?" Gasping mortally, he repeated: "W'at then, Lovey?"

For answer she bowed her head beside him, so that he could not see her stricken face, then laid her head on his, but only for a moment; even there his heart seemed to be throbbing.

"For my sake, sleep, Boshy," she pleaded, then stroked his brow till he slept, though lightly, and with an ease that almost disarmed her, till he began, as ever, to mutter about a pick and shovel. Waking suddenly, he asked:

"Lovey, ever 'ear tell of Scrammy 'And?" then irrelevantly, "I gut plenty t' do up theere, Lovey; soon ez I git roun' a bit we mus' be orf. There's plenty fer you t' know, an' I'll take yer and show of yer the very exac' spot. W'at 'ave I been a-tellin' yer?" he said abruptly, with a return to his old secretiveness.

"Only about us going away."

He seemed relieved.

"Sooner er later yer mus' know; but, Lovey, nut one word out ov yer lips t' no one. Remember, a still tongue makes a wise 'ead."

She promised.

"Didn' I tell yer about Scrammy 'And a-frightin' the old shep'e'd t' death fer his money?"

"No."

"Well, can yer reckerlec a-'earin' anythin' ov it up et Cameron Cameron's?"

"No, Boshy."

"Good Gord! then s'posin' I should some day be a cooker, yer don't know nothin', nor weer an napenny is to be foun'. Lord above me!" raising up his hands, "w'at em I a-goin' t' do wi' yer, if so be as I shouldn' pull roun'?"

"Dont, Boshy, don't worry; I'm all right."

"O Lord! yer know no more'n suckin' dove w'at's afore yer."

Breathless and weary, he lay back, but staggered up, and with sudden determination began preparations for their journey on the morrow. The futility of it stung her keenly, yet to humour him she made pretence of help; but he was soon exhausted.

"O Lord! me ole 'eart seems all of a skew-wif," he panted complainingly, lying down; but from his bed he directed her: "Me boots, Lovey — don't forget 'em, Lovey; but" — anxiously — "w'at about a-wearin' ov them?"

For days his swollen feet had worn only socks.

"Cut them and let them out, Boshy," she suggested humouringly.

"By 'eavens! them good boots." He was indignant at her proposal. "Leeches 'll do ther trick, Lovey, an' take down me feet. I'd soon git sandy blight in me 'eels a-wearin' an' a-walkin' in boots now."

He dosed, and again woke to ask the same question about Scrammy 'And.

"Reckerlec all erbout Scrammy 'And, Lovey?"

She nodded.

"An'," shaking a warning finger at her, "an' thet a still tongue makes a wise 'ead, an' thet a dorg ez brings a bone 'll kerry one back, so lis'en to no yarns nur tell none."

She would be careful.

"Oh yes," querulously, "w'ile I'm a-nex' an' a-near an' a-nigh yer."

She tried to stroke the trouble from his brow, but he moved his head for her to cease.

"Nut now, nut now; you lis'en t' w'at I say. I'm a-goin' t' tell yer."

He sat up, but she caught and held his swaying body, and gradually the effort to concentrate weakened him into forgetfulness. With half-closed eyes and open mouth he slept for a few moments.

"W'at erbout a pick and shovel?" he asked, sitting up the moment he waked.

She said she could soon get them.

"Nut out theere, Lovey. In the name ov Gord, nut out theere, or Civil 'll drop down; 'e's a-watchin'."

"Not out there," she promised.

He then kept waiting for her to unfold her alternative.

"Weer else can yer git 'em, then?"

"Get what, Boshy?"

"Oh, my Lord!" he moaned, "theer yer are: yer fergit everythin'; yer won't try t' reckerlec a thing." He thrust out his hands and frantically fastened his fingers in his hair. "I've lef' it too late. W'at will she do? w'at will she do?"

Loosening his hands and wiping away his tears, she begged him to be calm and trust her. She remembered everything he had ever told her — every word, everything, she emphasized.

"Now let's see w'at yer do know, then," he said suspiciously.

"Begin with Scrammy 'And?" she stipulated anxiously.

"Right yer are," he encouraged.

She went on: "Who frightened the old shepherd to death for his money."

"Lovey, talk liddle," he whispered, drawing her face down to him. "Lovey, think Scrammy gut the ole shep'e'd's money?"

"Yes," taking her cue intuitively.

"Stick to thet, Lovey ov mine," joyfully. "Think the'e wuz much?" eagerly.

She thought so.

"Ah yes," complainingly; then sagely, "Remember w'at comes over the divil's back goes under 'is belly; an' a narrer getherin' often gits a wide scatterin' — reckerlec thet. Now go on."

Her face was crimson and her breathing as strenuous as his own, but, strive as she would, she could not, mentally even, stumble along with the desired description.

"Come, now, weer d' yer think Scrammy," dropping his voice, "or me a-planted it? Speak liddle, ez you used t' say."

"Rest now," she coaxed.

"Rest! Me rest!" he repeated angrily — "rest, an' you nut knowin' nuthin'? Come now, Lovey, don't be lazy: weer d'ye think ther money wuz planted?"

"I don't know," she wailed.

"Oh my Gord! w'at 'll I do? W'at 'll I do?"

In a frenzy of purpose he stood up. Ursula, facing him, rose also.

"Go back t' wen yer wuz liddle," he commanded. "Can't yer see Nungi and Queeby, an' yer father, afore 'e wuz buried, an' ther yeos and lambs and ther wattle flow-wers, an' you a-chewin' and a-chawin' of ther wattle gum, an' a-getherin' of ther fi'-corners."

"Five-corners," corrected she, going back.

"Go orn!" he implored, suddenly breathless. "Go orn, Lovey!"

Her visualizing eyes were fastened on his hypnotic face. Hers grew ghastly with intensity.

"I can see a little river."

"Creek, Lovey."

But, unheeding, she went on: "I can see a little river. On the other side there's a hut with no door, and the roof nearly off."

"Twuz, but nut now. Someun 'as a-burnt most on it," Boshy interrupted, but almost under his breath.

"Over away from it," waving her hand indicatively, "there are some trees."

"Them's ther myalls, Lovey."

"Under them I," straining her head forward, "can see two graves."

"Yer mother an' father's; an' ther ole shep'e'd's."

"The palings are down and some men are there. They," doubtfully till she tip-toed — "yes, they have picks and shovels. They, they," stumblingly, but Boshy was speechless — "yes, they are throwing up the dirt. They are opening the grave—"

A choking squeal from Boshy silenced her.

"Christ! Gord! Me money — they've foun' me mo——"

In the old helpless manner he threw up his arms. She staggered, but caught his swaying body, and slid with it to the ground. Then, though she loosened his neck, his laboured breath reached only half-way up his throat; as though spent, it sighed in a thwarted throttle. Aided, it rose again successively in a seething gurgle that forced his mouth apart. She caught and rested his helpless head against her shoulder and listened — but he was still; then she wiped the blood from his nose and mouth. Drops had fallen on her hands and wrists, but they were left.

Mina, coming in later, could not distinguish the living from the dead.

11

BOSHY'S will was duly produced from an unexpected quarter, for with his usual cunning he had gone by a detour to the lawyer's private residence. Meeting there the wife, he told her much of his perplexities and anxieties for his Lovey's future. Her sympathy begot his confidence, and with her he had deposited his will, which, from beginning to end, contained but one beneficiary, Ursula Ewart, who was sole legatee to seventeen hundred and eighty-four pounds (£1,784), hidden — where Ursula knew, he testified. Despite her protestations, many agreed that of a surety the girl must know, and searches for Boshy's money — as thorough and as unavailing as those for the old shepherd's — raged for weeks in Boshy's room, Ursula's, all over the house, and for an unreasonable space around.

Recalling his Bush ramblings, the ex-parson wandered many times and oft; aided by his walking-stick, all hollow logs and stumps were explored. At length this gave place to personal espionage of Ursula's every movement.

Less than Boshy's savings would gain the legatee the goodwill of any small town. Besides, many argued, that was merely the sum stored by Boshy; who could tell what he had with him when he died? Sufficient only to bury him was found; but he had been notably cunning and sly, and had trained this girl, whose tragic brown eyes now seemed to hold some mystery. Was she not deep, going about pretending that she didn't know where the money was? What an actress she would have made! Still, each vied in outward kindly attention.

Mina stayed almost nightly with her, because, despite Mrs Stein's importunity, Mr Civil constituted himself the girl's guardian, giving the substance of a conversation with Boshy as his warrant. None outdid him in considerate attention.

"Trust none of them my de-ear," he advised, his small eyes agleam with double meaning. "They are all self-seekers — every one."

He saw this heiress one day assiduously repairing her well-worn clothes.

"That's right, my de-ear, save your money; don't waste it on things that perish," he commended.

She looked at him. She had told him so often that she had none; but she had told all who questioned her the same, yet all agreed she would have made a fine actress. And she understood them.

"Do you mean my father's money, Cameron Cameron told Boshy he had sent to aunt to keep for me?"

"No, no; there was no money sent to your aunt, my dear — Boshy's money. Don't touch it yet — too many Paul Prys; by-and-by, you understand."

One night his stealthy footfall woke her, even before his gentle tapping. She put on her dressing-gown and slippers; and, opening her door, candle in hand, went past him; then she faced him, her raised candle level with his eyes.

"What?" she demanded.

He was fully dressed, though the hour was late, and the sleek blackness of his freshly-dyed hair and brows threw out his sallow pallor.

"What?" again she challenged.

Twice his long hand went to his throat, but, though his lips parted, his tongue only clicked with a dumb dryness. To gain time he made a hand motion for silence, making a pretence of listening for some sounds; but his ears were not helped by his eyes. These smouldering lasciviously under his raised, dye-clogged eyebrows, were set as though fed by those of the girl, blazing with a tigerish hate into his.

"Good time to — er — 'r find his money, my dear — your money," he said, between breaths.

He waited for her to speak, but her set mouth seemed frozen.

"No — rather not, my dear? Well, another night," he said, hastily translating her speechlessness. "Say good-night to me," thrusting out his face.

He advanced to her, misled by her passiveness.

She aimed a heavy blow at his leering face with the candlestick, but he dodged it, and, terrified of a noisy scene, he rushed to his room.

As he lay fully dressed on his bed he heard her

movements for some time; then came a stillness that he, with all his cunning, misunderstood.

On the afternoon of the next day, after many long hours' wanderings, she sat by the river, concealed by some briar-bushes. Andrew and Hugh Palmer were expected, and long since, she had seen the dust of travelling sheep. Mina, soon after dinner, had walked to The Range to meet and welcome the drovers, and Ursula saw her now walking beside Andrew, both leading his horse. Hugh Palmer was not in sight, but after Andrew and Mina and the dog-driven sheep had crossed, he came along at a brisk canter. Catching sight of the bare-headed girl, who had mounted a flood-jettisoned log, and was absorbed in watching the two passing, he guided his horse to her; but when she saw him she shrank again among the briars.

"You, Ursie! What's up?" he asked, quickly dismounting.

She rose; her sun-scorched face was deathly, but she seemed calm.

"Mr Civil came to my room last night, Mr Palmer."

The orphaned look in her eyes struck the best in him.

"Curse him, the dog! Never mind, Ursula, you'll be all right now we're here. No hat?" he asked divertingly, looking at her sunburnt face.

She shook her head.

"I came away in the night."

He took a partially emptied flask from his pocket and poured some brandy into its tin shield. She took it, strangely obedient, meaning to drink it; but the smell nauseated her, though she knew he was reeking with it.

"Wait," he said, "and I'll water it for you."

With manly tenderness he would have placed her on his horse, but she resisted.

"Give me your little hand, then."

So hand-in-hand they went in the twilight to Stein's.

"Fust der 'andt, den der 'ardt," Mrs Stein observed to watching Andrew.

One afternoon a few days later, Palmer and Ursula were sitting on a stool outside, where they had spent many hours since their coming to Stein's. Palmer, with wine-begot sentiment, found a wavering pleasure in trying to probe the depth of her elusive mind; its elusiveness fascinated and enthralled him. He knew from the papers that Cameron Cameron had taken, and Boshy so much regretted, that her origin on her father's side threw back to the Spanish invasion. There was little in Cameron's possession that had escaped his son-in-law. He took a side look at the girl beside him. No particular beauty distinguished her face, but the dainty harmony of it and her body, appealed irresistibly to him. His dead wife had brought him a home but no money, and though he knew from her father's will that Ursula some day would have money despite Cameron's intrigues, yet there would be first a tussle; and he loathed all exertion, mental or bodily. Full fed, with a satisfied stomach, and no duty but inclination, which was now to sit watching her — this for the time seemed to fulfil all desire. For the ease with which he could ring-bark and sap the crude tastes begot by the readings of her callow days was an unending marvel and solace to him.

Ancestry, he thought gloatingly — but instinctively he kept this knowledge jealously. Quickly he realized that to meet her noonday reason a tale must be possible and logical. But he liked best when her twilight mood saw only the poetical; then her soul shone through her face like a star, joyfully radiant or mystically shrouded. This afternoon, in accord with it and her, he began with Ulysses and Penelope. Then next, to watch how at his bidding he could radiate joy or grief from her mood-flecked face, he took Charon and his mystic river and silent freight. Then the beast in him stirred, and he, for the first time, tested her with voluptuous scenes between Anthony and Cleopatra. Vainly did he feelingly paint the perfumed love passages of the passionate pair. The Puritan strain from her mother asserted itself, and this girl beside him saw nothing but lawlessness in the lotus-loving queen's infatuation for another woman's husband, and unfaithfulness in Anthony. Impatiently Palmer got up, and, most unusual for him, walked briskly away. When some time later he returned, she was still sitting there. He noticed the spiritual aloofness of her face, and though he shifted the disinfecting clove in his mouth, he forebore to speak. It was early autumn, and like a regretful sigh, the warm mist about them was floating to the valley of the shadow below.

"See," she said, sighing and pointing to the mist, "the summer's passionate essences float to a mirage ocean where Charon waits."

"River, Ursula," he corrected, holding out his hand for hers, which she, absorbed, withheld.

But this action dispelled her mood, and abruptly she said: "I want to work for my living; tell me how?"

"So you want to work, do you?" he asked, to quell his disquiet. "Oh Lord! work!" and he grimaced in disgust, for to work even for himself was appalling.

Almost earnestly for him he wished for a few hundred pounds a year with this girl; then the reformation he had so often promised himself would be possible, but now how impossible and far off! Who but she cared for the Latin or Greek classics with which he had dazzled her? Hand and body work was what others wanted, and horse sense. As an object-lesson to ear and eye, he turned from inward to outward contemplation.

Below them from the cultivation paddock came the sound of Mrs Stein's mustering incantation to the turkeys. "Cri-li-lati-turi-i-didi-wit-wom-wom."

"Tom — tom!" echoed the empty tin dish she drummed.

"Gool-gool, gool, dee-ri," responded the gulled turkeys, flocking to her decoy.

In the paddock below them Peter Stein, Mina's uncle, bent and twisted by undue labour, staggered stiffly and unwillingly behind a jolting plough. Peter's one vice accounted for his outdoor task: he was trusted with any work but wine-making or bottling. There was a saying that two men and a boy could not watch nor keep him sober in the wine-season.

Principally to avoid the labour, Mina copied his vice, and several times practised it with such success that, her mother, though giving no reason, often barred her going on this duty in the wine season.

But other likes or dislikes were nothing to Mrs Stein, and Mina, though she would have shirked it, was now sand-scouring the milk buckets. Gus was away on his afternoon milk delivery, but Mr Stein was still in sight, driving the cows to their night's grazing. When he came back, if no moon, he would light the swinging lanterns in the milking yard; then he and Peter would clean up the yard and bails for a morrow that would begin long before dawn, for all in this busy household.

"For how much?" Palmer asked himself, his eyes going from Mrs Stein's work-worn face to the bandaged, swollen leg showing beneath her tucked-up skirts; "for what purpose or pleasure is she labouring?" Then aloud:

"Ursula, here comes Mrs Neal. Ha! ha! Look at her trying to squeeze through the fence. I'll bet she doesn't."

The fat proprietress of the Shearers' Rest could not pass, and Peter, though he saw, did little without being told, so waited for her shrill summons to come and let out another panel. Mrs Stein, who expected her, had now, with the aid of the empty dish, deluded her brood to the drying-green near Ursie and Hugh Palmer, and stood with them awaiting the bi-yearly, waddling coming of her customer. It was an open and audible transaction; volubility of the untoward influence of friendship on business, was the foil of the landlady of the Shearers' Rest; firmness and brevity was Mrs Stein's.

Mrs Neal, according to her statement, had been besieged by poultry vendors, yet, from habit and motives of silly sentiment, had come to Mrs Stein. But she couldn't dream of giving as much for this lot as she did for the last, every one of which died disappointingly poor. Neighbourliness was all very well, but she had a duty to herself; besides, the bad times didn't, rightly speaking, allow for poultry on the table. Still, she took, and was acceded, great pride and credit in and for her table; and as Mrs Stein had reared these; and for the sake of friendship for an old neighbour and many other circumstances — well, now how much would Mrs Stein take?

"Same prize," was Mrs Stein's laconic answer. Through minding her brood she must have missed much of her customer's speech, yet when the crux "How much?" came, her "Same prize" was readily forthcoming.

Throughout the whole interview her watchful eyes found work for her hands and guidance for her tongue.

"Go t' sleep, Peder, choost do! Yor ged a goot supper thad way," she bawled; and Peter, thirsty soul, who was eagerly awaiting the order to drive the feathered flock to the Shearers' Rest, grabbed the plough handles and went on, knowing this command would come later, although there seemed no prospect of a deal coming off. For Mrs Neal apparently had abandoned all negotiations, but appeared fully compensated for her unusual exercise by the beauty of her surroundings, seemingly, from her appreciation, seen now for the first time.

Bending painfully by reason of her bad leg, Mrs Stein had industriously filled the decoy dish to overflowing with chickweed, weeded from the vegetable beds; at the same time keeping at bay her clamorous brood, and replying, when necessary, to her sentimental friend's discourse.

"Goom on, Peder; chook yurself aboud ant pud dese turkeys der bed."

Victoriously she turned away, cutting short with "Goot day" Mrs Neal's vivid praises given even to the seedy turnips.

Peter's horse, like himself, always awaited moving orders. It was safe to leave him stationary while Peter helped his sister-in-law drive the still expectant turkeys into an unaccustomed pen — a task that brought Ursula to their assistance. The chickens burst unitedly into a hungry clamour, as Mrs Stein, with the full dish in her hands, leant over the yard to count them. They were all there. She turned away, and emptied the dish into another pen.

"Are you going to feed them?" Ursula anxiously asked Peter.

He stopped and, looking at Mrs Stein, inquired, "Veedt 'em?"

"No; they are soldt."

"GOOD to be you two," Mina said to Ursula and Palmer.

"Better to be another two I know." Hugh Palmer's eyes held more than his words. Mina, standing on the bench, laughed, then, shading her eyes, looked townward.

"See anyone you like better than yourself?" His double meaning was keyed this time for Ursula, but Mina half understood.

"Yes — Ursie."

Ursula for the first time noticed that Mina's eyes, looking down into hers, were the colour of green grapes, and that her little teeth were pointed like Jim's cross-cut saw.

"Andrer's goin' to call for my dress for the party. We're goin' to have a little party."

"For two?" chaffed Palmer.

"When?" asked Ursula.

"To-night. Didn't I tell you long ago? Ole Falkenmeyer's comin' to play. Here's Andrer."

Mina went off with showy delight to meet him, and to avoid them Ursula went to her room.

Standing by her bedroom window, she wondered why she stayed in a household where even Andrew, the friend of her childhood, now kept purposely out of her life, and her out of his. She wanted nothing but advice from him or anyone. Long ago Boshy had sewn a five-pound note in the flap of her winter coat "for a rainy day". To-morrow she would pay Mrs Stein for her week's keep, then——

"W'at are you goin' t' wear?" Mina burst in — she never knocked.

"I'm not going," said Ursula, without looking at her.

"Course not, — sulk in your room an' tell Andrer and Mr Palmer I never told you. I know you," said Mina bitterly.

Ursula rose.

"I'm not like you, any way."

"Me? W'at 'ave I done? W'at's wrong with me?"

"Urgh!" said Ursula, in strong disgust.

Mina's mouth opened and her lower lip fell. She looked inquiringly at Ursula, who, watching her, thought her unduly agitated.

"Oh, that's me gentleman, is it?" Then between short breaths: "You, you! W'at are you? an' ole Boshy an' ole Civil, an' Andrer even, if ther truth was known?"

"You're mad," said Ursie, wondering at her sudden outburst. The sound from outside of the well bucket rapidly descending broke the hostile pause.

"Shut up! there's Andrer," said Mina, drawing back hastily from the window till he passed with a bucket of water, then she went after him.

The hungry discontent of the unfed turkeys distracted Ursula from herself. From her seat at the window she went into the kitchen, where all were busy preparing for the supper-party. Old Mrs Falkenmeyer had cut off the crusts of several loaves before slicing them for sandwiches.

"Ach! I 'af 'ardt to vurk," she complained to Ursula; "alvays, alvays I 'af 'ardt to vurk."

Ursula gave willing help, piling up huge plates of substantial sandwiches, then into a dish she swept the loaf crusts.

"Keeb all crus' for der fowl," admonished the old woman.

"Yes, oh yes," gladly agreed Ursula.

Making a détour she went, sheltered by the rows of decadent scarlet-runners, to the turkey-pen; then noiselessly scattered her gleanings among them, huddled in an unaccustomed corner. Disappointed that none attempted to eat, she crept round to them, meaning by disturbing to entice them. The sound of Mina's voice held her.

"Don't be a fool; she doesn't." That was Hugh Palmer.

"I tell you she does know. She——"

Ursula stood straight, and rattled the dish against the pen, looking into it.

Palmer alone came over to her.

"That you, Ursula?"

"Yes," said Ursula simply, ignoring the obvious.

"Mina's in a great state of agitation; she had planned a surprise to-night, and she thinks you and I know about it."

"I don't, then."

"No, nor——"

The late moon was level with the wide, child-like eyes

looking up at him. He looked away from them, for their sincerity challenged his insincerity into silence.

"They'll not eat at night," he said, with abrupt irrelevance.

Then he looked at her, and his eyes and mouth took a new light and shape as placing a trembling hot hand on hers, he asked:

"Ursula, will you marry me?"

She was quite unembarrassed.

"No, oh no; if I can't be an actress, I'm going to write a book."

Her manner snapped his intensity, and he laughed.

"That's right, little woman, you'll do something yet; there's stuff in you."

Despite his coppery breath, she stretched out to him the hand that a moment back she had withdrawn.

"Mr Palmer, you really think so?"

She seemed part of the radiant moonlight in her exultation.

"By God, I do!" he said solemnly. "You have all the instincts; you want only experience, but" — looking at her tenderly — "you must fall in love first."

Old Falkenmeyer drew the bow along his fiddle critically.

"Come on," said Palmer, "you'll be late."

"I'm not going, Mr Palmer; I'm in black for Boshy."

"You needn't dance. Don't dance with any of them, they're either colts or fools. We'll sit in a corner and talk," he said, leading her inside.

Now old Falkenmeyer's fiddle feelingly quavered a few notes, then sonorously heralded the preliminary bass of the first set. Daddy Stein, standing in the middle of the room, clapped his hands for attention.

"Ladtties andt gentlemens, chooss your pardners for der — der——"

"Firsd sed er kiddrills," Mrs Stein rasped.

The numerous guests surprised Ursula. All had made some brave attempt at festive finery, but she, in her present exultation, felt not of them, and would have gone back but for Palmer.

"What do you care for these cattle?"

And feeling that she did not, she went into an angle. Hugh Palmer brought her a seat and stood behind her, she watching the gathering, he watching her.

Andrew led the much-bedecked Mina to the top; then followed Jam Toohey with his selection, Pat the Jew's gorgeous daughter, and duly others, till top and bottom and both sides of the first set were formed. Talking between Ursula and Palmer was impossible, nor had either wish to speak. To the experienced man, the boorish gaucheries of these countrymen and maids in their methods of pleasuring, but accentuated his own failure and fall; he looked down at the girl near him. It was unwise, for many reasons, to keep markedly near her, but he felt he must, if only for a time. Her face was a puzzle; it reflected neither disgust nor anger. The music had sent her mentally triumphing over a glorious future, if not conceived, then quickened by Ashton's circus. She saw neither room nor dancers, but a vast theatre filled with homage tributers, and for her, though for what rare attribute was not clear.

A half-audible oath from Hugh Palmer, and her chair being drawn further into the corner, recalled her. The first set was ending in a mad gallop; its guerdon, tiring each other down. All sense of pleasure had gone; nearly all faces had exchanged the weak smirk of gratified distinction in participating in the very first set for one of giddy but grim determination to outdo and be last. Gradually the couples decreased till only three remained — Mina and Andrew; Sergeant Toohey's son with the Fuchsia; Widow Neal's daughter and Percy Snade, a local bank clerk. He, a Captain of the Volunteer Regiment, to show his contempt for the company, or his knowledge of military etiquette, kept on his spurs. From various signs, Ursula could see Andrew was for ceasing; but Mina, fiercely determined, forced him on.

"Mina vill vin! Vell don, Mina! Go id, Mina!" shouted old Stein encouragingly.

Hugh Palmer noted with an indescribable feeling of impotence, tempered by relief, that the glow had gone from Ursula's face. She was quite oblivious to him and very silent and still, moving only when Mina's intentioned incursions right into her corner made it necessary to shrink closer to the wall.

Suddenly there was a shriek as Percy Snade swished past Mina, with the best part of her muslin-flounced skirt entangled on his spur-rowels. Instantly the music ceased and the parties disengaged, while Mina, in unconquerable passion, blurted:

"Yer beast! yer brute beast! yer duffer brute!" advancing to him with hands clenching and unclenching like claws.

"Now den, Mina, dond looze yer 'ed," said her father, holding her back so that she could only claw at Snade's laughing partner, to whom, womanlike, she had shifted the blame.

"How green her eyes are!" thought Ursula, and more than ever her teeth seemed saw-edged.

"No good der cry aboud spilled milk. Pud on yer green," said Mrs Stein, who had left her occupation of serving drinks to see what caused the commotion. "Andt, young mans, if you wandt der dance again any mores, dake off yous spurs."

"A dastardly action," Jam Toohey remarked to Palmer, "coming into a ballroom with spurs on."

Some of the girls gathering round Mina, offering pins and advice in the restoration of her skirt; but it was beyond this, and she disappeared to change. There was a meaning pause, broken by old Stein again clapping his hands.

"Ladtties and gentlemens, once more, der nex' dance vill pe a song."

"Goot on yer, ole sour crouts," encouraged Teddy Neale, the dissolute droving son of the proprietress of the Shearers' Rest, who had come too late for the first set and had already sought and swallowed a pint of consolation, though Mrs Stein said afterwards that he was "haff drung wen 'e koms".

"Now then, toon up again," he bawled, having selected his partner.

"Silence," weakly demanded Jam Toohey in his father's official manner.

"Was that fur me, Jam?" asked Teddy, threateningly advancing.

"No, certainly not, Teddy," Jam denied, edging closer to Palmer.

"Generally a sign er rain w'en frogs croaks, ain't it, Mr Palmer?" said Teddy, retiring to his seat beside his sweetheart, gentle, trembling Teresa, Jam's sister.

"Now then, let 'im go, Golligah. Give it lip!" he shouted, but the silence continued. "Waitin' for me, I suppose, t' give you a leg up. Well, here goes for a start," he said, standing up.

The Cobar Road is a beggar of a road,
  For on it there's neither grass nor water;
I met an ole gin with her 'ead caved in,
  And she wanted me to marry 'er daughter.

"Chorus," he bawled, but instead gave them a few minutes' brisk step-dancing.

Before its echoes had ceased, a stout woman, Babyfinder Thompson, rose and stood beside her husband, seated with a concertina poised on his knee. But Teddy had his plans.

"Now then, Teresa, giv' 'em me old favourite, 'Bole Maryann', an' gi' yer Sergeant Daddy a tap."

"Sing 'Jewnita', Teresa," advised Pat the Jew's daughter Fuchsia, thereby currying Jam's favour.

"Sing w'at I tell yer, Tressy," ordered Teddy.

Weakly obedient to him, she, in a voice in utter variance with the theme and rollicking tune, began:

The Bobbies they run after me
  To catch me if they can,
But there's none of them smart enough
  For bold Maryann.
    Chorus: Fry the Bobbies in the pan,
      Fry the Bobbies in the pan.

As a filial protest Jam walked outside, but though Teresa looked appealingly at her sweetheart Teddy, he insisted in its finish. Then with much ostentation the Babyfinder's husband rose and dexterously sent angling through the room some congested chords. His wife had risen before the finish of the last song; she coughed, cleared her throat, sniffed, smoothed the front of her best dress, then in a long-distance range began:

Ther bibee wors sleepin', eets mother wors weepin',
Eets father wors ploughin' ther deep ragin' sea.

She sang it through, and before the weak applause had ceased, forestalled an encore by starting another. The virtue we lack is the one we covet or assume; therefore, despite her vigorous interpretation and execution, the following song was a tribute to "Gentil Hannie Lisle".

Wave willers, murmur waters,
  Goldin sunbeams smile;
Hearthly music cannot wakin
  Gentil Hannie Lisle.

However, at its conclusion, and apparently to test the earthly futility to rouse "gentil Hannie", her spouse rose to his feet and made a daringly gymnastic musical display, producing at the same time the tune unbrokenly. Beginning at arm's length above his head, travelling an incredible distance down his spine to within jumping range from back to front, then from the front to the starting-point above his head. Like his bigger half, not waiting for encouraging plaudits, with startling abruptness he began a vocal and instrumental duet:

I went ter T-O-W-N—

he sang, and spelled T-O-W-N, as did the concertina—

Me name was B-R-O-W-N;
They took me D-O-W-N
When I went to T-O-W-N.

It was a long song independent of the instrumental repetitions, but rollicking Teddy Neale, who had again drenched his troublesome throat, soon interrupted.

"Damn it now for a fair thing; better go down an' 'ire ther School o' Arts. Give someone else a show. Toon up, ole buck, an' give us a polka," he ordered old Falkenmeyer, and dragged drooping Teresa into the middle of the floor.

When Mina, more composed, returned, she came over to Ursula, and Palmer directly asked Mina to dance. As they turned away she looked back at Ursula in malignant triumph. Andrew had disappeared, but Gus Stein, standing near, immediately came into Palmer's place, while Daddy Stein from the middle of the room loudly besought Ursula to "Come ouder yer corner, siddin' there likge a liddle 'Orner, andt dance."

"Come on, Ursie," begged Gus Stein, taking her by the arm.

"I won't dance to-night, Gus."

"That's because 'e didn't ask you," pointing to Palmer.

"He did," she asserted. "He — it's got nothing to do with you who asked me."

"You needn't tell me what I know," he said bitterly.

He sat beside her, nervously biting his incipient fair moustache, and early as it was she could smell the wine on his breath and felt sorry.

"Gus, why do you take wine?" she asked.

"Oh Lord! I like that from you, I do. You that won't look at a man unless he does."

"I don't know what you mean," she said.

"Well, ask Andrew, then. Ursula, look 'ere, now," he was boyishly eager. "Say I swear off, will you give me a show? I'm dead nuts on you."

She did not answer him, for the nature of his words outdistanced his personality. "That's twice to-night I've been asked to marry", was the gratifying circumstance that held her. Certainly neither was her ideal, but, later, when she had done some great thing, there would be a possibility even of her ideals. She took refuge now from Gus's importunity, in the noisy, colliding movement of the dancers. Palmer had been swift to drop out, Jam Toohey, too, soon followed, and came to her importuning for a dance. His sister, too, would have been glad to stop, but her boisterous admirer was still twirling her round and round, for the polka had given place to a valse. Andrew joined Gus.

"Are you not dancing?" he asked Ursula.

She shook her head.

Then someone called him, and he replied with such surprising jocularity and recklessness that wonderingly she looked at him. His hair was cut close, showing a white margin all round his head; his eyes blazed excitedly, and his face was flushed unduly. He was unusually confident, and seemed altogether strangely alien and changed.

"Not dancing, Ursie?" he said again.

As before, she shook her head.

"Why?"

"Oh, ask 'im," said Gus Stein, pointing to Hugh Palmer, now talking to Mina — "ask my grandaddy, and 'e'll tell you why."

He laughed discordantly.

She looked up at Andrew, half expecting to see her resentment reflected in his face. For a moment his dilated eyes unmeaningly met hers; then she turned away from their unsympathetic glitter, feeling desolately alone.

"We've no show, old feller" — Gus Stein brought his hand resoundingly down on Andrew's back — "no show against——" He threw his body forward, and sank his neck into his upraised shoulders, in forcible imitation of Hugh Palmer. "By Christ! 'e's like — like — wot's 'e like, Andrew?"

"The bull on Keen's mustard," added Andrew, applauding Gus's graphic mimicry with a loud, reckless laugh.

Looking at Palmer shudderingly, Ursula saw the awful resemblance which Gus had demonstrated and Andrew had avowed.

"You've hit it, Andrew, old boy — the bull on the mustard-tin. After you with the mustard, please, miss," Gus said mockingly to Ursula; then again his and Andrew's laugh rang out.

"What's the joke?" asked Palmer, coming to them.

"Too sultry for you," answered Gus, in offensive tones.

"Mr Palmer, will you come out to the veranda?" asked Ursie, in purposeful attention.

"Certainly."

He bowed and gave his arm.

"Hook yer mutton, Andy, for ther next spin," advised Ned Neale, noisily bearing down on them with his partner, as Palmer and Ursula left.

Ursula was silent. Even by the night-light Palmer thought she was very pale, but he was in no mood to sympathize. Her open preference was rather disconcerting, and he was half afraid of his previous impulsiveness, though mingled with it was a subtle sense of satisfaction in this triumph over Andrew and Gus. She was ashen, though burning with bitterness and anger against Andrew, yet coldly a-quiver with an indefinable sense of loneliness, loss, and resentment. Revolting to her as he was to-night, had Palmer asked her to marry him then, she would have said "Yes". He, as though her mood radiated to himself, felt the danger and was silent, even definitely drawing her back to the door to watch the ever-increasing frenzy of these revellers. The noise was deafening, again and again, in obedience to their clamorous demand, old Falkenmeyer had changed tune and time, till, beaten and exhausted, he ceased. Then Neddy Neale, dragging his dazed partner, swished past where Palmer and Ursula stood. Gus Stein, with Pat the Jew's daughter and Andrew with Mina, still kept the floor, but now the rat-tat-tat accompaniment knuckled from the bottom of a tin dish by Dave Heely, Neale's drover mate, till, tired out, even he ceased.

Then the dancing husband of the singer, importuned, momentarily disengaged his partner to grab his concertina, and with this resting on the girl's back, he kept the dancers going, till also he, though much encouraged, wearied. Dry-throated and panting, some of the wine-maddened performers tried to hoarsely bellow independent tunes, which in turn yielded to impotent yells. Vainly Daddy Stein objected; but, though Mrs Stein came from time to time to the doorway, she was grimly silent; nor was she knitting, Ursula noted. Never before had she seen Mrs Stein's hands idle.

"God, they're crazy!" muttered Palmer.

Ursula's face shrank grimly, her mouth contracted into a set line. Palmer felt his remoteness from her, and consistently felt relieved and angry.

"Look out for your mundooeys," yelled Ned Neale.

Ursula stepped nearer Palmer, and at that moment Andrew and Mina violently collided with her, sending her reeling into Palmer's arms. She fought free of his crushing clasp, pushing him from her with open disgust for his breath and body.

"She's only throwin' 'er rubbish w'ere she throws her love," laughed Mina, breathlessly, to Andrew, but intently watching them.

Looking at Ursula's terrible little face, Hugh Palmer thought there was little to choose between the suppressed tempest of Ursie's now and Mina's unsuppressed passion earlier. Andrew had disappeared, but Mina, fanning herself, was coming towards him.

"Good-night, Mr Palmer," Ursula said perfunctorily; but now even he seemed to be waiting for Mina.

Sleep Ursula could not, for the noise of their maddened cries penetrated even into her little room. She was utterly powerless, she knew, to stop it; and from time to time she rose and restlessly looked into the night. The hungry are supposed to sleep soundly; but it was not so with the stupidly fasting turkeys, though now their complainings seemed a trifle that could find no place in her mind. She turned her ears from their metallic piping to sounds from the front of the house. From there she heard someone come stumbling through the back passage leading to the wine-cellar — Peter, she guessed. It took some time for him to find what he sought; but at length she, listening intently, heard his glug, glug. It was Peter drinking out of a bottle, too gratified and intent to hear the swift steps that meant the coming of Mrs Stein. Crash came the bottle to the stone floor, followed by the sound of Mrs Stein in a subdued, concentrated fury, pounding Peter and cursing, as she always did when excited, in German. Peter, already half stupefied, was dully complaining, quite impersonal in his resistance. Ursula heard him slide to the floor, and Mrs Stein, when she went, left him there. Later, when Ursula tried to reach the heavily sighing and groaning creature, she found the door locked and the key gone.

Gradually she, too, slept, and when she awoke the spring dawn was dewily ascending, heralded by the twittered delight of bush-birds and the loud arrogance of the still perched roosters. A vivid sense of past and coming trouble gripped her, blended with a far-away but subtle feeling of familiarity. Before, somewhere and time ungraspable, blurred and beset with bewildering details, she had lain alone in bed, listening to gladsome bird voices, mingled with a sense of distressed humanity. Then came the scene she had described to Boshy, but now that stood out boldly and clearly. She could not — must not — dwell on Boshy's tragic end, and for distraction she looked round.

In the far corner stood Mina's bed undisturbed.

"They have kept it up all night," thought Ursula. Was it late, she wondered? While wondering, she could distinguish a confusion of angry voices — Mrs Stein's, Daddy's, Palmer's. Mina was noisily crying, but, in effect, it seemed to Ursula to be as impersonal as Peter's moans. Many times she heard Andrew's name, but not his voice, in denunciation of some act he had done. She did not speculate as to the cause of this disturbance. Of a sudden a thought took possession of her, that some time to-day she would go quietly away and never see Andrew nor any of them again. Those tiresome turkeys could now see and were eating the food she had found for them; so, tranquillized, she noiselessly drew down the window-blind and again slept.

Some hours later she was sitting outside under the group of willow-trees near the well. Below her in the house paddock, Gus Stein, rounding up the horses, was bawling for Peter to come and help him. Looking about for the invisible Peter, Ursula saw Mr Civil going along a footpath back to town. Before coming to the slip-rails, she saw him turn and also look in all directions. Instinctively she felt that it was for her, and a trembling fear shook her; and, cowering, she hid till this black bird of ill omen was out of sight.

Then from the house came a group to her — Mrs Stein, Daddy, Mina, Palmer, and Andrew. Her mouth set frozenly; this very day she meant, with neither stinging words nor reproaches, to part for ever from Andrew.

When Mrs Stein stated her case, she waited as if in expectation of speech from Ursula. All seemed to have chosen Ursula for judge, or she arrogated that function to herself.

"He must marry her", was her verdict.

Mr Stein, unperceived, had slipped away while his wife made her charge against Andrew.

"Yes," agreed Mina's mother, "thad is righd enoff, andt 'e aff marry 'er allreedy, andt wod den?"

Her English was not so good as usual, and her face was almost flushed. She looked at Mina disapprovingly, who had raised her drooping head to shoot a triumphant glare into Ursula's eyes, wide with horror.

Andrew, Mina's husband! Ursula turned from her to him. The veins in his forehead stood out stagnantly; his blood-red eyes looked mournfully, helplessly at Ursula's, filling swiftly with maternal solicitude. His purple lips were moving, but speechlessly, and tremblingly his great hands went to and from his bare, pulsating throat. Water that had been poured over his dazed head dripped from it still.

"Andree, Andree!" screamed Ursula, rushing to him. "What's the matter? What have they done to you?"

Again he tried to speak, but not to her, and his hands clutched his throat to free the speech stuck in it.

"Have a drink, Andrew," aimlessly invited Palmer.

Ursula decided in a swift look that he was little less composed than Andrew. Her eyes, fastened questioningly upon Palmer, visibly increased his agitation. He dropped his head and kicked at a tuft of grass.

"You get him one!" she demanded sternly.

"Ged warder, no more wine; 'e haf dring doo much wine," commanded Mrs Stein.

Palmer brought out a dipper and cup, and, filling the cup, handed it to Andrew without looking at him.

"Sit down, Andrew," said Ursula, hoping that his unsteady hand, holding the water, would then reach his mouth.

"Now then, dring up ther warder, then shuck yerself aboud. Wod's goin' t' be don'?" said Mrs Stein.

"You leave him alone. What more do you want, if he has married her?" demanded Ursula fiercely.

"When" — Andrew cleared his throat — "did I — marry her? Catch me marrying her!" he gasped huskily.

"Misder Palmer, you widness id. Listen to 'im torg. I dell

you, sir, id wass marry 'er or de lockup andt der jail andt der 'ang-rope."

Andrew drew the back of an invoking hand across his brow. So spurred, he recalled a recent scene as one coming to, after falling from a great height, might recollect the sight of those watching the tragedy.

"Were you there, Ursie? No," he decided before she spoke. "But you were" — indicating Palmer — "and old Civil and Gus. No, not Gus." He turned his head away from Mina to her mother. "You dosed me. Talk about the hang-rope, if I had been in my senses, before I'd marry you" — pointing to Mina, with his head turned away — "I'd hang a week."

Gus Stein, with face deathly, rushed to them.

"Mother! Mina! poor old Peter's dead!"

"So iz Queen Ann," said the unmoved mother. For in the light of this living tragedy the sudden death of drunken Peter lost all importance. Andrew, deaf and oblivious to Ursula's tender pleading, was battling impotently with a torrent of angry declamation. Again his virile blood seethed, purpling and distending neck and face and brow. Again his hands fought for words to denounce this plot and plotters, till Ursula caught them, calming him instantly.

"Ursie! Your dear little hands!"

His bloodshot eyes looked hopelessly into hers, aching yet ashine with sympathy; then the tempestuous blood spurted from his mouth and nose. Palmer brought out his handkerchief.

"Not yours, not yours!" Andrew shouted.

13

THE tilt hooding the spring-cart was insecure — even the jolt from the down-and-up curving river bend near the house had brought it down twice. This was the third start. Peter had been an adept with tilts, as old Stein had said so often that morning, while he, Palmer, and Gus, had dubiously laboured at this elusive task. But Peter would rig no more tilts, and primitively old Stein and Gus lamented this, as they missed his services. Mrs Stein cut short all such comments by an over-vehement list of his failings; and finally it was her secure fingers that gave the requisite binding pass, and firm twitch, that had withstood the crucial descent and ascent of the river-bank. Mrs Stein's well-trained fingers could work without her eyes, else, though anxious, she would not have watched.

Mina, forced from home by her mother, was on the way to the husband, who, after recrimination and repudiation, had secretly gone to his Bush home. Ursula, urged by Mrs Stein constantly, and spurred by an indefinable impulse, had consented to go also.

"Vell, dat vas vod I call a glean sveep, Mina, Pomer, Urzie, and" — turning to where Peter lay — "poor oldt Peter," said Peter's brother.

He waved his hat in token of Ursie's hand seen through the back of the tilt, then followed his wife dutifully to the back of the house. In addition to his regular duties he now had Peter's — Mrs Stein had Mina's. When this was discussed as a difficulty by Mina's father, "Oh, Lordt! Mina vork!" Mina's mother said, and actually ceased pinning back and up her skirts to raise her brow and hands. "Oh, Lordt!" The repetition finished the sentence eloquently.

Mina's father, too, raised his hand, and beginning at the point where Peter lay, he circuited to the now hidden travellers.

"Vell, anyvays, id's a clean sveep," he repeated.

Mrs Stein now was swiftly but surely removing the egg-trays from the incubator. In mild surprise old Stein watched her.

"Goin' ter schange 'em?" — indicating the eggs.

"Give a 'andt," was her reply, and together they pushed the incubator into Mina's room.

"S'posin' Andrew clear oudt agen oncet more from up there, vere vill Mina sleeb ven she come back?"

"She comes back 'eres no more," she said decisively.

"Budt s'posin' 'e clears oudt."

"Less rubbish more room, andt Mina comes back no more," she reiterated.

When he, fagged by his double duties, was returning that afternoon, he saw smoke ascending from outside.

"Vot game now she play?" he asked himself, as he distinguished his wife near one of the pig-scalding coppers. Doubt and even fear dwelt in his eyes, travelling from her tucked-up skirts down to her bare feet. But they rested without emotion on the bandages emphasizing her swollen leg.

"Chrise! Peder's best 'at on yous 'eadt. You lose no dime," burst from him.

"Vell, vill 'e anymores vand id? Gus vill nod vear id, 'e say; andt you karnt. Vill I leave id to rodt?" She pressed it firmly on her head for answer.

She had Mina's bed and bedding outside as a finality.

He angrily looked at her, but she was engrossed in active examination of the mortised crevices of the bedposts. Stooping, he picked up the two she specified for him to carry.

"Nise mother you are, I mus' say," he fired at her.

"Andt you 'ave a nise dotter, I mus' say," she retorted.

"Mine. Chrise! Ain't she yous dotter, doo?"

"No" — shortly. Then challengingly: "Am I der man cat? Vos I ever got aboud?" — most excellently she mewed.

"Vell, 'oo vas? Nod me," he defended.

"Yous sister."

"Ach, Brenda!" he breathed in relief.

"Yes, an' ven she leafe I dake down 'er pedt; andt id, too, vass crawlin'." Her English suffered when she was angry.

From the crevices of the last post she withdrew a chocolate speck, squirming on the point of a long pin.

"This von vos nod borned into der vorld yesterday. Bud

if Mina vos 'ere she say so. Egscuses, egscuses — alvays dat. Ach! she go to 'ell bud she comes 'ere no more."

As they jolted along, in the creaking old cart, Ursie daily watched Mina for signs of uneasiness. If Mina felt any misgivings she betrayed none on the journey. With her head on a bag of seasoning herbs, given by Daddy Stein, she slept the best part of the day, waking refreshed and hungry when the cart stopped for their midday or evening meals.

Ursula either walked or sat well forward, trying to escape from the nauseating smell of the herbs. Dizzy with an effort to distract her thoughts she would try to search for Boshy's landmarks, so often described. Besides, she too had travelled along them, though, to her, ages ago. Boshy had told her that he had wandered off the track last time. At dark he had camped, taking for his pillow a little rise that he thought was a deserted ant-heap; next morning he discovered it was a grave. Maybe that little mound was it — or that beyond, for there were many. Rarely they sighted some isolated boundary rider's hut, and early one morning they passed "Gi' Away Nothin' 'All". Palmer pointed it out. Twice they had struck a wine shanty, but it was not the shearing season, consequently neither had its staple commodity — a circumstance, in the first instance, unimportant to Palmer, who then, with characteristic generosity, produced his well-supplied barrel. But though equally importuned, he had none to spare for the last.

What would Mina do if Andrew would not have her? had troubled Daddy Stein, who had secretly discussed it with Ursula; for Andrew had sworn that he would never live with Mina. Night and day now it haunted Ursula, yet there lay his wife, seemingly unthinking of the alternative, and certainly unafraid and unconcerned - - "And," thought the overwrought girl, "she is puffing breaths of the aggressive seasoning in my face."

"Stop; let me get down and walk."

Then she would walk for hours, and though she had often to do so, Palmer would uncomplainingly draw rein, and slacken the horses' speed to her pace. Generally such halts would waken Mina, who welcomed them only if they meant meal-time, waiting to alight till Palmer had prepared the fire, and Ursula spread the food. Mina had ears and smiles for his jokes, and understanding for many an innuendo mystic to Ursula. That Ursula should dislike the smell of the seasoning herbs in the cart, or the pungent pennyroyal at intervals surrounding them, amused her. Surreptitiously she inserted a sprig of it into Ursula's pint of steaming tea. Its violent result convulsed her with merriment.

"Still, as mother 'ud say, 'Sick after supper saves no meat,' " she laughed, though her merriment instantly vanished when concerned Palmer forced Ursula to swallow some brandy.

"We'll sight the homestead to-morrow, Ursula," one day he encouraged, for her worn, white face touched him.

With that day her heart shrank, and instinctively she turned to look at Mina, but Mina was outwardly unconcerned.

"Pine Point." He indicated a sweeping curve of giant primeval pines, the extreme point of which had screened a semicircle of river-split plain. The cart stopped, and Ursula, overborne by a strong but trembling impulse, steadied herself by the tilt, and stood up on the shaft. Immediately, under the glare of actuality, the mist of her ever-recurring sub-consciousness dissolved. Every detail that met her eyes was familiar, and always had been, dreaming or waking; of a truth, she might have told Boshy that she remembered. There was the old hut: the door faced the river, but she could plainly see the gap in the broken roof. This side of the river, though dwarfed by distance, still mouldering, were the myalls, scantier maybe, but there. Beneath them she knew what, though none now laboured as in her memory. On the other side, outlined by the sentinel pines, was the home of her childhood; beside it the paddocks. From them she turned to where the well and troughs used to be. The sheep were all round both, and she could see the wim ascending and descending — worked by whom?

Breathlessly she sat down, and yoked by mutual agitation she turned to Palmer. A purple hue had overspread his face, and the guilty grimness about his mouth quietened her different emotion. He made no reply to Mina, who, to manifest her careless freedom, talked louder and smiled continuously, but with her mouth only, Ursula noted.

As they neared the well Ursula saw the wim cease; so did Palmer, and again his face changed, but he continued to drive till they crossed the river. Without a word he handed the reins to Mina, then slid down and disappeared under the river-bank.

Instantly Mina ceased to smile.

"Has he gone to tell Andrew?" asked Ursula.

"'Ow do I know where 'e's gone to?" she said, lashing the horses. But Ursula, though she watched for his appearance at the well, noticed that Mina's eyes went the other way.

Involuntarily Ursula looked for the myall logs; both, unchanged, were there. Tumbledown Jimmy was dead, she knew, for Boshy had told her how the blacks had buried him alive.

In front of the house the horses stopped, but both women kept their seats, their eyes fixed on the closed door, as though waiting for it to open to welcome them.

"Jhust you git down and open the door," said Mina, assuming authority to cover the trepidation that her "jhust" betrayed.

Ursula struggled down, and Mina followed; then both stood aimlessly before the front-door.

"Open it! Open it!" Mina's hands worked in harmony with her command. Both women tried, but neither could open it.

Overborne by a sense of familiarity, Ursula went round to the back-door, slipped her hand through the opening showing, and slid back the bolt.

"What will we do with the horses?" before entering she asked.

Mina nodded towards the river.

"'E'll see to them w'en 'e comes. Quick! let's get in; 'e's comin'."

Hastily they both entered.

Near the top of the back-door was an almost unused, rusty bolt, which Mina forced across. Ursula saw her spring high to reach it, and heard its harsh creak, then stood with her back against the table, despoiled of its original top, long ago, by Boshy. Her hands grasped the one replacing it. Mina sat on the sofa on the other side.

The noise of galloping hoofs: the scrunch of a hasty foot sliding from the stirrup along the sand: then an authoritative rap and shake at the front-door. A sense of her deceit struck and sickened Ursula, as she saw a hand thrust through the back-door, as hers had been. It was bolted above; he did not know, but she did, yet she was powerless to speak and say so. Above the emotional din in her ears she could hear someone demanding the door to be opened. Intently she watched how the outside force widened a crack from the bottom, till, with a splintering crash, it burst open.

Through a mist, caused apparently to her, by her own breath, she saw Andrew — saw him look at her, and realized that the horror and agony on his face was caused by her gasping breath. She saw him tower, then shrink, yet she could not spare him. It was fate that he should suffer, and, great God, pity him! for how he must be suffering, and again he might burst a bloodvessel. She groaned and her hands went out to him, then dropped; he was Mina's husband.

Oh, that terrible smell of blood! Yet she must stir it, or it would be ruined. Virtuously her hand went out, circling in a vain endeavour to keep away Mina's husband.

14

FOR Ursula's sake, there was no word spoken by Andrew of the home-coming of Mina, who gave no grateful sign. With Andrew in sight, she made pretence of performing some household duty, ceasing with it half through when he disappeared.

Queeby was dead, and Nungi had taken for wife a young gin, but his merciless marital reign died with Queeby. So it was all tasks heavy and unpleasant were left to Ursula, for Gin Woona closely copied Mina in eye services, the difference being Woona's were practised for Mina, as Mina's were for Andrew.

Andrew now slept in Boshy's old workshop, Mina in the bedroom, and Ursula on the sofa in the front room.

Palmer at rare intervals called, carefully stating that his business was with Andrew, and going to him wherever he was to be found.

The long days were empty of all but household work; still here, as ever, Ursula was spellbound with a compelling sense of waiting, Andrew and she scarcely spoke. If he by chance saw her carrying or lifting a heavy burden, he was swift to relieve her; but it was an unusual happening, for Mina did one thing thoroughly, and that was watch. Helpful action from her always signified to Ursula that Andrew was in sight.

The whole thing must end, the girl said to herself every day, and she must get away. When and how, though, always belonged to to-morrow.

"It's in my blood. What has come to me? Why have I changed? What am I doing here? Why is it always to-morrow?" she moaned. Then her mouth drew into a thin line. "I will make it to-day," she decided; "I must tell him."

But it was night before he came home, so again she shrank from what she knew would be a shock to him. She would wait for a time when he would not look so tragically weary. Then, when she had gone to meet him with this to say, the divining wild fear in his eyes had silenced her. Mina, as ever, watching, only saw her pass him without speech, and go swiftly towards the river.

Still, Ursula's inner consciousness comforted her that the time was only deferred. Then, consoled and sustained by such human complexity, she decided to immediately act; and, looking across the sheep-yards, she saw Andrew coming; it was an unusual hour, but he wanted a branding-iron. She went to meet him, and when he stopped she saw the old look of fear dart into his eyes, but she was resolved nothing must prevent her.

"Andrew — I——"

"I know, Ursula. Wait till I come back. It will be better — things, I mean. I'm going to Queensland in a day or two; the station there is my own. You must have money, plenty of money, then you can go where you like. Go to London, Ursie, and write your book," he said, smiling grimly.

She was silent, for she knew when he had spoken that she really had never meant to go.

Together they turned to the house. Mina was standing by the table; she had a hood on, and had pulled it well over her eyes, but Ursula saw how wicked her mouth was.

"Andrew is going to Queensland, Mina."

"You, too?" asked Mina viciously.

It was midnight before he went to his room that night. Then Ursula wondered, did he sleep? she did not. As he, dry-mouthed, tried to eat breakfast next morning, she saw how a few hours had changed him.

All day he, with Nungi and his black boy, were busy with the sheep; then night again found him, till the small hours, busy in his bedroom and office.

"Why do you work so hard lately?" Ursula had ceased to call him by any name.

He looked at her with the old boyish light of their free days.

"Putting my house in order," he quoted.

"Will you be long away?" burned on her tremulous lips. Certainly she might ask this, and explain that she did not wish to remain here; but as she thought it she felt that any tangible desire was dead.

A "hand" from Cameron Cameron's was coming to manage the place, in pleased confidence Mina told her; Nungi and his gin were to remain as they were. Rain had replenished the river, so that the wim and the well rested; food in abundance was everywhere, encroaching even on the trodden track to the river and the sand patch before the house. It was well with beast and bird, and the musical callings of both were good to hear. Management under such conditions would be easy. Mina said Palmer would find it so.

"Palmer! Is *he* coming?" asked Ursula.

"Part of this place belongs to him as well as to Andrew," was Mina's evasive retort.

"Boshy used to say it was mine," rose to Ursula's lips. She restrained herself from taunting, not even saying:

"In Queensland Eulari is Andrew's own."

Mina, over-eager to trip her, waited, but she was silent.

All that day Ursula took refuge from herself in ceaseless work. In the dusk she saw the black boy yard some horses, then overhaul the pack-saddles — so to-morrow would be the day.

She knew to a moment when Mina's sleep began, and waited always for the sign, then she felt free to think; and this night it seemed to Ursula that Mina, too, must be wakeful. Andrew did not make even a pretence of going to bed, for late though it might be before Mina slept, even then he had not gone to his room. Leisurely the long hours ticked into nothingness, yet there was no sound from him. Would he go in the night, as he did before from Stein's, without a word? Ursula's heart quickened agonizingly, though she lay still, tingling with the thought. Suddenly, an uncontrollable impulse mastered her; she rose and, shrouded with the counterpane, passed barefooted, without sound, into the night.

The moon had almost sunk to a level with the stockyard, where her eyes turned. Standing near the old myall logs, she saw Andrew. He was bareheaded, but otherwise ready for his journey. He stood motionless, though he had seen and known her first, but from his eyes came beams of light as though to guide and draw her to him.

At the head of his shadow she stopped, her eyes fixed on his, and blazing as though fed by the same flame. All about her fell the dazzling moonlight, greedily enveloping her lest his shade, stretching towards her, should dull its gleaming power on her face, throat, and bare feet. Her hands were outstretched to him, his to her, yet both were motionless, for about them was a stillness, stagnant and omnipotent as death — and it was Death's moment, thought, and desired the girl — when suddenly, from a far point in the river, with the solemnity and clarity of Gabriel's trumpet, came that Bush-call, which few, even of its chosen, are privileged or fated to hear. In a span of sound it floated high over them, mournfully dying as it sank towards the lagoon, miles away in the scrub.

Both had followed the sound with their eyes, but the light had died in Ursula's when they again sought Andrew's, and his shadow had conquered the moonlight. She raised her fallen hand in voiceless farewell, and in the same way his went out to her.

Did Mina know Andrew was gone? Though he had not come to breakfast, she had not remarked, and a new sensation kept Ursula from speaking his name. Guiltily, from time to time, she took swift inquiring looks at Mina, who was dressed more carefully, and had fresh plaited her hair. Many times she went to the front, and, shading her eyes, took a steady survey of the working centres on the plain beyond.

"Set for three," she said to Ursula, who had prepared the dinner-table for Mina and herself.

The girl trembled violently. She must tell her Andrew was gone.

"Andrew," she forced from her dry lips — "Andrew ——"

"Palmer," snapped Mina; "'ow sly you are, w'en you know Andrew's gone. Didn't you see 'im off."

But though they waited till long past the usual hour, Palmer did not come, and as night did not bring him, Mina went down to Nungi's hut for news. Palmer had camped for the night at One Tree Hut, the half-caste told Mina.

"W'y?" she angrily demanded.

Nungi, hungry and weary, had come to a fireless and supperless hut, and, after fire-making, was busy preparing supper for himself and Woona — she sitting calmly watching him.

"W'y didn't he come home?" re-asked Mina.

Nungi was too hungrily cross to be respectful.

"Oh, missus, arst me somethin' easy. Palmer's all right; 'e's got plenty tucker an' blankets, an' Dildoo ter wait on 'im, so 'e won't catch cole, nur go 'ungry t' sleep. I wish ter Gord I stayed there meself stead ov comin' 'ere." Going on his knees, alternately with mouth and hat he fanned the smouldering fire into a blaze. "If I never come 'ome she'd never make no fire," he complained, indicating the unmoved Woona. Weariness had made him reckless, but he hastily and pacifically added: "An' then you'd go 'ungry t' bed, yer see, an' feel orl over alike t'morrer, wouldn't yer, Woona?"

But she, tyrannical in her youth, only glared at him.

"She ain't strong, an' don't eat much," was his loud excuse to Mina, unamiably watching both, and disappointed at Nungi's giving in.

"Isn't she? Tur! she's strong as a horse, an' 'as 'ad her tea up at the house long ago," enlightened Mina, as she went out.

When a few paces outside, she paused to listen to the virulent abuse of the now tongue-loosened Woona. There was only the distinction of sex between the well-qualified nouns that Woona impartially divided between Mina and Nungi. Nor had he any defence for himself nor for his mistress.

When Mina went in again, Woona was still squatted among the ashes; she was silent as Mina entered, but her black eyes rolled defiantly and her lower lip fell snarlingly.

"You low, black brute!" stormed Mina; "I 'eard all you said. Nungi, get your whip and thrash 'er. Go on — go on this minute."

Nungi moved back from his wrathful mistress towards Woona.

"She's got no dam sense," he cried, in excuse of his gin; "dunno wot she's torkin' about — no more savvey 'en a suckin' dove. Queeby——"

Mina picked up a stool.

"Then I'll teach the black cow" — raising it threateningly.

"Come, now, none er that, missus," almost coaxed Nungi, getting out of line of the missile's target — Woona. "You——"

Mina faced him.

"You take it, then!" — hurling it at him.

He ducked dexterously, and the stool crashed to its own detriment against the wall.

Unnoticed, Woona had seized a stick from the fire-place; she took deliberate aim, and sent it straight at Mina, striking her with staggering force across the face. In distressed horror Nungi's eyes rolled from one woman to the other. Expecting an attack Woona had another stick in readiness. She was muttering in her native tongue, and her whole attitude was a defiant challenge to Mina, now intently regarding her.

"Better go 'ome, missus," Nungi broke the pause to advise.

Mina, breathing heavily, passed her hand before her eyes to brush away the stars floating before them. Woona gave her weapon a defensive flourish.

"Go 'ome, missus, or she'll 'it yur again. I can't stop 'er," pleaded Nungi — "no good ov me tryin'; on'y get it meself."

"Shut up, you!" said Mina. "Tell me the truth, Woona, an' I won't touch you."

"Huh!" sneered unafraid Woona, till Mina suggested—

"Woona, 'oo told yer t' 'it me? Was it Ursula?"

"Tole meself," replied Woona promptly.

Nungi had made a personal disclaimer as soon as he grasped the nature of the question.

"No one tole 'er, missus; she done it 'erself. She's got no more sense——"

"Shut up!" again commanded Mina. "Now, look 'ere, Woona; if you'll tell me true 'oo tole yer to 'it me, I'll give yer something. Upon me soul an' body, I will!"

"Tell 'er yu'll gi' 'er a bottle ov rum, missus," insinuated Nungi interestedly.

Woona's mind had worked only in self-defence, and

instinctively feeling there was no more need she lowered her improvised waddy, and looked at Nungi in a way that made Nungi uneasy though he was guiltless.

"Missis, if you was t' cut 'ome like blazes, and clap a bit er raw meat on your eyes, they woulden' go black nur bungy. That's wot I do w'en she 'its me."

"Will they go black?" Mina asked in alarm.

"Black as 'ell," was his emphatic confirmation.

On the door-threshold Mina turned, and her eyes fastened on Woona in concentrated malignity.

"I'll pay you out, me black strumpit, if I got t' wait a year. See if I don't."

There was a light from Andrew's room, and she went hastily but quietly to the side furthest from the door and peeped in. Hugh Palmer was rolling blankets and pillow into a swag. She waited, watching till he had finished and came out carrying it. Then she, standing in the shadow, asked, "What er you doin'?"

He almost dropped the swag in his surprise, and for a few seconds stood disconcertedly silent.

"It's better for me to camp over there" — jerking his head towards the plain across the river.

She, too, was silent, but only for a moment. Then she threw out her short, thick arms impatiently.

"Well, I didn't know you was such a cur."

"Think what you like," and he reshouldered his swag.

Without any attempt to alter her opinion, he would have passed on to his horse fastened to a tree in the scrub, but she followed him determinedly.

Worn out, Ursula had gone to bed, and of the early night, beyond that Mina had gone to the hut, she knew nothing, waking only by Mina coming to the room. Had she been crying? Ursula wondered, as she watched her bathing her eyes; and was it for Andrew?

"Mina, what's the matter?" she called sympathetically.

"I fell over a log," replied Mina, in a voice free from tears.

"Did Mr Palmer come home, Mina?"

"I dunno," she answered.

"Yer see, miss," said Nungi to Ursula next day, as they

met on the river track, "if ther missus 'ad cut 'ome at oncet and clapped on a bit ov raw meat over 'er eyes, none of yous 'ud 'av knowed she was 'it. But no, she mus' go meeorkin' roun' wi' Boss Palmer till all hours. That's the worst of Woona, she alwers goes fur a poor b——'s eyes. But, Lord, she's got no more sense 'en a fool! Now, Queeby——"

He looked at the girl, ashen and trembling before him.

"Miss, don't you be a cocktail. One thing, 'ooever she tackles, Woona 'd never tetch you," he reassured.

But, leaving her bucket of water, Ursula sped home.

"Mina!" she almost shrieked, "Mina, where are you?"

Mina had hastily hidden in the chimney recess outside — from what danger she was not sure — and there Ursula, almost beside herself, found her with her back to the wall, and instinctively on the defence with hands and feet.

"Don't come a-nigh me, Ursie! If you're bit, there's no cure for snake-bite!"

"I will — I will!" stormed Ursula. "I will never leave you out of my sight, day and night. You are Andrew's wife, Mina; remember, Mina, you're Andrew's wife!"

This was the beginning of an espionage by Ursula that bespoke the mettle of martyrdom.

"You are Andrew's wife, Mina," was her only explanation to Mina's stinging taunts.

Then Palmer added his veiled suggestions regarding Ursula's born capacity in filling the rôle of private detective, and afterwards Mina continually addressed her as "detecter". "Lookin' for me, detecter?" or "'Ere I am, detecter".

"'Oo are you doin' yer dirty work for?" she asked one day. "One thing, you'll never ketch me!"

Ursula looked into the green eyes with their baleful gleam, and a sense of sickening horror almost overcame her.

"Faint, do; but I wouldn't if I was you, 'cause ther's no one 'ere t' pick you up," provoked Mina.

"I'll leave here the first chance I get," Ursula vowed solemnly.

It was a sudden resolution, but it ripened; and though Mina received it with indifference, not so Palmer, who instantly ceased tormenting.

Meeting her one day as she came from the river, he noted the change from girlhood to womanhood.

"The bush is ageing you," he said.

"The bush?" she asked.

He flinched.

"Have you begun your book yet, Ursula?"

"How could I here?"

"By God! no one ever had a finer chance. Two women and one man, with the Bush for a background!" He laughed mirthlessly. "Ah, you'll have to marry first, Ursula," and he sighed. "O Lord! if I had met you ten years earlier, and I were ten years younger and you ten years older, things would have been different."

"Not so far as I'm concerned," she answered proudly, passing him.

"Wouldn't they? I've ten times Andrew's personality," he sent after her, watching with a grim satisfaction how his shaft quickened her pace.

She had written to Cameron Cameron, telling only of her wish to return to town; but Andrew's marriage had alienated his father, and the weeks dragged on — no reply came. Occasionally a dealer's cart would penetrate to their remoteness, and once, soon after they had first come, a dealer had brought his wife. If such occurred again, she would go back with them; and for this she waited.

In the long, empty days and lonely nights she struggled against her nature, and in the end conquered herself. It was a mental feat that kept all introspection and retrospection, if not at bay, quiescent. A quiet sadness settled on her; she scarcely spoke unless in guidance to Woona, who was now more obedient and, in a stumbling way, more thoughtful of Ursula.

She was sitting one afternoon outside on the myall log, and inside Mina slept, so all was peaceful. Ursula's relaxed eyes were on the wide plain, on which the domed sky rested securely, and in an assertive flash the great sweeping circle recalled Ashton's circus. Her heart bounded.

"Good God! what a life here!" she groaned, and covered her eyes.

Unrestrained mentally she faced the reality — instead of

world-wide fame — "Mina's keeper", "detecter", visualizing the attitude of intense hatred of the sometimes thwarted and baffled Mina.

Intolerable! Oh God! she must not think, and, rising, she fixed her eyes and mind again on the plain.

Pyramids of clouds now fringed its edge, and the centre had hazed into a sandy mist. From the further side, quicksilver lakes of sheep formed into momentary circles that split into streams, then, dividing, trickled into single file and made for the river. There was a brooding stillness and sadness indefinitely suggestive of town Sabbath; for the bark of the dogs, anxious to pilot the unwilling flock to the wim instead of the river, was spent in the distance. From habit the sheep would head for the river, but, though it was early spring, the winter had been droughty, and the river was only a string of dangerous water-holes. The dogs, as ever, conquered, and the sheep, against their will, were driven to the troughs round the wim.

After the governed mob had passed, Ursula thought she could hear a faint call, and the crows, keener and quicker than she, were already circling in a preparatory swoop. They guided her to the dried saggs at the river's edge, where she found a lamb newly dropped, and deserted, maybe willy-nilly, by the ewe.

As she, with the ungainly creature in her arms, was making for home, Nungi on horseback overtook her. He had strapped before him a sheep for killing, which hung in an unresisting, listless bow across the saddle — limp, it seemed to Ursula, with the foreknowledge of its doom. Her arms tightened on the lamb she was carrying, such would not be its fate, she determined.

"'Ell ov a trouble t' poddy, miss, them lambs, but Queeby used t' poddy any Gord's quantity," remarked Nungi.

Ursula watched his eyes glazing reminiscently.

"Lord! Queeby used t' poddy ez many ez fifty or sixty every lambin'."

"What did she do with them?"

"Oh, ther boss 'e'd buy 'em, an' I used t' snavel ther rino.

S'elp me Bob, I've been for a fortnight at a stretch at Tambo on the spree, an' dam well never see daylight the 'ole time!"

Again his eyes became regretfully reminiscent.

"No chance ov them times now. Ketch Woona poddy one lamb — not even get up orf ov 'er unkers! I got t' dam well light the fire and poddy 'er meself, an' not so much ez thenk yer for it. She gimme a bit ov er spree? No dam fear ov Woona — But, Lord! I can't expect 'er t' knock 'erself about, for she's got no more sense un a lamb 'erself."

"Think she'll show me how to poddy this one?"

"Like rain," was Nungi's confirmation. "She'll do any morsel thing for you, miss — clean gone on you; like Queeby there, ain't she?"

Nearer the house Palmer joined her.

"What? Have you found your treasure-trove, Ursula?" he asked banteringly, but looking with envious interest at the instinctive maternity of her sheltering arms.

Then, as she scornfully moved onward, he, to delay her, asked:

"Did you know old Civil half guessed where Boshy's money was planted?"

She said, "No."

"Do you know, Ursula?" he asked earnestly.

"You know I don't," she answered curtly, and moved on, anxious to find her lamb.

There is no animal more devoid of affection than a sheep. Ursula was quick to see this, but the very helplessness of this small creature, and its dependence on her for its life, begot her tenderness. Besides, she welcomed anything that gave interest to her empty-days. Gradually they were becoming more so, for now Mina seemed to sleep all day, and Palmer left at dawn after a breakfast prepared and laid overnight, also eaten alone, and it was often dark when he returned. Even then, apparently, office work claimed his attention directly after his meal.

Both wine and spirits had been among the waggon-load of supplies that had been sent for the coming shearing. The wine was placed in a loft over the carefully locked storeroom, Mina keeping the keys. Several times Palmer had asked for them lately, and once to Ursula's surprise

Mina had refused to give them. Uneasily Ursula watched both, then a sudden intuition explained Mina's frequent visits to the storeroom and her long sleeps, followed by her uncritical apathy when awake.

"Give them to him, Mina. Take them, Mr Palmer," besought Ursula frantically.

He was gravely silent, but Mina laughed.

"'Im" — pointing to Palmer — "'im mindin' the keys! — pot callin' the pan black," said Mina.

That night Ursula's violently beating heart unaccountably woke her. Had Mina called? She rushed to Mina's bedroom door, but it had a barrier. She called "Mina!" and while she waited she heard the hide-hung window shutter strike the outside wall noisily and flap to. A footstep on the sand outside gave a dulled slide: her pet lamb bleated in sudden agony: and someone lurched against the wall, then went hastily into Palmer's room. Ursula forced back the barring stool, and entered Mina's room, which was reeking with spirits. Mina, though not snoring, was apparently sound asleep.

"Mina!" she called, shaking her roughly.

Again the lamb bleated.

Ursula thrust her head through the window. Beneath it, with its back close to the wall, and its feet stretched out stiffly, lay the lamb. Hastily she bent and lifted it, but the crushed creature instantly died in her arms. Carrying it into the front-room, she laid it in the fire-place, and without her usual careful thought for the sleeper, she washed the lamb's blood from her hands, then, dressing herself, lay on her bed awaiting daylight.

At dawn she began to collect and pack her possessions, and Woona, as usual, came and lighted the kitchen fire. When the breakfast hour was past, and none appeared, Ursula venturing inside for an explanation, found Mina's bedroom door again closed. Ursula wondered how, for she had left it open, and all therein ever since had been silent.

Later, Nungi, wild-eyed and strangely excited, came ostensibly for the day's orders. Then Ursula found that Palmer also had kept his room, and Nungi intimated that, though he had tried, he could not waken him. With cabalistic signs Woona accused Nungi of having done something wrong, and, with the same silent subtlety, Nungi intimated that this unspoken charge should be laid against Palmer instead of him.

"Wot's t' be done, miss, 'bout them yeos an' lambs in ther draftin'-yard?" he asked Ursula, with a show of anxiety to be at his duty.

"Better ask Mr Palmer," she advised.

"'E's asleep, miss; I tell yer I been tryin' t' wake 'im till I'm wore out. 'E's regler blin', an' deaf, an' dumb. Wish I 'ad a drop ov ther same pizen for these damn cramps," he added, rubbing his stomach and bending double in a feigned distress, that his expectant eyes and watering mouth contradicted.

Ursula knocked at Mina's door, then turned the handle: to her surprise it was again secured, and equally so was the window. So also she found Palmer's, but Nungi, deceived as to her intentions and because of his personal interest, invited her to look through the cracks as he had done. Across the bed, partly dressed, lay Palmer, and one of his stockinged feet hanging out of the bed was blood-spattered — the position of both bespeaking his drunken stupefaction.

"Busted yer poor little lamb wi' 'is big foot," said Nungi. Then he earnestly assured her that the black bottle on the table was empty, and Woona resentfully drew her attention to a hollow reed that Nungi was standing on in an endeavour to hide it. It was long enough to reach the bottle inside, and cunningly bent to enter its neck.

Tamely Nungi picked it up and broke it, volubly reaffirming that there was not a drop in the bottle, nor had there been "fust thing ters mornin'; an' spit me death, miss, if I 'ad a toothful," he said to Ursula.

"Nungi, you must go down for Mr Cameron."

"Not on Shanks's pony," he said sullenly.

"Ride what you like, but you must go."

Woona added her command, and, thwarted, he went sullenly to "'unt up a norse".

When Woona, hours after, returned to their hut, he was there.

"Nungi knows better, w'erever 'e learnt it, not t' go

down alonger Camerons. Christ! let 'im" — jerking his head towards Palmer — "ketch me at it, an' I'd think a tree fall on me. Nungi's got ernuff sense t' come in out o' ther rain long afore a t'underbolt 'its 'im."

Woona took him literally.

"No rain," she said.

"Be Gord, no!" he agreed, "an' no signs ov any. An' I'll see Palmer, ther boosy b— furdermore, afore I water all them yeos an' lambs meself. Plenty t' do in 'ere, aint' there, Woona?" he remarked to conciliate her. "No good ov you, and me bustin' ourselves. Yer git none ther more thanks in ther long run."

He hid all that day, but late in the afternoon of the next day, when Ursula was returning from burying her lamb, she surprised Nungi lying under a shelving bank. He rose up, suggesting by his simulated air of stiffness that he had accomplished a long riding journey. Boss Cameron, he told her, was out when he got there, so he had left Ursula's letter for him. "An' as no one there ask't me ther way to me mouth, I turns roun' an' come straight back." Then hastily to discourage her searching gaze he added, "Dam shame about yer poor liddle lamb, Miss."

"Nungi, did you disturb old Baldy and my father's graves?" she asked accusingly.

"Spit me death, miss if I tetch em. W'y, 'Oly Ghos'," he truthfully said, "I wouldn' go 'ithin cooey of em for all you'd gi'e me. Me rouse up ther debbil-debbil," and looking at his fear-charged eyes, she knew he spoke the truth.

She had gone that morning to unyard the ewes and lambs, and coming back had paid her good-bye visit to the little enclosure, and found that the graves had been opened by careless hands that had left convincing proof.

Inside the mouldering skeleton of the old hut she found several broken pickle-bottles. Their tops sealed by sheep basil, preserved with a tan of pitch, had been broken hastily, and lying among them were many scraps of age-discoloured paper with Boshy's characteristically rude writing and figures. She had no time for thought, and had only hastily gathered them together and hidden them.

Ursula knew that Palmer had been astir at dawn, but not

to attend to his usual duties, for she pityingly had freed the thirsty, uncared for sheep; many of these were now bogged in the various water-holes along the river.

As Ursula entered Mina was sitting on the table drumming on it with a vibrant knife-handle.

"Been for a constitootion, Urse?" she remarked defiantly.

It was all so hopeless that Ursula was silent, and she passed into the kitchen, where Woona, in sullen obedience to Mina's command, was resentfully busy, frying slices of salt beef in a pan of water.

"She wants me t' go 'untin' fer boggabri down on ther billabongs," she complained to Ursula. Then, as her complaint met with no response, remarked, "Been buryin' yer liddle lamb?"

Ursula nodded.

"Teddy, ther mail-boy, went by jus' now, 'e say wot 'e bin gibbit letter b'longin' you, to Boss Palmer."

"Where is he?" asked Ursula excitedly.

"Boss Palmer's gone down alonga river."

Ursula rushed out, and though she searched up and down the river he was not there; but later she saw him yard a horse, then come in to await supper. Ursula deferred her question and kept her eyes from his face, but she was conscious that intentionally his manner, assumed or otherwise, reeked with reckless defiance even to a complete disregard of the watchful Mina. As he sat at the head of the table, instinctively Ursula's eyes rested on his trembling hands, till a sudden discovery that the edges of two shirts were showing at his wrists, sent her eyes with swift inquiry to his. The effect was an influence that shattered his self-control. He replaced his cup with a noisy clatter. "What are you staring at? Do I owe you anything?" he asked, his face purpling in his futile attempt to meet her eyes fearlessly, and before she could reply he scrunched his chair back against the wall and went out.

Gratification at his hostility kept Mina gloatingly voiceless, but her sodden eyes gleamed at Ursula exultingly, and unaffected by Palmer's practically untouched plate, she went on with her meal, swallowing huge mouthfuls with noisy relish. Almost as harshly Ursula freed herself from her chair, and went out by the same door, meaning to ask him had there been a letter for her. It was useless to knock, his room-door was wide open and his horse was gone from the yard.

Mina had followed her, so almost together they went round to the front; this commanded a view of the roadway, along which hastily rode Palmer. Down the river-bank he disappeared for some time; when he reappeared on the other side he was leading a pack-horse.

A lower lip of blood-hued haze lay along the horizon, and from the sun sinking in it a flaming tongue protruded across the plain, till it caught man and horse, in a fine effect, as he drew rein and looked back at the house. Seeing both women he turned his horse to face them, and standing in his stirrups took off his hat, flourishing it in a sweeping circle that included both. With elaborate precision he singled out Ursula, and sending her a shower of kisses, he gave a farewell flourish and galloped onward.

Ursula heard a dry click catch Mina in the throat. Ursula's eyes were now on her. Dismay had conquered her caution; she stood in utter abandonment, with both hands raised to shield her eyes from the sun.

Ursula, leaning against the wall, pressed down her bursting heart. Into her eyes came the look of one who, spellbound, stands beneath a falling mountain. Her dilating pupils perfectly reflected the pregnant woman, still standing in the same attitude, watching the rapidly disappearing horseman.

15

In a night stormy but only with wind and dust, about a month after Palmer's departure, Ursula went for Woona. All gins are skilled midwives, and under her auspices the child was born. It was weirdly shrivelled and small, as the child of a big womb usually is. With Woona's aid Ursula had washed and dressed it in the clothes that had done service for all Mrs Stein's family — her sole wedding endowment to her daughter.

If the helplessness of the motherless lamb had appealed to Ursula, what was the lamb compared to this tiny creature, by reason of its humanity, more helpless? When Ursula handled this atom, its shrivelled hands, as if for protection, would clutch and hold her with a grim tenacity peculiar to infancy. But of infants and their ways what should Ursula know, though she speedily interpreted every movement of this one? Kissing the tendril fingers — at first because Mina, its mother, did not — but later with a rapture begot by its breath on her breast. The beat of its wee heart held against her own, sent her intense maternity surging like the spring sap in a young tree. Mina's keen eyes were watchful as ever, and instinctively Ursula strenuously endeavoured to disguise her love, finding that it endangered the infant. When she woke in the night thinking of it she smiled. "If only it were mine!" she longed, then turned her face in hiding to the wall.

Now it was sick, Mina said, and in swift alarm Ursula bent over it as it slept, her ear to its mouth. She turned her face the other way, for the sinister look on Mina's, watching her, broke her concentration. She laid a testing finger in the little one's palm, and though it slept, as ever its hand closed round it. It was safer for both, she knew, that Mina could not see her face. Shaking a negative head, she said it was not sick; but, unconvinced, Mina moved away, and that night for the first time demanded the care of it.

Then it seemed to Ursula that only her body slept, for the slightest sound or movement from the woman and child in the next room woke and drew her in. Then Mina began closing the door between them, so Ursula redoubled her vigilance. What was that to-night? She sat up instantly, and a sound of smothered fluttering sent her in swift alarm to the door. It was barred, and the inside was in darkness. "Mina, Mina!" she screamed, beating against it, "let me in, let me in!" In the waiting moment she heard the muffled fluttering increase. She rushed out, calling piercingly, "Woona, Woona!" and round to the bedroom window, and with the strength of two wrenched the shutter from its hide hinges; then, bounding through, stripped the bedclothes covering the face of the mother and child. Mina's arm was resting heavily across the little one's mouth when Ursula freed it. It was gasping feebly, and as she raised it she heard its breathless struggle and felt its stiffened body and clenched hands.

"What's the matter?" asked Mina, though also panting breathlessly, making a pretence of being rudely awakened.

Without replying, Ursula, holding the child, lighted Mina's lamp. A strange fear silenced Ursula, for she knew intuitively did she but license the speech scorching and shaking her, this would license action in the unnatural, desperate woman watching her with those terrible, inhuman eyes. Even now uncontrollably her powerful, hairy arms and hands were twitching murderously.

"Wot are yer doin' in 'ere?" she challenged.

"In your sleep, Mina, you nearly smothered the baby."

Watching her as one watches a springing snake, Ursula, with the child, backed into the next room, and took up a position where she could see but not be seen. So screened, she saw Mina's hand steal out and her fingers suddenly snuff out the lamp wick, after the manner of old Daddy Stein. The lightened creak of Mina's bed was further warning, and Ursula's hold on the child tightened, as she noiselessly made for the door; but even from there came the outside sound of bare feet, then a whisper:

"Missy, missy!"

It was Woona's voice. Thankfully Ursula let her in.

"Baby very sick, Woona," she said loudly, shivering with relief. "Light the lamp, and make big fella fire out there," pointing to the kitchen. "We'll bogey [bath] it."

When by the lamplight Woona saw the pallid terror of Ursula's face, alarmed, she asked:

"On'y that fella baby, you bin bogey Missy?"

"Only baby, Woona."

"Mine think it you sick, too," said Woona.

Together they went into the kitchen, and from inside it Ursula made a silent sign for Woona to listen. Mina, though equally cautious, was again betrayed by the lightened spring of the creaking bed. Since she was astir, better and safer for them to be where they could watch.

"Bring the water inside, Woona," said Ursula, and with it they went back.

Now the bedroom door was closed, but Woona sent a suspicious survey into all likely and unlikely corners of this room; then, radiating her relief, went briskly on with her work.

Gradually the little one's breathing had become more regular. Ursula, swift to know, felt its strained body relax in composure. God was good! but never for a moment, day or night, would she leave it out of her arms or sight. Now, while she bathed it, Woona held low the lamp, so that its full light fell on the infant's face. Suddenly Woona, with a native word, held it even lower, pointing excitedly to bruises on the swollen nose, and from them to the discoloured finger-prints on one cheek. Again she spoke excitedly, and again in her own tongue; then raising her head, she faced her hut, and sent a cooee that echoed and re-echoed. Instantly the bedroom door opened and Mina entered. She was whiter than Ursula, who, snatching up the infant, stood at bay facing her. Even in her agitation the flattened space between Mina's brows struck Ursula more vividly than the green malignity of her venomous eyes.

"Shut up, you black dingo!" she hissed at Woona, though her eyes were fastened on Ursula. "Wot are you doin' to it?"

Without replying, but watching her, Ursula rolled a blanket round the child. Woona was about to cooee again, when her keen ears heard the coming of Nungi. Instead she called to him that the front door where he was knocking was unbarred.

"Is it?" sneered Mina. But the back one was, and Nungi, swifter than she, had entered.

Woona gave him a warm welcome, then in native language told him something that sent his eyes uneasily rolling from the infant's face to Mina's right hand, clenched in impotent frenzy, then to her distorted face.

"Christ, missis! you do look snake-'eaded. Git yer neck stretched playin' that game," pointing to the child's face, he said, friendly advice in his tones; and as Mina only panted breathlessly, he took her speechlessness as a tribute to his advice. Turning from her to Ursula, he touched the little one's discoloured cheek. "Dam shime t' 'urt ther poor little b——, jus' as it was jus' beginnin' to know yer, too, missy."

"Hush, Nungi! the baby's sleeping; she's better now. It was an accident. Go back to bed, Mina," said Ursula.

"Give it to me."

Mina extended her arms authoritatively. Ursula, raising her head, looked unflinchingly into Mina's shifty eyes.

"It was an accident," she meaningly repeated and emphasized. "Sit down, Woona and Nungi, and you go back to bed, Mina."

Mina went into the bedroom, and closed the door. For hours the three sat round the fire, each in a position to watch the bedroom door; for each knew that, although Mina had closed it, she only did so as a shield for her scrutiny, unequally distressful, but as barren for her as for them. When the receiving creak of her bed, and soon after her reassuring snores, told them it was over, at a sign from Ursula, Woona noiselessly rebuilt the fire; then shortly after her head fell affectionately on Nungi's shoulder, and she, too, slept. His head gradually took a reposeful lean-to against then wall, then Ursula was the only watcher. Occasionally a convulsive sob would shake the little one, but the arms it already knew would tighten round it. Its groping, fearing fingers met Ursula's; its face nestled in her neck; so soothed and comforted, it would quiveringly sigh its reassurance and content. And every sigh that quivered to Ursula's bending ear, every breath breathed on her bared breast, quickened and nourished this resolve — to shield and shelter it with her life.

At dawn she aroused Woona and Nungi to duty, for before and since the birth of the child she had tried to look after everything outside and in. Palmer had been gone nearly two months, and though she had time and again written to Cameron, none had replaced him. By Nungi, Palmer had sent her father's will, and a note saying where she would find some money hidden. Andrew, he said, was coming soon. Tremblingly she wondered when, and went to reread Palmer's letter, but though she had hidden it with her father's unread will, both were gone.

She followed Woona into the kitchen, where already beneath the ashes smouldered a pile of glowing coals, that was soon, under Woona's skill, a roaring fire. Before it Ursula held the child, while Woona heated some milk; but the little one's lips were so rigidly compressed that Ursula could scarcely coax the spoon between them, and then she saw despairingly that it could not swallow. Motioning Woona to watch for Mina's coming, she went to the back of the kitchen, to think out some plan to protect this child. She would go to Mina, and ask her to renounce it to her; with it she would go away, and none need ever know that it was not hers. When Andrew should return, — though her face flamed at the thought, she did not flinch — when Andrew should return, Mina could tell him the child was hers (Ursula's); and this very day she would start for Camerons. So resolved, she went to seek and tell Mina, and guided by Woona, she went to a familiar crack.

A pair of freckled, scaly hands, groping along the beams of the bedroom, utterly unnerved her, and for a moment fear paralyzed her, then she crept closer. She saw those long fingers, that Boshy loathed, feel gropingly for something. Ah! what was it, that they had found? As though she, too, was not sure, Mina brushed the dust from it, and examined further by look and smell. It was what she sought; for, satisfied, she placed it in her bosom and went on dressing.

Woona had silently and swiftly backed away; and her ebon face, Ursula saw, had changed into leaden flabbiness with some horrible fear. There is no colour line in love, and though a-quiver with ungovernable fright, for Ursula's sake black Woona went graphically through the final death contortions of the poisoned mangy pup. Then with the speed of a wild animal, she made for the scrub, where Nungi was supposed to be scrub-cutting for the starving sheep; and, despite her burden, Ursula, equally terrified, instantly followed. But, though she turned the child's face across her shoulder, she found that the wind as she ran, caught the little one's breath, and she felt it strain and stiffen. Stopping for a moment, and screened by a tree, she looked back at the house. At that moment she saw Mina mount the butcher's block, with intent to locate the fugitives; then came a lusty cooee from Woona to Nungi, which, Mina hearing, instantly acted upon. To add to Ursula's terror, she saw that this breathing respite had not tranquillized the child, yet she dared not stand still, with its unnatural mother on her track. Again Woona cooeed resoundingly, and this time another look showed Mina running from the house towards the sound. Bending low, Ursula went swiftly as she dared to where Mina might pass wide of her; then, again hidden, she waited in breathless anxiety, that was increased to distracting horror when she saw the sun blaze and reflect on and about the axe's head that Mina had snatched from the wood heap. Suppressing a horrified shriek, Ursula sped away from her, back to the house; past this she fled across the river; passing her father's grave, she ran along the track to Pine Point. Looking back once, she thought that she was safe, for Mina was not to be seen; encouraged, onwards she ran to the myalls near, and stopped to examine the child, now struggling more strenuously, though only at intervals. It was ill, surely; yet what could she do to save it — she flying with it from that terrible woman? O God! there Mina was; she had only been hidden by the river-bank. Where were Woona and Nungi? She must get to them.

With a mind to try and double back so as to find them, when she reached Pine Point, she entered that part of the trackless scrub. Stumbling through the thick undergrowth with her precious burden, she pushed onward. Fearful of her pursuer, she dared not stop even to look at the ailing one, or to listen, knowing she had only her start against this murderous woman, with twice her strength, unburdened, and with that deadly weapon. Once, when the undergrowth gripped her, she drew breath and looked at the now twitching child. At the moment an internal spasm stiffened it, though no moan came from its cruelly indrawn lips. She raised her face, but heaven was hidden by the interlocking trees; so she bent her head to listen, but there seemed no following sound. Maybe Mina had passed while she had waited, still, what would she do with this stricken child? Dread drove her back, while she thought, but not far, for paroxysm after paroxysm, each swifter and more violent, seemed to wrestle for the soul that the locked lips of this wee one refused to surrender. Fearless now of her enemy, Ursula sank for the moment, intent only on saving the child. With her own dried tongue, she bent to moisten into relaxation its indrawn blue lips, and breathing on the clenched, congested hands, tried as unavailingly to lessen their terrible tension. Fiercer and fiercer grew the unequal fight, till gradually Ursula saw that all effort failed to still or soothe one quiver. Then the mighty King of Terrors wrestled but with one. Where had she read that only the old die easily? Her lamb had; but this lamb—— Ah! now it was over: though its lips were still closed and its hands clenched, it was still. She laid it along her cradling body, then she, too, was motionless and as emotionless as their surroudnings, for not a leaf stirred: sun-sleep was upon the scrub. So she had held Boshy, only then her back rested against the wall, now against a tree. She was thankful for one thing — there was no blood, for of all the nauseating things on earth, none were so appalling as blood to her. Mina had come when Boshy died; if only she would come now! Where was she? Rising, she called, "Mina, Mina!" Then, without waiting for a reply, with the child in her arms, she went on; but not for long, for even in this dense scrub the heat of the sun penetrated scorchingly, and surely her burden had grown heavier. She was only partially dressed — that was well — but, without looking, she covered the little one's head and discoloured face with her skirt. Strange that she did not want to kiss it. She would bury it beside her father, she decided, not out here. The lamb she had laid at his feet, but this dear thing in her arms

— she quivered chokingly, then conquering her emotion, she looked at the dead child. It might even yet recover if only she could reach Woona, and they together get hot water.

This purpose possessing her, hopefully she pushed onward swiftly, fighting the dense tangle of undergrowth which caught her at every step. Had she passed through it in her first flight? she now wondered. Oh, how could she know, with so little to guide her? For, looking back, the vines and leaves, as if to baffle her, had closed over even her last steps. One blessing, the sun here was less powerful, for the branches locked and entwined overhead, as did the brush of undergrowth.

She let fall her skirt, that was sheltering the head of the child. How calm and collected she was, fearing nothing now, free even from her haunting terror of snakes — those silent, creeping horrors! Yet how she had dreaded them up to this time! And now, looking at the child, she feared not Mina — no, not even Mina. Still, it was better not to think of her, but try to get out of this scrub; but when and how?

Perhaps if she laid the little one down for a few moments, and climbed (Andrew had taught her) to the top of one of these trees, she might be able to see her way out to the plain. She hesitated, then she carefully laid the baby down, first making sure that no creeping, venomous foe was near; and selecting one tree, she began its ascent, her eyes fixed on the child. Supposing Mina crouched hiding, waiting to snatch it?

Recklessly she jumped down, and, with a mingled cry of love and fear, caught up the child and again stumbled along. With an effort at composure, she tried to delude herself by the thought that the beloved little one might not be dead — it was very strong. But once she knew definitely it was, she would bury it somewhere — not here — then find Mina and kill her! Yes, if the child was dead she would kill Mina; that was just. Even the Bible said, "Blood for blood;'. Shudderingly she thought she could smell blood. Now for the present she must banish such thoughts, for the one great thing to do was to get back again.

Stopping, she tried to get the bearings. If only she knew

what way she had come! But she could not decide. However, she must be wrong, or by this she would see the plain. She turned another way, and by degrees many others, determinedly keeping at bay the distracting consciousness that she was bushed.

About noon, exhausted and painfully thirsty, after long scrutiny, she decided the baby must be dead. For a long time she sat, and through her dry mouth tried to breathe into its nostrils; nothing could pass through its locked lips, nor could the tip of her little finger worm its way into the sealed palms. Perhaps it would be as well to bury it for a time only, till she found Woona or Nungi; but where? Laying it down tenderly, she groped beneath the matted vines, but felt only hot shifting sand. Beside a large pine-tree was a bare, loose heap; carrying the body to this spot, she laboriously scraped a hole long and deep enough. Then again, with it across her knees, and for a longer time, she went through all methods of reanimation known to or invented by her. It was dead, so she laid it in its cot of sand, with its pain-distorted face to the hidden skies; then slowly began covering it, feet upwards. Tearing a strip from her skirt, she shrouded its face, and, looking away, blindly pushed over it the sand; still without looking, she turned and walked back a few paces, but marked the spot, so that she would know where to guide someone. She tore up vines and broke twigs, and covered it lightly, then rested awhile, stretching her stiffened arms. How weary she was, and how thirsty! But now, without her burden, she would get on quicker and get back — she must before dark. Making landmarks to guide her return, slowly she went on — not far — only a few paces, for, oh God! how could she leave it alone? Sobbing tearlessly, she rushed back, disinterred the child, then with it for hours distressfully stumbled onward.

Australian daylight dies with short shrift, and in this mighty scrub the pall of darkness fell with startling abruptness. She knew it would be madness to seek home, so, selecting a sparse spot, she shrouded the dead and laid it beside her. She sat with her aching back resting against a tree, realizing that were it light, and she for sure on the right track, her weary limbs could have gone no further. If dew fell — and it might in this clearing — it would moisten her dry tongue and mouth, and in this prayer her tongue clicked, dry and sore, against her swollen palate. This still night was not chilly, and, even if it were, could not matter to the dead child, yet she covered it with her skirt. She was not hungry, though she had eaten nothing all day; but she was very, very thirsty and weary. Still, dew might fall. And now, till dawn, she must rest — to sleep would be best, but she knew she could not sleep. The little body, so still and quiet, was growing cold. So her aunt and Boshy had been; she also must be, for she was shivering. Well, better cold than heat for thirst, and in the dawn she would again go in search of home. Could she leave this little one, carefully hidden? — looking at the shrouded form. But need she think of that till the morning? Yet better to think of anything or anyone, if it held in check her thirsty misery. Mentally she selected many intimate past incidents, resolutely discarding the obtrusive present. Long ago, when she was little, she had strayed too far and got lost till nearly dark, but then she had called and called Andree, and he had found her and carried her home.

Andrew — for a long time in that past she forgot the present, till the bitter reality recalled her with a shock the more cruel from being suspended. Not again would she dwell on him; instead, on her cruel thirst — oh, when would the dew fall? But just this she might debate, since she was on the forbidden subject — should she, if Andrew were to come now, claim this dead child as her own — hers and Palmers? for that was what such avowal meant. No, she decided; there was now no need. Would she rather have the child dead than face Andrew with it as her own? The tender clasp of its fingers round hers; its breath upon her as it lay the night before in her arms, and with infant instinct groped for her breast — no, no, no! The child — the child, even with dishonour!

Taking it in her arms, she held its stiffening body to her sore heart, till a trembling agony seized her. Then, as she placed it again beside her, she determined not to touch, nor even think of, it till the morrow. How long would the dawn be in coming? Yet if she rose to walk about to still her mind, she must uncover the child. She tried vainly, by various devices, to divert her thoughts; then, drawing off her skirt, swathed the body, walking afterwards round and round it, with her dry mouth upturned for the desired dew. How slow it was in falling! Perhaps those tree-tops, almost shutting out the sky, caught and kept it. For a moment the desire to climb to their tops and rob them possessed her; but there was the child — some stalking wild beast might seize or molest it. She must not.

Oh, but was ever night so long? Though lately there had been many that had tried her sorely, yet the night when that dear dead thing had come, and she, for a time alone and uninstructed, had been forced to minister to its unnatural mother, even that night had not seemed so long; and others since had been spent in anxious vigil. Ah! but all circumstances had been different, and the child had been nestling and warm, and she herself neither shivering nor thirsty. Still, she must keep a firm grip on herself and conquer all emotion, for her task on the long-deferred morrow would be neither easy, nor, because of her dead burden, light. She would again rest and try to calmly consider some guiding feature, passed in her flight, that in retracing she might recognize, and so be guided; but all that she could visualize was the path to the crossing over the river — it and the track to Pine Point. Still, now that her fear was gone and she reasonable, outlets to any of these might be possible in the daylight, but with it the first thing she would seek would be water.

When would dawn come? This awful stillness was stifling her. Oh for any sound that would break it! Even that solemn night-call that none but Andrew and she could interpret, would she welcome. Why were birds and beasts so voiceless? Surely here must be their haunts and lairs. Yet she, in walking round, was careful, mindful to move softly, lest she set even the leaves whispering, which was worse, for such might be a signal to shoals of stealthy foes covertly watching her. Should she for distraction go through her child-life? Immediately Ashton's circus sprang from the past, mocking the present intolerably. It served her need, for it took time to conquer her disquiet.

Day dawn was as stealthily swift as its death. When the boom of a brooding emu heralded it, Ursula went on her knees in voiceless prayer; then, burdened by the stiffened, cold child, went towards the sound. Her rustling approach betrayed her to the watching male bird. With a sonorous warning to his hatching mate, he fled, and later Ursula saw the sitting bird rise suddenly from her nest and run swiftly, though not to join her cowardly mate, but at a discreet distance to watch, even as Miriam, thought Ursula. She found in the nest thirteen eggs, warm to her cold hand. She would take one: it might moisten her parched mouth and so ease her burning throat; but a small one would do. Replacing the egg she held, she selected the smallest, yet it was smoother and more delicately tinted than the others; it might one day be a beautiful bird, and faithful like its prospective mother — she would not take that one. From so many, one could make little difference, and thirteen was an unlucky number. Her thirst and the terrible task before her surely justified her — yet she hesitated. The hen bird still watched, and bravely had ventured to come nearer its nest. Ursula would take an egg right away before she broke it, and perhaps the emu might not miss it. Selecting one, she moved away. What a contrast, the deadly cold of the child to the blood warmth of the egg! she believed it was making her feel sick and faint. Ah! and the robbed bird was standing disconsolately over, not on, its nest. Thank God! it was not too late. Hurrying back, and calling her intention encouragingly to the again fleeing bird, she restored the egg.

The sun-bleached bones of some animal were the next objects that she saw. Ah! why had it wandered from its fellows, and how had it perished? she wondered. Thirst, she decided.

And, merciful God! how dreadfully dry her own mouth and throat were! What would she do if she did not soon find water, or what would become of her? She took a critical survey of her surroundings. A cobweb, night-spun, hung in an insidious circle from branch to branch, facing her. Early as it was, its first victim struggled in its gummy meshes. Fascinated, she stook shaken ungovernably by its horrible suggestiveness, while above and about her the trees shivered meaningly. Yes, here in the Bush, Nature was frankly brutal, and meant her to know that she, too, was trapped hopelessly, as the poor fly. In her haste to free it, one of its wings broke off. This recalled that Sunday afternoon, long ago, when she had wantonly crippled the hornet and flies. How could she upbraid Nature? Sorrowing acutely for her earlier sin, she moved onward, till the necessity for some plan for her movements stopped her. Across her tangled track a tree, uprooted, as though top-heavy, rested slantwise against its fellows. Carrying the child she crawled along it, aided by the branches and vines, hoping from its highest point to see the plain. She could not, for there was a slight rise, and trees higher shut out all but the sky. Nor was there any dew nor moisture even on their tenderest tips. Still, from this height she might take her bearings from the sky, for the brighter glow would mean the east — their house on the plain's edge faced that way. But how distractedly her head buzzed in the effort to determine its locality. Perhaps this dizzy height was making her giddy. She descended to think better below. But even here, visualizing as strenuously as she could, and after a long struggle, no way seemed certain, for as she invoked tracks from her hot head, the tragical incidents of her flight dispelled them.

Then, abruptly as the dark and light changes came the heat. The sun, though hidden, sent piercing tongue-shafts, till even the tough trailing vegetation drooped, showing the hot sand beneath. The blood seethed scorchingly in the girl's veins; hot wave-wings quivered before her strained eyes, and buzzed about her ears and temples. The child alone was unaffected, as she stumbled wearily along, penalized by its dead, cold, unresponsive weight, she knew that, and was definitely thankful. Were it alive, it too must suffer, and was ever agony greater than this? Surely her head would burst. Was it swollen? — feeling it. Not much, thank God! she decided, but she must rest and again try to think of a way to water — then out to the plain.

Now, those emus — why had she left them? for they must be within a reasonable distance of water. Besides, if all else failed, and this awful torturing thirst continued, she would be forced to take one egg; but could she find the way back to the nest? it was just before she reached this rise. She would try, and vaguely she wandered about, but not for long — mind and body began to claim and force rest. Would she try to find the emu's eggs first? No, go on; try to get out to the plain. But was not that the cobweb which she had wrecked? Had she without knowing turned back, or was it another web? Calmly, and again undismayed, the spider was industriously respinning in repair. It was the same. Yet she thought that she had gone forward; she must mind, for never had she been good at locality. Jim used to say that she would get lost in the house paddock.

Jim, Fanny, her aunt, Mr Civil — and mentally twist and turn as she would, yes, Andrew — there they all were: but because of her strenuous repression, Andrew was multiplied. Quirr, quirr! her hot head buzzed, and her dry mouth opened chokingly, and she called him till she was dumb, till she could neither hear nor see. Yet above all a sense of her own lawlessness was uppermost. Oh, God! how hopeless and bewildering everything was! From then every moment seemed to weaken her, and add to the weight she bore in her stiff arms; and her thirst — her thirst! No way seemed clear, nor which way to turn. But if she began to think of herself she would not keep calm. Now she seemed to be ascending, and uphill was ever weary work; rest a little she must.

Was it late in the day? she wondered. She hoped, then feared it was; another night spent like the last, would, she knew, unhinge her mentally. No; such thoughts were foolish and distressing. Just now she had exaggerated the distance she had walked, till the spider and web had convinced her, and it was so with the time. It could not be late, though it was burning hot, and a long, long time since she had even tasted water; and she—— Oh, mercy! mercy! where could she, would she find water! Where? Where? What was the use of groping in the sand at her feet for water; she had put down the dead baby, and had been talking to herself. That was a bad sign. Was she going mad? No, it was her head — her hot head — was that swelling, and buzzing from weariness, weakness, and thirst.

When before had she lain down the child? — she could not remember so doing, but now it rested her. In future when she rested she would lay it down beside her. But supposing she forgot it — her head was not always quite clear. Oh! — snatching it up and stumbling along — she would not, could not, should not. She knew this last fear was a fancy, and she closed her eyes to shut it out. But now of a surety there was blood. Oh, thank God! no — only a streak of sunset. But this red flash had sent such a droughty blast into her open mouth. Oh! she must go on — go on and find water. She would turn this way: it was less entangling. But after a few wearying minutes she began to think it worse, still she stumbled on, for at least she was going in a fresh direction.

But was that not again the same spider and web? Of a certainty, yes.

Should she kill this magnetic spider, and so end its baleful influence? Incentively the trees hissed "Yes, yes". Motioning for them to be silent, she steadily watched the insidious spinner, now as if divining her purpose, merely an indrawn inert black speck but acutely watching her. Its attitude instantly recalled that long-past Sunday. What right had she to expect mercy, and she still with the same cruel instincts? Turning away, she went onward, mindful only that she did not again go near the spider.

What sound was that?

"Andrew!" burst impulsively from her. She listened, but there was no reply. Yes, yes; she distinctly heard a voice say "Israelites". Then her heart gave a suffocating bound, for, God have mercy, she had mistaken her own voice, as aloud she had been praying that she might be God-guided out of this wilderness, as were the Israelites. The shock nerved her, and she ran aimlessly till she fell, and for a time lay, but making a barrier of her arms, that the child should not be crushed.

Somewhat strengthened, she rose and moved on, but without a plan. If only Andrew—— But determinedly she beat back that predominant wish, for it was worse than her insistent thirst — worse, for it was wickeder. To get away from it she walked again, anywhere, anywhere.

Now, perhaps, she would get out again to the plain. Was there any sign of it yet? She could see if there was, for her head was clearer. Now, too, she had made good progress, and the dreaded spider trap was behind her. That was well. Thankfully she moved on. Oh the cruelty of it! She was back — there it was! there it was! Sobbing, she sank down to hide it from her despairing eyes. Was she losing her senses completely? Was it not her fancy? Let her try to think calmly and clearly as a test. This dead child that she carried, and whose face she had not seen for hours; yes, that was right. The baby was Mina's, and Mina — wait a moment — was Andrew's wife. But no — she would not think of that. Oh, God forgive her! not Andrew. Yes, she was perfectly sane, but till she got out of this she had better not think of anyone. No, for her head was again bursting. How like the sound of that hornet beating against the skylight! No; the sound of the emu it was, only hers was a double beat that sprang from both temples and increased her tiredness and unendurable thirst. Oh for just one small mouthful! Now if she had a cupful, first she would drink a little, then wet her temples. What a waste of time to sit there thinking of these things! Was it late? She closed her eyes to rest them, that they should when open the better determine if there was a change, but a scorching red flame flared through her closed lids, and, screaming, she rose, and, without the child, ran stumblingly. Coward, coward, that she was — she went back to it, and waited till her heart stilled. Ah! now, indeed, she was becoming disorganized, for certainly for hours — indeed, all day — she had been wandering about, without a plan.

At length, repassing the empty grave that she had hollowed for her chilly burden, the cobweb, the leaning tree, and other objects, convinced her that she was walking in a circle. She might as well sit still. It was getting late, but, thank God! cooler, but if night were coming a fire would be better than the thick darkness and awful quiet of the one past. Yet no, not a fire: it would only increase her thirst. Besides, if she dozed, it might creep up and set her alight. Again she ran, till barred by fatigue. Was ever agony so great as this thirst? Why, even Christ on the cross could not endure thirst and loneliness, though He suffered all other agonies uncomplainingly. But when He said "I thirst, I thirst", a sponge dipped in vinegar was held to His lips. Vividly the scene stood out. Why did she hold up her lips? Who was there to wet hers? One thing was certain, if instead of going on she stood there thinking about herself, she would perish — die of thirst. Die! that was the word; she had kept it at bay before, but now it was useless to try, dangerous also, for fear of death must spur her on. But she went a few paces only; then again saw the leaning tree.

What a most peculiar thing that was, the leaning tree which earlier she had passed — oh, surely long ago — days and weeks ago; and why did she pass it? Why? she wondered, and her enfeebled mind rested in this futile query. Oh — screaming — she knew why. She was lost in the Bush, and, as long ago, she called, "Andree, Andree!" Now, now, she was growing like a child. A child! Worse, for when a child she had conquered herself, and had governed her desire to scream after that Sunday, standing out even now as a force that shaped her destiny. She thought coherently about it for a few minutes. Would she now like to be Henry McGrath, dead, drowned; no thirst, no pain — no Andree? No, no; thank God! no: she was alive, and but for her aching head and burning thirst—— Oh, why did she think of that? — she walked rapidly. The sand here was surely deeper and hotter. Yes, for some storm long past, alas! had felled almost a pathway in this wilderness, and there were blazed trees bordering it. Who had barked them? And why? Where would it lead? she wondered. It seemed like a track, and she went along it hopefully till a new danger threatened — a snake, coiled reposefully; she was very close before she saw it, for its colour scheme was a tribute to its environment. Noiselessly it raised its head, and steadily its green eyes watched this invader, and when convinced that she was a menace, a forked tongue protruded from its head, swinging to and fro pendulously. Keeping her eyes upon it, fearfully she backed away for some distance, and as it did not pursue, she turned and ran a few paces. But was she between it and its nest? If so, it would catch her, no matter how swiftly she ran.

Besides, she must go back and do battle with it. One thing, she had not screamed and had felt little fear; that was well, to conquer the emotion of fear. Now she would go back and fight it, for never could she feel safe with such a fatal foe at large. She went back, or she thought so, but there was no snake. She was too late. All her life she had done this thing to everyone — to herself — even to Andrew. Surely there could be no harm in thinking of him when it was in self-condemnation. How long had he been away? Could she remember? Thirteen months exactly, and this dead child was a month old. The fright had done her good, and now, while her head was clear, she must make her way out. While she was counting, let her reckon how long it was since she last drank? Oh, it was such a ridiculously long time that she laughed. That was best, to laugh! She would do that whenever she thought of it — laugh; but the Bible, the bitter, mirthless Bible, said tears were better than laughter. She could not cry, even though this little one she loved lay dead in her arms.

She walked backwards and forwards, as though to soothe her lifeless burden, till, tripped by the vines, she fell. She lay still, till suddenly she recalled the snake. Stifling a scream, she rose and rushed along heedlessly till exhausted. "Mercy! mercy! Water! water!" she called, then waited, but there was neither.

Now, again, she would make her greatest effort to be calm, and think and plan. What she wanted to find was—— [visualizing giddily]. Where was the dead plain split by the empty river? Ah! all the plains was trackless now, lying dead, with its many sun-sucked open lips, dry as her own, turned to the relentless sky. Yet she had seen on it the green grass, undulating like a sea. How clear her mind was — the sea! looking steadily before her. Oh, oh! for her heart-beats nearly smothered her. Nonsense! she could not see the sea nor plain, and, beside, the sea was salt and the plain bare. No movement now on it but balls of roley-poley, hurled along by dusty whirlwinds. Even the noisy galahs that nested in the trees along the river-bank were gone. But — trembling violently — not the snakes. Often, how often, she had crept out in the night, and, quivering with the brooding silence, looked across the great stretch of land, and from it turned to the sleeping house. And that night of nights when he left — ah! that was her shame and this her just punishment! She struck her dry mouth, hungry even now, and sobbed fiercely.

Thank God! if she had wept then, it had been when the lights were out. God! was that a snake! No; only a trailing coil of sarsaparilla, but very snake-like. And why should she torture herself? Those lustrous things (regarding them earnestly) were glittering leaves and not rain-drops. There was no water, nor snakes, only vines; but there was no need to stand still tempting them. She ran till her nervously throbbing heart nearly suffocated her. Now! Now! She was becoming disorganized; running made her open her mouth — her hot mouth, dry as the plains. And the weight of this dead baby, but — she ground her teeth and clenched her hands — she would carry it to the end. No fancies now; she remembered everything. She was lost, or Bushed — no, had just missed her way and would find it by-and-by. There were no snakes but that one back there, which, looking back, she did not fear. First, she must find water, even before the plain or river. Still, even that had water-holes — filthy, evil-smelling, and studded with dead sheep — yet the water, the green, slimy water-holes, swam before her temptingly. Resolutely she closed her eyes. It was only burning sand, not water; nevertheless, her hands met it. She steadied herself by a sapling. She was not mad, only light-headed, and unable to think safely. The glare this way was dazzling her. She faced another way and laid the child down, then with her uncertain hands she pressed hot circlets round her hotter head. She believed it was swelling, and very soon it would burst. Now, where was the plain? To the east, where the sun rose. Well, there was the sun; but though it was past noon, she did not remember, and, taking up her burden, she went westward.

Again, and by degrees oftener, she fought and conquered her frenzies. She was not on fire, but her skirt nearly caught that blazing streak along that creeper. A little while back and she would have thought it a snake on fire. Was it? was it? She gathered her skirt tightly round her. No use that, for there was another burning snake and yet another. Breathlessly she flung her skirt off, and, demoralized by the blood-red, she stripped off, all but one, to swathe and uphold the child.

She stood and looked in terror at those coiling creepers; after all, they might be sleeping snakes. One thing, snakes were supposed to be deaf; giddily and laboriously she tried to step free and not disturb them. What if her noisy boots should wake them! She drew them off. Ah! that was wise, for they had not moved nor wakened; but the burning heat of that blistering sand on her feet — oh, she must get back to water! She shrieked, and a wild disorder mastered her. She ran, calling, "Water! water!" Then for a merciful interval all faculties became suspended, and she fell and lay with her head on the child.

Had she found water? Surely something cool — feeling the cold body — then groping beyond, she hoped that when she touched the water it would not seethe and boil. She crept forward — yes, she must crawl along the plank carefully, and not rush into it and get bogged, like those eyeless sheep.

Oh, those awful crows. The crows! They were there, and had been for some time, circling round her. She shut her eyes, and threw out her burdened arms, beating back those black brutes. Getting up, she ran till she fell; then, lying face downwards, with one arm and hand she held the baby's closed eyes protectingly to her bosom, with the other hand preserving her own precious eyes.

Water, water, everywhere water, and not a mouthful to drink, because she dare not open her eyes, so near were those crows' cawing hoarsely, "I'll 'ave 'er eyes out! I'll 'ave 'er eyes out!" She would creep with her eyes so close to the ground, so close that they—— Ah! again the snake, its head and tongue hidden, but betrayed by flaming flashes of crimson along its sinewy length. Down with the dead baby, till her burning hands uprooted and tore it apart; then — regarding her victim — there was no blood either. Of course not: snakes were bloodless. How strong she was to be able to tear it to pieces, and she gloated for a while, and alone went onward; but remembering the child, she went back, guided to it by her fibre victim. She strangled many tough-throated enemies afterwards, but her greatest she could not banish — the crows; yet even they, though circling and cawing insistently, were, because of her increasing weakness, sometimes ignored.

Oh, if only it would rain and fall into her parched, upraised mouth! God of heaven! — no, God of earth! — send rain, and let it fall on her hot head and thirsty mouth. She waited expectantly, but only the "I'll 'ave 'er eyes out!" of the crows answered her. Ah! — bitterly — when would God hear or answer her? When had He ever? To Him she would pray no more. What was that up there descending from that tree? (watching a gohanna). The devil? Yes, surely. She could not pray to him, but might tell him of her fearful need. She began, but at the sound of her voice the reptile deftly reversed his head and tail, and crawled nigher heaven. She waited till he had stopped, and, with his head turned over his shoulder, looked down on her. Now, if he would listen, she would confess, since now she did not love Andrew. No, all that was past. Ah, how foolish she was! What did sin matter to the devil, for, as though in disbelief and derision, his scaly majesty had thrust out his tongue at her, and climbed higher.

His unbelief and thrust-out tongue gave tone to her savagery. No matter how high he climbed, she would make him hear.

But it was only for "Water, water, water!" that she called, till her dry throat throttled her words, and she fell, and so lay in giddy stupefaction, then suddenly became possessed of a peculiar knowledge.

Ah! now she was in hell, and could see the flames of hell shooting round her. However, she felt she must put them out; but throughout her rain of dust and brambles, she shouted defiance at the devil, again watching her, till speech died and she again fell, and lay so long that the crows ceased cawing, but circled lower.

Then instantly and marvellously the burning sand changed to water. Water, water! She had been calling and praying for water, and she in a bath — not cold, certainly, but water. Gloating silently, she laved handfuls of hot sand over her, her mind alternating sanely and insanely. Not so much, or she would drown — no, smother. Now, now, what about that dead creature? Where was it? Into this bath with it. Where was it? — feeling about. Then she again forgot it. Ah! this was tasteless, unsatisfying water, and blinded her aching eyes without cooling her hot mouth; still, she must drink it. No, she must struggle up — staggering to her feet — for she would neither like to drown nor smother.

Oh, the horrible droughty dust! the wretched sheep must be rushing the water.

"Back! back! you thirsty, eyeless brutes, raising such stifling clouds of dust. Back! back! or by the Lord I will grab one of you by the throat and — and——" No! no! never; she would not drink blood. Poor frightened wretches! Come on! come on! she must make way for them, but she must make haste and get away. What was she groping for? What had she lost? Ah! the child — the dead child. God be praised! there it was, and unhurt by the crows, perched quite close to it. She had baffled them, but she could not go far while the earth rocked so, nor could she see. Great God! what was wrong with her eyes? — feeling them. Had the crows—— "Haw, haw!" they cawed mockingly, as they ascended, but only a few feet. No, only the dust from those sheep had filled her eyes and her mouth. Dry! dry! wiping it out — drier and hotter than the brick oven where long ago she had hidden from God, and now God was hiding from her. Huskily and hoarsely she called Him, then waited, watching the sky. But there was neither sign nor sound till the crows cawed, "Cor-pus Chris-ti! Cor-pus Chris-ti!" "Body of Christ!" she invoked. Yes, there, on that tree, begotten of what Bush-mother, hung the crucified Christ — eyeless, with a tangle of wild hair and beard, His white arms extended crosswise, and His bare body glistening bloodlessly, save for the red blood that had trickled and clotted from His wounded side.*

* "Christ on the Cross" is frequently to be found on trees in the Australian Bush — a tangle of shredded bark for hair and beard surrounding an eyeless face. The white-armed boughs stretch cross-like, and even the wounded side is represented by the crimson congealed gum.

She laid the child between them and knelt: appeal in her upraised hands: in the strained eyes sympathetic, reverent awe; but her droughty mouth was dumb. As from emotion, the drooping spearheads of the sentinel leaves quivered, she also, but Christ kept silent and still; she lowered her eyes. Along His glittering bare skin a bulldog ant crawled intently toward the speared side. Her heart bounded indignantly. How dare it? With trembling tenderness for Him, she drew it off.

It stung her — no matter; but had it stung Christ? And she laid her burnt swollen lips where its hold had been on Him, then again raised her eyes to His. But He could not see with those sightless eyes. Ah! the awful crows! They were there, hovering over her head, had not lost sight of her since she fell first. Ever and ever should she stay by Him and keep them off. And the flies! Oh, horrible! horrible! — watching intently those eyeless sockets. Had she, like poor Mary, come too late? Hastily she broke off a bough to beat back those buzzing horrors.

In the greatness of her work she forgot her droughty pain. Always and always she would stay beside Him. None should touch Him. No soldier dare again thrust a spear in His side. Stay — His side! What flowed? Blood — and — water — flowed — water! Her mouth gaped. Blood — and — water! Water! Violently her heart beat; stealthily she took a step nearer the wounded side, mouthing something. Back a step, then again forward. Maddeningly fierce was the struggle. No, no, dear Christ; fear not, for she would not drink His precious blood. Sobbing, she fell at His feet. She was thirsty, dear Christ — how thirsty! — and tears were salt, feeling her dry eyelids, and involuntarily placing her fingers on her tongue. How swollen it was — more swollen and painful than her stung hand! Ah! that bond between them; and she rejoiced that she had dared that for Him: now forgiveness. Never such a face as hers, imploringly upturned to Him.

From above His head a strip of bark descended — a sword. Submissively she bowed her guilty head, but it fell clear. Still she waited, her lips voicelessly twitching. How merciful He was! and mercy ever begot her penitence. But

— but though He knew her need, He moved no hand to hold a sponge, dipped even in vinegar, to her burnt lips. Ah! how could she forget? He also thirsted for water. "I thirst"; and they gave Him a sponge dipped in vinegar, but He could not drink that. Dear crucified Saviour! she would bring water. But first, where was the sponge (groping for it), because how else could she carry it? And if her own lips were only cooler, she would find water quicker. Fumblingly she groped and groped, till the burning blood gushed from her nose and mouth; then, mercifully, her tired senses swooned, and she fell with her head resting on the tree.

Her mind was clearer when she recovered, but she woke to the same holy purpose. In this tender Shepherd's care she would leave this lifeless lamb till she found water; then in her palms, hollowing them, she would carry it to Him.

Exalted with this divine mission, she went downhill, her soothed senses unnaturally acute, keenest of all sight. The blazed trees, along the track instinctively selected, held no meaning for her. No thought now for whether she were going right. Swiftly down Mount Calvary Hill slope she went; nor had she wonder when, in the hollow beneath, she saw the lagoon. Only she turned round to cry to Him that she had found it, and would return speedily. Stay, let her first be sure, lest she deceive Him, for what could be worse than her past fancies? No, this was no fancy. Water, water, water! Knee-deep she went into it, clutching it greedily, then clenching her hands determinedly, for her swollen tongue kept apart her teeth. Not one drop would she drink till He first drank, then bade her! Down, down dropped her burning head and desiring, droughty mouth to it, yet resolutely she fought. Out went her hollowed palms — full, nay, they were overflowing; then, surely, she might stoop and drink the drips. Oh, shame on her — she that would cheat Christ! Listen — yes, He was calling her name!

"My Christ, I come, — I come!" she called back.

No heed how to find Him, and speedily as her palms, cradling the precious water, permitted, she went on. Oh, sad that she dared not run, but she——

Why had those crows so suddenly uprisen? What prey had they found to mutilate here? What great swollen creature was that lying there, blocking her way? Was it one of the Marys? No; none of the Marys had red hair. See, here on the ground lay a tuft of it, and the woman's clenched hands were full of it. She was fearful, but she must go closer. She looked intently at the distorted face. The eyes were gone — but the familiar pointed teeth were showing in the widely gaping mouth.

For a second she resolutely battled to beat back her sense of recognition; then she wrestled with her sense of duty. This water she had so carefully carried was for the thirsty, waiting Christ, not for this woman, her enemy, whom she had hated. How cruelly bitter was this battle! — bitter from uncertainty. "For inasmuch as you did it unto the least of these——"

"Mina — poor Mina!" who had not been guided to the water as had she. Pityingly, into that open mouth trickled every drop she held.

Alas! even now she had not done right. She had only wasted the water, for Mina was dead, and the deceived Christ was again calling her name.

Who were these carrying the dead child coming from Him towards her? Two soldiers? No; one was a centurion. She thought the tall one was like — like—— Why, even the soldier, the dark one, with the dead child, was like, so like—— But if the women of Jerusalem were dark, so must the men be. But this other, bearded, was fair and merely burnt with the sun. Surely he was only—— No! no! she — closed her eyes.

Oh, of all the bitter cruelties that her fancy had played on her, surely this was the cruellest! But she would not be deceived; they were merely the soldiers come for the body of this woman. She must not betray Mina, or they would cast her dead body to the dogs, like Jezebel's.

"Soldier" — speaking to the dark man, then slowly turning to the other — "and centurion, I will come to Christ next. This poor woman — this" — watching intently the tears raining from the centurion's eyes — "I — I" — moving back from his outstretched arms — "I——"

"Ursie!"

A great sob broke from her; then —
"Andree!——"

THE END

Verse

1897-1919

Editors' Note

Barbara Baynton is not known at all as a writer of poems but the ten poems included here show her to have been interested in verse throughout her career. While none of the poems quite approaches the achievement of the early stories or the best parts of *Human Toll* they are interesting for the light they shed on Baynton as a writer and as a personality. On the one hand they demonstrate her versatility as a writer, a characteristic insufficiently acknowledged. On the other hand, as pieces apparently occasioned by personal circumstances, they reveal something of her more private side suggested by a reading of *Bush Studies* and *Human Toll*. Several of the poems for instance refer to the death of a young baby and, presumably, they were evoked by the death of her infant son, the only child of her marriage to Dr Baynton. In others there is a pervading sense of loss and even betrayal and an occasional depth of engagement that does recall the intensity of *Bush Studies*. Here too it is an intensity that tempts the reader to speculate about the kind of experience on which it seems to be based.

Apart from the poems printed here there are two others, never published, which are preserved, in manuscript in Baynton's own hand, in a collection of A.G. Stephens's papers in the Hayes Collection, Fryer Library, University of Queensland. In another hand is the note "Typed 26/10/99 1/- pd": the poems were presumably intended for publication in the *Bulletin* . Five others were published in the *Bulletin* : "A Noon, an Eve, a Night" (27 February 1897); "Good-Bye Australia!" (12 August 1899); "Day-Birth" and "To-Morrow" (9 December 1899); and "To My Country" (15 March 1902). The first two were signed

"B.B.", "To My Country" "B. N.S.W.", the others "Barbara Baynton". The Hayes manuscript versions of "Day-Birth" and "To-Morrow" show signs of Baynton's revisions, minor in the first case, more substantial in the second. These revisions are all incorporated in the *Bulletin* version which is the one printed here. Another, quite different poem also called "To-Morrow" was printed opposite the title page of *Cobbers* (London, 1917): no other publication of it has been discovered. The other four poems appeared in various special Summer Numbers of the London weekly, the *British-Australasian* . These Summer Numbers, which began in 1912, contained many poems, stories and essays by Australian writers, especially those living in, or visiting, Great Britain. The Chomleys (Charles Chomley was Martin Boyd's uncle) who edited the magazine were friends of Baynton and were among the very small group who attended her third wedding in 1921. The dates of publication of these poems were: "To-Morrow's Song" (24 July 1913); "The Broken Bough" (16 August 1917); "Rare Banqueters" (September 1918); and "In Rama. The Bush Mother" (September 1919).

A NOON, AN EVE, A NIGHT

A noon, an eve, a night,
He heard them with shut ears,
And saw it with shut eyes.
Before the new delight
Fled spectral, white-faced fears,
Grim-mouthed with agonies.
A noon, an eve, a night
He lived in Paradise!

A thousand miles away
His feet had trod the land,
A barren, lonely plain,
Where heat-waves, night and day,
Rolled o'er a burning sand
That knew not any rain.
A thousand miles away—
And madness in his brain!

At last a Paradise,
A noon, an eve, a night,
Burst on him where he lay.
He saw a fountain rise,
With sprays of water bright,
And heard his children play.
At last a Paradise,
A thousand miles away.

A noon, an eve, a night,
A thousand miles away,
Within a lonely land,
He saw the waters bright,
And heard his children play
Around the marble stand.
A noon, an eve, a night—
And Death crept down the sand!

GOOD-BYE, AUSTRALIA!

Good-bye to it all!
God still holds the land, haply;
Still holds me — its toy.

First, our one child died;
And the heart-broken mother
The summer sun slew.

Last flood drowned the stock;
Then the fires took home, fencing . . .
Her garden is gone.

So I will leave it.
The blue waters roll the ship
In the dull, sad bay.

Forget you, loved hearts! . . .
This dead wattle holds your dear
Memory ever.

Good-bye to the grave
On the hill; for the far isles
Are calling. Good-bye!

DAY-BIRTH

Pain-girt she stood and cried aloud—
I heard the sea.
In agony her strong head bowed—
Dew sprinkled me.
Night's red lips turned to east from west,
Her right hand drew them to her breast,
Her fair full breast — again the dew:
(I thought of you).
She sighed content — I heard the breeze,
Its rustling banners all unfurled.
Below a wanderer's smoke upcurled
And amorous sought the quivering trees.
She smiled, Morn-Mother, victory won,
And oped her eyes — I saw the Sun.

TO-MORROW

To-morrow?
Nay, I shall not fear — this is to-night—
Nor sorrow.
Beside thee kneels thy son — first mine, then thine.
Amid the gloom thy face gleams white,
Nor need we light
If thou but ope thine eyes — so shall mine shine.
Thy lips shew not where, moaning, mine have pressed.
The arms that folded lie upon thy breast
Stretch forth, Beloved! for thou are not dead . . .
Yet still, so still! Thy restless head
Furrowed the pillow ere but one hour sped.
Beloved! ever didst thou love the night . . .
Sleep on! I will not sorrow—
This is to-night — nor fear to-morrow.

TO MY COUNTRY

A wind-blown, shimmering, shifting, awful waste,
Fringed by a broken edge of green and grey—
A ghastly field for devilish winds at play;
A painful tale of desperate men that faced
The loathly hell, of hard-won pathways traced
In dull white bones, of a race whose long decay
Gives warning to the pallid crowd to-day
To seek a land by greener beauty graced:

Australia! thou whose dust, made flesh, has given
Power to my soul to warn thy people now,
To me these horrors are a thing of naught.
O, nurse of serfdom, how shalt thou be shriven
Of threadbare knees and dust-enshrouded brow,
Mother of slaves who dare not speak their thought?

TO-MORROW'S SONG

As bird I'll be, with burnished wing—
I'll cleave the sky of sunny spring.
From wintry woe, regretfulness—
My joyous song, forgetfulness.

Ah, then! ye tears blood of sorrow—
Die to-day, welcome to-morrow
That shrouds the face of memory.
Ah, then! Ah, then!! my heart and me.

And if — away I shall not think—
Nepenthe from the rose I'll drink.
The one you loved with velvet tongue,
The one I kissed when you were young.

TO-MORROW
(From *Cobbers*)

To-morrow I'll sail in a shadow-ship
With a phantom obedient band,
Who'll murmur not when past ports we slip,
For we'll never, we'll never land.

Muzzled, marooned on an empty shore,
O mariners, the wind shall be,
With his lusty roar he'll hurl no more
To the crypts of an angry sea.

Of the purple gloom I'll make my bed
And forever I'll cease to pray,
For I'll sleep till mem'ry thinks I'm dead:
Oh, I'll sleep to the doom of day.

THE BROKEN BOUGH

Too frail seems my shelter for this night
Of wind and storm and subtle fears,
I creep and quench my quavering light,
While rain falls like forsaken tears.

"Come out! Come out!" yells the wind to me,
"And watch me winnow my autumn toll,"
But I only bow submissively,
And strive to hide my stricken soul.

Then in a pregnant moment bleak,
A ghostly presence grew in the gloom;
A kiss familiar fell on my cheek,
While incense of sorrow filled the room.

All aghast I knelt, but not to pray,
Tho' wind and rain gave me armistice;
For why should the broken-hearted pray—
Who scorn love's afterbirth — called peace?

I know not if hours or moments sped,
To my heart, it was eternity,
When sudden some bell tolled for one dead,
On the outer door fell soft knocks three.

And when I opened wide the door,
The wind, and the rain, and the storm was gone.
And the moon shone brighter than before,
Lest I should miss one sight forlorn.

For the roses had vanished from the spot
Where you plighted your faithless troth to me;
And even the blue-eyed forget-me-not
Was away with the wind — to Arcady.

But in the path — where you stood that day—
Lay a broken bough — full meaningly.
Then my heart rejoiced — in woman's way—
For my soul had scorned this tryst with thee.

RARE BANQUETERS

The fruits of my youth lie about me
   On the wild, waste earth 'neath my feet.
Disdainful the birds fly above me,
   So that none save the canker-worms eat.

Rare banqueters these, in worm fashion,
   And besheathed in their symbol of flesh,
They feast on my primitive passion—
   And embroider their honeycomb mesh.

Maker, Thy methods baffle mankind,
   For Thou setteth his heart as a cup;
Then willeth the worm — the deaf and blind —
   Shall have *sesame* to it — and sup.

IN RAMA. THE BUSH MOTHER

With scythe agleam into thy garden go,
   Where all the flower of youth doth bloom,
   No shrift, nor sacrament, nor tomb;
But still their rich, ripe blood must flow,
Nor heed'st thou Rachel's cry of woe.
Oh, Death!

Now for thy vaunted chivalry,
   While thy last sacrament she sips,
   Close thou her lonely eyes and lips,
Take thou — oh, take her tenderly—
Then gloat upon thy victory.
Oh, Death!

Articles and Correspondence
1899-1921

Editors' Note

This sample of Baynton's non-fictional work exemplifies her interest in culture, social problems and nature. The letter to Melba is reprinted from Agnes Murphy's biography, *Melba* (1909). It is interesting to compare the adulatory tone of this "fan letter" with H.B. Gullett's report, in his "Memoir of Barbara Baynton", that when they got to know each other Baynton and Melba "cordially detested and vigorously maligned [each] other".

" 'B.B.' to the *Bulletin*" appeared in the *Bulletin* on 23 December 1899; "Indignity of Domestic Service" in the *Sydney Morning Herald*, 10 June 1911; "The Australian Soldier" in the *British-Australasian*, 28 November 1918; and "Australian Spring" in the *British-Australasian*, September 1921. The last of these was signed Barbara Headley. "The Australian Soldier" provoked a number of reactions from correspondents acknowledging Baynton's patriotism, but decrying her "odious comparisons" and defending the British soldier and his officers. The remarks in " 'B.B.' to the *Bulletin*" were in response to a note in the "Personal Items" column of the previous week in which it was indignantly reported that George Lambert's painting was to be reproduced and used as a Christmas supplement to a Sydney firm's trade paper. The *Bulletin* called this "a sordid piece of sacrilege" and asked if it would have been allowed had the artist not been an Australian.

In the rare interview given to the Sydney *Home* in September 1920, Baynton acknowledges a debt to Lawson's work; she also refers to a novel in progress called "Wet Paint" of which no trace can be found. The intention expressed at the end of this interview, of selling up her English property, was soon changed — in February 1921 Baynton was married to Lord Headley in London.

Apart from the pieces printed here there are a number of letters from Baynton held in public library collections. Barbara Baynton's executors however have not agreed to permit their publication.

In the Dixson Library, Public Library of New South Wales, there is a letter from her congratulating Sir Samuel Griffith on his appointment as Federal Chief Justice, and asking him to preserve a place in his life for his literary interests. She reports with pleasure the success of *Bush Studies*, and she confesses to a deep "egotistical" desire to be remembered by readers of the future.

The Hayes Collection in the Fryer Library, University of Queensland contains, among the papers of A.G. Stephens the literary editor of the *Bulletin* from 1894 to 1906, eight letters from Baynton to Stephens. All of the letters are in manuscript in Baynton's own hand and are dated between 9 November 1896 and 24 January 1906. They trace the development of a friendship over a decade. In the early letters Baynton is respectful, even diffident, and always defers to Stephens's judgment. She seems to have relied heavily on his advice, accepting his suggested revisions without question and acknowledging her lack of experience in revision and proof-reading. The letters that have survived are clearly no more than a fragment of an extensive correspondence. They are a part of a considerable friendship, and are important for the insight into her mind and into the friendship between author and editor rather than for the snippets of information they contain. Many of the letters are brief, even hurried, and imply or refer to other letters, conversations, and visits. Over the period the warmth increases and so does the level of personal reference and even banter. A couple of the letters refer to one Essie, who was evidently a housekeeper or companion, whose regard for Stephens is always passed on.

But several of the "snippets" of information are interesting. In a note of 9 November 1896, Baynton suggests that "What the Curlews Cried" would be an appropriate title for the story we know as "The Chosen Vessel". Stephens (whom for some time she addressed as Stevens) did not accept her suggestion. A day later she was writing to him again to thank him for the *Bulletin*'s cheque and the honour of publication: the story appeared on 12 December. She also, most importantly, accepts Stephens's decision to omit part of this story (the Hennessey section obviously) — though by the time *Bush Studies* was published she had changed her mind.

In a number of later letters she reports with some obvious pleasure that *Bush Studies* is selling well and is well-reviewed; she regrets relinquishing her interest in it. Stephens is thanked fulsomely for his review of the book. In February 1903 she refers to a "long story" she has been working on (possibly *Human Toll*) and is anxious to discuss literary matters with Stephens. A few months later she tells him that despite a long illness, occasioned by her throat ailment, she has been working well and that he'll be "surprised" at the results. On a more personal level she discusses the move from Woollahra to Ashfield, the effect this will have on her work, and the arrival of her portrait by Sir John Longstaff. The move was apparently a response to her recurrent illness.

In January 1906, evidently quite ill, she writes to Stephens, then newly arrived in London, from Switzerland where she has been undergoing a "health cure". Eight months of "enforced idleness" have delayed her work seriously and she refers to having with her (perhaps for some time) the proofs of *Human Toll*. She hopes that Stephens will find a position in London and learn to like that city to which she herself plans to return briefly in March. No later letters are presently known but it would be surprising if the correspondence had ceased at this point.

"B.B." to The Bulletin

Re your remarks on Lambert's picture, "Across the Black-soil Plains", and its reproduction by an ironmonger's paper. "Across the Black-soil Plains" isn't a "great" picture — it's only a good picture, clever and faulty. No mere transcript-picture, devoid of imagination, was ever "great", in the highest sense; and this isn't depreciation, for I admire Lambert's picture in its way and to its degree, and wish N.S.W. Gallery had more like it. Again, if Lambert had only sold his picture for 100d. instead of £100 he would still have no commercial right to complain that the purchaser reproduces it. When you sell all rights, you sell — all rights. Lambert would have a craftsman's right to object to the reproduction if it was an inferior reproduction, and misrepresented his picture. As the picture is photographically reproduced about as well as can be done in Sydney, what is he growling about? The "ironmonger's" paper? Well, if I were Shakespeare, I would be quite content to be given away with a pound of tea. Shakespeare would improve the tea; and the tea wouldn't hurt Shakespeare. There's nothing degrading in being an ironmonger: an honest ironmonger is as good in his way as an honest artist. As Lambert's work is Australian, and good, the artist should be glad to let it be known everywhere. Why shouldn't the common bush person enjoy it in reproduction if he can't see it in original? "Ironmonger's puff!" If the *Bulletin* had issued the picture as a journalist's puff, would Lambert have howled? How is a journalist better than an ironmonger, abstractly? Would the Gallery let a fishing firm reproduce "The Sons of Clovis"? Certainly, if the Gallery knows its business of disseminating art and cultivating artistic instincts, and if the reproduction fairly represents the picture. Better artists than Lambert draw for advertising-posters.

[*Bulletin* still thinks Lambert's grievance a substantial one. Association counts for a great deal, and, if Lambert objects to his picture being introduced to the public per ironmonger's advt., his objection is perfectly reasonable.—Ed.B.]

Letter to Nellie Melba

London
15th Nov. 1907

Dear Madame Melba,

Five years ago I came to London, and as with all Australians, my fear of the unknown evil of this great city was my dominant feeling. Then on my first Saturday night I went to hear you sing, and you stirred some depth in me that made me oblivious to all personal danger — even to the fact that at the close of the performance I had got separated from my two companions; for I was alone in the opera house waiting, hoping for you to come back once more. One of my friends had the latchkey, the other had my purse; yet when I gradually realized the position, I was utterly indifferent. Nothing mattered since I heard you sing. I gave my cabman a ring and told him to call in the morning. Then, as I could not make anyone hear, I went down the area steps. Some thoughts are more refreshing than sleep, and these were mine till the dawn came.

Many times since I have heard you, for now with my daughter I live in London, and to us both the experience of your singing is always the same — an exaltation that soars above life, or even death.

I trust you will soon come back to reign over us aforetime, and bring confusion to those enemies begotten by your greatness.

Some day we may meet. Till then and after, may the God who made you, He of your Scottish forebears, keep you safely. With the love of two you have never seen

Faithfully your admirer
Barbara Baynton

Indignity of Domestic Service

"Do use your influence to send out a shipload of good servants. There are none to be got here for love or money. All the old ones are too independent, and the young ones are all going to the factories."

In short, with a difference, it was the old Macedonian cry. "Come over and help us", that time and again was wafted to me across the wide watery way between Australia and England. But help is wanted in England also for I have had experience of housekeeping in both countries, and am fully seized of the manifold demands attached to the adjective "good", and I state authoritatively that it no longer sheathes every known virtue of domesticity in England.

No, the utterly servile, obedient, self-negating servant now belongs to where it fits — the obsolete or decadent generation. Decidedly there is the distinction — desired by those who love the sounding brass and tinkling cymbal of power, conveyed by the European "Madam", "Ma'am", and "Sir", as against the friendliness, or, perhaps, familiarity of the Australian "Mr" and "Mrs". But the veneered deference of the British workers for their employers is disappearing slowly, but as surely as the one-time general curtsey.

"Education" is the English lament. "Education — the Board Schools are to blame for teaching them above their station. There are no good servants now. They all flood to the shops and tea-rooms, offices, and even factories, rather than come well paid to a comfortable home."

And, compared with a few years back, domestics are well paid now in Britain, and wages are steadily on the increase.

The old scale of £12 per annum, entailing a quarter's notice, and paid quarterly or spent, at the mistress's will, on clothing, prevails only in remote villages — and there even, it is only the ground-down products of "The Man with the Hoe" who are content to work for this pittance. And there are tales of how sometimes, even in those stagnant spots, where life and land alike are moss grown, the shrill blare of the factory whistle has penetrated. For there is an immutable law that at some time, however rare, leisure be given to all animals, higher and lower, to think, so the factory whistle sometimes causes the family drudge to down kitchen tools and join the renegade domestic ranks, which factory workers so largely are.

The solution is apparent — mankind is naturally gregarious, and factory life, at its worst, teems with companionship, not only coming and going to work, but at mealtimes, and again on all holiday occasions. And even in England, factory work ceases from about 2 p.m. on Saturday till Monday morning, with an hour daily for dinner, and every night free, or overtime paid for, and with the Parliamentary decree of four bank holidays yearly.

No hated caps, or other "I serve" insignia, and, above all, that paramount privilege, men as masters.

It may sound disloyal to my sex, yet, it is a common truth; show me a woman in power, and I will show you a despot. Indeed, in my anti-suffrage canvass in London, my surest and most successful weapon for anti-votes was to just ask shopgirls, "Would you rather have a woman over you than a man?"

Now, put factory conditions against those hedging the duties of the "general". Begin with her outings. In England these are one night a week, and every other Sunday afternoon, spent generally at her parents' home, if she has one, where it is her custom to assist her mother in some sordid capacity. Consider the monotony of the daily routine. Scrubbing and scouring her kitchen, cleaning rooms she enters for that purpose only, lighting fires, cooking food of which her portion is the unpalatable refuse — this article could not contain the day, and, worse still, the night's demands on the ordinary general. "It is the little foxes that spoil the grapes", and it is the petty tyrannies of the mistress that sink the "family drudge" into the dull-headed, heavy-heeled creature she is. She knows that neither day nor night belongs to her, nor is any hour in the twenty-four absolutely hers. Nor does any portion of the premises afford her sanctuary from her ofttimes exacting mistress. Recall her when, as within your rights, you paid a surprise visit to her kitchen; her startled attitude always is one of defence, begot by the bondage of fear. If your mood is captious, your unjust complaints may show her your ignorance, but she must be discreetly dumb. Though sometimes when she gets or gives notice she dares, with language decidedly her own, to limn her disconcerting estimate of you. So her obedience is only seeming, and her respect from her lips only and as unnatural to her nature as it is to cook food that she never tastes. And what uplifting influence can ensue from what she eats amongst the usual malodorous surroundings.

Carlyle, the cynic, says man is a "cooking animal". And the recipes handed down to us from long dead days, show that our Foredames must have kept their subtle hold over him by much knowledge of what ministered to the comforts of the inner man; moreover, antique instructions for lace washing, renovating, remedies, whatsoever appertained to skilful housekeeping, was also in their ken; while the large basins, sometimes to be met with in our precious possessions of old china were manufactured for the mistress's use in washing up their choicest breakfast and tea sets. But modern housewives with the besetting sin of the beckoning bridge tables, have neither love nor leisure for this womanly occupation, though they thereby relieve even practised hands of an unnerving responsibility.

The servants in large establishments are generally the offspring of old retainers, but the sullen power of discontent creeps in even at these pretentious portals. The housekeeper, the butler, the ladies' maids, through the housekeeper's key, have an "open sesame" to the delicacies in the otherwise locked larders; but certainly this is the principal factor of the lower servants' grievance. Hotels, tea-rooms, and shops become their objective, and though these occupations for ever debar them from a return to patrician halls, they seldom want to take up their old life with its dreary routine, for who, having tried domestic duties, dare gainsay its monotony.

Monotony — that is the keynote of domestic revolt. Since I have been in Sydney I have heard of a Chinaman appearing in his Sunday suit in the middle of the week, and being asked to explain, said: "Too muchee washee-up", only he emphasized it with unprintable fervour. "Washee-up all day, washee up all night, allee same next day, allee time washee-up."

Regard the soda-shrivelled skin surmounting the par-boiled flesh of the washer-up's hands. The lye-burnt and discoloured nails, the laundry-enlarged joints, think upon these things; then say, with what womanly handicraft will this worker's inflexible fingers plan the garments of her offspring, should she become a wife and mother. This is the secret of the success of the kitchen literature.

The narrative containing the perils of the peerless Paulina takes the place of the nimble needle. The romance may have a sinister influence, but for the time it lifts the engrossed servant out of her surroundings. Small wonder if in middle life she resorts to some stimulant for this purpose.

The shop girl does feel the strain of set hours and continued standing, and the fastidious caprices of women customers, but her efforts to serve are not confined to our sex; there is the male customer to break her monotony, and sharpen her palate with the spice of life, variety — this subtle mind cure.

I was very young when I got my first lesson in metaphysics; an elder brother had taken a younger one and me an unwisely long walk, and on the return journey we both knocked up, and demanded to be carried; his ingenuity met the situation. "Knocked up, are you; then you must ride home." He cut us two stick horses, which we mounted, and with the aid of two switches flogged the rest of the way, as we thought, out of our steeds.

"Servants are like children, and I treat them accordingly," one arbitrary mistress told me once, but I am sure she never stopped to think if they regarded her in the light of a bad stepmother, nor are domestic duties well and intelligently performed the accomplishment of a child. Most of us housewives, at one time or other, have had to enter the kitchen and try our 'prentice hand at preparing meals, therefore we know the strenuous exigencies that encompass every action of well-rendered services.

Manhood suffrage in Australia most certainly limited the working man's labours to eight hours. Our sex have had the coveted blessing of the franchise for many years, but in all these years there has never been a concerted earnest movement to make the Eight Hours Act apply to household workers, though I know something has been done for shopgirls and factory workers.

The domestic life is in the — to women — political wilderness just the one oasis which they understand, and the personal inconvenience ensuing to themselves, which the Eight Hours Act applied to domestics would entail. Yet, considering the absolute necessity of domestic duties, the marvel is by what unnatural means it occupies its present undignified position. It is selfish thoughtlessness that has made girls leave this most womanly pursuit for the demoralizing factory life, with its pernicious, far-reaching after-effects. For domestic service, as it now is, is but a survival of slavery, and acknowledging it's the slave that makes the tyrant — how does the magnanimity of the mistress stand?

The present system existing between mistress and maid is threatening the very foundations of home life. The axe is laid at its roots with a severing menace. To protect this human birthright employers must surrender obsolete prejudices. The kitchen must be classed among the high places, and those who steer this helm of home must be called no longer "servants", but "benefactors", for a competent cook has much to do with the making of a Christian.

The Australian Soldier

An Appreciation and a Tribute

At this moment there is not a nation who warred, who does not admit that the Australian soldier for bravery, initiative, endurance, and great tendernesss, has no equal. In impartial witness of this take toll of some of their actual achievements in conquering, but for them, the unconquerable. As to their lawlessness, have their accusers ever calmly considered the unenviable circumstances that encircled the lot of the Australasian soldier when he found himself alone in the country of cold suspicion? The English instinctively are distrustful of strangers. I do not say that among the thousands of our boys who have placed the welfare of the Empire, and its necessity, before their own, there have not been a few who may for, generally speaking, a drugged space have careered along the broad way, that for them, poor fellows, certainly led to Hell.

When the European soldier gets leave, he goes home to parents, wife, or relations. He, at least, goes home. How often does that apply to our shy wayfarers? What signifies home to them? The deserted Christ in his bitter Gethsemane, was not more desolately lonely than thousands of my countrymen. And while on the saintly subject, I may remark that even that Divine Leader had among his few followers, one black sheep. The Australian soldiers generally speak no foreign tongue. One day he leaves the thunder of guns and shells, and the deadly poison gas. When he leaves these and other atrocities created by the worse than cannibal Huns, and comes for a short respite, say, to London, small wonder that the prowling harlot, even if she speak but broken English and borders on the half-century, finds these boys easy victims.

Official records must bear me out in this. I maintain that England owes the Australian mothers an unpayable debt in not providing a vigilant committee to meet, and attempt to safeguard these bush-born boys, shy and untamed as the wild birds of their own country. As to lawlessness — I have taken to both my homes, town and country, here, Australians from every colony and also New Zealanders, and have selected them promiscuously literally from the highways and hedges. I purposely have lost count how many now, for so many will come back no more, that I only press forward. My point is that, though some of these overseas boys were Woolamalooites, Rockpushites, and New South Wales men from my own country, and a like class from other colonies, and though they may have stayed a day or a month, not one of these boys ever abused my shelter, nor did an offensive action, nor said an indecent word, and from my heart I testify that not one ever left me after a long or a short stay, but that I felt their debtor, for their gratitude, and later on, their mothers', has enriched me as long as I live. Lawlessness — show me the true student of my countrymen who does not acknowledge that this misnomer is really their brave contempt for danger and death. Yea, death, even under the most subtle guise that the cauldrons of Hell have brewed — poison gas.

Major-General Sir J. Monash, in his spirited and affectionate interview with a Press representative at the front a few weeks back, surely explains for ever that other unjust and ungenerous accusation; want of discipline. Further, many other leaders assert that they consider it is the Australian soldier who makes the officers what they are, for they know they can depend upon them to a man. But here again, our officers are recruited generally from the ranks, and achieve their promotion from brains and brawn, while the English officers are mostly selected from the mentally unfit of the aristocracy. This is where our boys differ terribly from their English comrades. God made the English Tommy, but mechanical abnegation of his individuality unmade him. I lament this surrender, and would not for one moment attempt to rob these dogged heroes of one iota of what is their just and melancholy due.

I glory in and am grateful for every heroic deed done by our allies, and if I were not I should be mindful to disguise this want of appreciation, or suffer in the hearts of my countrymen; these, the world's finest fighters, whose deeds have placed our land among the foremost of all people. These great souls, as merciful and as full of compassion for a beaten foe, as they are brave.

I wish I could give you a few uncensored stories told to me by impartial people of this singular link of bravery and compassion that characterizes the Australasian, but we must wait yet long for the narrative of their wonderful deeds and actions, "full of the marrow of fat things." Take Gallipoli, for a base. Who taught the Turks t'were better to ape tenderness and mercy, even if they did not feel it, for all the teachings of the Koran with its immortal — "He made ye, and ye have compassion on one another."

Here is a little weak instance compared with some I hold:- A taxi man once demanded a 10s. fare for a 10d. drive from Trooper Jim Tasman, who you may remember has since "gone South." Poor Jim was ignorant of all written figures, but he had taxied the same way before, and he ventured to raise a small demur, but the ruffian insisted till a bystander interfered on Jim's behalf. Besides protecting Jim, he instituted proceedings against the driver, whom the magistrate severely reprimanded, and for all the ruffian's plea of wife and family, fined him and prohibited him from applying for hire for a month. I noticed neither Jim nor the other two boys staying with me showed the slightest satisfaction at the course of Justice, and a few days later I found that Jim and the others had made good the fine and had even taken supplies to the family. Immoral, perhaps, but very compassionate.

At the risk of partiality I quote H.S. Gullett, an extract from a letter to me:- "I wish you could see our beautiful, wonderful boys . . . old wine in new bottles . . . there never will be another Australian Imperial Force. Only a new free country could have bred these heroes."

Saith John Masefield of our dead in Gallipoli: "They died as they lived, owning no master on earth."

Mrs Barbara Baynton: Interview in Home *(September 1920)*

Those who have interested themselves in Australian literature will remember the two remarkable books by Mrs Barbara Baynton, which were published in London some years ago. *Bush Studies* was a collection of realistic short stories and sketches astonishingly virile in their treatment. *Human Toll* was a long story of a drab and ugly phase of Australian country life, told with considerable force and ability. These books are more like Maxim Gorky's stories than anything of Henry Lawson's, but they owe nothing to the Russian author.

After a long absence in London Mrs Baynton returned to Sydney recently, and had a good deal of interest to say about the changes made in English life by the war. Like every patriotic woman in England, she helped in the war work done at home, which made such a material difference in England's contribution to the Allies' cause, lending her home as well as her services in aid of the wounded Australians — eight thousand of whom went through her houses. Her impression of the effect of the excitement of war upon the character of men and women was that it was bad; they were unsettled and restless, more inclined than ever to take life as a gamble and get the most out of it while they might. Soldiers coming home on leave wanted to crowd the hours with pleasure, for to-morrow they might die; the women played up to them, and this forced gaiety, enhanced by the American colony in London, continued after the war was over.

"Easy money," said Mrs Baynton, "was the curse of the war. It will be some time before England gets over the effect of it. They are a fine people, though, and can do things splendidly when they want to. I admire the Tommies for their dogged determination, but I don't think they are so wonderful as the Australian soldiers. In spite of all that has been said of them, I don't think full justice has yet been done to the A.I.F.

"The English made a huge blunder in sending them to train at such a place as Salisbury Plain many of them fresh from the heat of Egypt, to be dumped on to soggy and exposed ground, and there over and over again paraded in wind and rain for inspection by pompous officers and visiting Australian officials. It was the same in France; the visiting politicians were a perfect nuisance to our men. They had to put up with a lot of useless ceremony and so-called drilling, which might be useful to brainless machines, but only irritates intelligent men. However, it is no use growling now. The A.I.F. put up with it handsomely, but privately they didn't like it, and no one can say they didn't fight splendidly.

"The most impressive military man I met in England was Sir Harry Wilson, Chief of General Staff. He is a very tall man, quiet, unassuming, and wonderfully clever. At Lady Wilson's house I met many interesting people — soldiers and civilians. She, too, is an unostentatious person, and was a great war-worker. I have met a great number of remarkable men in my time, but I have never met anyone like our Prime Minister, W.M. Hughes. He has the clear vision — a rare thing; a wonderful memory for facts, and unfailing humour.

"While in London I read any Australian books I could get, and was much impressed by Leon Gellert's *Songs of a Campaign*. The earlier poets I read again, and could always go back to Henry Lawson's prose and verse. Lawson was the first to set forth Australian life, and his *Star of Australasia* deserves the highest praise. I remember thinking, after reading *While the Billy Boils* that here for the first time a man had shown that the Bush was worth writing about, and it was a great encouragement to me when I started to write.

"Some of our Australian artists have made a big name in London. Longstaff's portrait of Sir George Reid struck me as his best work, and I know that Sir George was greatly pleased with it. Power's horses delighted me; they were refreshingly real. I saw a number of Burgess's seascapes, which I thought very good.

"Whenever I had leisure I went to the Galleries. Much of the new art is puzzling, but Epstein attracted me greatly. His 'Christ' is a thrilling piece of statuary. And, remember, it was a Jew who made this gaunt, majestic figure. His 'Mother and Child', which at first seemed a shapeless lump of rock, revealed itself as an extraordinarily powerful thing; I'll never forget it.

"One thing which makes me regret being away from London is the art exhibitions; there was always something to be seen. I am glad that art has advanced so much here lately: it is a good sign of the advancing culture of the people. And our soldiers have shown that Australians are really a wonderful people; they don't know what heights they can scale until they try."

Mrs Baynton published in London *Cobbers*, a collection of stories containing most of those which had appeared in *Bush Studies*. She now has under way a novel, to be called "Wet Paint", in which the bush, Sydney society and London scenes will appear, and it will be merrier than the work of her younger years. Mrs Baynton left for London last month to sell her property there, and will then come back to settle in Australia.

Australian Spring

The "boom, boom" of a faithful paternal emu heralds the dawn. His mate, in response, rises stiffly from maternal duties of the night — stretches her cramped legs and wings, then unerringly makes for their tryst, where her dutiful spouse has her breakfast awaiting her. While she eats he clumsily settles himself upon the warm eggs. After the mother emu has eaten she stalks about with her graceful undulating walk. The rising sun tips the tender spring leaves of the eucalyptus, crimsoning them with a warmer glow. Their pointed fingers stir in the soft breeze that seems to absorb the morning mist.

Every bird is astir, foraging for breakfast for the clamorous birdling. The horses are the first of the quadrupeds to awake. Then the cows leisurely arise and stand in a dreamy silence, before sending out an echo to the ma-aa of their penned calves. The sheep are the last to wake. The bark of a vigilant dog rouses the hurdled flock, though doubtless his master has sent him about his work. It is hard to say when a dingo sleeps, for he is a notorious night prowler and thief.

From the sunny side of a dead tree a bright-eyed lizard crawls cautiously out, and, after a careful survey, assures himself that no enemy is near. Swiftly then he descends and makes for the bare bark of a fallen tree, where he waits patiently for his meal of insects and flies. From the banks of a lagoon frogs croak hoarsely their "quoit roight". The watching crows, perched near the tree top above my head steadily regard me. Mentally, I compare the furtive cunning of these pariahs of Australia with the insolence of the crows of Colombo, "whose tameness is shocking to me", especially when they swoop down, and without fear or ceremony, and through my bedroom window, steal the biscuit from the saucer of my morning tea. They say that birds and beasts unacquainted with man are unafraid. I wonder how they got their heritage of fear — probably by bitter experience. The rapacity and cruelty of Australian crows leave the Colombo crow a gentleman, and, like all Bush folk, I loathe them, so I remain motionless, stretched on the fragrant grass, my hand ostensibly covering my peeping eyes. The crows are in mutual but silent conclave. They nod intelligently and make movements of assent and dissent. They make movements with their wings remarkably like a clergyman thrusting his hands under his tail coat. Am I dead or only asleep? is the burning question. A leader is chosen, and he silently descends to a lower branch. He noiselessly snaps off a dead twig. His aim is true, and it falls on my shielding hands. I remain motionless, and apparently oblivious. Emboldened, two others join the leader. With equal skill and aim three larger pieces are allowed to fall on my face. Very encouraging is the verdict. They are all together now, and on the lowest limb of the tree. With concerted swoop they descend, just as I spring to my feet to throw a-stick at them, but they are already again at the top of the tree, cawing hoarse curses at me. This is a good season, so they must work for a living. There are no starving fallen sheep, and no bogged animals stud the lagoon.

To turn from them to more amiable members of the feathered tribe. Among the Bush minstrelsy, the butcher's bird melody is supreme, though the coachman's whip, with its sweet lingering cadence, challenges it closely, and next in tunefulness comes the magpie. I wonder why the laughing jackass always laughs from a leafless myall tree; it is a fallacy that there are snakes — the jackass's traditional prey — in dead myalls. I have imitated these birds since childhood, so I go to join them. Surprised and curious, they listen to me for a little and then soar skywards.

I wander on to gather a bunch of our "scentless flowers". I wonder if the man who wrote of them and of our "songless birds" had a perpetual cold in his head and wool in his ears.

There is no need for me to pick wattle; it grows around the homestead. But there is the perfumed pink and white heath in bloom, the bell-shaped epacris, more delicate and soft than any I have seen. Here also are masses of our wild clematis, akin to the English syringa in scent. The cat and dog orchids, first harbingers of early spring, are nearly over, but I can still find some in sunless spots, just peeping shyly from their green snoods. The strong-scented pink native rose is not one of my favourites; but I love the wood violet, with its exquisite lingering scent. Later on we shall have the stiff waratah, the gigantic lily, the sweet-scented wild apple blossom, and many others I have missed. Those who really know the Australian Bush find in it endless interest and variety at any season of the year, and to such a one an early spring morning amid Australian birds and beasts and flowers is a season of delight as keen as can be enjoyed in any of those older countries whose spring their poets sing.

Select Bibliography

WORKS OF BARBARA BAYNTON

Books

The Chosen Vessel. Sydney: F. Cunninghame, n.d.

Bush Studies. London: Duckworth, 1902. Another edition with "A Memoir of Barbara Baynton" by H.B. Gullett, and "Barbara Baynton's Stories" by A.A. Phillips. Sydney: Angus & Robertson, 1965; reprinted 1972.

Human Toll. London: Duckworth, 1907.

Cobbers, with a foreword by George Reid. London: Duckworth, 1917.

Uncollected Prose and Verse

Stories and Sketches

"The Tramp", *Bulletin*, 12 December 1896, p.32. Later revised and published in *Bush Studies* as "The Chosen Vessel".

"Trooper Jim Tasman", *British-Australasian* (London), Summer Number, 21 July 1916, p.28. Later published in *Cobbers* with slight revisions.

"Her Bush Sweetheart", *British-Australasian* (London), Summer Number, September 1921, pp. 38-39. [Signed The Lady Headley.]

"Australian Spring", *British-Australasian* (London), Summer Number, September 1921, p.24. [Signed Barbara Headley.]

Non-Fiction

"To the Bulletin", *Bulletin*, 23 December 1899, p.7. [Signed B.B.]

Letter to Dame Nellie Melba, 15 November 1907, in *Melba: A Biography*, by Agnes G. Murphy. London: Chatto & Windus, 1909, pp.301-2.

"Indignity of Domestic Service", *Sydney Morning Herald*, 10 June 1911, p.4.

"The Australian Soldier: An Appreciation and a Tribute", *British-Australasian* (London), 28 November 1918, p.14. For responses to this article see under "Biographical and Other Notes".

"Mrs Barbara Baynton", *Home* (Sydney), September 1920. Interview.

Poems

"A Noon, an Eve, a Night", *Bulletin*, 27 February 1897, p.3. [Signed B.B.]

"Good-Bye, Australia!", *Bulletin*, 12 August 1899, Red Page (in "Under the Gum Tree"). [Signed B.B.]

"Day-Birth", *Bulletin*, 9 December 1899, p.16.

"To-Morrow", *Bulletin*, 9 December 1899, p.16.

"To My Country", *Bulletin*, 15 March 1902, p.3. [Signed B. N.S.W.]

"To-Morrow's Song", *British-Australasian* (London), Summer Number, 24 July 1913, p.4.

"To-Morrow", printed opposite title-page of her *Cobbers*. London: Duckworth, 1917.

"The Broken Bough", *British-Australasian* (London), Summer Number, 16 August 1917, p.12.

"Rare Banqueters", *British-Australasian* (London), Summer Number, September 1918, p.16.

"In Rama. The Bush Mother", *British-Australasian* (London), Summer Number, September 1919, p.12.

Manuscripts

Lady Barbara Headley: Papers: 1907-1938. MS3077, National Library of Australia, Canberra. [Correspondence, legal and financial papers.]

A.G. Stephens Papers in the Hayes Collection, Fryer Memorial Library of Australian Literature, University of Queensland includes typescripts of "Squeaker's Mate", manuscripts and typescripts of the poems "Baby", "Mateless", "Day-Birth", and "To-Morrow", and several of her letters to A.G. Stephens.

Mitchell Library, Sydney, holds a manuscript and typescript version of "Squeaker's Mate".

Letter to Sir Samuel Griffith in S.W. Griffith: Correspondence, 1903-1914. MSQ191, Dixson Library, Sydney.

Stories reprinted in Anthologies

"The Tramp"

in *The Bulletin Story Book: A Selection of Stories and Literary Sketches from the Bulletin (1881-1901)*, edited by A.G. Stephens. Sydney: The Bulletin Newspaper Company, 1901, pp.148-53.

in *Australian Short Stories*, edited by George Mackaness. London: Dent, 1928, pp.12-17.

in *Australian Round-Up: Stories from 1790 to 1950*, edited by Colin Roderick. Sydney: Angus & Robertson, 1953, pp.129-33.

in *It Could Be You*, edited by Hal Porter. Adelaide: Rigby, 1972, pp.63-67.

"Scrammy 'And"

in *Australian Short Stories*, edited by Walter Murdoch and H. Drake-Brockman, London; Oxford University Press, 1951, pp.36-58.

"Squeaker's Mate"

in *A Century of Australian Short Stories*, edited by Cecil Hadgraft and Richard Wilson, London: Heinemann, 1963, pp.72-85.

in *The Penguin Book of Australian Short Stories*, edited by Harry Heseltine. Ringwood: Penguin, 1976, pp.63-77.

in *The 1890s: Stories, Verse, and Essays*, edited by Leon Cantrell, St. Lucia: University of Queensland Press, 1977, pp. 216-30.

"Billy Skywonkie"

in *Twenty Great Australian Stories*, edited by J.L. Waten and V.G. O'Connor. Melbourne: Dolphin Publications, 1946, pp.71-87.

in *Short Stories of Australia: The Lawson Tradition*, edited by Douglas Stewart. Sydney: Angus & Robertson, 1967, pp.82-94.

in *Best Australian Short Stories*, edited by Douglas Stewart and Beatrice Davis. Melbourne: Lloyd O'Neil, 1971, pp.70-82.
in *Classic Australian Short Stories*, edited by Judah Waten and Stephen Murray-Smith. Melbourne: Wren, 1974, pp.17-29.

"The Chosen Vessel"

in *Short Stories of Australia: The Lawson Tradition*, edited by Douglas Stewart. Sydney: Angus & Robertson, 1967, pp.75-81.
in *Best Australian Short Stories*, edited by Douglas Stewart and Beatrice Davis. Melbourne: Lloyd O'Neil, 1971, pp.63-69.

"Die Erscheinung" ("The Chosen Vessel")

in *Eine Frau im Busch und andere Australische Erzählungen*, edited by Frank Auerbach, Tubingen: Horst Erdmann, 1970, pp.48-56. [German translation by Frank Auerbach.]

WORKS ABOUT BARBARA BAYNTON

Bibliography

Krimmer, Sally. "A Bibliography of Barbara Baynton", *Australian Literary Studies* 7, no.4 (1976): 430-33.
"Annual Bibliography of Studies in Australian Literature", *Australian Literary Studies*, 1 (1964 -).

Commentary

Barnes, John. "Australian Fiction to 1920", in *The Literature of Australia*, edited by Geoffrey Dutton. Ringwood: Penguin, 1964, p.167; rev. edition, 1976, p.182.
Barrett, Charles. "Barbara Baynton's Books", *Melbourne Herald*, 20 July 1929.
Blake, L.J. *Australian Writers*. Adelaide: Rigby, 1968, p.110-11.
Cantrell, Leon. *The 1890s: Stories, Verse, and Essays*. St. Lucia: University of Queensland Press, 1977, p.xxx.
"Callisto". "The Bush Stories of Barbara Baynton", *Wentworth Magazine*, June 1928, 39-41.

Dixson, Miriam. *The Real Matilda: Woman and Identity in Australia 1788-1975*. Ringwood: Penguin, 1976, pp.77, 185-86, 191-92.

Ellingsen, Peter. "A Film is made 'black as hell' that won't pay", *Australian*, 14 January 1974, p.3.

Elliott, Brian. "The Backward Glance", *Australian Book Review* 5, no. 7, (May 1966): 134-35.

Ewers, John K. *Creative Writing in Australia*. Melbourne: Georgian House, 1945, p.50.

Green, H.M. *An Outline of Australian Literature*. Sydney: Whitcombe & Tombs, 1930, pp.108, 117-18, 135-36.

———*A History of Australian Literature*. Sydney: Angus & Robertson, 1961, Vol. 1, pp.561-62, 564, 646.

Gullett, H.B. "Memoir of Barbara Baynton", *Bush Studies*. Sydney: Angus & Robertson, 1965 (Reprinted 1972), pp.3-25.

———"Memoir of Barbara Baynton", *Sydney Morning Herald*, 12 February 1966, p.18. [Condensed version of above.]

Hadgraft, Cecil. *Australian Literature: A Critical Account to 1955*. Melbourne: Heinemann, 1969, pp.94-95.

Krimmer, Sally. "New Light on Barbara Baynton", *Australian Literary Studies* 7, no. 4 (1976): 425-30.

Lindsay, Jack. "Barbara Baynton: a Master of Naturalism", in his *Decay and Renewal*. Sydney/London: Wild & Woolley/Lawrence & Wishart, 1976, pp.262-66.

Miller, E. Morris. *Australian Literature: From its Beginnings to 1935*. Melbourne: Melbourne University Press, 1940, Vol. 2, pp.506-8.

Moore, Inglis. *Social Patterns in Australian Literature*. Sydney: Angus & Robertson, 1971, pp.78-79, 136, 167-68.

Palmer, Nettie. *Modern Australian Literature (1900-1923)*. Melbourne: Lothian, 1924, pp.11, 15, 18.

———*Fourteen Years*. Melbourne: Meanjin Press, 1948, pp.22-23.

Palmer, Vance. "The Australian Soul: Three Authors Who Have Found It in Their Writings", *The Book Monthly* (London), October 1914: 860-64.

———"Writers I Remember: Barbara Baynton", *Overland*, no.11 (Summer 1958): 15-16.

———"Barbara Baynton", *Intimate Portraits and other Pieces, Essays and Articles*, edited by H.P. Heseltine. Melbourne: Cheshire, 1968, pp.83-87.

Phillips, A.A. "Barbara Baynton and the Dissidence of the Nineties", *Overland*, no.22, December 1961, pp.15-20.

Reprinted in his *The Australian Tradition*, 2nd edition. Melbourne: Cheshire-Lansdowne, 1966, pp. 32–42; and in *The Australian Nationalists: Modern Critical Essays*, edited by Chris Wallace-Crabbe. Melbourne: Oxford University Press, 1971, pp. 149–58.

——— "Barbara Baynton's Stories", *Bush Studies*. Sydney: Angus & Robertson, 1965, pp.29–42.

Schulz, Joachim. *Geschichte der Australische Literatur*. Munich: Max Hueber, 1960, pp.55-56.

Summers, Anne. "The Self Denied: Australian Women Writers — Their Image of Women", *Refractory Girl*, no.2 (Autumn 1973): pp.4-11.

——— *Damned Whores and God's Police: The Colonization of Women in Australia*. London: Allen Lane, 1975, pp.37, 312.

Tennant, Kylie. "Short Stories of a Bygone Era", *Sydney Morning Herald*, 19 March 1966, p. 15.

Contemporary Reviews

In an A.G. Stephens Scrapbook in the Mitchell Library, Sydney, there are many clippings of reviews and other references to Barbara Baynton. The asterisked items may be found in that Scrapbook. All but the last five refer to *Bush Studies*.

*"Current Literature: *Bush Studies*", *Sydney Morning Herald*, 10 January 1903, p.4.

*"*Bush Studies* by Barbara Baynton", *South Australian Register*, 10 January 1903.

**Adelaide Advertiser*, 17 January 1903.

**Daily Mail* (London), 20 January 1903.

*"Junius" (Frederick Cecil Rhodes). "New Books", *Town and Country Journal*, 21 January 1903, p.59.

**Glasgow Herald* 22 January 1903.

**Academy and Literature* (London), 24 January 1903.

*"Some Australian Books", *Age* (Melbourne), 24 January 1903, p.4.

*"Literature: Publications Received", *Queenslander*, 24 January 1903, p.187.

**Manchester Guardian*, 25 January 1903.

**Sydney Mail*, 28 January 1903.

**Leader* (Melbourne), 31 January 1903.

"Recent Publications", *Evening News*, 31 January 1903, p.4.

**Athenaeum* (London), 7 February 1903.
**Literary World* (London), 13 February 1903.
Stephens, A.G. "One realist and another", *Bulletin*, 14 February 1903, Red Page. Reprinted in *A.G. Stephens: His Life and Work*, edited by Vance Palmer, Melbourne: Robertson & Mullens, 1941, pp.109-13; reprinted in *A.G. Stephens: Selected Writings*, edited by Leon Cantrell, Sydney: Angus & Robertson, 1977, pp.198-99.
——— *Bulletin*, 28 February 1903, Red Page. Reprinted in *A.G. Stephens: Selected Writings*, edited by Leon Cantrell, Sydney: Angus & Robertson, 1977, pp.200-03 as "*[Bush Studies]*"
**Evening Observer* (Brisbane), 14 February 1903.
**Darling Downs Gazette*, 20 February 1903.
Australasian, 11 April 1903.
**Goulburn Evening Post*, 17 March 1903.
Bookfellow, 21 February 1907, p.4.
The Publisher and Bookseller (London), 23 February 1907, p.434.
Stephens, A.G. "The Bush", *Bulletin*, 4 April 1907, Red Page. [Review of *Human Toll*.]
"Notes". *Australian Weekly Magazine*, 6 June 1907, p.13. [Review of *Human Toll*.]
V.I.C. "Barbara Baynton: *Cobbers*", *British-Australasian* (London), 17 July 1917.

Biographical and Other Notes

"Women", *Bookfellow* (Sydney), 7 January 1899.
**Sydney Morning Herald*, [1904].
Bookfellow (Sydney), 21 February 1907, p.7.
Johns, Fred. *Fred Johns's Notable Australians: Who's Who in Australasia*. Adelaide: Fred Johns, 1908, p.67.
"England and the Australian Writer: Barbara Baynton's Experience", *Sydney Morning Herald*, 6 July 1911.
Johns, Fred. *Fred Johns's Annual: Who's Who in Australasia*. Adelaide: Fred Johns, 1912, p.41.
"The British Officer", letters to the editor from "An Australian in the Air Force", and Louise E. Edwards, *British-Australasian* (London), 5 December 1918, p.12. These and the following two items are responses to Baynton's "The Australian Soldier: An Appreciation and a Tribute".
"Democracy and Strength", editorial, *British-Australasian* (London), 12 December 1918, p.3.
"Personal", *Table Talk* (Melbourne), 6 March 1919, p.6.

"Phyllis". "In the Looking Glass", *British-Australasian* (London), 18 March 1920, p.15.
"Marriage: Lord Headley and Mrs Baynton", *The Times*, 12 February 1921, p.13.
"Wedding: Lord Headley and Mrs Baynton", *British-Australasian* (London), 17 February 1921, p.11.
B[oyd], M[artin]. "Australian and New Zealand Homes in England: No. 7 — The Residence of the Lady Headley, 6 Connaught Square, W2", *British-Australasian* (London), 24 November 1921, p. 13.
"High Court of Justice . . . Lord Headley's Suit Settled", *The Times*, 28 February 1924, p.5.
"Court Circular", *The Times*, 6 June 1924, p.17.
Palmer, Nettie. "Price Warung, Barbara Baynton", *Illustrated Tasmanian Mail*, 14 September 1927.
——— "Barbara Baynton", *Illustrated Tasmanian Mail*, 26 June 1929.
Argus (Melbourne), 29 May 1929.
"Lady Headley: Death in Melbourne", *Sydney Morning Herald*, 29 May 1929, p.19.
"The Late Lady Headley: Australian Author and English Peeress", *British Australian and New Zealander* (London), 30 May 1929, p.13.
Swinhoe, E.M. (ed). *Burke's Peerage*. London: Burke's Peerage, 1936.
"Barbara Baynton", *Kyneton Guardian*, 7 December 1944.
Serle, Percival (ed). *Dictionary of Australian Biography*. Sydney: Angus & Robertson, 1949, Vol. 1, p.65.
Palmer, Vance. "Fragment of Autobiography", *Meanjin* 27:1 (1958): 5.
Tennant, Kylie. "Miles Franklin: Feminist whose men were men", *Sydney Morning Herald*, 25 July 1974, p.14.

ADDENDUM 1988

Commentary

Astley, Thea. "The Teeth Father Naked at Last: the Short Stories of Barbara Baynton", in her *Three Australian Writers: Essays on Bruce Dawe, Barbara Baynton and Patrick White*. Townsville: Townsville Foundation for Australian Literary Studies, 1979, pp. 12–22.

Frost, Lucy. "Barbara Baynton: An Affinity with Pain", in *Who Is She? Images of Women in Australian Fiction*, edited by Shirley Walker. St Lucia: University of Queensland Press, 1983, pp. 56–70.

Iseman, Kay. "Barbara Baynton: Woman as 'The Chosen Vessel' ", *Australian Literary Studies* 11 (1983): 25–37.

Moore, Rosemary. " 'Squeaker's Mate': A Bushwoman's Tale", *Australian Feminist Studies* 3 (Summer 1986): 27–44.

Webby, Elizabeth. "Barbara Baynton's Revisions to 'Squeaker's Mate' ", *Southerly* 44 (1984): 455–68 (includes transcript of Mitchell Library manuscript/typescript version, with Baynton's corrections).

UQP AUSTRALIAN AUTHORS

The Australian Short Story
edited by Laurie Hergenhan
Outstanding contemporary short stories alongside some of the best from the past. This volume encompasses the short story in Australia from its *Bulletin* beginnings in the 1890s to its vigorous revival in the 1970s and 1980s.

Writing of the 1890s
edited by Leon Cantrell
A retrospective collection, bringing together the work of 32 Australian poets, storytellers and essayists. The anthology challenges previous assumptions about this romantic period of galloping ballads and bush yarns, bohemianism and creative giants.

Catherine Helen Spence
edited by Helen Thomson
An important early feminist writer, Catherine Helen Spence was one of the first women in Australia to break through the constraints of gender and class and enter public life. This selection contains her most highly regarded novel, *Clara Morison*, her triumphant autobiography, and much of her political and social reformist writing.

Henry Lawson
edited by Brian Kiernan
A complete profile of Henry Lawson, the finest and most original writer in the bush yarn tradition. This selection includes sketches, letters, autobiography and verse, with outspoken journalism and the best of his comic and tragic stories.

Christopher Brennan
edited by Terry Sturm
Christopher Brennan was a legend in his own time, and his art was an unusual amalgam of Victorian, symbolist and modernist tendencies. This selection draws on the whole range of Brennan's work: poetry, literary criticism and theory, autobiographical writing, and letters.

Robert D. Fitzgerald
edited by Julian Croft
Fitzgerald's long and distinguished literary career is reflected in this selection of his poetry and prose. There is poetry from the 1920s to the 1980s, samples from his lectures on poetics and essays on family origins and philosophical pre-occupations, a short story, and his views on Australian poetry.

Australian Science Fiction
edited by Van Ikin
An exotic blend of exciting recent works with a selection from Australia's long science fiction tradition. Classics by Erle Cox, M. Barnard Eldershaw and others are followed by stories from major contemporary writers Damien Broderick, Frank Bryning, Peter Carey, A. Bertram Chandler, Lee Harding, David J. Lake, Philippa C. Maddern, Dal Stivens, George Turner, Wynne N. Whiteford, Michael Wilding and Jack Wodhams.

Joseph Furphy
edited by John Barnes
Such is Life is an Australian classic. Written by an ex-bullock driver, "half-bushman and half bookworm", it is an extraordinary achievement. The accompanying selection of novel extracts, stories, verse, *Bulletin* articles and letters illustrates the astounding range of Furphy's talent, and John Barnes's notes reveal the intellectual and linguistic richness of his prose.

James McAuley
edited by Leonie Kramer
James McAuley was a poet, intellectual, and leading critic of his time. This volume represents the whole range of his poetry and prose, including the "Ern Malley" hoax that caused such a sensation in the 1940s, and some new prose pieces published for the first time. Leonie Kramer's introduction offers new critical perspectives on his work.